The Life of
JAMES OTIS
of Massachusetts

A Da Capo Press Reprint Series

THE ERA OF THE AMERICAN REVOLUTION

GENERAL EDITOR: LEONARD W. LEVY

Brandeis University

The Life of
JAMES OTIS
of Massachusetts

BY WILLIAM TUDOR

DA CAPO PRESS · NEW YORK · 1970

A Da Capo Press Reprint Edition

This Da Capo Press edition of
The Life of James Otis
is an unabridged republication of the
first edition published in Boston in 1823.

Library of Congress Catalog Card Number 70-118203

SBN 306-71936-3

Published by Da Capo Press
A Division of Plenum Publishing Corporation
227 West 17th Street
New York, N.Y. 10011

Manufactured in the United States of America

The Life of
JAMES OTIS
of Massachusetts

J. Blackburn pinx.t 1755.

A.B. Durand sc.

JAMES OTIS.

Published by Wells & Lilly — 98 Court st. Boston.

THE

Life of James Otis,

OF

MASSACHUSETTS:

CONTAINING ALSO,

NOTICES OF SOME CONTEMPORARY CHARACTERS AND EVENTS

FROM THE YEAR 1760 TO 1775.

BY WILLIAM TUDOR.

BOSTON:
WELLS AND LILLY—COURT-STREET.

1823.

Contents.

CHAPTER VIII.

CHAPTER IX.

CHAPTER X.

CHAPTER XI.

CHAPTER XII.

CHAPTER XIII.

CHAPTER XIV.

CHAPTER XV.

CHAPTER XVI.

CHAPTER XVII.

CHAPTER XVIII.

CHAPTER XIX.

CHAPTER XX.

CHAPTER XXI.

CHAPTER XXII.

CHAPTER XXIII.

CHAPTER XXIV.

CHAPTER XXV.

CHAPTER XXVI.

CHAPTER XXVII.

CHAPTER XXVIII.

CHAPTER XXIX.

CHAPTER XXX.

Preface.

THE period of time under review in this volume, is one of the most remarkable in the political history of the world. The transactions of that epoch owe their importance, not so much to their individual magnitude or splendour, as to their prospective character, and inevitable consequences. The minds of men were every where excited to investigate their civil and political condition; ancient abuses began to lose that sanction which a blind, hereditary reverence had long given them; and the intelligent citizens of every nation became convinced that they possessed certain indefeisible rights, of which they had been forcibly deprived in ages of ignorance and barbarism, and which were now withheld by a claim of prescription, founded on that very usurpation. The struggle that ensued from this revival, produced the American revolution first, and afterwards that of France. These great events were signalized by actions and results, as different as were the circumstances of the two countries in which they occurred. But the spirit of the age still advances; it visits every region where commerce, intelligence, and enterprize can penetrate, and will be sooner or later universally triumphant. The unholy purposes of the Holy Alliance may effect some partial and momentary checks, but the re-action will be proportionate. Even the unfortunate Italians, overwhelmed for a time, and forced to renounce their scheme of reformation, while they look at Spain, Portugal, and Greece, may exclaim with their countryman Galileo, rising from his recantation, *Pero si muove!* *It moves notwithstanding!* Even among nations that are farthest in the rear in this course of amelioration, there are some individuals who believe that governments are made for the people, and not the people for governments. The great principle which originates and secures all liberty and social improvement, the principle of representation, is now the wish of every country, and it will be finally obtained, unless all example of its advantages be effaced from the earth.

The spirit which predominates in particular eras among civilized nations, will often be promoted, at the same moment, by incidents that have no striking similarity, and which are entirely disconnected with each other. Thus, about the same time that Otis argued the cause of the *Writs of Assistance,* and wrote his Vindication of the Massachusetts Legislature, Rousseau published his *Social Contract.* The novelties, the mixture of truth and extravagance, and the glowing eloquence with which these were conveyed in that celebrated performance, made it generally read on the continent of Europe, and tended in a very remarkable degree to excite the disposition on that continent to examine and reform political institutions, by which, after the lapse of a generation, some of them were riven to their foundations. The animated arguments of Otis, awakened at the same moment, a close and attentive watchfulness in America of every movement of government; and united the idea of taxation and representation, inseparably, in the mind of every citizen.

It so happened, from the plan of the British ministry in their experiment of taxing the colonies, that the attention of the people of England was strongly directed to the discussions in this country. The question was to be first settled here, and the friends of liberty, or the followers of arbitrary principles, equally watched this scene of action. Their sympathy was actively shewn by the clamors that were made, with partial success, for relief from the accumulated abuses that crushed the people of Ireland; and a similar feeling originated the questions of par-

liamentary reform, which so many eminent men have
from that time to the present, successively attempted
and relinquished in England. This long and momentous struggle began in Massachusetts, and her capital
witnessed most of the leading measures, till it terminated in actual war. There, the innovations project-
ed by the ministry, inflicted the greatest injury;
there, the most active and able of their partisans
were stationed, and the main body of their forces
was concentrated ; there in fine, from various circumstances, the ministry and the sovereign resolved " to
try the question."

It was, therefore, in the British North American
colonies, and especially in Massachusetts, that the
statesmen and the politicians of England, were occupied, in the attack and defence of the opposite maxims of government, which they had adopted.

From 1763 to 1775, Massachusetts was the scene
where all the dearest interests of the colonists were
most powerfully assailed, and to which the public
characters of America and England looked with deep
solicitude. It was the system attempted to be enforced here, which was to destroy or to establish
principles of the widest bearing, and the most lasting
importance.

The question concerning the rights of the colonies,
directly affected the interests of the whole empire.

It was the defence of these rights that engaged the
purest and highest minds in the mother country, in
a long series of efforts.   It was in this cause, that in
either branch of the British senate, the finest models
of eloquence were produced which modern times
can boast; and it was in the support of these rights,
that the greatest statesman of his time, with the
truest foresight, wisdom, and magnanimity exclaimed, " *I thank God that America has resisted!*"

It is difficult to repress enthusiasm in considering
the conduct of the men, who opposed the arbitrary
designs of the British ministry, and who in a great
crisis of human affairs, had the sagacity and firmness
to discover and maintain the right course.   Our admiration is the greater, because their conduct originated, not so much from the feeling of actual oppression, as from a true foresight of the intolerable evils,
that would be the future consequences of precedents which were the more to be feared, as they
were insidiously and plausibly introduced.   Their
resistance too, was made from the highest convic-
tions of duty, and as the event proved, with an exaggerated, yet not unnatural apprehension, of all the
dangers that might have occurred from the contest.

Nor should this admiration be confined to Americans, but may be justly felt by liberal men of every
country, since it was the cause of all mankind.   Even

high-minded Englishmen may regard the termination with complacency ; while the regret they must
feel, will not be, that their government was foiled
in the attempt, but that it was ever undertaken.
Unquestionably, the greatest statesmen, and a very
choice, though not numerous part of the nation, felt
it to be a civil war, in which they took side with
the party oppressed. The results, contrary indeed
to expectation, have been so advantageous to England, that none but the most slavish bigot to arbitrary government, can do otherwise than rejoice at
them.

It never fell to the lot of a braver, more humane,
or more virtuous people to contend in a cause, that
would ultimately effect the condition of every country. Their leaders were fitted for the station that
was assigned to them, and when in after times, their
inextinguishable principles and unfading example,
shall make their destined way throughout the world,
they will be revered by future ages among the
general benefactors of mankind.

Even now, though placed too near their colossal
merit to discern all its excellent proportions, some
idea may be formed of their value, by considering
the miserable scenes of rapine, cruelty, fickleness,
and apostacy, that have been exhibited by the various actors in revolutions before the eyes of the pre-

sent generation. The revolutionary patriots of America were courageous, moderate, plain, and incorruptible, and imbued with a deep sense of religion, which guided and guaranteed all their conduct. They were, in fact, " the men of Plutarch," formed in a school of primitive simplicity and unyielding principle, which made them the ornaments of their own age, and will secure to them the admiration of posterity.

To those persons who have not fully examined the events and the characters that prepared the American revolution, this anticipation may seem too confident, perhaps extravagant. But if they will trace back the currents of public opinion on all subjects of political reform and amelioration, they will find how many of them began their course on this continent, between the years 1760 and 1776; though their primary fountains must at last be sought in the reformation, the commonwealth of England, and the English revolution. It will be found what vast consequences have followed the exertions of American patriotism, what excitement has been caused by its example, and how much human happiness has been increased by its labours. When the consideration of these high services shall be divested of all the envy and the familiarity of contemporaneous observation, it is not difficult to imagine in what scale

they will be placed, compared with the great actions of history. It is a quaint and trite remark, that
no man is a hero to his own servant, and on the same
principle, the number of servile or of feeble minds,
that fill up the ranks of society, can never overlook
the petty infirmities which come within their scope of
intellect; and are quite incapable of estimating the
character of eminent men, whose memory will be
preserved, when the surrounding crowds shall have
passed into the same oblivion that has covered the
innumerable millions of their predecessors.

While the plain principles of justice were contended for on this side the water, in the most distinct and open manner, and with a steadiness and
inflexibility suited to the occasion, the conduct of the
ministry was encroaching, disingenuous and obscure,
arrogant at one moment, and hesitating at another.
Most of the illustrious names in modern English history were to be found on the side of opposition.

The ministry were, through the whole period,
destitute of any elevated or extensive views, though
they held the reins of power at a moment, when
these qualities were peculiarly desirable. They
seem throughout to have been composed of intri-
guing courtiers, or mere business men, without genius
or energy enough to carry into effect, even their own
narrow and tyrannical system. This judgment has

been too often passed upon them to be now reversed. The instances of it are familiar to every reader,
but the following description, while it is less known,
is not inferior in force and truth to most others.
Sir Samuel Romilly, in a speech in parliament in
1780, thus described the administration that produced and prosecuted the American war.

" As statesmen, it is not easy to distinguish their
characters ; for no one minister has appeared to be
the author of any particular measure.   All that has
been done, has had the apparent approbation of the
whole administration, and there are persons who go
so far as to assert, that the real authors of all the
proceedings against America are still behind the
curtain.   Of the whole administration, however,
taken together, the principal characteristics are
want of system and irresolution.   The latter, indeed, is but a consequence of the former.   Having
little, confined views, they seem never from the first
to have formed any comprehensive plan, and this
original defect has proportionally increased with ill
success ; perplexed and confounded with the mazes
and dangers into which they have run, like children, they rather turn away from what affrights
them, than endeavour to prevent it.   They ward
off the present evil that presses on them, but leave
the morrow to provide for itself ; and may be truly

said, according to the latin phrase, *in diem vivere.*
Their plan of operations, (for systems, they have
none,) changes with every new occurrence. With
every various accident, every various passion takes
its turns to rule them. Regarding only the immediate object before them, they magnify its importance,
and are now confident of success, now plunged into
despair. The idol they erected yesterday, is cast
down to day, and perhaps, will be enshrined again
to-morrow. In prosperity, they are proud, contemptuous, and overbearing; in adversity, supple, mean
and abject. At the commencement of the struggle
with America, they treated the refractory colonists
as a despicable gang of ruffians; but the moment a
league was formed with France, they prostrated
themselves at the feet of those *rebels* they had
spurned, and offered them much more than had
ever been demanded. But the panic was soon dissipated by a gleam of success; ministers resumed
confidence, and one of them was imprudent enough
to hint even in the house of commons, that unconditional submission was alone to be listened to—*quid
libet impotens sperare, fortunaque dulci ebrius.* Nay,
but last winter, flushed with the successes of lord
Cornwallis, they were in imagination masters of all
the southern provinces, and masters so absolute, that

they thought it time to send out again lord Dunmore, to chastise, not to govern, Virginia."

No study can be more useful to the ingenuous youth of the United States, than that of their own history, nor any examples more interesting or more safe for their contemplation, than those of the great founders of the republic. Yet it may be feared that this department is too much neglected by them, or only superficially examined. There are certain sentiments indeed, that are learned by rote, while a few prominent names and facts are known and repeated exclusively. When a well known foreign journal* in all the triumph of insolent ignorance, asked, " *Who Patrick Henry was ?*" we only smiled at its impertinence. But are we entirely exempt from the reproach of neglecting our own annals, for less valuable history ?†

---

* Quarterly Review.

† It may be safely affirmed that no man can thoroughly understand the origin of the American Revolution, without a critical perusal of the *Massachusetts State Papers*, that no statesman should be without them, no lawyer who pretends to rise above the lowest classes of the profession, should be destitute of a copy, yet the volume that was published two years since, cost only a dollar, and almost the entire edition remains on the printer's hands. Nearly the same result followed the republication of the celebrated essays of *Novanglus* and *Massachusettensis*, they were written during that interesting period, which immediately preceded the battle of Lexington, and which contain the arguments on each side, stated with great learning and consummate ability, forming a masterly commentary on the whole history of American taxation and the rise of the revolution.

The reader will be disappointed, if he expects to find in this volume, more than mere fragments of the life of James Otis. After a diligent and widely extended search, but little comparatively has been recovered of his private life, or of his public services ; yet before the year 1770, no American, Dr. Franklin only excepted, was so much known, and so often named in the other colonies, and in England. His papers have all perished, none of his speeches were recorded, and he himself having been cut off before the revolution actually commenced, his name is connected with none of the public documents that are familiar to the nation. It is owing to this combination of circumstances, that the most learned, the most eloquent, the most ardent, the most influential man of his time, is now so little known, that to many persons the following language of President Adams, seemed exaggerated. " I have been young, and now am old, and I solemnly say, I have never known a man whose love of his country was more ardent or sincere ; never one who suffered so much ; never one, whose services for any ten years of his life, were so important and essential to the cause of his country, as those of Mr. Otis, from 1760 to 1770."* Language equally strong was used by the

---

* Letters to the late W. Tudor, Esq.

late Chief Justice Dana, when speaking of him, in one of his charges to a grand jury ; and similar opinions were held by all those who acted with him, and were witnesses to his talents and influence.

His manuscripts being all lost, a more copious use has been consequently made of some of his printed works and official reports, in order to give a distinct idea of his manner, as well as his ability and services. A more accurate impression will be thus obtained, than could be received of most men from their printed works, because few persons were more frank and fearless in giving their opinions to the public; and they were, besides, thrown off so rapid-ly, and published with so little revision or correction, that they exhibit a very lively picture of his mind. In seeking for materials, the search has been like attempting to recover the parts of a mutilated an-tique statue; here and there a fragment might be found, a hand in one place, a foot in another, and though we might confidently exclaim, *Ex pede Her-culem !* still the symmetry of an entire restoration is hopeless.

Some sketches are given of his colleagues, but many who are worthy of commemoration are omit-ted, because the volume had grown beyond the original design. Many characteristic and interesting

anecdotes of the same period, remain to be collected.
Many curious illustrations of individual character and
of historical events abound in that era; in which, like
all others of high excitement, the lights and shadows
are strongly cast, and the actions of men stand forward in bold relief.

ALLYN HOUSE PLYMOUTH.

Chapter I.

Introductory Remarks—Origin of the Otis Family—Birth and Education of James Otis.

THE memorable contest between Great Britain and her colonies in America, which in its progress involved the chief maritime powers of Europe, and terminated in the independence of the United States, was gradually prepared by events, and by the situation and character of the parties. Circumstances had slowly developed, for a series of years, the discordant interests of the parent country, and the colonies, and convinced thinking men in both, that some change must ensue. Whether there were many remedies to be tried, can now be only matter of speculation, but the course adopted by the British statesmen, left their opponents the choice of only this alternative,—entire separation or political servitude. The crisis had been too long foreseen to deter by its magnitude, and too well understood to permit hesitation. Respectful, and even imploring petitions, were followed by angry discussions and stern protests : to these succeeded the scenes of actual warfare. The whole action advanced with a slowness of movement, and progressive increase of interest, that were suited to the grandeur of a drama, whose spectators were all the nations of Europe, and the consequences of which were to have a wider bearing on the welfare of mankind, than any event in modern, or perhaps in ancient times.

For a war of this nature every species of exertion was required. The most profound and earnest discussion of all the principles of government, the prerogative of the crown, the jurisdiction of the Parliament, and the rights of the colonies, naturally preceded and for a time accompanied, the struggle in the field. Talents of all kinds were put in requisition, and as the effort on the part of the colonists was not made for territory or plunder, but for principle, the knowledge, the zeal, the firmness of the citizens in their civil capacity, were no less necessary to their success, than bravery and skill in arms. The features of civil and foreign warfare were blended. It was a civil war, as it was carried on against subjects who renounced their allegiance ;—it was foreign in some of its aspects, because it was waged by the mother country, amongst distant settlements, to whose inhabitants the invading troops appeared like foreign mercenaries, who came to spoil them without remorse.

In the ordinary disputes of party, or the quarrels between nations, it little affects reputation, on which side men may happen to be. The objects in dispute are then narrow and transient; the party which is in the shade, at one moment, may bask in the sunshine at the next; the fortress or province that is lost in one war may be regained in another; while the statesmen and commanders who are at the head of operations cause no peculiar result by their efforts, and their names being connected with no great era in the affairs of mankind, merely serve to swell the common annals of the world, without attracting any strong interest or lasting remembrance.

The American revolution furnishes an impressive lesson, to shew how different are the consequences, when the contest is one, that forms an epoch in history, by its permanent influence on the interests of the human race. The choice between parties at such a crisis is of vast moment; it involves home, fame and country—Oblivion may be mercy to the vanquished; and magnanimous minds will grant an amnesty to all who were honest though misled; while their fortunate rivals are borne in triumph through the nation they have saved. By this mighty event, one party became the citizens of the

freest nation upon earth : while the unfortunate fragments of the other, were doomed to exile from the
place of their nativity, forming a sort of political ex-
travasation, and were rewarded for all their sacrifices by an eleemosynary pension, or by a grant of
lands in some bleak region of colonial subserviency.
The talents of the individuals may have been equal ;
yet in this case, the names on one side are already
forgotten, while those on the other are daily acquiring renown, by the wider experience of the advantages they obtained for their country.   The characters of the great leaders in the American revolution,
are gradually emerging from the jealous level of
their own times.   As this sinks away, they will become daily more conspicuous, and when their contemporary age shall be enrolled among the past ;
these founders of a nation will remain the lofty
land-marks of history, sublime as the mountains of
the globe appeared in all their majestic elevation,
after the waters of the deluge had subsided.

The philosophical observer will not often believe
in prodigies, nor imagine that the powers of human
intellect greatly vary at different periods.   While
the envious detract from all merit, he will render
justice to great services without being impelled by
a blind admiration.   No age perhaps has been
wholly deficient in men, who were capable of reach-
ing the highest attainments, or performing the noblest actions, yet it is only some congenial seasons
that call these faculties into exercise, and afford to
superior minds the opportunity of connecting their

names with enduring recollections. It is eminent good fortune for such minds to exist in those times, when some lasting improvement is taking place in human affairs; when principles are to be established, that will spread and develope themselves through a long succession of ages. The American revolution constitutes one of the epochs from which will be dated a vast amelioration in the destiny of man : and the fame of many illustrious men who were en- engaged in its cause, will continually increase as the operation of its consequences is extended. Their talents and virtues were exhibited in the senate or the camp, in the forum or the field, with undaunted zeal and heroic constancy. One of the most emi- nent of these patriots for his civil services, and one of the earliest and boldest asserters of the great principles which led to our national existence, was JAMES OTIS, of Massachusetts, to whose life and cha- racter this volume is devoted.

The family of Otis has produced some eminent persons, and its several branches are now widely extended. They all derived their origin from John Otis, who came over from England with his family, at a very early period of the Colony, and was one of the first inhabitants of Hingham. His grandson John Otis* was born A. D. 1657 and removed when a young man to Barnstable, where his talents soon made him the most respectable individual in the

---

* See Appendix B.

county : He was eighteen years at the head of its militia, twenty years a representative, and for twenty one years in the Council of the Province. He was also for thirteen years chief Judge of the Common Pleas, and also Judge of Probate ; a combination of offices sometimes enjoyed by the same individual in the early stages of our settlements, before the population became crowded, and when the functions of office did not require incessant labour. The successful discharge of such various employments is an evidence of his capacity and integrity, which joined to his wit and affability secured him great influence : he died November 30th, 1727. Two of his sons were known in public life, John and James. John Otis was a representative for Barnstable; and afterwards of the Council till his death in 1756. James Otis, born in 1702, was a man of great distinction and influence, but more indebted to the native energy of his mind, than to a regular education, for the acquirements he possessed. He became eminent at the bar, and was at one period a candidate for the bench of the Supreme Court, a circumstance which it will be necessary to notice more particularly hereafter.

He married Mary Allyne in Connecticut, and had thirteen children, five sons and eight daughters, several of whom died in infancy. The second son, Joseph, remained at Barnstable, where his children held different public offices, and one of them now inhabits the family mansion at Great Marshes,

Samuel Allyne was his youngest son. Of the daughters, Mercy, the eldest, married General James Warren of Plymouth, and Mary married Mr. John Gray, the other daughters died unmarried.

His employment in public stations was affected in a very considerable degree, by the course followed by his celebrated son. He was at one period a Justice of the Common Pleas and Judge of Probate, joining to these offices that of Colonel of the Militia, as his father had done before him. Colonel Otis, as he was generally called, was several times negatived as a Councillor, by Governor Bernard; but being constantly rechosen, was afterwards approved by Governor Hutchinson, and sat at the Council Board during the first years of the war. He died in the month of November 1778.

James Otis, the eldest son of Colonel James Otis of Barnstable, descended in the fifth generation from John Otis, the first of the name in this country, was born in the family mansion at Great Marshes, in what is now called West Barnstable, the 5th day of February 1724–5. His father, having always regretted his own want of a classical education, was the more anxious that his children should have every opportunity to secure all its advantages. His son therefore was prepared for college under the care of the Rev. Jonathan Russell, the clergyman of the parish, and entered at Cambridge in June, 1739 During the two first years of his college life, his natural ardour and vivacity made his society much courted by the elder students, and engaged him

more in amusement than in study ; but he changed
his course in the junior year, and though yet in his
boyhood, began thenceforward to give indications of
great talent and power of application. He took the
degree of A. B. in 1743, and that of A. M. in due
course, three years afterwards. The only record
of his having any part in the public college exercises, is that of a syllogistic disputation on receiving
his first degree.

The period is past when any traits of his youth can
be known from personal observation. All the persons who might have cherished in their memory such
incidents of his early years, as at that period often
indicate the future character of eminent men, have
paid the debt of nature. The few traditions that
can now be gleaned are extremely scanty. At
school, and at college excepting his first two years,
he was serious in his habits and steady in application. When he came home from the latter during
the vacations, he was so devoted to his books, that
he was seldom seen, and the near neighbours to his
father's dwelling would sometimes only remark his
return, after he had been at home a fortnight.
Though enveloped in his studies, and marked with
some of the gravity and abstraction, natural to
severe application, he would occasionally discover
the wit and humour, which formed afterwards striking ingredients in his character. A small party of
young people being assembled one day at his father's
house, when he was at home during a college vaca-
tion, he had taken a slight part in their sports, when

after much persuasion, they induced him to play a
country dance for them with his violin, on which instrument he then practised a little. The set was
made up, and after they were fairly engaged, he
suddenly stopped and holding up his fiddle and bow,
exclaimed " So Orpheus fiddled, and so danced the
brutes!" and then tossing aside the instrument, rushed into the garden, followed by the disappointed
revellers, who were obliged to convert their intended dance, into a frolicksome chase after the fugitive musician.

Chapter II.

*His Preparation for the Study of Law—Letter on that Subject—
His Entrance into the Profession—Literary Pursuits—Two Private Letters—His Marriage and Family—Professional Anecdotes.*

AFTER leaving college in 1743, Otis devoted
eighteen months to the pursuit of various branches
of literature, previously to entering on the study of
jurisprudence. He always regretted that he had
not given a longer time to the acquisition of general
knowledge, before he directed his attention exclusively to reading law. The learning he acquired in
this preparatory study, was afterwards of the greatest use to him. He inculcated on his pupils as a

maxim, "that a lawyer ought never to be without a volume of natural or public law, or moral philosophy, on his table, or in his pocket." His own expressions in the following letter, will place this subject in a strong light: though only a sketch of the advantages resulting from the course he recommends, yet they are ably stated and come from him with peculiar weight. The letter was addressed to his father, on the subject of his younger brother* Samuel Allyne Otis studying law. It was written in 1760, and may be inserted here appropriately, though it is anticipating the regular course of dates. In conversing with his brother on the subject of this study and speaking of the books in this science and its modern improvements, he told him, " that Blackstone's Commentaries would have saved him seven years labour poring over and delving in black letter."

" It is with sincerest pleasure I find my brother Samuel has well employed his time during his residence at home, I am sure you don't think the time long he is spending in his present course of studies, since it is past all doubt they are not only ornamental and useful, but indispensably necessary preparatorys for the figure I hope one day, for his and your sake, as well as my own, to see him make in the

---

* Samuel Allyne Otis took his degree of A. B. at Harvard University in 1759. He became a merchant; and at the first organization of the Federal Government, he was chosen Secretary of the Senate of the United States, which office he held through all the changes of parties till his death in 1814. The Hon. Harrison Gray Otis, now of the Senate of the United States, is his eldest son.

profession, he is determined to pursue. I am sure the year and a half I spent in the same way, after leaving the academy, was as well spent as any part of my life; and I shall always lament that I did not take a year or two further for more general inquiries in the arts and sciences, before I sat down to the laborious study of the laws of my country. My brother's judgment can't at present be supposed to be ripe enough for so severe an exercise, as the proper reading and well digesting the common law. Very sure I am, if he should stay a year or two from the time of his degree, before he begins with the law, he will be able to make a better progress in one week, than he could now, without a miracle, in six. Early and short clerkships and a premature rushing into practice, without a competent knowledge in the theory of law, have blasted the hopes of, (and ruined the expectations formed by the parents of) most of the students in the profession, who have fell within my observation for these ten or fifteen years past."

" I hold it to be of vast importance that a young man should be able to make some eclat at his opening, which it is in vain to expect from one under twenty five : missing of this is very apt to discourage and dispirit him, and what is of worse consequence, may prevent the application of clients ever after. It has been observed before I was born, if a man don't obtain a character in any profession soon after his first appearance, he hardly will ever obtain one. The bulk of mankind, I need not inform you, who

have conversed with, studied and found many of
them out, are a gaping crew, and like little children
and all other gazing creatures, won't look long upon
one object which gives them pleasure ; much less
will they seek for entertainment where they have
been twice or thrice disappointed. The late eminent Mr. John Reed, who, by some, has been perhaps justly esteemed the greatest common lawyer
this continent ever saw, was, you know, many years
a clergyman, and had attained the age of forty, before he began the practice, if not before he began
the study, of the law. Sir Peter King, formerly
Lord high Chancellor of England, kept a grocer's
shop till he was turn'd of thirty, then fell into an
acquaintance with the immortal John Locke, who
discovered a genius in him, advised him to books
and assisted in his education; after which he took
to the study of the common law, and finally attained
to the highest place, to which his royal master
could advance a lawyer. I think I have been told
the Lord Chief Justice Pemberton, or some one of
the Chief Justices of England, was a bankrupt, and in
the Fleet prison for debt, before he even dreamed
of being a lawyer. I mention these instances, not
as arguments to prove it would be most eligible to
stay till thirty or forty, before a man begins the
study of a profession he is to live by; but this inference I think very fairly follows, that those gentlemen availed themselves much of the ripeness of
their judgments when they began this study, and
made much swifter progress than a young man of

twenty with all the genius in the world could do; or
they would have been approaching superannuation,
before they could be equipped with a sufficient
degree of learning, once to give hope for the success they found, and then such hope would vanish,
unless they could get a new lease of life and understanding."

" I have formed very sanguine hopes from Samuel's pursuing the plan I have taken a little pains to
project for him; and flatter myself, that though I
am not wholly disinterested in this matter, yet I
come as near being so, as can be expected from man.
—The great point in view with regard to myself,
for this you have taught me by your excellent example to consider my children, is in short this: I
have one son who may live to be to Samuel, what
Samuel is in one respect at least to me, and his
uncle's wishes may be of more importance to him,
than those of an elder brother can be to his uncle.
And as in the common course of things I have not
so great a probability of seeing this son so far, or so
well advanced in life, as I hope you will see all
yours, I think it my duty to secure him so far as is
in my power, such a friend and instructor as may, as
much as is possible, supply the place of a father; and
I know no better way of effecting this, than by spar-
ing no pains in seeking the intellectual welfare of the
uncle, who, had the ability and integrity of my in-
structors been equal to the paternal care and liberality of the best of fathers, would have found a
better assistant through the pleasant though long

journies of science, than I ever can expect to furnish
him with, in yielding him my well meant, however
weak endeavours."

In 1745 he began the study of the law in the
office of Mr. Gridley,* at that time the most eminent lawyer in the Province. After completing his
studies under him, he went to Plymouth, was first
admitted to the bar of that county, and entered
there upon the practice. But the narrow range of
country business could not long detain a character
like his, from appearing on a scene more suited to
his powers. After two years residence at Plymouth, which were occupied more in study than in
practice,† he removed to Boston, and very soon rose
to the first rank in his profession. His business as

---

* Jeremiah Gridley was one of the principal lawyers and civilians of this
time. He took his degree at Harvard College in 1725. He came to Boston
as an assistant in the Grammar School, for some time preached occasionally;
but turning his attention to the law, he soon rose to distinction in the profession. He set on foot a weekly journal, in 1732, called the Rehearsal, in
which he wrote on various literary as well as political subjects, but it lasted
only one year. He was a whig in politics, and as a representative from
Brookline in the General Court, opposed the measures of the Ministry. He
was however appointed Attorney General, when Mr. Trowbridge was promoted to the bench, and in that capacity was obliged to defend the famous
" Writs of Assistance," in which he was opposed and wholly confuted by his
pupil, Otis. He was a Colonel of the Militia, and Grand Master of the Free
Masons, and belonged to some other charitable associations. He died in Boston September 7th, 1767.—*Eliot.*

† He lived in Plymouth in 1748 and 1749, and kept his office in the main
street; his name does not appear on the records of the Town, except in a tax
bill in 1748, where he is rated at " 20*l.* personal estate and faculty," but it
is found frequently on the records of the Court, for those two years, as being
" of Plymouth."—In Boston he occupied successively three different houses,
one in School street, on the North side, next to the county property, the house
in Court Street which belongs to the Brattle Street Church, and the house
on the south side of the western entrance to Bowdoin Square.

a lawyer became very extensive, and his reputation was firmly established for learning, eloquence and the most high minded integrity. He was soon generally known in many of the other colonies, and often consulted from a distance; at one time he yielded to the urgent solicitations that were made to him to proceed to Halifax in the middle of winter, to plead the cause of three men accused of piracy, whom he defended so ably as to procure their acquittal. On this occasion he received a fee, which was said to have been the largest that had ever been given to any advocate in the Province. This compensation however, would have been an inadequate motive for accepting such a commission, if there had not been joined to it the flattering compliment of being sought from afar, and the increase of reputation that naturally attended on such a distinction.

Through all his professional engagements, he still retained his taste for literature, which was established on the sure foundation of accomplished scholarship. To aid the cultivation of classical learning, he supplied a deficiency which then existed, by composing a treatise entitled " The *Rudiments of Latin Prosody*, with a dissertation on Letters, and the principles of Harmony, in poetic and prosaic composition, collected from the best writers;" which was published in 1760.* This work forms a very complete treatise; and if it were used in all our latin schools at the present day, the stu-

---

* See Appendix C.

dents might hereafter escape the reproaches to which they are too generally obnoxious from their neglect of prosody. He also composed a similar work on Greek prosody, which remained in manuscript; and perished with all the rest of his papers. He was a passionate admirer of the Greek poets, particularly of Homer, and used to say, it was in vain to attempt to read poetry in any language without a thorough knowledge of its prosody. When the wish was suggested by a friend to whom he had lent the treatise, that it should be printed; he said " there were no Greek types in the country, or if there were that no printer knew how to set them." His o'her writings were political and will be noticed hereafter in regular order.

His literary taste was formed and matured by the most thorough classical study, and his tenets in criticism were those of the old school. He was fond of the society of young people, to whom he was indulgent and instructive. At a certain period it was the fashion to a degree of affectation, for many young men, to be talking about poetry and citing verses, but altogether from the English poets of the day. To a young gentleman* who was particularly intimate in his family, he remarked, " These lads are very fond of talking about poetry, and repeat-

---

* The late James Perkins, Esq. of Boston, who was intimate in Mr. Otis's family. Mr. Perkins has deceased since the passage in the text was written. He was one of the most eminent merchants in the United States, and distinguished not only by uprightness and intelligence in his profession, but by a taste for literature and attachment to its interests. He will be remembered for several liberal donations to public institutions.

ing passages of it; the poets they quote I know nothing of, but do you take care, James, that you don't give into this folly. If you want to read poetry, read Shakespeare, Milton, Dryden and Pope, and throw all the rest in the fire, these are all that are worth reading."

The following letters were addressed one to his brother, and the other to his father. Though they relate only to the ordinary occurrences of private life, they are inserted here, because with the exception of some copies of letters of business in an imperfect letter-book, these brief and familiar epistles are almost the only vestiges in his own hand writing, of his most extensive correspondence.

BOSTON, OCTOBER 11th 1752.

" DEAR BROTHER,

" I HAVE sent you what you wrote for; the buttons are more fashionable than plain. I would have sent you a better whip, but that you would not go to the price for one of the best. I am sorry to find by your letter that you are yet so weak. I am no physician, as I could wish, but recommend the advice of Sir William Temple, which is, care, temperance and patience. Whatever you do, engage in no pursuit of business till you find yourself strong; even thinking with any degree of intensness may be prejudicial. If you can, bring yourself to a moderate degree of cheerfulness, for I am of opinion that bodily infirmities may some times be greatly allayed, if not removed, by getting the mind into the easy, facetious frame—but above all things abstain from meat of any kind, and from any thing stronger than beer. I know as well as the best of the doctors. I hope with God's blessing to see you ere long in a better situation of health than ever you was, as I doubt not you will be, if you once get the better of your present indisposition.

I am your affectionate brother,

J. OTIS.

JOSEPH OTIS, ESQ."

BOSTON, APRIL 3d, 1758.

*HONOURED SIR,

" SINCE mine of this morning I have been sent for by the Governor, upon the receipt of yours by Mr. Coffin, and he hath sent the enclosed orders. He thinks it as strange as you do, that they don't know their own minds at York, however he saith you have nothing to do but obey orders, and whatever extraordinary expences accrue you shall be allowed, and that you may draw on him for money as you want it. By his order I send Barker with this which will all go into your account as it ought; I received these orders at sunset, and have desired Barker to ride all night, for fear of any delay—as our Court

---

* The style of this address is a trait of former manners. Our puritan ancestors and their descendants down to the last generation, in their intercourse with their children, discouraged familiarity: a severe restraint was imposed on them, and their duty was exhibited in the line of submissive reverence rather than in that of endearing affection. To have appeared unconstrained in the company of a parent, or to have used the style of modern times in writing " My dear Father," instead of " Honoured Sir," would have been considered indecorous, and a subversion of all discipline and respect.

sits to-morrow and my affairs here are situated, I could not come to Plymouth—Since my last have received fifty shillings for Lot Case's gun which brother Joseph knew nothing of, not having the certificate, so remains due to me 10 shillings besides what he is willing to allow me for my trouble, which don't care much about.

I am your dutiful son,
JAMES OTIS.

HON. JAMES OTIS, BARNSTABLE.

In the spring of the year 1755 he married Miss Ruth Cunningham, the daughter of a respectable merchant. The lady was very beautiful, and was possessed of a dowry which in those times was considered very large. They had three children, one son and two daughters. The son was named James, after his father; he was a boy of very bright parts, and some eccentricity, but his career was terminated before a just estimate could be made of his character. He entered at the beginning of the war, as a volunteer midshipman, and died after being a short time in the service, before he was eighteen. The eldest daughter Elizabeth, married Captain Brown, an officer* in the English army, of a good family in Lincolnshire, who, after the conclusion of the war, coming into possession of a handsome pro-

---

* Mr. Brown was wounded at the battle of Bunker Hill; he was then a Lieutenant, was promoted, and afterwards placed in command of one of the fortresses on the coast of England.

perty, resigned his commission. Mrs. Brown left
the country with her husband during the war, and
did not return to it again except for a short visit in
1792. This lady was in 1821, still living a widow
in England. The youngest daughter, Mary, married
Benjamin Lincoln, eldest son of General Lincoln.*
This gentleman was in the profession of the law, and
gave promise of great distinction, but died deeply
regretted at the early age of twenty eight. His
widow, who possessed fine talents and an agreeable
character, died suddenly at Cambridge in 1806.
They had two sons, Benjamin a physician, and James
Otis Lincoln, a lawyer, who like their father, were
cut off prematurely; the elder died in August 1813,
and the younger in August 1818, leaving a widow
and two children.

Few characters could be more unlike than those
of Mr. Otis and his wife, yet they were attached to
each other. Beautiful, placid and formal, she was
suited to the calm and monotonous routine of a
quiet existence, while his ardent mind, impetuous
genius, and energetic will, qualified him to direct the
leading events in a great crisis of national affairs.
Her feelings too were not in sympathy with his, on
political topics: the consequence was shewn in the

---

* General Lincoln, who commanded in Carolina and capitulated at
Charleston: afterwards received the sword of Lord Cornwallis when his
army surrendered at York-Town. As a military man, he was one of the
most distinguished in the revolutionary army; and as a private individual he
had that union of simple dignity and benevolent courtesy, which mark the
gentleman: as a citizen he was one of the most estimable that Massachusetts
ever possessed. An account of his life, remarkably well written, may be found
in the 3d Vol. 2d series, of the Mass. His. Soc. Collections.

marriage of her eldest daughter with a British officer, which took place after his unfortunate, mental
disorder. An alliance of this kind, though there
were no personal objections to the individual, and in
this case the match was unexceptionable, would
have been most repugnant to his feelings ; and afforded one of the examples to shew, how cruelly
the calamities of war, and especially of civil war, interfere with the natural affections of mankind, and
carry confusion and bitterness among the dearest
connections of private life. In his unfortunate state
of mind, when reason could not exert its influence to
subdue prejudice and hatred, this marriage was always a subject of exasperation. His wife, though
exposed to many painful trials, from his misfortune,
never lost her tenderness and respect for him.
While amidst all the diminution of income and embarrassment of his private affairs, from neglecting his
own concerns to take care of those of the public, he
sacredly preserved the fortune he received with
her ; and after her decease, which was very sudden,
on November 15th, 1789, in her 60th year, it was
divided between her daughters.

In connection with these family notices, a brief
account of his sister, a very distinguished woman
may be here introduced. This sister, Mercy Otis,
married the Hon. James Warren of Plymouth, a descendant of some of the first and most respectable
pilgrims, who founded the Plymouth colony. General
Warren and his wife were both of them earnestly
attached to the cause of the revolution, in which he

rendered many efficient services, one of sufficient utility, to connect his name with that event in a lasting manner. He was the author of the scheme for forming Committees of Correspondence, which he communicated to Samuel Adams, in 1773, who was making him a visit. Mr. Adams consulted with his friends on his return to Boston, the plan was adopted, spread with rapidity throughout all the colonies, and became one of the most powerful mechanical means, for uniting and directing public sentiment in favour of the Revolution. He filled many honourable and responsible stations,* and died at Plymouth in November, 1808, in the eighty third year of his age. Mrs. Warren had much of the same ardour of character that distinguished her brother, and their political sympathies were in complete unison. With a husband who was earnestly engaged against the arbitrary designs that brought on the revolution; and with a brother, who was for so many years the chief leader and adviser in all the councils of opposition, she could not fail to become acquainted with all the principles and occurrences of that period, in which her disposition led her to be deeply interested. Politics and literature always

---

* On the death of his father in 1757, he was appointed his successor in the place of High Sheriff for the County, and retained this place to the beginning of the war. He was a member of the legislature, and President of the Provincial Congress. In 1775 he was made paymaster general of the army, but soon resigned it. He was for several years speaker of the House of Representatives of Massachusetts, and afterwards a Commissioner of the Navy Board. At the close of the war he retired, but was afterwards chosen into the council: his last public employment was as an elector of President in 1804.

occupied a large share of her attention, and through her whole life, she felt a strong interest in public affairs, and devoted much of her time to writing. She published, in 1805, a history of the American Revolution, in three volumes; a volume of Poems containing two tragedies, and occasional verses addressed to children and friends, in 1790—and an anonymous political satire in the shape of a drama, called " The Group," in 1775; she maintained a correspondence with several distinguished individuals, and wrote occasionally in the newspapers anonymously. She died at Plymouth, in 1814, at the age of 86.

Some scanty gleanings from the field of his professional career, are all that can now be recollected, though the qualities and employments that made Mr. Otis the acknowledged head of the bar, must have produced a rich harvest of professional anecdote. The following is one of the examples of his conduct as a lawyer, that is often related in the part of the country where it occurred. He was employed in a suit in the county of Plymouth, to recover the amount of a bill, which the defendant alleged had been paid, but of which fact he could not produce any proof. Mr. Otis was not aware of the dishonesty of his client, who was the plaintiff and a man of reputable standing—but while the cause was under trial, the latter taking out his pocket book to look after some document that was wanted, Mr. Otis happened to see among the papers a receipt in full which had been given for this identical demand; which the plaintiff having by some means

got possession of, had now brought this suit to recover a second time. Otis immediately took him
aside, and said to him, "you are a pretty rascal,
there is a receipt for the very demand now before
the Court!" The man was confounded and acknowledged that it was so, but begged his advocate
not to expose him. Otis immediately went back
into the bar, and stated to the Court, that it was
unnecessary the cause should be carried any further,
a circumstance had occurred which had convinced
him the plaintiff's demand was unfounded, and begged his client might be nonsuited. Chief Justice
Hutchinson without knowing at the time, the particular reasons for Otis's proceeding, paid him
some natural compliments on his frank and manly
conduct, and took the occasion to remark, how much
time might be saved, if it were generally imitated.

During the trial of one of the causes in which he
was engaged on the Western Circuit; his attention
was much excited by the manner of one of the witnesses, a young woman of very pleasing and modest
appearance, who gave her testimony against his
client, with such uncommon distinctness and intelligence, that after it was concluded, Mr. Otis said,
that with the leave of the Court, and the consent of
the witness, he would ask her some questions.
Then telling her, how much gratified every one
who heard her must have been, with the remarkable clearness and propriety of her testimony, the
following dialogue took place: " Where were you
born, ma'am? In the next town, Sir—Where were

you educated?—There, Sir—Where have you tra-
velled?—never out of this county, Sir." Mr. Otis
raised his hands exclaiming,

" Full many a flower is born to blush unseen
And waste its sweetness on the desert air."

He espoused a cause gratuitously at Plymouth, that
arose out of a frolic on a " Pope day ;" some details
of which, furnish characteristics of the times. A
custom of English origin, prevailed in Boston, and
occasionally in other seaports of Massachusetts, of
celebrating the fifth of November, the day of the
well known Gunpowder plot, which was called
Pope day. It was attended here with extravagan-
ces and pasquinades, not unlike, by a whimsical ap-
proximation, the satirical and burlesque licentiousness, that is practised during certain days of the
Carnival in some Catholic countries. On one of
these occasions at Plymouth, there was a great deal
of noisy turbulence. The inhabitants had been
forced to illuminate their windows, some of which
had been broken, which excited a good deal of ill
temper, and led to a prosecution of the offenders.
Mr. Otis was applied to by the defendants, some
thoughtless young men, to plead their cause.
Thinking the prosecution to have been illnatured
and vindictive, he kindly engaged in their defence,
exerted all his powers of humour and argument, described it as a common, annual frolic, undertaken
without malice, and conducted without substantial
injury; obtained their acquittal and refused all fees.

This anniversary, which was got up originally with political views, to keep alive hatred and distrust towards the Catholics in England ;* was commemorated in this country in a solemn way, and finished a topic for occasional sermons and prayers, against popery. It sometimes included in its denunciations, a covert reference to the hierarchy in England ; which in succeeding to many of the possessions, and some of the ceremonies of the papal church, was also thought by our puritan forefathers to have retained a good share of its cruel intolerance ; an intolerance, that, with marvellous inconsistency, they practised on others, while grieving themselves under its effects. Boston was always the head quarters of the celebration, which was indeed seldom practised beyond the limits of Massachusetts ; but in process of time it degenerated into a turbulent, licentious frolic. The town was divided into two parties, called the *North-end* and *South-end*, who had each their " pope," as it was called. One of the party ringing a hand bell knocked at every house, and recited a short ballad,† to get some gratuity for

---

* Pope burning was first introduced in England on the anniversary of Elizabeth's coronation. In Scott's edition of Dryden, there is a curious account of the ceremony, with a plate representing a procession that was made November 17th, 1679. See Vol. 6, p. 222. and vol. 10, p. 370.

     † Don't you remember
       The fifth of November,
     The Gunpowder treason and plot;
       I see no reason,
     Why gunpowder treason
       Should ever be forgot.

a common purse, to defray the expence of a jovial supper for the principal performers.

The pageant was exhibited on a stage, mounted on wheels and drawn by horses. In front of the stage, was a lantern six or eight feet high, made with oiled paper, and covered with satirical inscriptions, alluding to the political characters or events of the day ; and sometimes a boy was placed inside of it, accoutred and dancing in an antic manner. Next to the lantern, was a small figure meant for the Pretender, suspended to a gibbet. In the centre was the Pope, preposterously dressed, and made as corpulent as possible ; and in the rear was a figure of the Devil, with an enormous tail, a pitchfork in one hand, and a lantern in the other. Beneath the floor, boys were placed, who held poles that went up through the principal figures into the head, so that they could turn the heads round, or raise them up to a level with the chamber windows of the houses. Occasionally some political character, obnoxious to popular ill will, was exhibited between the figures of the Pope and the Devil. Thus the marquis of Bute was caricatured by a boot suspended

---

From Rome to Rome
The Pope is come,
Amid ten thousand fears,
With fiery serpents to be seen
At eyes, nose, mouth, and ears.
Don't you hear my little bell
Go chink, chink, chink.
Please to give me a little money,
To buy my Pope some drink.

to a gallows : Commissioner Paxton,* who was a remarkably polite man, but very unpopular, was represented by a figure with this label—" every man's
humble servant but no man's friend"—Governor
Bernard was personified by a tomcod, a small fish
he was very fond of catching, and consuming in his
family, a fondness that was attributed to his parsi-
mony. The pageants of the two parties were pa-
raded about in the day time quietly ; but in the
evening they met in Union Street, which was the
line of demarcation between them. A struggle ensued with all the force they could respectively mus-
ter, and the object was to capture the " Pope" of
the other. This was commonly effected at the expence of some broken heads ; and if the South succeeded, the trophies of the contest were carried to
the Common and there consumed; if the *North* was
victorious, they were taken to Copps Hill, where a
benfire was had, followed by a jovial supper. The
sailors, mechanics, young men and boys of all classes,
took part in these scenes. A story is related of one
of them, that interested the feelings of the whole
town at the time, and was productive of much chagrin to one side, and of many a hearty laugh to the
other. The *South-end* had been unlucky for several
years in the contests, when some young men, resolved to retrieve its reputation. This they effected

---

* Charles Paxton was one of the Commissioners of the Customs, and actively discharged the duties of a very unpopular office. He was remarkable
for the finished politeness and courtesy of his manners : but this, which might
have been considered a merit at other times, was in the bitterness of party
struggles, turned sarcastically against him.

chiefly by stratagem. They went down in considerable numbers in the evening to the lower part of Middle Street, and vociferated the usual cry, "*North-end* forever!" Deceived by this watch-word, the Northend Pope was brought out, when only a few of its real partizans were present, who joined this convoy of the enemy, as soon as they had carried it a little way, the disguised party, being joined by a number of their friends, threw off the concealment, assumed their own cry of *South-end forever!* and carried the prize to a triumphal bonfire, in the Common.

The termination of these *Pope days*, exhibits a characteristic trait of those times, and the docility of what might be considered a thoughtless, mob. The patriots of the town saw the mischief of these dissensions, when they wanted the feelings of the citizens to be united in the great object of opposition to the measures of the British Ministry : they therefore brought about a reconciliation, and in 1774, had what was called an *Union Pope*, when the two parties, after great preparations, met with their pageants, and exchanging amicable salutes, proceeded to make a common bonfire, and terminated the frolic by supping together. This was in November, 1774. The next spring, the affairs of Lexington and Bunker Hill took place, and this foolish and turbulent practise, a striking mark of colonial subserviency, was never repeated.

Chapter III.

Extracts from the Professional Correspondence of Otis.

THE following extracts from a letter book containing copies of letters on business, are cited, because so few fragments of Otis's manuscript can now be found. In the absence of more interesting correspondence, they may throw some light on his professional character. The deep feeling of respect and affection for the mother country, is exemplified in a very expressive word, that was commonly used in speaking of it, before the Revolution. England was called *home*, not only by those officers whose appointment from thence made their responsibility center there, but even by those who had never seen that country, and had derived their descent through several generations of colonial residence. The word occurs several times in these business letters. —Thus in one dated in 1764, there are these phrases: " but has the cause continued, to know from home, if he is chargeable" and again " since the matter was concluded by them, and the terms sent home for approbation." In a letter to his sister, Mrs. Warren, in 1766 " the enemies of our peace entertain hopes that we shall get no relief from home." But the course of events a few years after, made this distant home a foreign country; and in defending their real home from the encroachments of arbitrary power, they found, that this only could be the true object of their attachment.

The extracts from these letters are taken in the order of their dates. It will be shewn by them, that his political engagements, and interest in public affairs progressively increased, till he speaks of giving up his professional pursuits altogether. The first extract is from a letter to " Mr. Francis Rybot, London," dated November 22, 1763.—" I pray that your orders may be explicit, that I may come under no blame, for when gentlemen send powers with orders to make demands, and in their letters express fears least a suit should be brought, as you seem to do in yours, the consequence is, that all severities are to be laid to those they employ, which is a thing no man could run the risk of. I shall never take upon me to exercise my lenity at another man's expense, nor run the risk of involving myself for other people. If therefore at any time you would have compliance with your orders, please to let me know whether I am only to demand, or in default of payment to sue, expressly."

" To Messrs. Johnstone and others, assignees," &c. he writes May 16, 1764. " I am sorry to tell you the London Gazette you send me, for the proof of the bankruptcy of Wright and Graham, and as an evidence that you were assignees, is of no more value than an old almanack in my opinion. If our courts would receive such a paper as evidence, it don't appear by the advertisement, when the commission issued, &c." To the same, " September

25th 1764. I supposed by you, first application to me, that I was only to act in my profession as a lawyer, and not as a merchant or factor, to settle accounts and vendue goods. However, it seems you expect both of me, without having ever taken care, to this moment, to furnish me with the proper papers to act in either quality. My request, is that you would make a new power to some able merchant here, for I utterly decline being any further concerned, than till you have notice of this opportunity to make and send out such new powers. I have no inclination to merchandize." This last idea is expressed in letters to two other correspondents. In letters to two of these clients, who had at his request transferred the agency of their affairs to a merchant, whom he had recommended ; he says to one in June, 1765—" My discharge from the burden of your affairs is the more acceptable, as my engagements to the public, and the difficulties on the trade of this country, and my private concerns, render it inconvenient for me to enter into more affairs than I have on hand."—To another—" I am glad of your resolution not to send me any other of your affairs, more especially as the times are rendered so difficult here, that it is a very invidious employ to collect debts for gentlemen on your side of the water, and my own private affairs and engagements in the public service, will not admit of my engaging any further in the concerns of others."

He writes to Mr. Arthur Jones—September 13th, 1766. " With regard to the late measures you re-

fer to in the former administration, if I have been
instrumental of any benefit to the interest of Great
Britain and her Colonies, which I ever consider as
the same, I shall think it the great happiness of my
life, and can only wish for further opportunity of
promoting that interest to the utmost of my poor
ability."

Oliver Delancy, Esq. of New York, wished to
engage him to act for the widow of Sir Peter Warren, for various claims. In reply, after giving some
account of the debtors, he goes on to say—" October
6th, 1766—I should choose to act only in my profession, in which way, you and Lady Warren may at
all times command and depend on my best services.
I should not incline to undertake as a factor for any
person, having within these two or three years had
more trouble and gained more ill will by two or
three *procurations*, I was prevailed on to accept,
than by all the transactions of my life. I should
think it best for you to substitute Mr. Hancock, as
there is no better man for your purpose if he will
accept. He will of course apply to me as Counsel,
especially if you desire it, and Lady Warren will by
that means be availed of all his and my power to
serve her. If you think it worth while to transmit
a copy of this, let my most respectful compliments
attend it, with the highest assurances of the regard
I have for the memory of Sir Peter Warren,* for

---

* Sir Peter Warren, was a British Admiral, and knight of the Bath. He
performed many gallant services, and was much known and esteemed in the
northern colonies. He commanded the naval force in the New England ex-

the services he rendered this country."—Mr. De-, lancy writes him in return, that it was at Mr. Hancock's suggestion he had been applied to, that the power of Attorney is made out, and in behalf of Lady W. urges the request that he would undertake the agency. He writes in answer, October 13th, 1766. " Sir, next to *surety-ship*, it has been the care of my life to avoid *trusts*, yet I am engaged in many more public and private, than I have capacity to discharge, as I could wish. It would give me equal pleasure to comply with your and Lady Warren's desire, but I clearly foresee so many difficulties that will attend the settlement of her affairs here, that I can by no means think of accepting the power you mention, at the same time if you think fit to substitute any person, I shall ever be ready and proud to assist him in my profession, if desired, but I must repeat that I cannot accept of any power to me alone, or jointly with any other."

In a letter to Mr. Rybot of July 27th, 1767— " In answer to yours of the 7th of January—I have waited on Mr. ——— and he tells me it will much distress him to be sued for the note of 300*l.* sterling ; in short it is impossible for him to pay it at present. He also informs me, that you have given no express orders to sue the note, and being of opinion it is not for your interest to press him at present, I have not commenced any action against him. I am convinc-

---

pedition against Louisbourg, in 1745. He died in 1752, in the 49th year of his age.

Our fathers were a good people
we have known of the people
and if you will not let
us remain any longer
we shall be a great people

ed he is an honest man and will pay you as soon as
possible. However, if you should think fit to pursue him, I desire you would send a power to some
other person, as he is an old friend, and I chuse not
to be concerned in any severity against him, or
any other gentleman."

In November, 1768 writing to the same—" But
as I wrote you before, I decline that, and all other
affairs of the kind, especially as the times are, and
as I am winding up my own concerns, in order as
soon as possible to retire from business."

To Mr. Arthur Jones, he writes—November 26th,
1768. " All business is at a stand here, little going
on besides military musters and reviews and other
parading of the red coats, sent here, the Lord I believe only knows for what. I am and have been
long concerned more for Great Britain than for the
colonies. You may ruin yourselves, but you cannot
in the end ruin the colonies—Our fathers were a
good people, we have been a free people, and if
you will not let us remain so any longer, we shall
be a great people, and the present measures can
have no tendency but to hasten with great rapidity,
events, which every good and honest man would
wish delayed for ages, if possible, prevented forever."

In two letters dated October 11th, 1769. There
is this ominous memorandum at the top : " on paper
of Boston manufacture."

His talents and learning placed him so much
above those of his own standing, that he had no

rival; and though civil to those about him, he was not very cautious in concealing the contempt he felt for political enemies, who were inferior to him in every thing, but the power of their office, and who were, for the promotion of their private advantage, he believed, conspiring to ruin the country. Having cited Domat, in the course of some discussion, Governor Bernard enquired, " who he was ?"—Otis answered, that, " he was a very distinguished civilian, and not the less an authority, for being unknown to your Excellency."

His mode of conducting causes, as an advocate, was consistent with his extensive acquirements. He argued with boldness, energy and decision, without resorting to many of the subtleties, and narrow expedients, that are allowable, and often employed in the common practice of lawyers. He was indeed conscious of his strength, proud and impatient of rivalry. Governor Hutchinson, whose favourable testimony must have more weight, as being that of an enemy, said of him; " that he never knew fairer or more noble conduct in a pleader, than in Otis; that he always disdained to take advantage of any clerical error, or similar inadvertence, but passed over minor points, and defended his causes solely on their broad and substantial foundations."

These desultory anecdotes and disconnected sketches of his private life, are selected from the few that can be now recovered. His professional reputation and influence, having been gradually established on the most solid foundations, were held in the first rank, before he began his career in public life, the date of which may be fixed, from his pleading the cause of the Writs of Assistance. His learning and eloquence, on this occasion, gave him precedence over every member of his profession; while his ardour and enthusiasm excited a corresponding feeling in the breasts of his fellow citizens, who placed him at the succeeding election in the legislature of the Province. From that time, he became, for a period of ten years, the chief counsellor, and leading orator, in the course of resistance to arbitrary encroachment, that brought on the declaration of independence. A cursory view of the administration of the Province, at this epoch, will shew more clearly the situation in which he was placed.

Chapter IV.

Political Situation of Massachusetts—Governor Shirley—Lieutenant Governor Phipps—Governor Pownal—Lieutenant Governor Hutchinson—Appointment of Governor Bernard—Colonial monopoly.

THE war which terminated in the Peace of 1763, was for several years almost the exclusive object of attention, among the people of the Northern Colonies; and as Massachusetts was not only the most considerable of these in wealth and population, but far exceeded her proportion, in contributions of men and money and efforts of all kinds in the public service, her government had a very leading influence in all the transactions of the day. Jealousy and animosity towards the French, was in no part of the British dominions more keenly felt. On the water, they met us as rivals in the fisheries, while on the land, all the frontier settlements from Novia Scotia to the Lakes, were subject, through French agency, to perpetual anxiety, and occasionally to the desolating incursions, and horrible barbarities, of Indian warfare. The enmity arising from these causes was aggravated and kept in activity, by a deep hereditary prejudice on account of their religion.

To overturn the power of France in Canada, was therefore the leading and engrossing wish in our politics ; and to effect this object we made voluntary sacrifices, that perhaps were never exceeded by any people, whose whole territory was not overrun.*   Mr. Shirley the Governor of Massachusetts, was indefatigable in stimulating the ministry, and the several colonies, to follow this course. He had discovered so much industry and ability in his government, although not bred to a military life, that he was made Commander in Chief of the military forces, after the death of General Braddock. The brilliant success of the expedition to Louisbourg, in

---

* At one period every third man was engaged in some branch of the sea or land service, and the taxes in Boston, amounted to two thirds of the whole income of the real estate.

1745, undertaken under his auspices, gave him a reputation for the management of military operations.* But the disappointments and defeats, that took place in the campaign of 1755, were attributed to his want of skill in the immediate command of the forces. He was succeeded by General Abercrombie for only a few months, and then by Lord Loudon. Under this latter commander, the Colonies were involved in the deepest depression. His arrogance and indiscretion led him into disputes, and almost to make war against those he came to defend; while his indecision and delay, inspired the enemy with confidence, wasted all the resources of the country, paralysed every operation, and exposed the colonists, to the greatest mortification and danger. This period of imbecility and mismanagement dissipated much of that illusion, which had been felt in regard to the British regulars,† as they were called. The bold tone and arrogant presumption, which the regular army always assumed over the provincial troops, and which was commonly submit-

---

* The capture of Louisbourg, by the Massachusetts troops, was a fair subject of triumph, and is often mentioned, in the subsequent annals of that province. That their idea of the importance of this operation is not singular, the following passage from Lord Chesterfield's works will serve to prove. " This conquest was certainly of great importance, and in the end procured peace; but it was magnified to such a degree, that the noble Duke, who was at the head of the Admiralty, declared, that if France was master of Portsmouth, he would hang the man, who should give up Cape Breton in exchange.
Chesterfield's works, v. 2. p. 283.

† This distinction between regulars and provincials, which arose while they acted together, was retained long after. In popular language, the common term for the British troops, during the revolutionary war, was the " regulars."

ted to as a matter of course, if not of right, joined
to the real advantages they possessed, from their
discipline and experience, gave them the reputation
of being invincible. The gross blunders, committed
by some of their generals* and the ill success of
most the attempts made by the regular army, were
contrasted with many efficient and gallant services,
performed by the provincials : and though the
praise in the official accounts was as lavishly given
to the former, as it was sparingly bestowed on the
latter, the provincials themselves could not be
blinded to the truth. The illusion, about the irresistible prowess of the British troops, was destroyed
in the minds of many at this period ; and the consequences were shewn a few years afterwards, when
these bodies were to be opposed to each other.

Governor Shirley, it was said, first received the
plan of the Ministry for taxing America ;† but his
knowledge of the people, and his wish to direct their
utmost efforts against the French, made him discourage the project, and prevented its being attempted during his administration. He had sufficient sagacity and influence, to lead public opinion

---

* Among the documents on this subject, the eloquent letters of Washington, on the conduct of the army, under Generals Braddock and Forbes, are
remarkable. Those who wish to study the history of this period, will read a
pamphlet by Lord Sterling, entitled "the conduct of Major General Shirley,
late General and Commander in Chief of his Majesty's Forces, in North
America, briefly stated" also another defending Lord Loudon, called "The
Conduct of a noble commander in America, briefly reviewed." These with
two or three other pamphlets, relating to military affairs in America during
that war, may be found in the library of the Historical Society, in the volume
of tracts marked, C. D. 17.

† Minot.

entirely to this great object, and continued to be
popular, in his government, notwithstanding the burdens that were laid on the country, and the ill success
of his later military enterprises. His recall has
been attributed, in part, to the intrigues of his successor, though the charge involves ingratitude at
least, if not treachery.* A long residence in the
province, gave him a clear insight into the character
of the people : and he succeeded in being popular
here, without losing the confidence of the ministry.
At a later period, he might perhaps have been involved in the difficulties which rendered some of
his successors odious : but one motive to the course
they pursued, an avaricious and grasping spirit, he
was exempt from. He was disinterested, and elevated above the sordid pursuit of accumulating
money. Though placed in situations that furnished
him many opportunities of enriching himself, yet he
died without fortune. One of the most important
services he rendered, was the abolition of the paper
currency in 1749, which was greatly owing to his
firmness and perseverance.

He left the country highly respected and beloved, and was sent to Paris, as a Commissioner, to settle the subject of boundaries : The powers he had
exercised here, of Governor of one of the principal

---

* Some details on this matter may be found in a memoir of Governor
Livingston of New York, entitled, " A Review of Military operations, in
North America from 1753 to 1756." It is a well written and very interesting
historical document, though allowances must be made for its party feelings.
It may be found in the 7th volume first series of the Massachusetts Histori-
cal Society's Collections.

colonies, with the supremacy over others in military affairs, made him rivals and enemies in abundance. The unfortunate events of the war were also laid to his charge; but the circumstance, that wholly destroyed his popularity here, the mention of which will throw light on the character of the times, was, that he married a second wife in Paris, who was *a Catholic!* In the language of Dr. Eliot, " this was disgusting to the province, as the people, at that time, detested the French and all popish connections." He did not however lose the confidence of the ministry, who gave him the Government of the Bahamas, in which place he was succeeded by his son. Governor Shirley returned to Boston in 1770, and died at his seat in Roxbury, the next year.*

Mr. Phipps,† the Lieutenant Governor, administered the government for a short period, after Shirley was recalled, till the arrival of Governor Pownall in 1757. This gentleman first came to this country as Secretary of Sir Danvers Osborne, Governor of New York, and was then appointed Lieutenant Governor of New Jersey. Shirley took him into his confidence, and communicated his plans to him ;

---

* He built the spacious mansion in Roxbury, called Shirley Place, now owned by the Hon. W. Eustis. In King's Chapel in Boston, there is a handsome mural monument on the North side, erected to his first wife and daughter.

† Mr. Phipps, was the nephew of Sir William Phipps, and inherited his fortune, he was made Lieutenant Governor in 1732, in which post he continued till his death April 4th, 1757. His talents were not of a class to make him conspicuous as a statesman, but in the discharge of his functions, he was esteemed a prudent, upright magistrate.

and he was accused of betraying this trust, by anticipating all the important information in his own communications to the ministry. He doubtless saw the defects of Shirley as a military commander, and in taking part with his enemies, Delancey and Sir William Johnson, he acted with private ingratitude, though it might conduce to the public good to effect a change in the command. He went to England in 1756. His connections were respectable, and his brother was Secretary of the Board of Trade.* He was there appointed Governor of Massachusetts. His politics were those of Chatham, and he came to his government full of zeal and animation to promote the grand and decisive policy of that minister, for putting an end to the contests with France in America, by depriving that power of all its North American possessions.

On his arrival in his government, he could not be greeted with much cordiality, by those officers of the customs, and other departments, who had been the friends of Shirley ; and who thought the new governor had used unfair intrigues to supersede him. Their politics also were not of the same school. He cared less about enforcing the obnoxious acts of trade, and the collections of the revenue from them, than for a vigorous prosecution of the war. To this point he directed all his ef-

---

* To John Pownal, Esq. Secretary of the Board of Trade, the world owes the preservation of a vast number of valuable documents relating to the Colonies, which were in a very neglected state, and in danger of being wholly lost.

forts, and gave many proofs of activity and address. He took into his confidence such men as Judge Pratt and Dr. Cooper, who had much popular influence, and he associated affably and readily with all classes of people. This conduct counteracted in some degree the prejudice he excited in a community, distinguished by a very severe tone of manners; in which the light and free conduct of a man of wit and pleasure, appeared wholly unsuited to the formal dignity, and cautious propriety, which was expected in their chief magistrates.*

Hutchinson was appointed Lieutenant Governor in 1758, and as he was then very popular, he was of great use in aiding the Governor, in his efforts to draw out all the resources of the province in the prosecution of the war. There was however neither similarity of manners, nor cordiality of feeling between them. Pownal associated very intimately with the enemies of Hutchinson, and the latter in his turn exerted himself to destroy the

---

* In one of the satirical pieces, it was objected to him, that he would sometimes, "sit in the chair, without a sword, in a plain short frock, unruffled shirt, with a scratch wig and little rattan."—Externals were all important in those days, and this neglect of the appropriate costume, was considered a very improper levity. The title of this pamphlet, which is in the library of the Historical Society, (C. c. 3.) is as follows: "Proposals for publishing by subscription, the History of the public life, and distinguished actions of Vice Admiral, Sir Thomas Brazen, commander of an American Squadron in the last age. Together with his slighter adventures and more entertaining anecdotes In three volumes in quarto, adorned throughout with cuts: being the judicious abridgment of the unwearied author's own most elaborate and costly performance, of thirty one volumes in folio. By Thomas Thumb, Esq. surveyor of the customs, and clerk of the Check.—1760."

Governor's popularity.* But these differences, fortunately, did not operate to impede the efforts of
the province in the prosecution of the war. Massachusetts, and the neighbouring colonies, strained every nerve in the contest, and the glorious campaigns
under Wolfe and Amherst, realized the comprehensive designs of Lord Chatham, and extinguished
the French power on this continent.

Governor Pownal began his administration in
Massachusetts, at a period when the country was
depressed, both from the great sacrifices and the
repeated disasters of the previous years. Under
the auspices of an energetic minister, the whole aspect of affairs was soon changed, and the conquest
of Canada, the great object of New England for half
a century, completely obtained. His administration,
though short, was eminently successful. But he
found all the principal officers of Government opposed to him; and the friends of Shirley endeavouring to make him odious for his conduct towards that
officer, and called in wit and ridicule to aid their cause.
He therefore, after two years residence, obtained
leave to exchange his government for that of South
Carolina, and left Boston in June 1760, the two

---

* Pownal had induced the legislature, to erect a monument, in Westminster
Abbey, to Lord Howe, who fell in the attack against Ticonderoga. Out of
of the many monuments, *voted* by legislatures in this country, this is nearly
the only one, that has ever been executed. In 1760 a monument was voted to
the memory of General Wolfe, to be erected at the east end of the town house,
in King Street. Hutchinson displayed, with considerable success, to the
minds of the members of the legislature, the enormous expense to the province
of this monument, which cost 250*l.*! If the Governor had remained longer,
it would have been a powerful instrument for destroying his popularity.

branches of the legislature shewing their respect,
by accompanying him to the place of embarkation.
He held this appointment but a short time, before
he resigned it, to be sent in an official capacity to
the combined army in Germany in 1762. After he
obtained a seat in parliament, he opposed all the
measures of the ministry which led to the war of
separation. He argued in favour of giving the
Colonies a representation in Parliament, considering
their situation to be analogous to that of the Counties Palatine in England. His views were in some
degree like those of Dr. Franklin, in wishing to keep
the empire together. Governor Pownal was a
member of the Royal Society and fond of scientific
pursuits. He died at Bath in February 1805, in
his eighty fourth year.*

Hutchinson, as Lieutenant Governor, administered
the affairs of the province about two months, till
the arrival of Governor Bernard, who was promoted to Massachusetts from New Jersey, which province he had governed very acceptably. He arrived at a fortunate moment, to enter upon his new
government, and public opinion was prejudiced in

---

* He published many parliamentary speeches, and political and scientific
tracts. His style is rather harsh and obscure. The best of his works was " the
administration of the colonies," in 1764, which went through several editions.
His first work was " Principles of Polity" in 1752; he also wrote a Memoir
on East India affairs : a memoir on drainage : topographical description of
North America : Letter to Adam Smith : a memorial to the sovereigns of
Europe, on the state of affairs between the old and new World : a memorial
addressed to the Sovereigns of America : on the study of Antiquities : description of Roman antiquities in Gaul : Intellectual physics : a treatise on
old age.

his favour. This harmony continued for a time, though he very early took exclusively into his confidence the officers of the revenue, and their connections, and made the Lieutenant Governor his chief adviser. This course led to great results. Shirley, though in principle a friend to prerogative, and the supreme power of parliament over the colonies, had skilfully avoided, as much as possible, all disputes on these subjects, and had conciliated parties, and balanced them against each other. Pownal, with different political sympathies, naturally confided in the leaders of the popular party, knowing that the officers of government must support his measures of course; and perceiving that the great object, both with the ministry at home, and the rulers of the province, was a vigorous prosecution of the war, he knew if he could promote this policy, he might neglect minor objects, with impunity both to himself and the public. The course of avoiding a collision with popular sentiment on the snbjects of revenue and taxation, which had thus been followed for a period of fifteen years, through the administration of these two governors, was departed from by their successor, almost in the outset of his career. The friends he adopted, and the counsels he followed, aggravated the difficulties between the mother country and the colonies, every year; and were a very leading cause, among those arising out of individual influence, of the ultimate resort to open resistance by the latter.

There is something so monstrous in the general

system of colonial monopoly, that we look back
with some degree of surprise at the attempt to fas-
ten on a free, intelligent and active people, the odious shackles of a rigid colonial system. From the
time of our resistance to such tyranny, down to the
present day, its injustice and impolicy have been
growing more and more apparent. The first great
blow it received, was the emancipation of the United States; and that event inevitably leads to its
final destruction. France, Holland, Portugal and
Spain, have successively seen this colonial power
torn with violence, or fall by its own weight, from
their hands; and the period is obviously not remote,
when in every instance, the subjects of the same
empire, whatever may be their location, will require
an equality of rights, in disposing of the produce of
their industry. The whole clumsy and oppressive
scheme of mutual restrictions and alternate monopo-
lies will be done away. The only case where they
can, or do now exist, is in regard to colonies whose
produce is altogether agricultural, rich in amount,
but comprising a very few articles: where the
population, being composed of a few proprietors and
a large body of slaves, is intrinsically too feeble
to resist either foreign aggression or domestic commotion; and therefore needs on every ground a
force from the parent country for protection. Yet,
the progress of enlightened views in political economy, and wider experience of the beneficent effects of
free intercourse, on the activity and industry of
mankind, must eventually bring all civilized nations,

even those who possess such colonies, to abolish the greater part of the restrictive system.

The most conspicuous example of its absurdity and injustice, that the world has seen, was shewn in the case of the British North American provinces, especially those of New England. The inhabitants were descended from that virtuous, but stern and inflexible part of the English nation, who could neither compound with, nor endure, the chains of ecclesiastical or regal tyranny ; and who sought and found, at their own risk and expence, a country where they might be exempt from both. This they purchased from its natural owners, cultivated with their own hands, and defended with their own blood. The colonies thus formed, deriving nothing from the royal government but the form of a charter, which that government violated at will, found themselves, in process of time, under the protection of that same government, as soon as they afforded an object to increase its patronage. The kind of protection growing out of this circumstance, and they hardly experienced any other, increased, as they flourished. It exposed them to wars occasioned by European quarrels, and entailed upon them numberless sacrifices and sufferings. The moment that the great cause of these misfortunes, the French power in Canada, had been destroyed, which was effected mainly by their efforts, they began to find that the protection, as it was called, of the parent country, was to receive a most portentous extension; it entered all their fields, penetrated all their dwellings, mingled with their food, regulated all their enterprises, and finally claimed a right, " to bind them in all cases whatsoever."

The northern colonies had no great staple of agriculture, to employ their labour and afford them wealth. Industry and enterprise might make them amends, by enabling them to secure the comforts, and gradually to accumulate the wealth, that would furnish the luxuries of life; but they found their exertions impeded in every direction. Even the fisheries, which formed a very important part of their employment, were put in jeopardy, by some of the regulations consequent on the " Acts of Trade." They seemed in fact to be made the victims of every separate interest in the Empire, and in all cases of rivalry they were the party to be sacrificed; they were not allowed to manufacture, because the manufactures of the parent country would be injured; they were confined in their navigation, because the shipping interest in England would suffer; they were not allowed to sell their fish for French and Spanish molasses, because the sugar colonies would not have the monopoly of supplying them; they could not import teas from Holland, because it interfered with the East India Company; they could not trade with Spain and Portugal nor any other nation, because it infringed the navigation laws.* Under this colonial system, thwarted

---

* Yet not satisfied with this exclusive possession of their trade, the English government claimed the right of unlimited taxation. " Whether," says Burke, " you were right or wrong, in establishing the colonies on the princi-

in every movement, they received no equivalent for their deprivations, and were constantly restive and refractory: the system indeed was wholly inapplicable to them, unless they were doomed to poverty, ignorance, and insignificance. Under such a system, it was truly remarked by Sir Josiah Child, and steadily inculcated by all his followers; " that New England is the most prejudicial plantation to the kingdom of England." Yet what a fine illustration is given by this very country, to the beneficent effects of a liberal spirit in the regulations of commerce, and the incalculable advantages of destroying colonial monopoly. Since this " prejudicial plantation of New England," has formed part of a free country, has been allowed full scope to its industry, sending its ships wherever the wind bloweth; it has increased in its consumption of English products a thousand fold, without costing England a dollar for government or protection.

---

ples of commercial monopoly, rather than on that of revenue, is at this day a problem of mere speculation. You cannot have both by the same authority. To join together the restraints of an universal internal and external taxation, is an unnatural union: perfect uncompensated slavery. You have long since decided for yourself and them; and you and they have prospered exceedingly under that decision."

Chapter V.

*Application for Writs of Assistance—Hutchinson appointed Chief
Justice—Dissatisfaction of Otis—Chief Justice Pratt—Oxen-
bridge Thacher—Opening of the Cause of the Writs of Assistance
by Gridley and Thacher.*

IMMEDIATELY after the conquest of Canada was
completed, rumors were widely circulated, that a
different system would be pursued, that the charters would be taken away, and the colonies reduced
to royal governments. The offices of the customs
began at once to enforce with strictness, all the acts
of parliament regulating the trade of the colonies,
several of which had been suspended, or become
obsolete, and thus had never been executed at all.
The good will of the colonists or their legislatures,
was no longer wanted in the prosecution of the
war; and the commissioners of the customs were
permitted and directed to enforce the obnoxious
acts. Governor Bernard, who was always a suppor-
ter of the royal prerogative, entered fully into these
views, and shewed by his opinion, his appointments
and his confidential advisers, that his object would
be, to extend the power of the government to any
limits, which the ministry might authorize.

The first demonstration of the new course intended to be pursued, was the arrival of an order in
Council to carry into effect the Acts of trade, and
to apply to the supreme judicature of the Province.

for *Writs of Assistance*, to be granted to the officers
of the customs. In a case of this importance there
can be no doubt, that Mr. Paxton, who was at the
head of the customs in Boston, consulted with the
Government and all the crown officers, as to the
best course to be taken. The result was, that he
directed his deputy at Salem, Mr. Cockle, in November 1760, to petition the Superior Court, then
sitting in that town, for " writs of assistance." Stephen Sewall* who was the Chief Justice, expressed
great doubt of the legality of such a writ, and of
the authority of the Court to grant it. None of the
other judges said a word in favour of it; but as the
application was on the part of the Crown, it could
not be dismissed without a hearing, which after consultation was fixed for the next term of the Court,
to be held in February, 1761, at Boston, when the
question was ordered to be argued. In the interval, Chief Justice Sewall died, and Lieutenant Governor Hutchinson was made his successor, thereby
uniting in his person, the office of Lieutenant Governor with the emoluments of the commander of the
castle, a member of the Council, Judge of Probate
and Chief Justice of the Supreme Court!† This

---

* Stephen Sewall, then Chief Justice of the Supreme Court, belonged to one
of the most respectable families in New England, which has produced several learned and able men. This gentleman stood very high in public esteem,
for his honour, integrity, moderation, and great benevolence. He died in
December, 1760; and the loss of this impartial, high minded magistrate, at
that critical period, was rightly esteemed a public misfortune.

† Besides these offices held by himself, one of his brothers in law was
Secretary of State, and then a judge of the Supreme Court, and a mem-

appointment was unexpected and alarming to all reflecting minds; because it was evident, that this important place could n t have been given to a man
who already held so many offices, some of which
were quite incompatible with the place of Chief
Justice, unless seconding the designs of government
in all cases, was to be the excuse and the return
for such extraordinary favours.

There were some circumstances of a personal
kind connected with this appointment, that formed
the ground work for very malicious and absurd misrepresentation. It was generally believed, that the
place of Chief Justice, whenever it should become
vacant, had been promised by Governor Shirley to
James Otis's father, and that revenge for the disappointment was the cause of all his subsequent opposition. The language that was imputed to him by
common report on this occasion, and which has
been transmitted down, was according to one ver-
sion, " that he would set the province in flames,
though he perished in the fire" or according to another, in part of a well known line, *Acheronta movebo :** though neither of these speeches was ever
authenticated. That Otis should have perceived,
as clearly as any man, the impropriety and the danger of giving so many incongruous offices to one individual; that he would readily infer that the nomina-

---

ber of the Council. Afterwards one of them was Commissioner of stamps,
and when Hutchinson became Governor, his sons were consignees of the Tea :
the greediness of this family was uniform.

† Flectere si nequeo Superos, Acheronta movebo.

tion could not have been made except from sinister
views, that he should have felt disgust and indignation at the rapacity which could seek for such a
monopoly of offices; that his quick and generous
feelings should be roused at what he might consider
an injury to a parent, is natural; but that his public
career should have been forever guided by this
transient emotion, is preposterous and impossible.
It supposes a degree of dishonesty inconsistent with
the powerful talents, which even his bitterest enemies acknowledged. If he had not been governed
by principle, and taken the side which duty dic-
tated, he was acting a part in sheer folly; for his
talents, which led all the measures of opposition for
a series of years, would have been retained on the
opposite side at any price, and if his purpose had
been only to revenge his father's cause, the certain mode of doing so, would have been to take
part with the government. The motives of human
conduct are seldom unmixed, and even the best men
may, through the infirmities of nature, have some alloy
with their noblest intentions. But there is no surer
mark of a base and envious mind, than the belief,
that narrow, sordid views, can be the exclusive
means of giving to eminent men a lasting impulse in
the career of public life.*

---

* In writing upon this topic, Mr. Adams remarks : " It is provoking, and it is
astonishing, and it is humiliating, to see how calumny sticks and is transmitted
from age to age. Mr. —— is one of the last men that I should have expected to have swallowed that execrable lie, that Otis had no patriotism. The
father was refused an office worth 1200*l.* old tenor, or about 120*l.* Sterling,
and the refusal was no loss, for his practice at the bar was worth much more;

The mercantile part of the community was in a state of great anxiety, as to the result of this question. The officers of the Customs called upon Otis for his official assistance, as Advocate General, to argue their cause. But, as he believed these writs to be illegal and tyrannical, he refused. He would not prostitute his office to the support of an oppressive act; and with true delicacy and dignity, being unwilling to retain a station, in which he might be expected or called upon to argue in support of such odious measures, he resigned it, though the situation was very lucrative, and if filled by an incumbent with a compliant spirit, led to the highest favours of government.

The merchants of Salem and Boston, applied to Mr. Pratt* to undertake their cause, who was also

---

for Colonel Otis was a lawyer in profitable practice, and his seat in the legislature gave him more power and more honour ; for this refusal, the son resigned an office which he held from the Crown, worth twice that sum. The son must have been a most dutiful and affectionate child to the father ; or rather most enthusiastically and frenzically affectionate."

* Benjamin Pratt, Chief Justice of New York, was gifted by nature with strong talent and energy of mind, and he affords a striking example how these may raise one from a humble lot, and make even calamity the foundation of prosperity. Mr. Pratt was bred a mechanic, and met with a serious injury that disabled him from pursuing his trade. He turned his mind to study, went to college, and took his degree at Cambridge, 1737. He studied law, and rose to great distinction at the bar. Through the friendship of Governor Pownal, he was made Chief Justice of New York, in 1761 ; and on his first arrival there, was looked at by the Judges and the bar with reserve and dislike, from his being brought from another province to preside over them. A cause of great difficulty which had been many years depending, being brought up soon after he had taken his seat, gave him an opportunity of displaying the depth and acuteness of his intellect, and the soundness of his judgment, and secured for him at once, the public respect. He wrote some political essays on the topics of the day ; and a few remaining fragments in verse of his composition,

solicited to engage on the other side; but he declined taking any part, being about to leave Boston for
New York, of which province he had been appointed Chief Justice. They also applied to Otis and
Thacher, who engaged to make their defence, and
probably both of them without fees, though very
great ones were offered. The language of Otis
was, " in such a cause, I despise all fees."

Mr. Thacher, the colleague of Mr. Otis in this
great cause, was at that time one of the heads of
the bar in Boston, was a fine scholar, and possessed
of much general learning. He received his degree
at Cambridge in 1738; he first studied divinity, and
began to follow a profession which had been that
of his ancestors for several generations, but his voice
being too weak for the pulpit, he gave it up to
study law. His family was one of the most respectable in the Province, and his own character and
manners were such, as to secure affection and esteem. Unassuming and affable in his deportment,
of strict morality, punctual in his religious duties,
and with sectarian attachments that made him, like
a large majority of the people, look with jealousy
and enmity on the meditated encroachments of the
English hierarchy, he was in all these respects fitted to be popular. To these qualities he joined
the most pure and ardent patriotism, and a quick
preception of the views of those in power. He had
been for a long time watchful of Hutchinson's ambi-

---

prove that he possessed both taste and talent for poetry. He presided over
the Courts of New York but two years, dying in 1763, at the age of 54.

tion, but when he heard of his taking the place of Chief Justice, he no longer restrained his feelings, but on all occasions spoke of him with the contempt and indignation, that his selfishness and sinister conduct deserved. The opposition of Thacher gave the government great uneasiness : his disposition and habits secured public confidence, and while his moderation preserved him from the imputation of ambition, his learning and ability gave weight to his opinions, and prevented him from being considered as under the influence of others. Such a man might be esteemed an impartial umpire between the government and the people, and his example had naturally great weight with them. There was no pretext for assigning any unworthy motive for the part he took ; and he was therefore the more to be dreaded. Mr. Adams says, " they hated him worse than they did James Otis or Samuel Adams, and they feared him more, because they had no revenge for a father's disappointment of a seat on the Superior bench to impute to him, as they did to Otis."

He published some essays on the subject of an alteration proposed by Hutchinson relative to the value of gold and silver ; in which controversy, as will be noticed hereafter, Otis took part on the same side. Thacher also wrote a pamphlet against the policy of the Navigation Act, and the Acts of Trade. This pamphlet is entitled " The Sentiments of a British American" printed in 1764. It is temperate, though earnest, and well written, the hardship and impolicy of these measures is very ably illustrated—His motto is a fable of Phœdrus, of which the close is a key to his sentiments——

Ergo quid refert mea
Cui serviam? clitellas dum portem meas.

He died of a pulmonary complaint, aggravated by his excessive anxiety respecting public affairs in 1765, after having been two years in the legislature from the town of Boston.*

The trial took place in the Council Chamber of the Old Town House, in Boston. This room was situated at the east end of that building, and like all the interior parts, has since undergone various alterations. At that time it was an imposing and elegant apartment, ornamented with two splendid full length portraits of Charles II. and James II. The Judges, in those days, in conformity to European practice, attached a part of their official dignity to a

---

* "Not long before his death," says President Adams, "he sent for me, to commit to my care some of his business at the bar. I asked him whether he had seen the Virginia resolves: "Oh yes—they are men! they are noble spirits! It kills me, to think of the lethargy and stupidity that prevails here, I long to be out. I will go out—I will go out—I will go into Court and make a speech, which shall be read after my death, as my dying testimony against this infernal tyranny, which they are bringing upon us." Seeing the violent agitation into which it threw him, I changed the subject as soon as possible, and retired. He had been confined for some time. Had he been abroad among the people, he could not have complained so pathetically of the "lethargy and stupidity," for town and country were all alive; and in August, became active enough, and some of the people proceeded to unwarrantable excesses, which were more lamented by the patriots, than by their enemies. Mr. Thacher soon died, deeply lamented by all the friends of their country."

peculiar costume, which in later times they have here discarded. Their dress was composed of voluminous wigs, broad bands, and robes of scarlet cloth. The judges were five in number, including Lieutenant Governor Hutchinson, who presided as Chief Justice. The room was filled with all the officers of government, and the principal citizens, to hear the arguments in a cause, that inspired the deepest solicitude.

The case was opened by Mr. Gridley, who argued it with much learning, ingenuity and dignity, urging every point and authority, that could be found after the most diligent search, in favour of the Custom house petition; making all his reasoning depend on this consideration—" if the parliament of Great Britain is the sovereign legislator of the British Empire."* He was followed by Mr. Thacher on the opposite side, whose reasoning was ingenious and able, delivered in a tone of great mildness and moderation. " But," in the language of President Adams, " Otis was a flame of fire; with a prompti-

---

* This summary account of Mr. Gridley's argument, is from President Adams' letters. In Minot's History, Vol. 2. p. 87. A short statement of his argument is given, which tends to shew that this writ was founded on statutes of the 12th and 14th of Charles II. ; and the authority of the Supreme Court in this Province to grant it, was to be derived from the statute of the 7th and 8th of William III., which gave officers of the revenue in this country the same powers as officers in England—And that in the execution of their duty they should receive the *like assistance*. The obvious meaning of this seems to be, that an officer in case of necessity should have a right to call for the same support from those about him in pursuance of his duty. It seems a most stained and preposterous inference, to make the general term, *like assistance*, mean a special and odious process called a *writ of assistance*, invented in the worst times of the Stuart tyranny.

tude of classical allusions, a depth of research, a rapid summary of historical events and dates, a profusion of legal authorities, a prophetic glance of his eyes into futurity, and a rapid torrent of impetuous eloquence, he hurried away all before him. American Independence was then and there born. The seeds of patriots and heroes, to defend the *Non sine Diis animosus infans;** to defend the vigorous youth, were then and there sown. Every man of an immense crouded audience appeared to me to go away as I did, ready to take arms against Writs of Assistance. Then and there, was the first scene of the first act of opposition, to the arbitrary claims of Great Britain. Then and there, the child Independence was born. In fifteen years, i. e. in 1776, he grew up to manhood and declared himself free."

"There were no stenographers in those days," to give a complete report of this momentous harangue. How gladly would be exchanged for it, a few hundred verbose speeches on some of the miserable, transient topics of the day, that are circulated in worthless profusion. Yet on this occasion, "the seeds were sown," and though some of them doubtless fell by the wayside or on stony places, others fell

---

* This allusion is to the *Alliance Medal,* struck in Paris. One side of which contains the head of Liberty, with the words *Libertas Americana,* 4th July 1776, and on the reverse a robust infant struggling with the serpent, attacked by a Lion, (England) defended by Minerva, (France) who interposes a shield with the *fleurs de lis,* and on which the Lion fastens: the motto, furnished by Sir William Jones, *Non sine diis animosus infans,* and underneath the dates 17 Oct. 1777.
19 Oct. 1781.

on good ground, and sprang up and increased and brought forth in due season, thirty, sixty and an hundred fold. Of the vigour of some of the soil that received this seed, the preceding quotation is a living and most eloquent proof. It indeed affords some compensation for the absence of contemporary records, and the subsequent neglect of this great leading transaction, that one of the hearers, after the lapse of sixty years, with all the authority which venerable age and illustrious services can confer, should have called the attention of his countrymen to the subject; and by a rare and felicitous force of memory, carrying back their regards over the course of two generations, have exhibited with a magical effect through the obscurity of time, an impressive and brilliant sketch, of one of the first struggles that led to their national existence.

Chapter VI.

Otis's Speech in the Cause of the Writs of Assistance.

ANXIETY and expectation were raised to the utmost in the minds of all parties, to hear the argument of Otis, which he began in the following manner.*

---

* The fragments of this speech are taken from Minot's History, Vol. 2. It seems from the letters of President Adams, that they were derived from

" MAY IT PLEASE YOUR HONOURS,

" I was desired by one of the Court to look into
the books, and consider the question now before
them concerning Writs of Assistance. I have accordingly considered it, and now appear not only in
obedience to your order, but likewise in behalf of
the inhabitants of this town, who have presented
another petition, and out of regard to the liberties of
the subject. And I take this opportunity to declare, that whether under a fee or not, (for in such
a cause as this I despise a fee,) I will to my dying
day oppose with all the powers and faculties God
has given me, all such instruments of slavery on the
one hand, and villany on the other, as this writ of
assistance is.

" It appears to me the worst instrument of arbitrary power, the most destructive of English liberty and the fundamental principles of law, that ever
was found in an English law book. I must therefore beg your honours' patience and attention to
the whole range of an argument, that may perhaps
appear uncommon in many things, as well as to
points of learning that are more remote and unusual: that the whole tendency of my design may
the more easily be perceived, the conclusions better
descend, and the force of them be better felt. I
shall not think much of my pains in this cause, as I
engaged in it from principle. I was solicited to

some imperfect notes, taken by him at the time, which were afterwards carried off by some individual, who " interpolated them, with some bombastic
expressions of his own," and printed them in a newspaper.

argue this cause as Advocate General ; and because I would not, I have been charged with desertion from my office. To this charge I can give a very sufficient answer. I renounced that office, and I argue this cause from the same principle ; and I argue it with the greater pleasure, as it is in favour of British liberty, at a time when we hear the greatest monarch upon earth declaring from his throne, that he glories in the name of Briton, and that the privileges of his people are dearer to him than the most valuable prerogatives of his crown; and it is in opposition to a kind of power, the exercise of which in former periods of English history, cost one King of England his head, and another his throne. I have taken more pains in this cause, than I ever will take again, although my engaging in this and another popular cause has raised much resentment. But I think I can sincerely declare, that I cheerfully submit myself to every odious name for conscience sake : and from my soul I despise all those, whose guilt, malice, or folly has made them my foes. Let the consequences be what they will, I am determined to proceed. The only principles of public conduct, that are worthy of a gentleman or a man, are to sacrifice estate, ease, health, and applause, and even life, to the sacred calls of his country.

" These manly sentiments, in private life, make the good citizen ; in public life, the patriot and the hero. I do not say, that when brought to the test, I shall be invincible. I pray God I may never be brought to the melancholy trial, but if ever I should, it will be then known how far I can reduce to practice, principles, which I know to be founded in truth. In the mean time I will proceed to the subject of this writ."

It appears that some of these writs had been issued, though by what authority is not stated; and the officers of the revenue were afraid to make use of them, unless they could obtain the sanction of the superior court, which had led to the application. It is impossible to devise a more outrageous and unlimited instrument of tyranny, than this proposed writ :* and it cannot be wondered at, that such an alarm should have been created, when it is considered to what enormous abuses such a process might have led. The following paragraph from the report of Otis' speech before quoted, will serve to shew what kind of instrument was here prayed for, and some results that might have been expected from it.

" Your Honours will find in the old books concerning the office of a Justice of the Peace, precedents of general warrants to search suspected houses. But in more modern books, you will find only special warrants to search such and such houses, specially named, in which the complainant has before sworn that he suspects his goods are conceal-

---

* " The form of this writ, was no where to be found ; in no statute, no law book, no volume of entries ; neither in Rastall, Coke, or Fitzherbert, nor even in the Instructor Clericalis, or Burns Justice. Where then was it to be found ? No where, but in the imagination or invention, of Boston Custom House Officers, Royal Governors, West India Planters, or Naval Commanders." President Adams' Letters.

ed; and will find it adjudged, that special warrants only, are legal. In the same manner I rely on it, that the writ prayed for in this petition, being general, is illegal. It is a power, that places the liberty of every man in the hands of every petty officer. I say I admit that special writs of assistance, to search special places, may be granted to certain persons on oath; but I deny that the writ now prayed for can be granted, for I beg leave to make some observations on the writ itself, before I proceed to other acts of Parliament. In the first place, the writ is universal, being directed ' to all and singular Justices, Sheriffs, Constables, and all other officers and subjects;' so that, in short, it is directed to every subject in the King's dominions. Every one with this writ may be a tyrant in a legal manner, also may control, imprison, or murder any one within the realm. In the next place, it is perpetual, there is no return. A man is accountable to no person for his doings. Every man may reign secure in his petty tyranny, and spread terror and desolation around him, until the tramp of the arch-angel shall excite different emotions in his soul. In the third place, a person with this writ, in the day time, may enter all houses, shops, &c. at will, and command all to assist him. Fourthly, by this writ, not only deputies, &c. but even their menial servants, are allowed to lord it over us. What is this but to have the curse of Canaan with a witness on us; to be the servant of servants, the most despicable of God's creation? Now one of the most essential branches of English liberty is the freedom of one's house. A man's house is his castle; and whilst he is quiet, he is as well guarded as a prince in his castle. This writ, if it should be declared legal, would totally annihilate this privilege. Custom-house officers may enter our houses when they please; we are commanded to permit their entry. Their menial servants may enter, may break locks, bars, and every thing in their way: and whether they break through malice or revenge, no man, no court, can inquire. Bare suspicion without oath is sufficient. This wanton exercise of this power is not a chimerical suggestion of a heated brain. I will mention some facts. Mr. Pew had one of these writs, and when Mr. Ware succeeded him, he endorsed this writ over to Mr. Ware: so that, these writs are negotiable from one officer to another; and so your Honours have no opportunity of judging the persons to whom this vast power is delegated. Another instance is this: Mr. Justice Walley had called this same Mr. Ware before him, by a constable, to answer for a breach of the sabbath-day acts, or that of profane swearing. As soon as he had finished, Mr. Ware asked him if he had done. He replied, Yes. Well then, said Mr. Ware, I will shew you a little of my power. I command you to permit me to search your house for uncustomed goods; and went on to search the house from the garret to the cellar; and then served the constable in the same manner! But to shew another absurdity in this writ, if it should be established, I insist upon it every person by the 14th Charles second, has this power as well as the Custom-House officers. The words are, " it shall be lawful for any person or persons authorized, &c." "What a scene does this open! Every man prompted by revenge, ill humou , or wantonness to inspect the inside of his neighbour's house, may get a writ of assistance. Others will ask it from self-defence; one arbitrary exertion will provoke another, until society be involved in tumult and in blood."

His argument in this cause lasted between four and five hours, and the summary of it can be best, and can now be only given, in the words of President Adams, who divides it into five parts as follows : 1. " He began with an exordium, containing an apology for his resignation of the office of advocate general in the court of admiralty; and for his appearance in that cause in opposition to the crown, and in favour of the town of Boston, and the merchants of Boston and Salem."

2. " A dissertation on the rights of man in a state of nature. He asserted, that every man, merely natural, was an independent sovereign, subject to no law, but the law written on his heart, and revealed to him by his Maker, in the constitution of his nature, and the inspiration of his understanding and his conscience. His right to his life, his liberty, no created being could rightfully contest. Nor was his right to his property less incontestible. The club that he had snapped from a tree, for a staff or for defence, was his own. His bow and arrow were

his own; if by a pebble he had killed a partridge or
a squirrel, it was his own. No creature, man or
beast, had a right to take it from him. If he had
taken an eel, or a smelt, or a sculpion, it was his
property. In short, he sported upon this topic with
so much wit and humour, and at the same time with
so much indisputable truth and reason, that he was
not less entertaining than instructive. He asserted,
that these rights were inherent and inalienable.
That they never could be surrendered or alienated,
but by ideots or madmen, and all the acts of ideots
and lunatics were void, and not obligatory, by all the
laws of God and man. Nor were the poor negroes
forgotten. Not a Quaker in Philadelphia, or Mr.
Jefferson of Virginia, ever asserted the rights of negroes in stronger terms. Young as I was, and ignorant as I was, I shuddered at the doctrine he
taught; and I have all my life shuddered, and still
shudder, at the consequences that may be drawn
from such premises. Shall we say, that the rights
of masters and servants clash, and can be decided
only by force? I adore the idea of gradual abolitions! but who shall decide how fast or how slowly
these abolitions shall be made?

3. " From individual independence he proceeded
to association. If it was inconsistent with the dignity
of human nature to say, that men were gregarious
animals, like wild geese, it surely could offend no
delicacy to say, they were social animals by nature;
that there were natural sympathies, and above all,
the sweet attraction of the sexes, which must soon

draw them together in little groups, and by degrees in larger congregations, for mutual assistance and defence. And this must have happened before any formal covenant, by express words or signs, was concluded. When general councils and deliberations commenced, the objects could be no other than the mutual defence and security of every individual for his life, his liberty, and his property. To suppose them to have surrendered these in any other way, than by equal rules and general consent, was to suppose them ideots or madmen, whose acts were never binding. To suppose them surprised by fraud, or compelled by force into any other compact, such fraud and such force could confer no obligation. Every man had a right to trample it under foot whenever he pleased. In short, he asserted these rights to be derived only from nature, and the author of nature ; that they were inherent, inalienable, and indefeasible by any laws, pacts, contracts, covenants, or stipulations, which man could devise.

4. " These principles and these rights were wrought into the English constitution, as fundamental laws. And under this head he went back to the old Saxon laws, and to Magna Charta, and the fifty confirmations of it in parliament, and the executions ordained against the violators of it, and the national vengeance which had been taken on them from time to time, down to the Jameses and Charleses ; and to the position of rights and the bill of rights, and the revolution. He asserted, that the security of these rights to life, liberty and property, had been the

object of all those struggles against arbitrary power, temporal and spiritual, civil and political, military and ecclesiastical, in every age. He asserted, that our ancestors, as British subjects, and we, their descendants, as British subjects, were entitled to all those rights, by the British constitution, as well as by the law of nature, and our provincial charter, as much as any inhabitant of London or Bristol, or any part of England; and were not to be cheated out of them by any phantom of " virtual representation," or any other fiction of law or politics, or any monkish trick of deceit and hypocrisy.

5. " He then examined the acts of trade, one by one, and demonstrated, that if they were considered as revenue laws, they destroyed all our security of property, liberty, and life, every right of nature, and the English constitution, and the charter of the province. Here he considered the distinction between " external and internal taxes," at that time a popular and common place distinction. But he asserted that there was no such distinction in theory, or upon any principle but " necessity." The necessity that the commerce of the empire should be under one direction, was obvious. The Americans had been so sensible of this necessity, that they had connived at the distinction between external and internal taxes, and had submitted to the acts of trade as regulations of commerce, but never as taxations, or revenue laws. Nor had the British government, till now, ever dared to attempt to enforce them as taxations or revenue laws. They had laid dormant in that character for a century almost. The navi-

gation act he allowed to be binding upon us, because we had consented to it by our own legislature.
Here he gave a history of the navigation act of
the first of Charles II., a plagiarism from Oliver
Cromwell. This act had lain dormant for fifteen
years. In 1675, after repeated letters and orders
from the King, governor Leverett very candidly informs his majesty, that the law had not been executed, because it was thought unconstitutional; parliament not having authority over us."

Taking a rapid survey of the terrors and vexations the colonists were exposed to under the reign
of Charles I. and their tranquillity under the Commonwealth, he came to the first fruits which they
tasted of the restoration, to the celebrated Navigation Act; and he dwelt upon this as the first in order, among those acts which were now to be enforced by the Writs of Assistance. The main provisions of this act may be comprised in a very few
words; nothing should be imported into any of the
English possessions in Asia, Africa or America, excepting in vessels belonging to the people of England,
Ireland, Wales or the Town of Berwick upon
Tweed, and besides being truly built and owned in
said possessions, the master and three fourths of the
sailors must be English; and no goods of foreign
production should be brought even in English shipping, except from the countries that produced them.

He expatiated on the narrow exclusive spirit of
this statute; but he would not deny either its policy
or necessity, at the time of its enactment, because
England was then surrounded by the power of

France, Spain, and Holland; nor would he blame the conduct of Governor Leverett,* and the Massachusetts legislature in adopting it in 1675, after it had laid dormant for fifteen years. It was a sacrifice they were obliged to make ; but he contended, that the sacrifice was a very great one on the part of the colonies in general, and of New England in particular, and above all to the town of Boston. He thought this statute ought to have been sufficient to satisfy the ambition and cupidity of the mother country, who boasted so much of her indulgence and affection for her colonies.

The navigation act, however, was wholly prohibitory, it abounded with penalties and forfeitures, but it imposed no taxes. The distinction therefore was vastly great between this and the Acts of Trade. Though no revenue was to be derived from this act, still it was intended to be enforced by these Writs, and houses were to be broken open and ransacked under their authority to enforce it. The Writs of Assistance were thus extended in a manner, which had never been contemplated. He dis-

---

* Governor Leverett was the son of Thomas Leverett, a ruling elder of the first Church, and one of the earliest inhabitants of Boston. He had been in military life abroad before he received employment here, which happened in 1642, when he was sent to demand satisfaction of the Sachem Miantinomo. He was one of Cromwell's commissioners in 1653, to make war against the Dutch at Manhadoes (New York.) He was afterwards constantly in the public service. He was in England at the restoration, and a useful advocate for Massachusetts with the King, who did not look with much complacency on a colony, whose attachments were far more republican than royal. Upon his return to Boston, he filled various offices, and was made Governor, in 1673, and was chosen annually till his death. He died greatly beloved and lamented, March 16th, 1678-9.

cussed most amply, all the effects, which the acts of navigation produced upon the colonies.

There are, it may be here observed, few statutes enacted by any nation, that have been more important, or excited more discussion, than the English navigation act. While the restrictive and monopolizing system was thought to be sound political wisdom, this act as forming an essential part of it, might be considered a masterpiece of policy; but in proportion, as wiser notions of national policy make their way into the councils of all civilized countries, and gradually eradicate the false and narrow principles of less enlightened periods, this act, which has been often relaxed in its operation, will probably so far as foreign trade is concerned, give way to the extension of liberal views in commerce; which all free and industrious nations find every day to be more and more productive of advantage to themselves, as well as to the world at large. Commerce is now gradually enlarging the prosperity and the rights of mankind; and wise statesmen begin to believe more fully, that the general prosperity increases individual advantage; and that nations gain not by depressing, but by a free intercourse with each other. This act did not meet with universal approbation at first, and in the language of Sir Josiah Child "some wise and honest gentlemen and merchants doubted, whether the inconveniences it has brought with it, be not greater than the conveniences." It is a curious circumstance, that this act which has been cherished with so much bigotry in England, and which inflicted so much injury and oppression on the Colonies, and especially on Massachusetts, should have originated from one of her own progeny, for such was its author, Sir George Downing, of whom President Adams speaks in the following manner.

" But it is high time for me to return from this ramble to Mr. Otis' quotations from Sir Josiah Child, whose chapter four, page 105, is " concerning the act of navigation." Probably this knight was one of the most active and able inflamers of the national pride in their navy and their commerce, and one of the principal promoters of that enthusiasm for the act of navigation, which has prevailed to this day. For this work was written about the year 1677, near the period, when the court of Charles II. began to urge and insist on the strict execution of the act of navigation. Such pride in that statute, did not become Charles, his court, or his nation of royalists and loyalists, at that time. For shall I blush, or shall I boast, when I remember, that this act was not the invention of a Briton, but of an American. George Downing, a native of New England, educated at Harvard College, whose name, office, and title appear in their catalogue, went to England in the time of lord Clarendon's civil wars, and became such a favourite of Cromwell and the ruling powers, that he was sent ambassador to Holland. He was not only not received, but ill treated, which he resented on his return to England, by proposing an act of navigation, which was adopted,

and has ruined Holland, and would have ruined
America, if she had not resisted.

"To borrow the language of the great Dr. Johnson, this 'Dog' Downing must have had a head and
brains, or in other words, genius and address : but if
we may believe history, he was a scoundrel. To in-
gratiate himself with Charles II. he probably not
only pleaded his merit in inventing the navigation
act, but he betrayed to the block some of his old
republican and revolutionary friends.

"But where is Downing's statute ? British policy
has suppressed all the laws of England, from 1648
to 1660. The statute book contains not one line.
Such are records and such is history."

From the navigation act the advocate passed to
the Acts of Trade, and these, he contended, imposed
taxes, enormous, burthensome, intolerable taxes; and
on this topic he gave full scope to his talent, for
powerful declamation and invective, against *the tyranny of taxation without representation.** From the

---

* "It happened," (says Burke in his speech on taxation) "you know,
Sir, that the great contests for freedom in this country, were from the earliest
times chiefly upon the question of taxing. Most of the contests in the ancient Commonwealths turned primarily on the right of election of magistrates ;
or on the balance among the several orders of the state. The question of
money was not with them so immediate. But in England it was otherwise.
On this point of taxes, the ablest pens and most eloquent tongues have been
exercised ; the greatest spirits have acted and suffered. In order to give the
fullest satisfaction concerning the importance of this point, it was not only
necessary for those who in argument defended the excellence of the English
constitution, to insist on this privilege of granting money as a dry point of
fact, and to prove, that the right had been acknowledged in ancient parch-
ments and blind usages, to reside in a certain body called a House of Commons. They went much further, they attempted to prove, and they suc-

energy with which he urged this position, that taxation without representation is tyranny, it came to be a common maxim in the mouth of every one. And with him it formed the basis of all his speeches and political writings; he builds all his opposition to arbitrary measures from this foundation, and perpetually recurs to it through his whole career, as the great constitutional theme of liberty, and as the fundamental principle of all opposition to arbitrary power.

The first of these acts of trade on which he commented was the 15th of Charles II. ch. 7. in 1663, entitled " An act for the encouragement of trade" one short section from this act may be given as a type of them all, shewing in the most undisguised manner, the remorseless spirit of colonial monopoly. " Sec. 5. And in regard his majesty's plantations beyond the seas are inhabited and peopled by his sub-

---

ceeded, that in theory it ought to be so, from the particular nature of a House of Commons, as an immediate representative of the people; whether the old records had delivered this oracle or not. They took infinite pains to inculcate as a fundamental principle, that in all monarchies, the people must in effect themselves, mediately, or immediately, possess the power of granting their own money, or no shadow of liberty could subsist. The colonies drew from you, as with their lifeblood, these ideas and principles. Their love of liberty, as with you, fixed and attached on this specific point of taxing. Liberty might be safe, or might be endangered in twenty other particulars, without their being much pleased or alarmed. Here they felt its pulse, and as they found that beat, they thought themselves sick or sound. I do not say whether they were right or wrong, in applying your general arguments to their own case. It is not easy indeed to make a monopoly of theorems and corollaries. The fact is, that they did thus apply those general arguments; and your mode of governing them whether through wisdom or mistake, confirmed them in the imagination, that they as well as you, had an interest in these common principles."

jects of this his kingdom of England, for the maintaining a greater correspondence and kindness between them, and keeping them yet more beneficial and advantageous unto it, in the further employment and increase of English shipping and seamen, vent of English woollen and other manufactures and commodities, rendering the navigation to and from the same, more cheap and safe, and making this kingdom a staple, not only of the commoditie of these plantations, but also of the commodities of other countries and places, for the supplying of them; and it being the usage of other nations to keep their plantations' trade to themselves."—The statute then goes on to enact that nothing shall be imported or exported from the Colonies, except from or to " England, Wales, or the Town of Berwick upon Tweed." It may be imagined from the ardent character of the speaker, what must have been the tone of his observations on these ordinances. Mr. Adams says, that " some of them appeared to me at the time, young as I was, bitter."

The main question constantly recurred, where is the authority for the writs of assistance? After all the search that had been made by all the members of the bar who had been employed on either side, the only instance where the words could be found, was in a statute of the 13th and 14th of Charles the second, which was cited by Mr Gridley, and which Otis denied to be either authority or precedent, or to have the least colour of either, in America. " The statute was entitled, " An act to prevent

frauds, and regulating abuses in his majesty's customs;" and in the fifth section, which had reference
to prohibited or uncustomed goods being found on
board of vessels after clearance, or in any place on
shore, it is provided for the seizure of those goods,
that, " it shall be lawful to or for, any person or
persons, authorized by *writ of assistance under the seal
of his majesty's Court of Exchequer*, to take a constable, headborough, or other public officer, inhabiting
near unto the place, and in the day time to enter,
and go into any house, shop, cellar, warehouse, or
room, or other place; and in case of resistance,
to break open doors, chests, trunks, and other pack-
age, there to seize and from thence bring, any kind
of goods or merchandize whatsoever prohibited and
uncustomed, and to put and secure the same, in his
majesty's storehouse in the port next to the place
where such seizure shall be made." Another act
was cited in connexion with this, that was passed in
the seventh and eight of William the third, chap.
23d. "to regulate the plantation trade."—This statute
expressly recited the act before mentioned of Charles
II. which it went to inforce, and that " like assistance" should be given to the officers as in the act
of Charles—the word *assistance* here occurs for the
second, and last time, in any statute.

But in the former of these acts, and in the latter,
if the construction can be allowed to authorize a
writ of assistance, these writs were to be issued under the seal of the Court of Exchequer, and were
returnable to it. Otis, after alluding to both these

acts, asked with triumphant confidence, "where is your seal of his majesty's Court of Exchequer, and, what has the Court of Exchequer to do here?" They had no warrant from the Exchequer in England, and could not assume to have any. It could not be pretended that the Superior Court of Judicature, court of assize and general goal delivery in the Massachusetts Bay, had all the powers of the Court of Exchequer in England and could issue warrants like that Court. No custom house officer dared say it, or instruct his counsel to say it. This Court, it is true, was invested with all the power of the Court of King's bench, common pleas and exchequer in England; but this power was given by a law of the provincial legislature, by virtue of the powers vested in it by the charter. Yet neither Hutchinson nor the other judges, dared say that this Court was his majesty's court of exchequer, because the principle would have been fatal to parliamentary pretensions.

Otis went still further than to deny the jurisdiction of the court of exchequer; its warrants and writs were never seen here, or if they were, would be only waste paper. Such a " writ of assistance" he said, might become the reign of Charles* the se-

---

* Chalmers in his Political Annals, relating the protection accorded by Charles to the followers of Gorton, against the tyrannical measures of the Massachusetts government, remarks; "What a contrast is there between the good natured, careless monarch of England, and the unfeeling and interested bigots of Massachusetts. When the failings of Charles II. are mentioned, it ought to be remembered, that during his reign, he exerted himself with more than usual vigour in protecting his subjects against the injustice and oppression of that government." Yet Chalmers, whose antipathy is very strong to the puritan forefathers of Massachusetts, when speak-

cond of England, and he would not dispute the taste of the parliament of England in passing such an act, nor the people of England in submitting to it; but it was not calculated for the meridian of this country. He insisted further, that these warrants and writs were even in England inconsistent with the fundamental laws, the natural and constitutional

---

ing of their intolerant conduct in another place, observes : " We think with less asperity of the persecutors of such men : and when we see them struggling with disease and famine in the wilderness, we are too apt to give them less of our pity, than humanity would otherwise bestow. There is nothing more irregular than the human mind when governed by unnatural impulses. The general Court, while persecuting all who differed from it in opinion, religious or political, ordained, " that all strangers professing the christian religion, who shall flee to this country, from the tyranny of their persecutors, shall be succoured at the public charge, till some provision can be made for them" and that body received with a benevolence that covereth a multitude of faults, the Scots ' whom the Lord had delivered into Cromwell's hands at Dunbar,' and who were transported to Massachusetts to suffer for their own credulity, and the folly of their rulers."

The intolerance exercised by the government in the first ages of the Massachusetts colony, is a sad instance of human weakness. Yet there are still more apologies for them than those mentioned by Chalmers. The sacrifices they made for conscience sake, and the dangers they exposed themselves to, serious enough in reality, but still magnified by imagination, could only be sustained by nourishing a solemn feeling of their being, like the Jews, a chosen people under the special protection of Providence. But the very belief in this divine protection, naturally made them think very harshly of those who differed from them ; and these " poor exiles to the utmost ends of the earth," in the language of the Massachusetts Government to Cromwell ; " these dear saints of God" as the deputies of the league in 1653 termed the inhabitants of Connecticut, exposed to the machinations of the Dutch and Indians at Manhattan, thought errors of faith, the most heinous of all crimes, were destined to afford a remarkable proof of the maxim, that the same spirit that will suffer martyrdom, will inflict it. As to Charles II. he was doubtless a much pleasanter companion than the puritan magistrates of Massachusetts, but it will be recollected, that " careless and good-natured" as he was, all his measures tended to the establishment of tyranny ; while the policy of the forefathers of New England, stern and bigotted as they were led eventually to the attainment of freedom.

rights of the subjects. If, however, it would please the people of England, he might admit that they were legal there, but not here.

The case of the petitioners was attempted to be made out, by a series of inferences and forced constructions of the most sophistical kind; whenever they could find the word " writ" or " continued" or " assistance" or the words " court of exchequer," they produced the statute, though it might be in express terms, " restricted to the realm." There were several acts of this kind passed under the Stuart kings, which were brought forward. Among these were, " an act for the regulation of the trade of Bay making, in the Dutch Hall in Colchester"—and an " act for the regulating the making of Kidderminster stuffs." There seems to have been no other reason for citing these statutes than their having contained permission " to enter, search, break open houses, shops, cellars, rooms, casks, boxes," &c. &c .and to seize and carry away " certain obnoxious articles." These odious and violent enactments, which have at all times perhaps, been too readily passed in England, were yet limited to some particular manufacture, which they were designed to encourage. Many of them were brought from different reigns, in which the rights of the subject were treated with little ceremony, in favour of establishing particular manufactures, and of destroying foreign rivalship, yet all these acts were confined to the realm, and their operation to very narrow limits within it. " The wit, the humour, the irony, the satire played off, by

Mr. Otis, in his observations on these acts of navigation, Dutch Bays, and Kidderminster stuffs," "it would be madness in me," says Mr. Adams, " to pretend to remember with any accuracy.   But I do say, that Horace's *Irritat, mulcet, veris terroribus implet*, was never exemplified in my hearing with so great effect."   All the statutes were noticed from Charles II. to George III. inclusive, that the crown officers thought could be made to bear on the question.   In the examination of these statutes, and especially of those called the acts of trade, he illustrated their spirit and tendency, by many references to Child, Gee, Ashley, and Davenant, whose works on Trade, and the Colonies, were a commentary on these acts. He shewed by many sound and striking observations, how unjust, oppressive and impracticable they were ; that they never had been and never could be executed ; and asserted what must have then been considered rather extravagant, though it was doubtless true, " that if the King of Great Britain in person were encamped on Boston Common, at the head of twenty thousand men, with all his navy on our coast, he would not be able to execute these laws.   They would be resisted or eluded."   When he came to the consideration, of " an act for the better security and encouraging the trade of his Majesty's sugar Colonies in America," passed the 6th year of George II. which imposed a very heavy duty on foreign sugar and molasses, and which statute contains the fol lowing language; " we, your Majesty's most dutiful and loyal subjects, the Commons of Great Britain, assembled in parliament, have *given and granted* unto your Majesty, the several and respective duties hereinafter mentioned," he laid down maxims which thenceforward became current enough. He demonstrated the importance of these two articles of molasses and sugar, the former of which, especially, was connected inseparably with the fisheries, with almost all the commerce of the colony, as well as its manufactures and agriculture, and he observed by calculation the great amount of revenue that would be raised by it. He further advanced principles, that must have been heard by his audience with very strong, but very different emotions, when " he asserted this act to be a revenue law, a taxation law, made by a foreign legislature, without our consent, and by a legislature who had no feeling for us, and whose interest prompted them to tax us to the quick."*

The last ground taken by him in commenting on these later acts of trade, was their incompatibility with the charter of the Colony. He went over the history of the charters. " Neither the first James nor Charles could be supposed to intend, that Parliament, which they both hated more than they did the Pope or the French king, should share with them in the government of colonies instituted by their royal prerogative." " Tom, Dick and Harry were not to censure them in their council." Pym, Hampden, Sir Harry Vane and Cromwell, did not surely wish to

---

* President Adams' Letters.

subject a country, which they sought as an asylum, to the arbitrary jurisdiction of a country, from which they wished to fly. Charles the second had learned by dismal, doleful experience, that parliaments, were not to be wholly despised. He therefore endeavoured to associate parliament with himself, in his navigation act, and many others of his despotic projects, even in that of destroying by his unlimited licentiousness and debauchery, the moral character of the nation." In pointing out the violent infringement of the charters, from Dummer's defence of the New England charters, he bestowed many just praises on that excellent work.*

In thus adverting to the history of the charters and the colony, he fell naturally on the merit of its founders, in undertaking so perilous, arduous, and almost desperate an enterprise ; in " disforesting bare

---

* This work entitled " a defence of the New England Charters by Jer. Dummer," was written in 1721, and in point of style or argument, may vie with any American production before the Revolution. Dummer was born in Boston, in 1699, and was the grandson of Richard Dummer, one of the fathers of Massachusetts. He was educated at Cambridge, and Dr. Mather, who was then President of the College, pronounced him one of the best scholars it had produced. He afterwards studied at Leyden, where Witzius, professor of theology, spoke of him in very high terms. He received a learned theological education, but afterwards turned his attention to politics. He was appointed agent of the Province in 1710, and to the disappointment of his countrymen and probably to his own injury eventually, he took the side of prerogative ; yet he held the place of agent eleven years, and was always steadily attached to his native home. He spoke several languages, and his talents and address gave him intimacy and influence in the highest circles. He was employed by Lord Bolingbroke in some important, secret negociations, and was promised high promotion, but the death of the Queen blasted all his hopes. His acquaintance with Bolingbroke contributed to destroy his religious principles. He published four theological dissertations in Latin, the defence of the Charters, and a letter on the expedition to Canada in 1712. He died in England in May, 1739.

creation ;"* in conciliating and necessarily contending with Indian natives, in purchasing, rather than conquering, a quarter of the glob.e at their own expense, by the sweat of their own brows, at the hazard and sacrifice of their own lives; without the smallest aid, assistance or comfort from the government of England, or from England itself as a nation. On the contrary, meeting with constant jealousy, envy, intrigue against their charter, their religion, and all their privileges. He reproached the nation, parliament, and king with injustice, illiberality, ingratitude, and oppression in their conduct towards this country, in a style of oratory that I never heard equalled in this or any other country."

After the close of his argument, the Court adjourned for consideration, and at the close of the term, Chief Justice Hutchinson pronounced the opinion: " The Court has considered the subject of writs of assistance, and can see no foundation for such a writ ; but as the practise in England is not known, it has been thought best to continue the question to the next term, that in the mean time opportunity may be given to know the result."†   No cause in

---

* Dummer, in his defence of the New England charters, in describing the country, as the first colonists found it, says : " The land itself was of a rough savage nature, incumbered with unprofitable woods, and of no use till by vast labour and expence subdued and cultivated. For to speak the truth, those parts were but *bare creation* to the first planters, and their labour *like the beginning of the world.*"

† When the next term came, Mr. Adams says, "no judgment was pronounced, nothing was said about writs of assistance. But it was generally reported and understood that the Court clandestinely granted them, and the custom house officers had them in their pockets, though I never knew that they dared to produce and execute them in any one instance." Minot's history

the annals of colonial jurisprudence had hitherto excited more public interest ; and none had given rise
to such powerful argument. When the profound
learning of the advocate, the powers of wit, fancy
and pathos, with which he could copiously illustrate
and adorn that learning, and the ardent character of
his eloquence, are considered ; and that the disposition to serve his clients, whose cause he had undertaken to defend gratuitously, was not probably lessened by the instant conviction that his family had,
with a view to this very cause, been injured by the
appointment of the presiding judge ; and that his
belief in the importance of the subject must have
been certainly enforced by all the personal sacrifices
he had made on this occasion, together with the
obloquy and ill will of the people in power which
would follow his course ; and, above all, a deep foresight of the meditated oppression and tyranny that
would be gratified by the success of this hateful application—when all these circumstances are recalled,
the power and magnificence of this oration may be
imagined. With a knowledge of the topics that
were involved, and the fearless energy with which
they were developed and elucidated, the time when
it occurred, and the accompanying circumstances ;
every person will join with President Adams when
he says : " I do say in the most solemn manner, that

---

says, " the writ of assistance was granted," and refers to the court records
for authority : Yet this was probably a mere form to save the pride of the administration ; and as nothing was afterwards heard of this odious instrument,
President Adams' opinion is unquestionably correct, " that they never dared
to execute them."

Mr. Otis' oration against writs of assistance, breathed into this nation the breath of life."

Chapter VII.

Results of the Cause of " Writs of Assistance"—Otis chosen into the Legislature—Anecdotes on that Subject—Thomas Cushing —Governor Bernard's allusions to the late Trial.

IN addition to the deep anxiety, which such a question as that of " Writs of Assistance," involving so extensively, not only pecuniary concerns, but political and civil rights, must inevitably have created; this trial was also accompanied with a peculiar interest, arising out of incidental circumstances of a personal nature, some of which have been already mentioned.   There were others very striking.   Otis was the pupil of Gridley, for whose character he felt a high respect, and for whose instruction he was sincerely grateful: and he never lost sight of these feelings in the course of the trial. " It was," says, the venerable witness so often quoted, " a moral spectacle more affecting to me than any I have ever since seen upon the stage, to observe a pupil treating his master with all the deference, respect, esteem and affection of a son to a father, and that without the least affectation; while

he baffled and confounded all his authorities, confuted all his arguments, and reduced him to silence!"
Nor was a suitable return wanting on the part of
the master. The same observer in another place
remarks; " The crown, by its agents, accumulated
construction upon construction, and inference upon
inference, as the giants heaped Pelion upon Ossa.
I hope it is not impious or profane to compare Otis
to Ovid's Jupiter; but, *misso fulmine fregit Olym-
pum, et excussit subjecto Pelio Ossam.* He dashed
this whole building to pieces, and scattered the pul-
verized atoms to the four winds; and no judge,
lawyer, or crown officer dared to say, why do ye
so ?"

" In plain English, by cool, patient comparison of
the phraseology of these statutes, their several provisions, the dates of their enactments, the privileges of
our charters, the merits of the Colonists, &c. he
shewed the pretentions to introduce the revenue acts,
and these arbitrary and mechanical Writs of Assistance, as an instrument for the execution of them, to be
so irrational; by his wit he represented the attempt
as so ludicrous and ridiculous; and by his dignified re-
probation of an impudent attempt to impose on the
people of America, he raised such a storm of indignation, that even Hutchinson, who had been appointed on purpose to sanction this writ, dared not
utter a word in its favour, and Mr. Gridley himself
seemed to me to exult inwardly at the glory and
triumph of his pupil."

An epoch in public affairs may be dated from this

trial. Political parties became more distinctly formed, and their several adherents were more marked
and decided. The nature of ultra-marine jurisdiction began to be closely examined; the question
respecting raising a revenue fully discussed. The
right of the British parliament to impose taxes was
openly denied. " Taxation without representation
is tyranny," was the maxim, that was the guide and
watch word of all the friends of liberty. The crown
officers and their followers adopted openly the pretensions of the British ministry and parliament, and
considering their power to be irresistible, appealed
to the selfishness of those who might be expectants
of patronage, and to the fears of all quiet and timid minds, to adopt a blind submission, as the only
safe or reasonable alternative. Otis took the side
of his country, and as has been shewn, under circumstances that made his decision irrevocable. He
was transferred at once from the ranks of private
life, not merely to take the side, but to be the guide
and leader of his country, in opposition to the designs of the British ministry. " Although" says President Adams, " Mr. Otis had never before interfered
in public affairs, his exertions on this single occasion secured him a commanding popularity with the
friends of their country, and the terror and vengeance of her enemies; neither of which ever deserted him."

His popularity was instantaneous, and universal;
and the public were impatient for the approaching
election, when they could make him a representa-

tive of Boston. Speaking one day on this subject, with a gentleman of great shrewdness and capacity, who was one of the delegation, a friendly conversation took place between them, in which the satire, if it bears a little hard on the character of those times, is perhaps not wholly inapplicable to most others. Otis observed, " They talk of sending me to the next General Court."—" You will never succeed in the General Court."—" Not succeed! and why not pray?"—" Why, Mr. Otis, you have ten times the learning, and much greater abilities than I have, but you know nothing of human nature."—" Indeed! I wish you would give me some lessons."—" Be patient and I will do so with pleasure. In the first place what meeting do you go to?"—" Dr. Sewall's."*— " Very well, you must stand up in sermon time, you must look devout and deeply attentive : Do you have family prayers?"—" No."—" It were well if you did: what does your family consist of?"—" Why only four or five commonly, but at this time, I have in addition one of Dr. Sewall's saints, who is a nurse of my wife."—" Ah! that is the very thing : you must talk religion with her in a serious manner, you must have family prayers at least once while she is in your house : that woman can do you more harm or more good than any other person; she will

---

* Dr. Joseph Sewall was pastor of the old South Church, ordained Sept. 16th, 1713. He was a strict calvinist, and eminent for his fervid piety, almsgiving, and his long and useful career. He preached for fifty-six years, and the last time on the evening that he completed his eightieth year. He died soon after, June 27th, 1769.

spread your fame throughout the congregation. I can also tell you, by way of example, some of the steps I take : two or three weeks before an election comes on, I send to the cooper and get all my casks put in order : I say nothing about the number of hoops. I send to the mason and have some job done to the hearths or the chimnies: I have the carpenter to make some repairs in the roof or the wood house : I often go down to the ship yards about eleven o'clock, when they break off to take their drink, and enter into conversation with them. They all vote for me."*

Mr. Otis was chosen almost unanimously a representative to the legislature, at the ensuing election in May 1761,† and on taking his place, being seated by the gentleman with whom he had held the preceding conversation, the latter said to him : " Mr. Otis you have great abilities, but are too warm, too impetuous, your opponents though they cannot

---

* At that period there were seven or eight shipyards in Boston, employing from twenty to seventy men each. After this gentleman who paid them these friendly visits, was chosen from the House into the Council, he omitted going to see them for a long time. On the next visit after this interval, one of them remarked to him in a significant way, " that since he had got into the Council, he did not come to see them so often." His answer with much good nature and knowledge of mankind, embraced all the slyness of the remark. " O yes, that was true, but my time is so much taken up ; and then you know, it is the House of Representatives, that chooses the Council."

† " On that week," says President Adams, " I happened to be at Worcester attending a Court of Common Pleas, of which Brigadier Ruggles was Chief Justice. When the news arrived from Boston, you can have no idea of the consternation among the government people. Chief Justice Ruggles at dinner at Colonel Chandler's on that day, said, ' Out of this election will arise a damned faction, which will shake this province to its foundation.' "

meet you in argument, will get the advantage by interrupting you, and putting you in a passion."— " Well," said Otis, " if you see me growing warm, give me a hint, and I'll command myself." Sometime afterwards a question of some importance arose, Otis and his friend, being on the Boston seat together. The former said he would speak, and the latter cautioned him against being irritated. He soon rose, and was speaking with great fluency and in a powerful train of reasoning, when Brigadier Ruggles interrupted him, he was growing warm in his reply, but his friend pulled his coat slightly: he scowled, looked round, took the hint, and moderated his tone. As he continued his argument, Mr. Choate of Ipswich, interrupted him again: this roused his temper, his coat was pulled a second time, when he turned round and said quickly in an under tone to his monitor ; " let me alone, do you take me for a school boy ?" and then continued his course with impetuosity, corruscating with sarcasms, and overwhelming his opponents with vehement argument and invective.

His colleagues in representing the town that year, were Royal Tyler, John Phillips and Thomas Cushing, all of them men of great weight in society. Mr. Cushing however, next to Mr. Otis, became the most known from the part he took in public affairs.

The grandfather and father of Mr. Cushing were both of them men of talents, and had both of them been distinguished in the stations they had filled in public life. His grandfather was long a member of the Council, and his father born in 1693 and educated at Cambridge, was chosen to various offices, the duties of which he discharged with ability. He was for several years Speaker of the House and held that office at his death in 1746, being then in his 53d year. He left a handsome estate to his son, and the reputation of a family which had long been engaged in the public service.

Thomas Cushing, was born in 1725, and his name stands on the Cambridge catalogue in the class of 1744. He engaged in political life, enjoying the general confidence of his fellow citizens, by an almost hereditary right, and under many advantages. He was supposed to possess less talent than his father, but his qualifications were well adapted to the part he had to play. When Governor Bernard in 1763 negatived James Otis, the father, as Speaker, Mr. Cushing was chosen in his place, and was annually called to the chair for many succeeding years. His name therefore appears to all the public documents, for a long period preceding the revolution. This gave him celebrity, and the reputation of taking the lead in affairs, to a much greater extent than he actually did. Dr. Johnson in his pamphlet " Taxation no tyranny," from the frequent occurrence of his name to public papers, was led to make this absurd remark ; " one object of the Americans is said to be, to adorn the brows of Mr. Cushing with a diadem."

Mr. Cushing was in fact a most useful agent in

public concerns, and perhaps more so, than if he had possessed very commanding abilities. He was decidedly patriotic in his principles, but extremely moderate and conciliatory in his conduct. He mixed with persons of different parties, and exhibited great urbanity in his intercourse with all classes. Though opposed to persons in the administration of the province, he was not personally obnoxious to them, so that in his office of Speaker, he stood between the popular party and the government, in a manner to prevent much inconvenient collision.

He was the friend and correspondent of Dr. Franklin, and received from him the famous letters of Hutchinson and others, that produced so strong an effect at the time. The moderate counsels of Dr. Franklin were received by him with very congenial feelings. He was steady in the course he adopted, possessing much prudence, little zeal, and no ambition of martyrdom, or desire for that species of pre-eminence, that insulates the possessor from all persons except his immediate partisans.

Mr. Cushing always took an active share in the concerns of the college at Cambridge, which conferred on him the degree of Doctor of Laws. He held various public offices, and died Lieutenant Governor of Massachusetts in 1788, aged 63 years.

At the first session of the legislature in 1761, on the last Wednesday of May, Governor Bernard fully acquainted with the excitement that had been caused by the question about Writs of Assistance, after advising the legislature, " to lay aside all divisions and distinctions whatsoever, especially those, (if any there be) that are founded upon private views," proceeds to say : " Let me also recommend to you, to give no attention to declamations tending to promote a suspicion of the civil rights of the people being in danger. Such harangues might well suit in the reigns of Charles and James, but in the times of the Georges they are groundless and unjust." The difference between these reigns, he then urges at some length, to shew the superiority of the present over the past. It is surprising, however, to find the Governor indulging in this ungrateful sneer at Charles and James, when certain acts of those sovereigns were the only precedents, that could be adduced to sustain the application for the writs of assistance, and their arbitrary edicts were to be made use of under a George, to revive an obsolete, odious instrument of tyranny. The legislature in their answer, were civil but firm. They knew nothing of any parties to which he alluded, and they assured him that ; " Your Excellency's recommendations will always have weight with us—Your recommendation, to give no attention to declamations tending to promote suspicion of the civil rights of the people being in danger, shall have its weight. It is our intention to see for ourselves; and it gives us pleasure to see that the civil rights of the people are not in danger; nor are we in the least degree suspicious that they will ever be under your Excellency's administration."

Chapter VIII.

Question relating to the Currency—Otis and Hutchinson take diffe-
rent sides—Extracts from Otis's Essays—Letter from Sewall to
Paine, and Answer—Jonathan Sewall—Robert Treat Paine.

It was discovered in 1761, that many of the Treasurer's notes then in circulation had been counter-
feited, and a session of the Legislature was held in
the autumn of that year, to devise a remedy for this
evil.   It was resolved to call them in and pay them
off in part, and issue new paper for the balance.
This course, which was wise enough in itself, brought
into discussion the questions, in what coin they should
be payable, whether in gold or silver, and at what
rates ? According to the standard, is was more advantageous to remit silver to England than gold, and
in consequence the province had been nearly drain-
ed of the former.   The council, with Mr. Hutchinson at their head, proposed to make gold a tender,
and to lessen its value, so that it might be remitted, and thereby tend to keep the silver coin from
being exported.   But the house maintained that gold
was already a legal tender, that there was no necessity of lowering its current price, and that there
would be great injustice in so doing.   Each branch
negatived the proposal of the other, and after a session of a fortnight, could agree upon nothing but to
separate.

This subject, which in the relations of debtor or creditor, touches almost every individual in a community, is one where alterations should be made with the greatest delicacy and prudence. On this occasion a great deal of discussion and warmth of feeling were produced. Its inherent difficulties were far from being diminished by a dispute as to the fact, whether gold was a legal tender. After the legislature was prorogued, the dispute was transferred to the newspapers, and was there chiefly managed by Hutchinson and Otis, who followed the opposite opinions which they had severally supported in the two branches of the legislature. Hutchinson argued in favour of enacting, that gold should be made a legal tender, at a diminished value. Otis contended against any diminution of the rate, and shewed that it was already a tender by law. The discussion was chiefly carried on by these two gentlemen, under their own signatures; one writer took the side of Hutchinson anonymously, who was supposed to be Mr. Bowdoin of the council, as he had maintained the same positions in that body.

Otis gave proofs of great learning and powerful reasoning, mixed up with many sarcastic allusions to his opponent; and Hutchinson avoided making a direct reply, but proceeded to give a curious history of the currency, and sought to mortify his antagonist by making no allusion to his pieces. Persons who are fond of considering these intricate questions of currency and its relative values, which still offer unexhausted fields of dispute, will find a great deal of learning and ingenuity displayed in this controversy. The arguments and authorities produced by Otis, would occupy too much space here, and it would be injurious to abridge them. The following extracts from the articles he wrote, contain only some of the incidental topics, and are selected as characteristic of the times.

" MESSRS. EDES AND GILL,

" Perhaps I should not have troubled you or the public with any thoughts of mine, had not his Honour the Lieutenant Governor condescended to give me a personal challenge. This is an honour that I never had vanity enough to aspire after, and I shall ever respect Mr. Hutchinson for it, so long as I live, as he certainly consulted my reputation more than his own, when he bestowed it. A general officer in the army would be thought very condescending to accept, much more to give, a challenge to a subaltern. The honour of entering the lists with a gentleman so much one's superior in one view, is certainly very tempting; it is at least possible that his honour may lose much; but from those who have and desire but little, but little can possibly be taken away. I am your humble servant.

JAMES OTIS, JR.

Boston, Dec. 19*th.*

" His Honour is of opinion that gold and silver cannot both be kept here, without 'lessening our imports' that plenty of money has produced luxury, luxury tends to poverty—' poverty to industry and frugality, these bring money again.' I am no merchant, but have been informed that increasing the *exports* is more advantageous to a country than lessening the imports. As to the revolution or wheel of fortune which his Honour has described, luxury is a very vague and loose term, if by it is meant, the importation of many foreign commodities. The more we have the better, if we can export enough to pay for them; poverty is so far from being the basis of industry and frugality, that it is too often the occasion of vices directly opposite. Poverty can no more produce riches, than it can furnish a man with the secret of the philosophers stone. I know it is the maxim of some, that the common people in this town and country live too well; however I am of quite a different opinion, I do not think they live half well enough. I should be glad to see here, as in England, tradesmen and yeomen worth their tens and their hundreds or thousands of pounds, for then, and not till then, we shall have gentlemen and merchants, worth their hundreds and their millions. The tradesman and the husbandman would do well to consider, that when they are for cramping trade, they are for killing a faithful servant, who is toiling night and day, and eating the bread of care for their good as well as his own; the merchant and the gentleman would do well to reflect that the hands of the tradesman, and husbandman, are their employers, and that unless they multiply and increase in their commodities and riches, the merchant will never flourish: *the mer-*

chant, manufacturer, and freeholder, should consider themselves as the most immediate and natural brothers in the community, that God and nature have made their interest inseparable, and when they will agree conjointly to pursue it, no mortal hand can ever prevail against them.

" Nature has been as kind to this Province, as to most in the world. This is demonstrable from its increase in people and trade, from its settlement to the year 1749, and yet we never raised our own bread. The balance yearly sent out in cash for wheat and flour, which we might raise as easily as the other colonies, has been often mentioned to our shame; and yet nothing has been done to encourage the raising of one, or the manufacturing the other. It is said we pay two thousand pounds sterling a year, only for flour barrels. It is humbly submitted, whether it is not highly incumbent upon the government to take this affair into their consideration, and grant a bounty for raising wheat ; the saving between raising and paying the other colonies for our bread, would in two years furnish a sufficient medium for all our other trade."

After a full discussion of the principal question, he concludes ; " Thus I have endeavoured, according to my poor capacity, to answer his Honour's reasons for lowering the price of gold, to prove the necessity of making gold expressly a tender, and have pointed out the only possible mode of keeping gold and silver plenty amongst us. Every political writer is allowed to lament the decay of public spirit; it is cer-

tain that in proportion to this decay, calamities of
every kind will invade a community : and amidst all
our disquisitions could we hit upon any method for
reviving this spirit among us, public embarrass-
ments that appear incurable, would vanish before
it. I am the humble servant of my country, and
hearty well wisher to all men.

JAMES OTIS, JR.

P. S. Very soon after his Honour published his
thoughts, he told me, he had " been cutting out work
for me in the papers," as near as I can recollect the
words, which I took as a personal challenge to answer him; if they were not so intended, I was mistak-
en : however, read in the preface challenge to *answer :* and those who think it can make any difference in the sense, may for Cooke the Cobbler, read
all mankind.   J. O.

Extract from the article in the Boston Gazette of
January 11th, in the preface, to which he says that
" it is not an answer to his Honour's piece of the
4th; that cannot come till he has finished, and then
he may be unanswerable, my apology for this is, the
extract from Mr. Locke, published the same day
with my answer.

" I shall not compare myself to either of those
great men, Mr. Locke, or Mr. Lowndes. But with
regard to the terms *delicacy and politeness,* it may not
be amiss to observe, that they are relative and admit
of no invariable standard. The present humour of a
Court, the prevalent fashion of the age, and a thou-

sand other accidents and circumstances concur to vary the idea annexed to those words. The delicacy and politeness of the Russian Court, would perhaps appear boorish in the present refinement at St. James'. The British courtiers, at Versailles may be looked upon with as much pity and contempt, as the true plain-hearted old Briton would be by a modern politician. In the days of our forefathers, power put on the grim visage of open force and violence. In this more delicate age, soft words, a smiling countenance, fair promises and other tickling blandishments, are the only sure means of obtaining those enormous degrees of power, which mankind are so fond of: whatever delicacy and politeness may dictate, good sense and good nature require that great allowance be made for the different ages, nations, education, advantages and natural tempers of men. In one word, I am no courtier; I know not how to give flattering titles to men, nor have I the least desire to offend them. If plain English and freedom of speech, are too hard for the digestion of any stomachs, those who labour under this infirmity have a right to please their palates, and will of course seek elsewhere for entertainment."

" Mr. Locke informs us, that Mr. Lowndes was no otherwise known to him, than by his civilities," and adds, that he had " a very great esteem for him," and so have I for his Honour, tho' no part of my respect arises from civilities I have received, but purely from his Honour's rank and merit. Mr. Locke in his disputes, uses greater freedoms by fifty

times, than ever I desired to use with his Honour,
and it would be no difficult task, to point out some
of them, in his controversy with his friend Lowndes.
However this might not serve me, as it may be said,
that greater freedoms are excusable between friends.
The Bishop of Worcester was greatly Mr. Locke's
superior in rank, tho' I must confess not so much as
his Honour is mine in abilities.   But it must be remembered that no man carries the atmosphere of
his commission, or public character, into a disputation:
if there was any rule of logic, in favour of that, the
very name of a Justice of the quorum, would be as
effectual to strike a poor plebian dumb, as the *ulti-
ma ratio regum* of Lewis the XIV. Most men,
had rather be silent all their days, than run the
risque of being thought worthy of hard names,
bonds and stripes, for every word that may happen
to displease the delicate ears of a superior."

" I return my most humble, and hearty thanks,
to his Honour, for his history of our currency, and
should promise myself great entertainment, if he
would gratify the public with a more general history of the Province, his Honour's long acquaintance
with our ancient records, must have furnished him
with many curious anecdotes, unknown to most
others.

" I entirely agree with his Honour, that *our standard* of silver, has ever been the same with sterling.
I could never see any necessity of altering the de-
nomination, and have often wondered at such alteration taking place; and am more fully convinced since

his Honour's opinion, that it was a very ill judged thing, tending only to confusion and disorder. It is a thousand pities, that so fair an opportunity as offered itself in 1749, for rectifying this error, should not have been embraced."

"His Honour observes, that in democratical governments, generally, there will be a bias in the legislature, to the number rather than to the *weight* of the inhabitants. It is presumed this may be true in speculation, but it cannot well be examined in practice : because strictly speaking, there never were many democratical governments in the world. I do not at present recollect one such government existing upon the face of the earth. The English government is by some indeed considered as democratical, others have not scrupled to call it an anarchy : but the best opinion is, that the true British constitution, as settled by the glorious revolution, is a *mixed monarchy*, or a composite of three famous kinds, viz. of *monarchy* supplied by the king, *aristocracy* supplied by the lords, and of *democracy* supplied by the commons. This, when the checks and balances are preserved, is perhaps the most perfect form of government, that in the present depraved state, human nature is capable of. It is a fundamental maxim in such a government, to keep the legislative and executive powers separate. When these powers are in the same hands, such a government is hastening fast to its ruin, and the mischief and miseries that must happen before that fatal period, will be as bad as those felt in the most absolute monarchy."

" It may happen to governments formed after this model, that in consequence of art and corruption, half a dozen or half a score men will form an oligarchy in favour of their families and friends. Instances may be found, where a man of abilities shall monopolize a power proportionate to all those of lord chief baron of the exchequer, lord chief justice of both benches, lord high treasurer, and lord high chancellor of Great Britain, united in one single person. There is no axiom in mathematics clearer, than that no man ought to be sole legislator of his country, and supreme judge of his fellow citizens. Should it be objected that in making these political reflections, I have wandered; my apology is, I went out of the way for the sake of his Honour's company,* whose observation on the democratical bias led me astray, if I have erred. By analogy it seems probable, that in an aristocratical government, the bias will be in favour of the weight, rather than the number of the inhabitants, but the more equitable way in all governments, is to set quantity against quality, and to keep as exact a balance between debtor and creditor, as the nature of the thing will admit. If it is possible that his Honour should intend a distant, light, *delicate* suggestion, that I am in the least warped by either of these biasses, he is very much mistaken. I desire neither poverty nor riches, and thank God heartily that I have nei-

---

* To feel all the pungency of this sarcasm, it should be recollected that Hutchinson had thus monopolized offices.

ther. *Mediocritate mea contentus sum.* My argument in more respects than one, runs counter to what the wise of this world call interest. This will not lie, and when a man speaks against it there is little reason to suspect his sincerity, however lightly we may think of his understanding. *Restituit rem* is a pompous motto, that I never expect to be complimented with, and I certainly will never assume it; but this, *non populi fasces non purpura regum flexit,* is what every man should take care to deserve, before he pretends to any degree of philosophy or patriotism."

He then proceeds to define the different kinds of government, and makes several extracts from Montesquieu to shew the mischief which results from uniting legislative, executive, and judicial powers in the same person, for the purpose of severe allusion to Hutchinson—and concludes with this paragraph.

" Oh! Secondat! thou wast surely inspired, or you could never have so exactly described the state of provinces, perhaps unpeopled, and of people unborn, when you first felt their miseries. Had France had many Montesquieus', Canada might never have been conquered. Should Great Britain play it away, when another Pitt appears, she may conquer it again.

JAMES OTIS."

The feeling of a community is easily excited on a topic that so immediately involves the interest of every individual. As the legislature had separated without coming to any decision, the anxiety of the public was kept alive as to the result; this discussion in the newspapers was therefore read with an avidity, that was not a little increased by the character of the principal writers. A curious exemplification of the general interest taken in this dispute, is afforded by the following letters, which were found among the papers of Governor Hutchinson. They afford a proof also of his care in collecting whatever related to the opinions of men, on events of the times. They seem hastily and carelessly written, and yet were full of meaning. The first letter is from Mr. Sewall to Mr. R. T. Paine, asking of the latter a little professional favour, while attending a county court. The questions in the postscript, which forms the principal part of the letter, shew what were the prevailing topics of the day; and the answer discovers a kind of shrewd caution, as well as ready wit.

" BROTHER BOB.

Pray be kind enough to deliver the inclosed to Catch-pole—and when you can give me an opportunity to cancel the obligation, please to command freely—Your hearty friend.

JONATHAN SEWALL.

Charlestown, 11*th Feb.* 1762.

" How is the harvest in your part of the vineyard? Which side do you take in the political controversies? What think you of coins? What of

Writs of Assistance? What of his Hon. the L.—
G.—? What of Otis? What of Thacher? What
of Cooke the Cobbler? What of patriotism? What
think you of disappointed ambition? What think
you of the fable of the Bees? What —— send me
your thoughts on these questions, and I'll send you
fifty more.

TAUNTON, FEB. 17th, 1762.

" FRIEND JONATHAN.

" Have just received yours, and shall take special
care of the inclosed. Your queries demand immediate answers, in which I hope you will find a satisfactory display of the orthodoxy of my mind.—*Que.* 1.
How is the harvest in your part of the vineyard?
Ans. The old account is reversed, for the harvest is
small and the labourers are many, and there are many little Foxes that spoil the vines.—*Que.* 2. Which
side do you take in the political controversies?—
Ans. The right side.—*Que.* 3. What think you of
coin?—*Ans.* What hungry men do of food, if they
can get any, never dispute the quality or the price.
—*Que.* 4. What of Writs of Assistance?—*Ans.*
Never was more in need of them, I shall soon apply
for one to get a *help meet.*—*Que.* 5. What of his Honour the L— G—?—*Ans.* As the son of Sirach said,
' all things cannot be in man because man is not immortal.'—*Que.* 6. What of Otis?—*Ans.* What the
Virtuosi do of Lemery's concave mirror, which burns
up every thing that cannot be melted.—*Que.* 7.
What of Thacher?—*Ans.* As Jacob of old said of

his son Dan, as a serpent in the way that biteth the horses heels, so that his rider falleth backward.— *Que.* 8. What of Cooke the Cobbler?—*Ans.* That he is dignified with that title, which many others deserve much more.—*Que.* 9. What of Bedlam for political madmen?—*Ans.* T'will by no means do, being already occupied by madmen of a more sacred profession.—*Que.* 10. What think you of patriotism? —*Ans.* As I do of the balance-master's act; very few have virtue enough (in the Roman sense) to keep themselves, perpendicular.—*Que.* 11. What of disappointed ambition?—*Ans.* Consult your own mind in having no reply to this question.—*Que.* 12. What of the fable of the Bees?—*Ans.* As it proves the good old word, " the *wrath* of man shall praise the Lord.—*Que.* 13. What——?—*Ans.* 'Tis the recapitulation of all your queries."

" Thus I have gone through my catechism, and according to the good rule of education, the next step is to learn it with the proofs, in which I shall hardly fail of success, if I keep to that standard. As for your fifty questions more, with which you threaten me, I beg you would observe a good modern rule of answering them yourself, as you go along; in the mean time conceive yourself obliged to answer these small queries. What think you of our——? of our act?—of that strange compound, soul and body? and of mankind? Expecting to see your agreeable Democritical visage, I subscribe, your fellow gazer and friend,   R. T. P."

Jonathan Sewall, one of the class of 1748, in the Cambridge catalogue, and for several years Attorney General of Massachusetts, was a man of fine talents and most honourable character. He was strongly attached to his country, and was early jealous of the arbitrary intentions of the British ministry against it. After the death of his uncle, who held the place of Chief Justice, as mentioned on a previous page, Mr. Sewall presented a petition to the legislature, relative to his estate ; the failure of which, he attributed, though erroneously, to the want of support from Otis and his father. Hutchinson, on hearing of his dissatisfaction, with his usual alertness to gain partisans, immediately courted his good will, praised his talents, and patronized his practice. Soon afterwards the office of Solicitor General was erected expressly for him, and he was won over to the ministerial party. Though he was always opposed to every measure of injustice against his country, he adhered to the side of the ministry, from believing as did many others, that the power of England could at any time crush the Colonies, and that resistance would only entail upon them the greatest calamities. Mr. Sewall left Boston for England in 1775, in which country he remained till 1788, when he came out with his family to Nova Scotia, and died soon after. One of his sons was appointed Chief Justice, and the other Attorney General, in Canada. Mr. Sewall wrote much in the newspapers ; and among others, a very able series of essays under the signature of *Massachusettensis*, (answered by President Adams, under the signature of *Nov-Anglus*,) has usually been attributed to him.*

Robert Treat Paine, the correspondent of Sewall on this occasion, was in the next class to him at college. He stood high in his profession, and took a decided part in politics. He had the good fortune to be one of the delegates from Massachusetts in the first Congress, and his name is enrolled among the signatures to the declaration of Independence; he continued in that Congress through the Revolutionary war. A voice whose tones were a deep base, and serious if not stern expression of countenance, gave him an appearance of greater severity than he possessed.† He was respected for his talents and integrity, which procured him the post of Attorney General, and afterwards of Judge of the Supreme Court of the state, which he filled for many years. He died in Boston, May 11th, 1814, aged eighty-four years.

To return to the question of the currency; it was settled at the next meeting of the legislature, according to the principles which Otis had maintained, and acts were passed to issue new treasury notes

---

* These Essays were republished in Boston, in 1819. There is a most interesting sketch of Mr. Sewall, by his friend President Adams, in the introduction to them, from which these minutes of him are derived. That he was the author of *Massachusettensis*, however, has been recently contradicted. A gentleman of high respectability in Nova Scotia, asserts on his own positive knowledge, that these papers were written by Mr. Leonard, formerly of Massachusetts, but since Chief Justice of Bermuda.

† He had kind feelings and a strong relish of humour, though with this peculiarity, that his perception of it was not quick, and the report of his laugh was sometimes not heard, till the flash of the jest had entirely vanished.

to replace the old ones, and making gold and silver a legal tender in all cases at the usual rates. But there was one circumstance attending these acts, that had more than a temporary interest : this was, the refusal of the legislature to make the crime of counterfeiting the notes capital. The act was at the next session of the legislature returned by the Governor unsigned, because the offence was not made capital, and thereby differing from every other part of the British dominions, to whose practice he urged them to conform. Otis was one of the committee on this subject, and in their answer to the Governor's communication, after agreeing in the mischievous and atrocious nature of the offence, they proceed to say : " At the same time, the house are very averse to capital punishment, in any case, where the interest of the government does not absolutely require it. And as they doubt not, some other punishment than death, will be sufficient effectually to deter from the commission of this crime, they cannot give their consent it should be punished with death." It is gratifying to find this early stand made in our legislature, against the prodigal use of sanguinary punishments ; a policy which is about being adopted in relation to the same crimes, by the wisdom and humanity of the English parliament at the present day.

In the winter session of 1762, the legislature made Governor Bernard a present of Mount Desert Island.* No opposition was given to this grant, which shews a

* Mount Desert is an island, fifteen miles long and twelve broad, on the coast of Maine,

good will towards him, and proves that the subjects
of dispute had not rendered him unpopular.

Chapter IX.

*Choice of a Colony Agent—Message of Governor Bernard respect-
ing Troops, and important discussion—Answer of the Legislature
drawn by Otis—Objections to it by the Governor—Otis' vindication and extracts from it.*

In the winter session of 1762, a new agent for the
Colony in England was chosen. This was an important trust, and for many years was placed in very
incapable hands. The first agents of Massachusetts
were Hugh Peters, Hibbins and Weld, appointed in
1641; from that period down, there were occasionally able men entrusted with these concerns. At no
period however, were there more inefficient agents,
than from the dismissal of Mr. Bollan* in 1762, to

---

* " Mr. Bollan" says President Adams, " was a kind of learned man, of
indefatigable research, and a faithful friend to America ; though he lost all
his influence, when his father-in-law, Governor and General Shirley, went out
of circulation. This Mr. Bollan printed a book very early on the " Rights of
the Colonies." I scarcely ever knew a book so deeply despised. The English
Reviews would not allow it to be the production of a rational creature. In
America itself, it was held in no esteem. Otis himself, expressed in the House
of Representatives, in a public speech, his contempt of it in these words : " Mr.
Bollan's book is the strangest thing I ever read ; under the title of ' Rights of
the Colonies,' he has employed one third of this work to prove that the world
is round ; another, that it turns round ; and the last, that the pope was a devil
for pretending to give it to whom he pleased."

the appointment of Dr. Franklin, in 1770; precisely the period when the greatest talents were requisite. During all the violent contests which took place in the interval, and which were maintained with such firmness and vigilance by the colonial legislature, a leading qualification for an agent was, in the minds of the majority, that he should be a dissenter. Mr. Bollan, who was an able advocate, and had rendered very great services in obtaining the reimbursement for the great expences of the Colony, was dismissed. Mr. Bollan had married the daughter of Governor Shirley, and Governor Pownal had endeavoured to supplant him by his brother the secretary of the board of Trade. He was accused of some remissness in his correspondence, but an important circumstance against him, characteristic of the times, was his being a member of the Church of England. Mr. Mauduit who was chosen his successor, was a dissenter.* Mr. Mauduit's brother was a hired writer in favour of the ministry, and he himself was unqualified for the office he held. Mr. Bollan was some years afterwards again employed as agent of the council. Otis, who had no sectarian bigotry, was opposed to Mr. Bollan, from his political connexions.

" All this I regretted. I wished that Bollan had not only been permitted, but encouraged to proceed. There was no doubt he would have produced much in illustration of the ecclesiastical and political supeistition and despotism, of the ages when colonization commenced and proceeded. But Bollan was discouraged and ceased from his labours."

The opinion of the English Critics, alluded to above, may be found in the Critical Review, for 1762, p. 190.

* Richard Jackson, Esq. a friend of Governor Bernard's, and agent for Connecticut, was associated with Mr. Mauduit.

A bill was brought forward in the legislature at the same session, to exclude the Judges of the Superior Court from holding a seat in the Council, or in the House of Representatives, and was lost by a majority of seven votes. This measure which would have materially impaired the influence of Hutchinson, and weakened the power of the administration, was of course most strenuously opposed by all their partisans, and called forth all the efforts of the former to defend himself, in his incongruous employments of Lieutenant Governor, Councillor and Chief Justice. Otis and all the members in opposition, demonstrated with unanswerable arguments, the incompatibility of these offices, and the dangerous abuses that must follow, from such a violation of the whole spirit of a free government. It is a striking proof of the progress that has been made in the science of constitutions, that a principle could not be sustained sixty years ago in a legislative body, which is now felt by every citizen, to form the basis of all political liberty and civil security : the separation of the legislative, judicial and executive functions, is a fundamental and undisputed axiom in all our governments.

The House of Representatives assembled in September 1762, at which session, though it lasted only a few days, some important occurrences took place. The Governor in his message, expressed his regret at being obliged to call them together at that unusual season, but that the public exigencies required it. He then communicated to them a requisition from Sir Jeffery Amherst, to maintain a certain number of men in the service, the following winter, during the absence of the regular troops. The Governor next proceeded to speak of the recent invasion of Newfoundland, and the anxiety that had been felt by those concerned in the fishery; and that he had in consequence by advice of Council, taken some precautionary measures, which had occasioned some expenses, the account of which would be laid before them.

When this message was taken into consideration, Otis delivered a speech, which he afterwards printed from memory, urging a compliance with the requisition. The whole tone of it is loyal and sincere, and it shows a readiness to second all the just views of government. He was made one of the committee for carrying the object into effect, and a bill was reported without any delay, appropriating the money to make the required levies.

On the 16th September, the Governor sent a message informing them, that to quiet the fears for the fishing vessels from the French expedition at Newfoundland, he had increased the armament of the Massachusetts Sloop, and putting on board fifty additional men, sent her out for the protection of the fishery. In the language of Otis, " A little paper only accompanied this message, with a short account of the difference to the Province, by the Governor and Council's enlarging the establishment, which amounted to about seventy two pounds. But no notice was taken of the commissary's and other bills, which must finally swell this amount much higher. However, it was neither the measure, nor the expense of it, that gave the house so much uneasiness, as the manner of it; that is, enlarging the establishment, without the knowledge of the house, and paying it without their privity or consent."

This message gave rise to a remarkable discussion, and this trifling expenditure may be considered as one of the preparatory causes of the Revolution. A few years before this period, it might not have been noticed; but since the attempt to enforce the acts of Trade, by the Writs of Assistance, the maxims laid down by Otis in that cause, that "taxation without representation was tyranny," and " that expenditures of public money without appropriations by the representatives of the people, were arbitrary, unconstitutional and therefore tyrannical," had created a watchful jealousy in the community, and a disposition to resist every encroachment on the part of government, in the management, of financial affairs. The public were thus taught to look at principles, and to resist every insidious precedent inflexibly. This state of feeling in America is thus finely described by Burke; " In other countries the people, more simple, of a less mercurial cast, judge of an ill principle in government, only by an actual grievance; here they anticipate the evil, and judge of the pressure of the grievance, by the badness of the principle. They augur misgovernment at a distance; and snuff the approach of tyranny in every tainted breeze."

Otis, from his first appearance in the house in 1761, had shewn such a superiority of talents, information and energy over every other member, that he took the lead in 1763, as it were of course." He engaged in this subject with great earnestness, remarking upon three or four other appropriations, that had happened under the present administration, where the Governor and Council had made expenditures without the knowledge, or contrary to the will of the house, and that it was necessary to put a stop to these dangerous practices. The message was referred to a committee of which he was chairman, who were instructed in their answer to remonstrate against the Governor and Council's making, or increasing, establishments, without the consent of the house. The answer drawn up by Otis, was as follows:

" MAY IT PLEASE YOUR EXCELLENCY,

" The House have duly attended to your Excellency's message, of the 11th inst. relating to the Massachusetts *Sloop*, and are humbly of opinion that there is not the least *necessity*, for keeping up her present compliment of men, and therefore desire that your Excellency would be pleased to reduce them to six, the old establishment made for said Sloop by the General Court.

" Justice to ourselves, and to our constituents, obliges us to remonstrate, against the method of making or increasing establishments, by the Governor and Council.

" It is in effect taking from the house, their most darling privilege, the right of originating all taxes.

" It is in short annihilating one branch of the legislature. And when once the representatives of a people give up this privilege, the government will very soon become arbitrary.

" No necessity can be sufficient to justify a house of representatives, in giving up such a privilege; *for it would be of little consequence to the people, whether they were subject to George, or Lewis, the king of Great Britain, or the French king, if both were arbitrary, as both would be, if both could levy taxes without Parliament.*

" Had this been the first instance of the kind, we might not have troubled your Excellency about it; but lest the matter should grow into precedent; we earnestly beseech your Excellency, as you regard the peace and welfare of the Province, that no measures of this nature be taken for the future, let the advice of Council be what it may."

When the passage in Italics was read, Mr. Paine, a member from Worcester, cried out, " *Treason! Treason!*" but after a most animated speech from Otis, the answer was passed entire by a large majority, and Otis was appointed one of the committee, to present it to the Governor.*

A report was immediately circulated through the town, that the House had sent a very improper

---

* A very curious parallel to this scene, occurred in the legislature of Virginia, three years afterwards, of which an animated account is given by Mr. Wirt, in his biography of Patrick Henry.

message to his Excellency, one that reflected upon
the king's person and government, and was highly
derogatory to his crown and dignity ; and that they
had desired him not to take the advice of his Council, in any case. In the afternoon a letter was addressed by the Governor to the speaker, sending
back the message, in which he says " the King's
name, dignity and cause are so improperly treated,"
that he " recommends earnestly, it should not be
entered on the journals as it now stands; if it
should be, he is satisfied they will again and again
wish some part of it were expunged ;" especially if
it should appear, when he entered upon his vindication, " that there is not the least ground for the in-
sinuation under colour of which, that sacred and
well beloved name is so disrespectfully brought
into question."* Upon the reading of this letter,
says Otis, it was moved to insert these words,
viz " with all due reverence to his Majesty's sacred
person and government, to both which we profess
the sincerest attachment and loyalty be it spoken, it
would be of little importance," &c. " But the same
gentleman who had before exclaimed, Treason !
now cried out, *Rase them ! Rase them !* The amend-
ment was dropped, and the sense of the message
not being altered," these " dreadful words, under

---

* " Bernard was no great thing, but he was not a fool. It is impossible to
believe that he thought the offensive passage treason or sedition, or of such
danger and importance as he represented it. But his design was to destroy
Otis. There is your enemy, said Bernard (after a Scottish General,) if you
do not kill him, he will kill you."—President Adams' Letters.

which his Excellency placed a black mark, were accordingly expunged, and the message returned by the speaker."

Three days afterwards the governor sent a message, vindicating his conduct, and maintaining principles that were by no means satisfactory to the house. The secretary after reading the message, gave notice, that his Excellency directed the attendance of the house, in the Council Chamber. They voted to insert his vindication on the journal. A committee of three, the speaker, Otis and Tyler, were appointed to prepare an answer during the recess, and the house was then prorogued.

Soon after this separation, Otis published a pamphlet,* giving an account of all these occurrences and justifying the course taken by the house. This production may be considered the original source, from which all subsequent arguments against taxation were derived. The great principles of constitutional liberty, are shewn to rest at last on this basis, that taxation and representation are inseparable : the specious pretences of public expedience, which were designed to mask the encroachments of arbitrary power are all torn away ; and

---

* The title is; " A vindication of the conduct of the House of Representatives, of the Province of the Massachusetts Bay : more particularly in the last session of the General Assembly. By James Otis, Esq. a member of said House.

     Let such, such only, tread this sacred floor,
     Who dare to love their country and be poor :
     Or good though rich, humane and wise tho' great,
     Jove give but these we've nought to fear from fate.
Boston, printed by Edes and Gill, 1762."

the vigilance of a clear sighted statesman, is exhibited in the utmost plainness and energy. " How many volumes," says President Adams, " are concentrated in this little fugitive pamphlet, the production of a few hurried hours, amidst the continual solicitation of a crowd of clients; for his business at the bar at that time was very extensive, and of the first importance, and amidst the host of politicians, suggesting their plans and schemes, claiming his advice and directions! Look over the Declarations of Rights and Wrongs, issued by Congress in 1774. Look into the Declaration of Independence in 1776. Look into the writings of Dr. Price, and Dr. Priestley. Look into all the French constitutions of government, and to cap the climax, look into Mr. Thomas Paine's Common Sense, Crisis, and Rights of Man; what can you find that is not to be found in solid substance in this Vindication of the House of Representatives ?"

The preface contains a frank statement of his motives: " The following Vindication was written, in order to give a clear view of facts; and to free the House of Representatives from some very injurious aspersions, that have been cast upon them, by ill-minded people out of doors. Whether the writer has acquitted himself as becomes a candid and impartial vindicator, is submitted to the judgment of the public; which is ever finally given without favour or affection; and therefore the appeal is made to a truly respectable, and solemn tribunal? At the same time that a sincere love is professed for all men, and the duty of honour and reverence towards superiors, is freely acknowledged, it must be allowed that one of the best ways of fulfilling these duties, is in a modest and humble endeavour, by calm reason and argument, to convince mankind of their mistakes, when they happen to be guilty of any.

" The more elevated the person who errs, the stronger sometimes is the obligation to refute him; for the errors of great men are often of very dangerous consequences to themselves, as well as to the little ones below them. However it is a very disagreeable task, to engage in any kind of opposition to the least individual in society; and much more so, when the opinions of gentlemen of the first rank and abilities, and of public bodies of men, are to be called in question.

" The world ever has been, and will be pretty equally divided, between those two great parties, vulgarly called *winners* and *losers;* or to speak more precisely, between those who are discontented that they have no power, and those who never think they can have enough.

" Now it is absolutely impossible to please both sides, either by temporizing, trimming, or retreating; the two former justly incur the censure of a wicked heart, the latter that of cowardice, and fairly and manfully fighting the battle out, is in the opinion of many worse than either. All further apology for this performance shall be sum'd up in the adage. *Amicus Socrates, amicus Plato, sed magis Amica veritas.*"

His Vindication begins with the history of the
session, the first message of the governor, his own
speech in favour of raising all the men and granting
all the money that was required; then the governor's second message about the fitting out the Massachusetts, and the answer to the house that was represented to be treasonable. His defence of this passage exemplifies the firmness and wit of the writer.

"In order to excuse, if not altogether justify the
offensive passage, and clear it from ambiguity, I beg
leave to premise two or three *data*. 1. God made
all men naturally equal.—2. The ideas of earthly
superiority, pre-eminence, and grandeur, are educa-
tional, at least acquired, not innate.—3. Kings were
(and plantation governors should be) made for the
good of the people, and not the people for them.
4. "No government has a right to make hobby
horses, asses, and slaves of the subject; nature having
made sufficient of the two former, for all the lawful
purposes of man, from the harmless peasant in the
field, to the most refined politician in the cabinet;
but none of the last which infallibly proves they are
unnecessary. 5. Though most governments are, *de facto*, arbitrary, and consequently the curse and scandal
of human nature ; yet none are, *de jure*, arbitrary.
6. The British constitution of government as now esta-
lished in his majesty's person and family is the wisest
and best in the world. 7. The king of Great Britain is the best as well as the most glorious monarch
upon the globe, and his subjects the happiest in the
universe. 8. It is most humbly presumed the king

would have all his plantation governors follow his royal example, in a wise and strict adherence to the principles of the British constitution, by which, in conjunction with his other royal virtues, he is enabled to reign in the hearts of a brave and generous, free and loyal people. 9. This is the summit, the *ne plus ultra* of human glory and felicity. 10. The French king is a despotic arbitrary prince, and consequently his subjects are very miserable.

" Let us now take a more careful review of this passage, which by some out of doors, has been represented as seditious, rebellious and traitorous. I hope none, however, will be so wanting to the interests of their country, as to represent the matter in this light on the east side of the Atlantic, though recent instances of such a conduct might be quoted, efforts, wherein the province has after its most strenuous during this and other wars, been painted in all the odious colours that avarice, malice, and the worst passions, could suggest.

" The house assert, that it ' would be of little consequence to the people, whether they were subject to George, or Lewis, the king of Great Britain, or the French king, if both were arbitrary, as both would be if both could levy taxes without parliament.' Or the same words transposed without the least alteration of the sense. It would be of little consequence to the people whether they were subject to George the king of Great Britain, or Lewis the French king, if both were arbitrary, as both would be, if both could levy taxes without parliament.

" The first question that would occur to a philosopher, if any question should be made about it, would
be, whether the position were true.   But truth being
of little importance with most modern politicians, we
shall touch lightly upon that topic, and proceed to
inquiries of a more interesting nature.   That arbitrary government implies the worst of temporal evils,
or at least the continual danger, of them is certain.
That a man would be pretty equally subjected to
these evils under every arbitrary government, is clear.
That I should die very soon after my head should be
cut off, whether by a sabre or a broad sword, whether
chopped off to gratify a tyrant by the christian name
of *Tom, Dick, or Harry*, is evident.   That the name
of the tyrant would be of no more avail to save my
life, than the name of the executioner, needs no proof.
It is therefore manifestly of no importance what a
prince's christian name is, if he be arbitrary, any
more indeed, than if he were not arbitrary.   So the
whole amount of this dangerous proposition may at
least in one view be reduced to this, viz : *It is of
little importance what a king's christian name is.* It
is indeed of importance that a king, a governor,
and all other good christians should have a christian
name, but whether Edward, Francis, or William, is
of none, that I can discern.   It being a rule to put
the most mild and favourable construction upon
words that they can possibly bear, it will follow that
this proposition is a very harmless one, that cannot
by any means tend to prejudice his majesty's person,
crown, dignity, or cause, all which I deem equally

sacred with his Excellency. If this proposition will
bear an hundred different constructions, they must
all be admitted before any that imports any bad meaning, much more a treasonable one. It is conceived
the house intended nothing disrespectful to his majesty, his government or governor, in those words.
It would be very injurious to insinuate this of a house
that upon all occasions has distinguished itself by a
truly loyal spirit, and which spirit possesses at least
nine hundred and ninety-nine in a thousand of these
constituents throughout the province. One good natured construction at least seems to be implied in the
assertion, and that pretty strongly, viz. that in the
present situation of Great Britain and France, it is
of vast importance to be a Briton, rather than a
Frenchman, as the French king is an arbitrary despotic prince ; but the king of Great Britain is not
so *de jure, de facto,* nor by *inclination ;* a greater difference on this side the *grave* cannot be found, than
that which subsists between British subjects and
the slaves of tyranny.

" Perhaps it may be objected, that there are some
differences between arbitrary princes in this respect,
at least, that some are more rigorous than others.
It is granted, but then let it be remembered, that
the life of man is a vapour, that soon vanisheth away,
and we know not who may come after him, a wise man
or a fool; though the chances before and since So-
lomon, have ever been in favour of the latter. Therefore it is said to be of little consequence. Had it been
no instead of *little,* the clause upon the most rigid stric-
ture might have been found barely exceptionable.

" Some fine gentlemen have charged the expression
as indelicate. This is a capital impeachment in politics, and therefore demands our most serious attention. The idea of delicacy in the creed of some politicians, implies that an inferior should at the peril
of all that is near and dear to him, (*i. e.* his interest)
avoid every, the least trifle that can offend his superior. Does my superior want my estate? I must
give it him, and that with a good grace, which is appearing to be, and if possible being, really obliged to
him that he will condescend to take it. The reason is
evident, it gives him some little pain or uneasiness
to see me whimpering, much more openly complaining, at the loss of a little glittering dirt. I must, according to this system, not only endeavour to acquire
myself, but impress upon all around me a reverence
and *passive obedience* to the sentiments of my superi-
or, little short of adoration. Is the superior in contemplation, a king, I must consider him as God's vice-
regent, clothed with unlimited power, his will the
supreme law, and not accountable for his actions, let
them be what they may, to any tribunal upon earth.
Is the superior a plantation governor? he must be
viewed not only as the most excellent representation
of majesty, but as a viceroy in his department, and
guarded with all the prerogatives that were ever exercised by the most absolute prince of Great Britain.
The votaries of this sect are all monopolizers of
offices, peculators, informers, and generally the seek-
ers of all kinds. It is better, say they, ' to give up any
thing and every thing quietly, than contend with a

superior, who by his prerogative can do, and (as
the vulgar express it,) right or wrong, will have
whatever he pleases. For you must know, that
according to some of the most refined and fashionable systems of modern politics, the ideas of right and
wrong, and all moral virtues, are to be considered
only as the vagaries of a weak or distempered imagination in the possessor, and of no use in the world,
but for the skilful politician to convert to his own
purposes of power and profit.

With these,

> The love of country is an empty name,
> For gold they hunger: but ne'er thirst for fame.

" It is well known that the least ' patriotic spark'
unawares ' catched,' and discovered, disqualifies a
candidate from all further preferment, in this famous
and flourishing order of knights errant. It must
however be confessed they are so catholic as to
admit all sorts, from the knights of the post to a
garter and star; provided they are thoroughly
divested of the fear of God, and the love of mankind; and have concentrated all their views in
dear self, with them the only sacred and well beloved name, or thing in the universe. See Cardinal *Richlieu's Political Testament*, and the greater
bible of the sect, *Mandeville's Fable of the Bees.*
Richlieu expressly, in solemn earnest, without any
sarcasm or irony, advises the discarding all honest
men from the presence of a prince, and from even
the purlieus of a court. According to *Mandeville*,

' The moral virtues are the political offspring which flattery begot upon pride.'

" The most darling principle of the great apostle of the order, who has done more than any mortal towards diffusing corruption, not only through the three kingdoms, but through the remotest dominions, is, ' that every man has his price, and that if you bid high enough, you are sure of him.'

" To those who have been taught to bow at the name of a king, with as much ardour and devotion as a papist at the sight of a crucifix, the assertion under examination may appear harsh; but there is an immense difference between the sentiments of a British house of Commons remonstrating, and those of a courtier cringing for a favour. A house of Representatives, here at least, bears an equal proportion to a governor, with that of a house of Commons to the king. There is indeed one difference in favour of a house of Representatives; when a house of Commons address the king, they speak to their sovereign, who is truly the most august personage upon earth: when a house of Representatives remonstrate to a governor, they speak to a fellow subject, though a superior, who is undoubtedly intitled to decency and respect; but I hardly think to quite so much reverence as his master.

" It may not be amiss to observe, that a form of speech may be in no sort improper when used *argu-endo*, or for illustration, speaking of the king, which same form might be very harsh, indecent and even ridiculous, if spoken to the king.

" The expression under censure has had the approbation of divers gentlemen of sense, who are quite
unprejudiced by any party.   They have taken it to
imply a compliment rather that any indecent reflection, upon his majesty's wise and gracious administration.   It seems strange, therefore, that the house
should be so suddenly charged by his excellency
with *impropriety, groundless insinuations, &c.*

" What cause of so bitter repentance, *again and
again*, could possibly have taken place, if this clause
had been printed in the Journal I can't imagine.
If the case be fairly represented, I guess the province can be in no danger from a house of Representatives daring to speak plain English, when they are
complaining of a grievance.   I sincerely believe the
house had no disposition to enter into any contest
with the governor and council.   Sure I am, that
the promoters of this address had no such view.
On the contrary, there is the highest reason to presume, that the house of Representatives will at all
times rejoice in the prosperity of the governor and
council, and contribute their utmost assistance, in supporting those two branches of the legislature, in all
their just rights and pre-eminence.   But the house
is and ought to be jealous and tenacious of its own
privileges ; these are a sacred deposit intrusted by
the people, and the jealousy of them is a godly jealousy."

The principles of this defence he fortifies, by
quoting Locke's Discourse on Government at some
length in a note.   His reason for doing so he de-

clares to be, least "some of the principles advanced
in the Vindication of the House, should be branded
with the odious epithets, *seditious and levelling*. Had
any thing to justify them been quoted from colonel
Algernon Sydney, or other British martyrs, to the
liberty of their country, an outcry of rebellion would
not be surprising. The authority of Mr. Locke has
therefore been prefered to all others, for these further reasons. 1. He was not only one of the most
wise, as well as the most honest, but the most impartial man that ever lived. 2. He professedly wrote
his Discourses on Government, as he himself expresses it, "to establish the throne of the great restorer,
King William, to make good his title in the consent
of the people, which, being the only one of all lawful governments, he had more clearly and fully, than
any prince in Christendom, and to justify to the
world the people of England, whose love of liberty,
their just and natural rights, with their resolution to
preserve them, saved the nation when it was on the
brink of slavery and ruin. By this title, our illustrious sovereign George III. (whom God long per-
serve) now holds. 3. Mr. Locke was as great an ornament under a crowned head, as the church of
England ever had to boast of. Had all her sons
been of his wise, moderate, tolerant principles, we
should probably never have heard of those civil
dissensions, that have so often brought the nation to
the borders of perdition. Upon the score of his
being a churchman however, his sentiments are less
liable to the invidious reflections and insinuations that

Highflyers, Jacobites and other stupid bigots are apt too liberally to bestow, not only upon dissenters of all denominations, but upon the moderate, and therefore infinitely the most valuable part, of the church of England itself."

After this comes governor Bernard's message, containing his vindication, which occupies about four pages, and in which he seeks to justify his conduct; first, on the urgency and expediency of the measure, and secondly, that he possessed the right constitutionally, to make the expenditure. Both these points of defence are examined and refuted. But the principal stress in the argument is laid upon the latter, and here the position assumed by the governor, is not only shewn to be untenable, but the dangerous tendency of such constructions pointed out with a clearness and force, that effectually roused the public attention to guard against every step of arbitrary power in future.

Governor Bernard met with more liberality from the legislature in the beginning of his administration, than any of his predecessors; but he seems in the course of it to have lost the good will of all parties. His disposition was irritable, and not placable; he had a very indiscreet arrogance of office, and was avaricious. In the course of his message, he alludes to his conduct in his government of New Jersey, where he had taken much more important steps with the advice of council only, and, when " the assembly met, received their thanks." In allusion to this, Otis observes: " Whether the assembly of this province

equal the assembly of New Jersey in gratitude or any other virtue, I shall not pretend to determine. But this I am sure of, that this province has been more liberal of its grants to his Excellency, than to any of his predecessors. Instead of any debate about *his salary*, three grants have been made in less than two years, amounting to near three thousand pounds sterling in the whole ; besides the very valuable island of Mount Desert, which the province thought they had a right to grant, subject to his Majesty's confirmation ; and which his Excellency doubtless will have confirmed to him. All this, with the ordinary perquisites, besides the *full* third of all the seizures, must amount to a very handsome fortune, obtained in about two years and two months."
" To conclude, would all plantation governors reflect upon the nature of a free government, and the principles of the British constitution, as now happily established, and practise upon those principles, instead (as most of them do,) of spending their whole time in extending the prerogative beyond all bounds ; they would serve the king their master much better, and make the people under their care infinitely happier."

Chapter X.

Jealousy respecting Episcopacy—Controversy on this subject—Dr.
Mayhew—Dr. Apthorp—Dr. Chauncy—Dr. Cooper—Dr. Byles.

THE allusion made by Otis in his Vindication, to
the church of England, in speaking of Mr. Locke,
was naturally suggested by a subject, that was blend
ed with all the uneasy feelings of the times. A jealousy of the designs of the English hierarchy was
kept constantly alive, by the indications given from
time to time of anxiety to extend its authority over
this country, and by the indiscreet conduct of some
of its missionaries. Fear, hatred, and a long course
of hereditary prejudices against this church, combined almost all the dissenting clergy of New England, in constant opposition to it; and naturally led
them to sympathize with those who opposed the
unconstitutional acts of political power. The intentions of the church and the king were often mentioned in conjunction, and when the ambitious designs
of the ministry under George III. began to be apprehended, an extension of the power of the church was
supposed to be connected with them. Episcopacy,
or the patriarchate in America, was said to have
been first proposed by bishop Sherlock in the reign
of George II., which was then very coldly received,
and he was never afterwards summoned to the
privy council.*

---

* See Critical Review, for October, 1764. Article, Mayhew.

No project perhaps could shew greater ignorance of the character of the New England colonies, than any attempt of the English church to extend its dominion among them.* The efforts of the Society for propagating the Gospel, when made, not among the Indians but among the colonists, were looked upon as designed rather to extend the forms and power of the church, than to diffuse the knowledge of truth. It could not be pretended that the gospel was not preached and practised, for this

---

* " If any thing were wanting to this necessary operation of the form of government, religion would have given it a complete effect. Religion always a principle of energy in this new people, is no way worn out or impaired : and their mode of professing it, is also one main cause of this free spirit. The people are protestants, and of that kind which is most adverse to all implicit submission of mind and opinion. This is a persuasion not only favourable to liberty, but built upon it. I do not think, sir, that the reason of this averseness in the dissenting churches, from all that looks like absolute government, is so much to be sought in their religious tenets, as in their history. Every one knows that the Roman Catholic religion is at least coeval with most of the governments, where it prevails : that it has generally gone hand in hand with them, and received great favour and every kind of support from authority. The church of England too, was formed from her cradle, under the nursing care of regular government. But the dissenting interests have sprung up in direct opposition to all the ordinary powers of the world ; and could justify that opposition only on a strong claim to natural liberty. Their very existence depended on the powerful and unremitted assertion of that claim. All protestantism, even the most cold and passive, is a sort of dissent. But the religion prevalent in our northern colonies, is a refinement on the principle of resistance ; it is the dissidence of dissent and the protestantism of the protestant religion. This religion under a variety of denominations, agreeing in nothing but in the communion of the spirit of liberty, is predominant in most of the northern provinces, where the church of England, notwithstanding its legal rights, is in reality no more than a sort of private sect, not composing most probably the tenth of the people. The colonists left England when this spirit was high ; and in the emigrants was the highest of all ; and even that stream of foreigners, which hath been constantly flowing into these colonies, has, for the greatest part, been composed of dissenters from the establishment of their several countries, and who have brought with them a temper and character far from alien to that of the people with whom they mixed." *Burke.*

community was indisputably one of the most religious in the world; and that the congregational
ministers were not deficient in learning, was shewn
by the ability with which they engaged in the controversy, against all the talents of their opponents.
Their resistance indeed was fortunate, and it aided
the cause of civil as well as religious liberty. From
the first origin of the colony, this jealousy of the
church had been kept alive by a series of ill advised
attempts to establish its power, but the congregational clergy and their flocks could not be ignorant of
the consequences, if these attempts had succeeded.
In the year 1763, when this contest broke out into
open publishing, the intelligent part of the public
was not so bigoted as to fear the mere forms and
names of things, but it was the power behind them,
on which their eyes were steadily fixed. Since the
independence of the country, episcopacy has been
fully established. When the first bishops were seen
in New England, though some strong prejudices
were startled at the name, yet the panic soon subsided, as it was found, than this title was borne by a
christian pastor without temporal power, who owed
his elevation to the free choice of his people. This
church, which could make no progress under foreign
auspices, has since increased in an equal proportion
with other sects, though its spirit is opposed to the
enthusiasm and fanaticism that seek to make prose-
lytes. The propositions for establishing episcopacy
were moderate and unobjectionable, but this mild
beginning could not calm the apprehensions of any

man who had ever considered the nature, and examined the progress of ecclesiastical rule, or who had seen its mischief when connected with civil government, and their pernicious effects upon each other.* On this occasion, it was most fortunate that it did not succeed. If it had once obtained a settlement, it would have gradually extended its influence. The government would have lent its aid to enlarge its own patronage and adherents; and the country might in time, have become like Ireland, burdened with the support of a double hierarchy, not to promote the interests of religion, but to serve the purposes of party.

A controversy began on this subject in 1763, and was continued with little intermission till the declaration of Independence. It arose from an article in a newspaper, on the decease of an episcopal clergyman in Braintree, reflecting with great coarseness on episcopalians generally, and on the Society in England for propagating the Gospel. This produced a pamphlet by Dr. Apthorp, rector of the church in Cambridge, defending the conduct of the Society for propagating the Gospel. Dr. Apthorp,† was a

---

* See Appendix C.

† The Rev. East Apthorp was born in Boston in 1733, and having passed through Master Lovell's school, went to the University of Cambridge in England. After taking orders, he was sent out to this country, in the service of the Society for propagating the Gospel. The church at Cambridge was erected under his care. The controversy in which he became engaged, rendered his situation irksome, and he went back to England. He was there made successively Vicar of Croydon, Rector of Bow Church, London, and Prebend of Finsbury. He published, besides sermons, two volumes of Discourses on Prophecy, delivered at the Warburton lecture, at Lincoln's Inn, and a volume in answer to Gibbon. Dr. Apthorp had many friends among the dignitaries of the English church, and was generally beloved and respected. His education

gentleman and a scholar, and his work was well written; a phrase in the beginning of it, however, that he would " settle the question once for all," shewed more sincerity in the belief of the goodness of his cause, than recollection of the usual result of theological discussions. He was answered by Dr. Mayhew, with a degree of energy and ability, that placed him in a high rank amongst polemics. This produced several answers, and among them, one by Dr. Secker, Archbishop of Canterbury. Dr. Mayhew wrote two pamphlets in reply to his opponents, and a very able review of the whole dispute was afterwards given by Samuel Adams. It was believed, that the design of establishing this church at Cambridge, was for the purpose of making converts among the students, and with ulterior views that excited the most acrimonious jealousy. The immediate predecessor of Dr. Mayhew had given up the congregational form to be ordained as an episcopalian; a circumstance not calculated to lessen his apprehensions of the encroachments of episcopacy. All his feelings and principles led him to engage actively, in what he considered the cause of civil, as well as religious freedom.

Dr. Mayhew, whose name will be found in the class of 1744 in the Cambridge catalogue, was descended from the first proprietor of Martha's vine-

---

and ecclesiastical engagements naturally attached him to the government of England, but he always rejoiced in the prosperity of his native land, and received with pleasure all those who came from it. He passed the last twenty-six years of his life at Cambridge, (England) afflicted with an almost total loss of sight, and died in April.1816, at the age of eighty-three.

yard,* and his family had furnished several men of
piety and talents; some of whom were distinguished
by their benevolent and effectual services, as missionaries among the Indians in that quarter.   It seemed
therefore to be a very appropriate duty in him, to
discuss the conduct of a missionary society.   Before
this controversy, Dr. Mayhew was extensively known
in America, and perhaps still more in Europe, by
the bold and vigorous character of his writings.
Among these was a sermon on the anniversary of
" Charles the martyr," preached in the year 1750,
which went through several editions in Europe, as
well as this country; and its wit, sarcasm and unhesitating assertion of the highest principles of freedom,
made all who read it, foes, or admirers.   A more flagrant instance of indiscretion could hardly have been
given, than the celebration of this holy-day by the
episcopalians in Massachusetts.   It has been struck
out of the reformed episcopal calendar in this country, and even in England it was endured reluctantly;†
but among the descendants of the puritans and Com-
monwealthsmen, it offered a direct provocation and

---

* The Earl of Sterling, who claimed all the islands between Cape Cod and
Hudson's river, appointed Thomas Mayhew of Watertown governor of Nan-
tucket, Martha's Vineyard, and the adjacent islands, and in 1641 granted to
him and his son Thomas, the Island of Martha's Vineyard, where he and
several of this family after him were devoted to the conversion and civilization of the Indians.

† Among other attempts that conscientious men have made to get rid of a
day, in the service for which that prince is compared to the Saviour of mankind, a bill was introduced into the house of commons March 1772, by Mr.
Montague, to abolish the 30th of January as " a day of fasting and humiliation," the votes were 97 yeas, to 125 nays.

insult to them, in addition to what they and others, considered blasphemy.

Dr. Mayhew was the intimate friend of Otis, and there was in many respects a similarity of character, as well as of principles. Both were men of ardent and impetuous dispositions, high minded, honest and indignant opposers of every kind of hypocrisy and oppression. Both were men of sound learning, energetic rather than elegant writers; impatient of disguise, and with an inclination to wit and sarcasm, that sometimes led them, in the warmth of discussion, to write some things, they would at a calmer moment have omitted. There is also a circumstance of sad resemblance; both of them were cut off from the public service in the vigour of life.

One or two passages taken from his sermon, "On the repeal of the Stamp Act in 1766," will shew in a lively manner, the feelings of that period, in regard to parliamentary taxation of the Colonies: they will also shew the patriotic zeal and intrepidity, with which he supported the cause of liberty and justice. Speaking of the repeal, he says; " We have never known so quick and general a transition from the depth of sorrow to the height of joy, as on this occasion: nor indeed, so universal a flow of either, on any occasion whatever. It is very true we have heretofore seen times of great adversity. We have known seasons of drought, dearth, and spreading mortal diseases; the pestilence walking in darkness, and destruction wasting at noon-day.—We have seen wide devastations made by fire; and amaz-

ing tempests, the heaven on flames, the winds and
waves roaring. We have known repeated earth-
quakes, threatening us with destruction. We have
been under great apprehensions by reason of formidable fleets of an enemy on our coasts, menacing fire and
sword to all our maritime towns. We have known
times, when the French and savage armies made
terrible havock on our frontiers, carrying all before
them for a while ; when we have not been without
fear, that some capital towns in the colonies would
fall into their merciless hands. Such times as these
we have known; at some of which, almost every
' face gathered paleness,' and the knees of all but
the good and brave, waxed feeble. But never have
we known a season of such universal consternation
and anxiety, among people of all ranks and ages, in
these colonies, as was occasioned by that parliamentary procedure, which threatened us and our
posterity with perpetual bondage and slavery. For
they, as we generally suppose, are really slaves to
all intents and purposes, who are obliged to labour
and toil only for the benefit of others ; or, which
comes to the same thing, the fruit of whose labour
and industry, may be *lawfully* taken from them
without their consent, and they justly punished,
if they refuse to surrender it on demand, or apply it
to other purposes than those, which their masters,
for their mere grace and pleasure, see fit to allow.
Nor are there many *American* understandings acute
enough to distinguish any material difference, between this being done by a *single* person, under the

title of an absolute monarch, and done by a far distant legislature consisting of *many* persons, in which they are not represented; and the members whereof, instead of feeling and sharing equally with them in the burden thus imposed, are eased of their own in proportion to the greatness and weight of it. It may be questioned, whether the ancient Greeks or Romans, or any other nation in which slavery was allowed, carried their idea of it much further than this. So that our late apprehensions, and universal consternation, on account of ourselves and posterity, were far, very far indeed from being groundless. For what is there in this world more wretched, than for those who were born free, and have a right to continue so, to be made slaves themselves, and to think of leaving a race of slaves behind them; even tho' it be to masters confessedly the most humane and generous in the world? Or what wonder is it, if after groaning with a low voice for a while, to no purpose, we at length groaned so loudly, as to be heard more than three thousand miles; and to be pitied throughout Europe, whereever it is not hazardous to mention even the name of liberty, unless it be to reproach it, as only another name for sedition, faction, or rebellion?"

Towards the conclusion of the discourse, he dwells on his own principles : " Having been initiated in youth, in the doctrines of civil liberty, as they were taught by such men as Plato, Demosthenes, Cicero, and other renowned persons among the ancients ; and such as Sydney and Milton, Locke and

Hoadley, among the moderns, I liked them; they seemed rational. And having learnt from the holy scriptures, that wise, brave, and virtuous men were always friends to liberty; that God gave the Israelites a king (or absolute monarch) in his anger, because they had not sense and virtue enough to like a free Commonwealth, and to have himself for their king; that the son of God came down from heaven to make us ' free indeed,' and that ' where the spirit of the Lord is, there is liberty;' this made me conclude that freedom was a great blessing. Having also from my childhood up, by the kind providence of my God, and the tender care of a good parent now at rest with him, been educated to the love of liberty, though not licentiousness, which chaste and virtuous passion was still increased in me, as I advanced towards, and into manhood; I would not, I cannot now, though past middle age, relinquish the fair object of my youthful affections, LIBERTY; whose charms instead of decaying with time in my eyes, have daily captivated me more and more. I was accordingly penetrated with the most sensible grief when about the *first of November last, that day of darkness, a day hardly to be numbered with the days of the year, SHE seemed about to depart from America, and to leave that ugly hag Slavery, the deformed child of Satan, in her room. I am now filled with a proportionate degree of joy in God, on occasion of her speedy return with new

---

* The day the Stamp Act was to have gone into operation.

smiles on her face, with augmented beauty and splendour—Once more then, hail! celestial maid, the daughter of God, and excepting his son, the first born of heaven! Welcome to these shores again, welcome to every expanding heart! Long mayest thou reside among us, the delight of the wise, good and brave; the protectress of innocence from wrong and oppression; the patroness of learning, art, eloquence, virtue, rational loyalty, religion! And if any miserable people on the continent—or isles of Europe, after being weakened by luxury, debauchery, venality, intestine quarrels, or other vices, should, in rude collisions, or now uncertain revolutions of kingdoms, be driven in their extremity to seek a safe retreat from slavery, in some distant climate; let them find, O! let them find one in America, under thy brooding, sacred wings; where *our* oppressed fathers once found it, and we now enjoy it, by the favour of him, whose service is the most glorious freedom! Never, O! never may he permit thee to forsake us, for our unworthiness to enjoy thy enlivening presence! By his high permission mayest thou attend us through *life and death*, to the regions of the blessed, thy original abode, there to enjoy forever, 'the glorious liberty of the sons of God!'"

This high and earnest tone, this solemn enthusiasm, were suited to the times; they animated the courage and perseverance of the hearers; they were worthy of men engaged in one of the most arduous, and by its consequences, one of the most important, struggles, that has ever been maintained to secure

the great principles of civil liberty. The sermon
from which these extracts were made, may be considered the dying testimony of Dr. Mayhew. It
was delivered on Friday, May 23d, 1766, and he died
on the 8th of July following, in the forty sixth year
of his age.*

Another distinguished clergyman in Boston, the
Rev. Charles Chauncy, was the coadjutor and successor of Dr. Mayhew in the episcopal controversy.
He was indeed partially engaged in it from the year
1762, when he preached the Dudleian lecture at
Cambridge, on the validity of Presbyterian ordina-
tion; from which time he gave the subject his
strenuous attention, with a perseverance that formed
one of the traits of his character. After Dr. Mayhew's death, the contest was maintained by Dr.
Chauncy, who published various tracts on the question, between 1767 and 1771.

Dr. Chauncy was born January 1st, 1705, and was
the great grandson of the learned Dr. Charles
Chauncy, the second President of Harvard College,
who came to this country in 1638, to escape the persecution of Laud. His descendant also possessed
great learning with the unyielding temper of his ancestor, and enmity to bishops came down to him
through two or three generations of dissenting ministers, as a kind of heirloom attached to his name

---

* Dr. Mayhew corresponded with several distinguished men in England.
His printed sermons form several volumes. He was instrumental in procuring
many additions to the library at Cambridge, from his friend T. B. Hollis, Esq.
in whose works there is a portrait and many notices of him.

and profession. In the episcopal controversy, he was opposing what he considered a scheme of government ; but he had on a previous occasion, been equally conspicuous in resisting the waywardness of popular feeling, in the case of the famous Whitefield. The progress of that preacher and his followers, he considered injurious to the cause of true religion; the enthusiasm of the ' Newlights,' their extravagant pretensions, their appeals to the passions, and the intrusion of itinerant preachers, he held in abhorrence. In 1742, he resisted the popular delusion in this case, with as much zeal and boldness, as he did arbitrary designs afterwards in the other. He also wrote on some disputed points in theology, in which Sandiman and Edwards were his opponents : He was considered one of the greatest American divines, and was well known to theologians abroad.

His political opinions harmonized with his feelings on ecclesiastical matters. No man was more open, decided and staunch, in favour of the rights of his countrymen. In his writings he was perhaps more calm than Dr. Mayhew, but in conversation equally vehement against oppression. He used to assert that our cause was so just, that if human efforts should fail, a host of angels would be sent to support it ; and when a smile of incredulity was expressed at this opinion, he persisted more emphatically in the assertion, and said he knew it.

He was a man of the most inflexible honesty, who felt the highest indignation at every thing like duplicity ; so that many trivial things in the common intercourse of society, he thought worthy of serious reprehension. He had so little idea of poetry, that he could never relish it, and wished that some one would translate Paradise Lost into prose, that he might understand it. The same plain and straight forward turn of mind made him like the old divines; and to dislike excessively, the florid, rhetorical manner of some of the French sermons. This aversion to mere oratory, was probably increased by his antipathy to Whitefield and the methodists; and led him to beseech God that he might never be an orator; a prayer, which some malicious wit remarked had been fully granted. Of few men could it be so truly said, that he was in earnest every moment of his life. He had the strictest principles of integrity in pecuniary concerns, and never would tolerate any deviation by individuals or the public, from fulfilling all their engagements. The plea of expediency had no force with him; he vehemently opposed all tender-laws, and every attempt to legalize depreciation. During the period that some great losses were experienced by the fluctuation of paper money, he preached the election sermon, in 1747, before the governor and legislature; on which occasion, he spoke in very plain terms of their duty, as honest men and legislators, and said, that if their acts were unjust, they would one day be called upon to answer for them. The discourse gave some dissatisfaction, and a discussion arose whether it should be printed. To a person who came to tell him of this difficulty, he answered; " It shall be printed, whether the General

Court print it or not; and do you, sir, say from me, that if I wanted to initiate and instruct a person into all kinds of iniquity and double-dealing, I would send him to our General Court."

As a student, his ideas were clear, his conception quick; as a theologian, he was learned and liberal; as a writer, plain, argumentative and vigorous; as a preacher, sincere, unaffected, and, at times, deeply impressive; as a politician, open, inflexible and patriotic; as a man, sudden and vehement in his temper eminently upright, with a seriousness suited to his profession, and an earnestness appropriate to a period, when the most essential rights of freemen were brought into jeopardy, and were to be secured for his country at last, only by the hazardous claim and triumphant assumption of national independence. In the whole progress of the discussion, from its beginning with the pen, to its termination by the sword, he never wavered, nor refrained from giving his sanction to the asserters of American rights; for the support of which, with the enthusiastic habit of primitive times, he placed the most full and devout reliance on the kind protection of Providence. He had the happiness to see the freedom of the nation established, and died, February 10th, 1787, in his eighty-third year.*

There was another gentleman of the same profession, a contemporary and friend of Dr. Chauncy, though their manners were very dissimilar, who was

---

* Dr. Chauncy printed about sixty sermons, several controversial tracts, and some volumes of theology.

an advocate for the same political principles, and
one of the most conspicuous and influential public
characters of that time. Dr. Samuel Cooper was
born in Boston, March 25th, 1725, and took his degree at Cambridge, in 1743. He followed the pro-
fesssion of his father, who died the year his son left
college, and his congregàtion and colleague, Dr. Col-
man, were so anxious to have young Cooper for a
successor to his father, that he was persuaded to
preach very soon after leaving college; but, at his
own request, was not ordained over the society wor
shipping in Brattle Street Church, till 1746. This
religious society contained several of the most distinguished individuals, either for their wealth or talents,
in the town; and was generally considered the first
among equals, of all the congregational churches.
The situation, therefore, placed its incumbent among
the leading circles of society : a circumstance of some
moment, where the social intercourse between the
clergyman and his congregation, was so intimate and
frequent, as it has always been in Boston. No person of his profession was better suited to adorn a
station of this kind, and to derive from it all the influence it was calculated to give.

     Dr. Cooper was a fine scholar, but neither an in-
dustrious nor profound theologian. He wrote with
elegance, and his delivery was eloquent. He had a
readiness of thought and flow of language, that gave
him great command over his hearers, whether in the
pulpit or in conversation. His manners were polished and courteous, and in the peculiar functions of his

office, he had great power to impress and to sooth. These qualifications secured to him the private affection and admiration of his parishioners; while his knowledge of the world, and the active part which he took in public affairs, procured him the esteem and confidence of many eminent public characters.

Dr. Cooper had very early written upon some political topics. In the year 1754 he produced a pamphlet, called "The Crisis," against the excise act, then before the legislature. He had been the intimate friend of Governor Pownal, and was considered one of his confidential advisers. From the commencement of the ministerial plan of taxation upon the colonies, he had taken a part on the same side with Mayhew and Chauncy. He frequently wrote in the newspapers against the measures of the administration, from the date of the stamp act to the Declaration of Independence. His zeal in this cause was unbounded, and his influence greatly increased by his caution and address.

Many of his contemporaries, either by the works which they have left, or by their share in political events, subsequent to the peace of 1783, occupy now, a more prominent station than Dr. Cooper, in the public mind. Yet, in looking at some of the writings and opinions of that time, there were not many persons who appear so conspicuous, or to whom a greater agency was attributed, in the opposition to the British government. There were not many individuals more admired by one side, and hated by the other. Few vestiges of the rank he thus held in public sentiment

now remain, because his exertions were principally
of a personal and temporary nature. He maintained
a very active agency in counsel, in conversation and
private correspondence; an agency that was most
powerful and salutary at the period, yet being attached to no public acts, nor to any considerable
works, is more dependent on mere tradition, than
that of many other patriots of the day. He was
considered by the British officers, and those who adhered to the cause of the parent country, to have a
very large share in that opposition to arbitrary measures, which gradually ripened into open resistance.
Having been frequently lampooned and personally
insulted, as the rupture drew near, he was probably
saved from some serious personal inconveniences, by
getting out of Boston, a short time previous to the
skirmish at Lexington.

Dr. Cooper was the confidential correspondent of
Dr. Franklin, who recommended to him the French
officers, who came with the forces of France to
this country. They were mutually pleased, and
though the hospitality of the inhabitants, to their
new allies, was both frank and general, yet ancient prejudices could not be at once eradicated,
and there were many persons who saw this intercourse with ill-will. Dr. Cooper had previously
learnt the French language; an accomplishment at
that time very uncommon; and its singularity in
a clergyman, was aggravated in the minds of
many persons, to whom it seemed a very popish sort
of acquisition. Among these officers were several
of the most distinguished noblemen in the service;

men, who, having been bred at the most refined court in Europe, found a singular contrast of manners in the almost primitive simplicity of our society. Each had the charm of novelty for the other; and though for a century and a half, all their political and religious prejudices, and the recollection of Indian warfare, had made every thing French, particularly odious to the northern colonists, yet these new allies were received in this period of trial, with the utmost kindness; and the reaction in the minds of some, carried their prejudices to the other extreme. Much of this feeling was owing to the natural gratitude for assistance, in a time of adversity: but the prudent and excellent conduct of the French officers, joined to the facility with which the people of that nation adapt themselves to different circumstances, contributed to remove ancient dislike, and to create a lively friendship. Dr. Cooper was greatly delighted with these new friends, papists as they were, and the feeling was reciprocal. They admired his talents and address; though educated in a colony, with the simple habits of a dissenting clergyman, they found in him a knowledge of the world and a cast of character, that under a different star, might have qualified him for a prelate and a courtier.

Dr. Cooper died deeply regretted, at the close of the year 1783, in the fifty ninth year of his age, leaving only one child, a daughter.* His death was

---

* His brother, William Cooper, the venerable town clerk of Boston, adhered steadily to the same political principles, and was one of the most zeal-

after a short illness, and by an apoplectic attack, which upon anatomical examination was attributed to obstructions caused by the use of snuff. He published nothing with his name, excepting a few occasional sermons. He was a good friend to literature, one of the founders of the American Academy, and an useful patron to Harvard College. He was cut off before the period of old age, but he lived long enough to have his most earnest desires accomplished, in seeing the independence of his country acknowledged and peace restored.

Though Doctors Mayhew, Chauncy, and Cooper, were more celebrated than any clergymen in Massachusetts, for the decided part which they took in the arduous politics of their time, yet there were also many others, who exerted all their influence in the cause of their country, and rendered great service by their opinions and example. The number among the congregational clergy, who took the opposite side, was very small : but among them there was one at least, who was too remarkable to be passed over in silence.

Doctor Mather Byles was born in Boston in 1706, and educated at Cambridge; his name will be found in the class of 1725. His father came from England, and his mother was related to two

---

ous patriots of the town, with the acts of which his name is connected in an official station, during all the eventful period of the revolution. He was first chosen town cle.k of Boston, in 1760, and was annually re-elected to that office, till his death in 1809, at the age of 88, having held that place by popular election, through various changes of parties, forty-nine years,

celebrated clergymen, Richard Mather, and John Cotton. After completing his studies in theology, he was ordained the first pastor of the Church in Hollis street. He was twice married; his first wife was a niece of Governor Belcher, and the second a daughter of Lieutenant Governor Tailer.

Dr. Byles was a scholar, and fond of literature, he contributed many essays to the New England Weekly Journal, and several occasional poems, some of which were collected in a volume. He corresponded with Pope, Lansdowne and Watts; the former gave him an elegant copy of the Odyssey, and the last always sent him his works, as they were published. Beside these Miscellaneous Essays, in prose and verse, which he composed for recreation in his leisure hours, he published a few occasional sermons, the last of which was printed in 1771.

Dr. Byles avoided politics in his pulpit, and on being asked, why he did not sometimes preach on that subject, he answered; " I have thrown up four breastworks, behind which I have intrenched myself, neither of which can be forced. In the first place, I do not understand politics; in the second place, you all do, every man and mother's son of you; in the third place, you have politics all the week, pray let one day in seven be devoted to religion; in the fourth place, I am engaged in a work of infinitely greater importance : give me any subject to preach on of more consequence than the truths I bring to you, and I will preach on it the next sabbath." These reasons would have been deemed, by every one,

quite sufficient at another period; but in those times
the voice of the people was held to be the voice
of God, and the general feeling was, that he who is
not with me, is against me. If, however, there had
been only this negative conduct to blame, he would
have experienced no difficulty ; but his well known
feelings and opinions on political questions, and his
sarcastic expression of them, created a strong ill will
against him.

In 1776 his connexion with his congregation was
dissolved; for any disaffection to the cause of his
own country, or leaning towards England, could no
longer be tolerated. In 1777, he was denounced in
town meeting, as an enemy to his country, and afterwards was tried before a special court. The charges against him were, that he remained in the town
during the siege, that he prayed for the king, and
received the visits of the British officers. In a different kind of contest, this conduct might not have
been considered a very heinous offence ; and even
then, was not attended with any very dangerous
consequences to him. He was sentenced to confinement with his family, on board a guardship,
and to be sent to England with them. On being
brought before the Board of War, he was treated
with respect, and he was ordered to be confined to
his own house for a short time.

As there seems to have been nothing absolutely
treasonable in his conduct, it may be doubted, whether
he would have experienced any inconvenience on ac
count of his political sentiments, if he had not pro-

voked enmity in other ways. He possessed in a remarkable degree, a ready and powerful wit; a quality
which commonly excites more envy than good will, and
unless accompanied with great discretion, is often an
unfortunate gift. He sometimes exerted this talent,
where good nature would have refrained, and left a
lasting sting by a transient jest. He exhibited this
love of ridicule in various ways. On one occasion,
when sentenced to be confined to his own house,
with a sentinel over him, he persuaded this sentinel
to go on an errand for him, promising to take his
place. This he did very faithfully, and to the great
amusement of all who passed, the Doctor was seen
very gravely marching before his door, the musket
on his shoulder, keeping guard over himself.

He had the greatest readiness at a pun or repar-
tee, and many instances of these, and of his sarcastic
humour, are still repeated. A few of them will give
an idea of his manner. After his trial, he was sentenced to confinement in his house, and a guard
placed over him : this was done for a short time, and
then the guard was removed; on some further complaint, a sentinel was again placed over him : he was
soon freed, and no further noticed. In speaking of
these transactions, he said " *he had been guarded, re-
guarded,* and *disreguarded.*" Directly opposite to his
house, still standing at the angle of Nassau street,
which was formerly without pavement, there was a
very bad slough in wet weather. It happened one
day, that two of the selectmen who had the care of
the streets, driving in a chaise, stuck fast in this

hole, and were obliged to get out in the mud to endeavour to extricate their vehicle. Dr. Byles came
out, and making them a respectful bow said; " Gentlemen, I have often complained to you of this nui-
sance without any attention being paid to it, and I
am very glad to see you *stirring in this matter* now."
In the year 1780, a most extraordinary obscurity
pervaded the atmosphere on a particular day, which
is always designated as " the dark day." The darkness, though perhaps not greater, than what happens
for a day or two in London almost every year, from
an accumulation of fog and smoke, excited astonish-
ment among people accustomed to a clear atmosphere ; and in some timid minds, a good deal of alarm.
A lady who was a neighbour of the Doctor, though
above any superstitious fears herself, yet sent her
son, a young lad, with her compliments to him, to
know if he could account for the uncommon appearance of the day. His answer was ; " my dear, you
will give my compliments to your mamma, and tell
her that I am as much in the dark as she is"——A
ship from London brought out 300 street lamps, for
the town of Boston. It chanced that on the same
day, a female neighbour, who was a *new light* with a
weak mind and whining manner, that was not very
pleasing, called to see him. Wishing to get rid of
the visit, he soon asked with a tone calculated to
excite curiosity, if she had heard the news ? " O, no!
dear Doctor, what news ?" " Why three hundred *new
lights* have come over in the ship that arrived this
morning from London."—" Bless me, I had not heard

of it."—" Yes and the selectmen have wisely ordered them to be put in irons immediately." His visitor at once hurried away in great anxiety to make further inquiries. A person with this disposition to sarcasm, must sometimes expose himself to retorts of the same description, as occasionally happened to him. Having paid his addresses unsuccessfully to a lady, who afterwards married a gentleman of the name of Quincy; the doctor on meeting her said, " so madam, it appears you prefer a *Quincy* to *Byles*" —" Yes, for if there had been any thing worse than *biles*, God would have afflicted Job with them."

Dr. Byles was in person tall and well proportioned, and with a commanding appearance. His voice was strong and harmonious, and his delivery graceful. His political principles were odious to the great majority of his fellow citizens; and his sarcastic, pungent wit created many a laugh, and many an enemy. He lived in retirement the last twelve years of his life, and died July 5th, 1788, at the age of eight-two.

Chapter XI.

Question respecting the salary of the Attorney General—Edmund Trowbridge—The Acts of Trade—Instructions to the Agent—Otis' " Rights of the Colonies"—Choice of an Agent—Inactivity of Otis—Motives of his Conduct.

BESIDE the memorable dispute with the governor relative to expenditures, in which Mr. Otis took such a leading part; he was also chairman of a committee of the same house, on another topic connected with constitutional principles, and in which the house of representatives felt a strong interest. In 1762, Edmund Trowbridge,* the attorney general, pre-

---

* Edmund Trowbridge was born at Newton, near Boston, in 1709, was graduated at Harvard College in 1728. He bore during a part of his life the name o Goffe, after an uncle, but afterwards resumed his paternal name. He was one of the most learned lawyers in Massachusetts, and was first appointed attorney general by governor Shirley, in 1749, and was continued in that office till 1767, when he was promoted to the bench of the supreme court. He was the principal judge in the trial of captain Preston and the soldiers, for firing on the people on the 5th of March, 1770. His application to his profession had been originally very severe, and his knowledge of the law was profound. Hutchinson, while on the bench, visited him very frequently, and derived much assistance from his learning and readiness to impart it. But in the case of Judge Trowbridge, as in some others, the governor ceased to be grateful, when the individual refused compliance with any of his wishes. He urged Trowbridge to continue on the bench at a time, that the tenure of the office from ministerial innovations on the charter, was extremely unpopular with the country at large, and was disapproved of by Judge Trowbridge himself, and this for the purpose of nursing and supporting his brother, Forster Hutchinson, whose inexperience required some assistance. He refused very firmly to accept the appointment against his principles, and the governor then treated him with supercilious coldness and neglect. Judge Trowbridge leaned in his politics to the government side, without however becoming obnoxious to

sented a petition to be remunerated for his official services, which was referred to the next session. It was taken up in February, 1763, and negatived. Five days afterwards, Otis moved a reconsideration, and the subject was again committed to him and six others—a long report, drawn up by Otis, was made, in which the prayer of the petitioner was refused, because the house had no share in his appointment, and it had been repeatedly decided in former cases, that the house had a right to participate in the choice of this officer. The report contained an elaborate argument to shew that the attorney general was an officer to be appointed by the general court ; and, of consequence, refused " to grant any salary or pay, to any person officiating in said office, whom they had no hand in choosing." The committee added, " that they are satisfied that Mr. Trowbridge has behaved with fidelity, integrity and industry, in said office." The question relating to the compensation, was then referred to the next session of the legislature. In June, 1763, it was taken into consideration, and after some debate, 300*l.* were voted for his services. This transaction shews the watchfulness that prevailed on every subject, connected with the rights of the people. Otis, in this affair, contended strenuously for the principle that was involved ; but at the same time was an advocate

---

his fellow citizens, by whom he was respected for his ability and uprightness. General Warren offered him a pass, or card of safety, in 1775, but be declined accepting it, saying he had nothing to fear from his countrymen, and he was never molested. He died at Cambridge, 1793, in his 84th year.

for granting to the officer, the remuneration that was honourably due to him.

On the accession of George the third to the throne of England, the inhabitants of the colonies generally, and of the northern ones especially, were never more cordially disposed to form part of the dominions of the English monarch, on terms of equality and common favour with the rest of his subjects. At the same time, perhaps, there was never a moment in the history of Massachusetts, a colony, remarkable for a jealous care of its rights, and very intractable under foreign controul, when every encroachment and every assumption of power, would have been so keenly and instantaneously resisted. The question about the Writs of Assistance, the opposition to a trifling expenditure in fitting out a guard vessel, on at least plausible pretences, had excited universal attention to financial questions. The objections to the incongruous employments, that were held by lieutentant governor Hutchinson, and the minor question about the appointment of the attorney general, produced a general discussion as to the constitutional tenure of office. The controversy in regard to episcopacy, had roused all the ardent feelings connected with religious or sectarian attachment. The impending restrictions on commerce, which would fall with ruinous weight both on the trade and fisheries of the province, kept the trading part of the community in constant anxiety. All these causes together, made the patriotic majority so numerous, that the legislature of the Province would do nothing to aid the sinister designs of the ministry; and wherever the government attempted to lay its hand, a bristling impatience instantly announced resistance.

In the latter part of 1763, the alarm became excessive, at the idea, that the navigation acts, and the acts of trade, were to be strictly enforced. The ministry began to put their intended system of taxation in operation, by a strict execution of these trade laws, which would give them external taxes, while the system could be matured for raising an internal revenue. The custom-house officers were ordered to enforce every regulation, and the officers of the navy were employed in the same service on the coast, so that their vessels were converted into custom-house tenders. "Orders for the strict execution of the molasses act were published, which are said to have caused a greater alarm in the country, than the taking of Fort William Henry did in the year 1757."* This comparison is not exaggerated, though the loss of Fort William Henry, which seemed to leave the northern colonies entirely at the mercy of the French and Indians, was one of the most disastrous events they had ever known. The vast importance that was attached to this homely commodity, molasses, could hardly be understood in England, or in the other colonies; and the clamour that was made, drew after it a degree of ridicule, by the supposition of its being a chief article of food, that is

---

* Minot's History.

not yet wholly obliterated. At that time, the importation of molasses was connected with the prosperity of almost the whole trade of New England. The molasses was received from the French islands in payment for fish; their islands afforded the only market for a considerable part of the produce of the fisheries, which was unsaleable any where else. If, then, this quality of fish could not be sold, the fishery could not be continued for the other sorts alone, that were culled for the European market. The question, therefore, involved almost the whole of the fisheries. The molasses, also, was distilled in large quantities, for home consumption, and for the African trade; and in various ways, it contributed essentially to the means of making remittances to England for her manufactures. The reason assigned for inflicting all this extensive evil upon the country, was to benefit the planters in the English islands, by the consumption of some additional portion of their productions; but the true motive, undoubtedly, arose from the design of taxation, which might be most easily commenced by a system of external revenue. The town of Boston, at their annual meeting in May, appointed a committee to draw up instructions* to their representatives, which directed them to use every exertion to maintain the rights and privileges of the province, and to resist all attempts to lay taxes upon them without their consent. Memorials of a very pressing kind were presented by the mer-

---

* These instructions are printed at the end of Otis's Rights of the Colonies.

chants of Boston, Salem, and all the other chief
ports, praying for protection against the danger.
These memorials against the sugar act, as it was
called, were referred to a committee of which Otis
was chairman, and he made a report, June 13th,
1764, containing a letter of instructions to the agent,
Mr. Mauduit, from which the following extracts are
taken, which bear evident marks of his manner.

" Volumes have been transmitted from the Province in relation to the sugar act, to little purpose.
If a West Indian, or any other, by influence, is to
govern and supersede our most essential rights as
British subjects, what will it avail us to make remonstrances, or the most demonstrable representations of our rights and privileges. You ' hope, however, there will be found a general disposition to
serve the Colonies, and not to distress them.' The
sudden passing of the sugar act, and continuing a
heavy duty on that branch of our commerce, we are
far from thinking a proof, that your hope had any
solid foundation. No agent of this province has
power to make express concessions in any case without express orders. And the silence of the province should have been imputed to any cause, even
to despair, rather than be construed into a tacit
cession of their rights, or an acknowledgment of a
right in the parliament of Great Britain to impose
duties and taxes upon a people, who are not represented in the House of Commons."

" The letter of the 11th of February is still more
surprising. We conceive nothing could restrain

your liberty of opposing so burthensome a scheme, as that of obliging the Colonies to maintain an army. What merit could there be in a submission to such an unconstitutional measure? It is time enough for us to make a virtue of necessity, when we are obliged to submit to so unreasonable an establishment. Is there any thing in your power of agency, or in the nature of the office, that can warrant a concession of this kind? most certainly there is not. We are extremely obliged to Mr. Grenville, ' for his kind expressions of regard to the Colonies.' But we can't conceive it any vast favour, that he will not think of ' any thing from America for the relief of Great Britain,' nor can we conceive it to be exactly agreeable to equity and justice, that America ' should be at the whole charge of its own government and defence.'

" The northern Colonies have, during the late war, exerted themselves in full proportion to that of Great Britain. This province in particular, had in one campaign on foot seven thousand troops. This was a greater levy, for a single Province, than the three kingdoms have made, collectively, in any one year since the Revolution."

The letter then goes on to say, that the colony had defended itself for more than a hundred years, that it was now at great expense to protect itself against the Indians—that in this situation, it was grievous to be obliged to pay for the support of large forces in other colonies. " And granting the time may come, which we hope is far off, when the British parliament shall think fit to oblige the North Americans, not only to maintain civil government among themselves, for this they have already done, but to support an army to protect them; can it be possible that the duties to be imposed and the taxes to be levied, shall be assessed without the voice or consent of one American in Parliament? If all the Colonists are to be taxed at pleasure without our consent, will it be any consolation to us, that we are to be assessed by an hundred, instead of one? " If we are not represented, we are slaves : nay, at this rate, the British Colonists will be in a worse condition than those of any other prince : for besides maintaining internal provincial governments among themselves, they must pay towards the support of the national, civil and military government in Great Britain. Now it is conceived, that no people on earth are doubly taxed for the support of government.

* * * * * *

" The actual laying the stamp duty, you say, is deferred 'till next year, Mr. Grenville being willing to give the Provinces their option to raise that or some other equivalent tax, ' desirous,' as he was pleased to express himself, ' to consult all the ease, the quiet, and the good will of the Colonies.'

" If the ease, the quiet, and the good will of the Colonies are of any importance to Great Britain, no measures could be hit upon, that have a more natural and direct tendency to enervate those principles, than the resolutions you inclose."

" The kind offer of suspending this stamp duty in the manner and upon the condition you mention, amounts to no more than this; that if the Colonies will not tax themselves as they may be directed, the parliament will tax them."

*   *   *   *   *   *

" You are to remonstrate against these measures, and if possible, to obtain a repeal of the sugar act, and prevent the imposition of any further duties or taxes on these Colonies. Measures will be taken that you may be joined by all the other agents."

" Ireland is a conquered country, which is not the case with the northern Colonies, except Canada : yet no duties have been levied by the British Parliament on Ireland. No internal or external taxes have been assessed on them, but by their own Parliament."

" It may be said, that if the Parliament have a right to lay prohibitions, they can certainly lay duties, which is a less burthen. Why then has this not been done to Ireland ? Many prohibitions have been made by the British Parliament on Ireland, yet we can find no precedent of a duty imposed on them.

" Further, let it be remembered, that equity and justice require, that the power of laying prohibitions on the dominions which are not represented in Parliament, should be exercised with great moderation. But this had better be exercised with the utmost rigour, than the power of taxing : for this last is the grand barrier of British liberty : but which if once broken down, all is lost.

" In a word, a people may be free and tolerably happy without a particular branch of trade, but without the privilege of assessing their own taxes, they can be neither.

" Inclosed you will have a brief state of the rights of the colonies, drawn up by one of our members, which you are to make the best use of in your power, with the addition of such arguments as your own good sense will suggest.

" The house rest assured nothing will be omitted, that may have a tendency to save the province from impending ruin."

An order follows, that a draught of "the Rights of the British Colonies" should be sent to the agent: and another, that Mr. Otis and others named, be a committee to write to the other governments, during the recess, to acquaint them with these instructions, to obtain a repeal of the sugar act, to remonstrate against the stamp act, and in behalf of the house, to desire the other assemblies to join with them in the same measures.

There was about this time a degree of hesitation and uncertainty in the conduct of parties, as to the course which they should pursue. The weak and inefficient manner, in which Mr. Mauduit, the province agent, defended their interests in England, made the house resolve on choosing a new agent. The lieutenant governor, who had so justly incurred the suspicion of the leading members in the legislature, appeared suddenly to have recovered his influence. He was chosen agent by a great majority, to the surprise of the public at large. The previous instructions to the agent were suppressed, as being too strong in their language: and the interests of the colony were to be committed to a man who

well knew their value, but who had shewn himself
ready to aid the most arbitrary measures. Governor Bernard, however, by some scruples unfortunate
for his own views, would not consent to the absence
of the lieutenant governor, without permission from
the ministry. He was obliged, therefore, to decline
the appointment. Through his influence the choice
was postponed till the next session, that he might
in the mean time obtain leave from the ministry;
but his opponents having recovered from their trance
in the interval, he was disappointed in his hope of
being re-chosen.

The conduct of Otis at this period, was an object
of general animadversion, and the public murmurs
against him grew louder and louder. Having been
the acknowledged leader and adviser of the opposition, his conduct was watched with great closeness.
His father, colonel Otis, received a judicial appointment in his county ; a suspicion began to arise in
the public mind, that there was a compromise between the chief individuals on both sides, by which,
resistance to ministerial measures was to be less
stern and inflexible. Otis published a work entitled,
" *the rights of the British Colonies asserted and proved*,"* in which he made some concessions to the power of parliament, that were thought inconsistent
with the principles, which he had so triumphantly
supported on previous occasions.

" The rights of the British colonies" attracted
much attention at the time ; as well from the theme,

---

* See Appendix.

at the character of the author. The work affords proofs of his merits and defects as a writer; it discovers learning, wit, and argumentative strength; and at the same time carelessness, haste, and a disdain of revising thoughts, thrown off with the rapidity of a powerful, impatient spirit. The work gave satisfaction to no party; the English Journals spoke of it according to the bias of their particular views, but without entire blame or approbation.*

The zealous patriots in this country dissented from his admission of complete parliamentary supremacy : while the officers of the crown scowled at

---

* Several allusions were made to this work in the debates in parliament : the two following are extracted from a debate in the House of Lords in February 1766, " on the disturbances in America." The observations of another speaker alluded to by Lord Mansfield, were probably not recorded.

Extract from Lord Lyttleton's speech :—"If the colonies are subjects of Great Britain, they are represented, and consent to all statutes." " But it is said they will not submit to the stamp act, as it lays an internal tax : if this be admitted, the same reasoning extends to all acts of parliament. The Americans will find themselves crampt by the act of navigation, and oppose that too."

" The Americans themselves make no distinction between external and internal taxes. Mr. Otis their champion scouts such a distinction, and the assembly shewed they were not displeased with him, by making him their representative at the Congress of the states general of America."

Extract from Lord Mansfield's speech. " With respect to what has been said or written upon this subject, I differ from the noble lord, who spoke of Mr. Otis and his book with contempt, though he maintained the same doctrine in some points, although in others he carried it further than Otis himself, who allows every where the supremacy of the crown over the colonies. No man on such a subject is contemptible. Otis is a man of consequence among the people there. They have chosen him for one of their deputies at the Congress, and general meeting from the respective governments. It was said the man is mad. What then? one madman often makes many. Massaniello was mad, nobody doubts it; yet for all that, he overturned the government of Naples. Madness is catching in all popular assemblies, and upon all popular matters. The book is full of wildness. I never read it till a few days ago; for I seldom look into such things."

his lofty and unlimited claim for his countrymen, of the fullest and highest rights of British subjects. The question included principles which even his powerful mind in vain attempted to unite; they were irreconcilable. If the parliament was supreme, and there was no representation of the colonies, that power as regarded them, was absolute and arbitrary, and they might have been lawfully crushed under restrictions and taxes. It would have been safer for Otis to have taken the ground which he had formerly maintained, that the acts of parliament were not binding on the colonies; because there still remained between this position, and the abyss of independence, as it was then considered, the protecting expedient of a representation in parliament.

The ultimate view of the author was, no doubt, to have a representation of the colonies in Parliament, though he alludes satirically to Governor Pownal's work on the "Administration of the Colonies," which recommended the adoption of this plan. The scheme of a colonial representation was a favourite one with many minds, and might perhaps have been adopted, if the ministry had renounced their pursuit of immediate taxation. What the consequences would have been is now only a subject of idle speculation; but, it is very certain, that 'the colonists would never have been satisfied with the chimera of virtual representation. Yet in claiming their own proportion, they would have resisted the pretensions of others, that would inevitably have produced great alterations in the composition of the

British Parliament. With regard to Otis, he was, as usual, accused of madness, which from the first moment of his political career, was the reproach resorted to by those, who could not doubt his talents, who dared not suspect his integrity, who were astonished at his boldness, and confounded by the contagious enthusiasm of his eloquence. Though an imputation of madness previously communicated to our minds against a stranger, will attach suspicion to every movement and expression which he may make, however calm or rational, and on this occasion, as has been seen, was readily admitted, yet a discordant theme, an almost contemptuous carelessness of style, and a vehemence of thought, seemed to furnish some colour for the allegation.

What were his motives for relaxing his opposition, or acting in the spirit of compromise in the legislature, and almost entirely abstaining from interference in private meetings on political affairs, can now be only matter of conjecture. The wavering conduct of the legislature, was partly owing, perhaps, to the uncertainty of what were the eventual designs of the ministry, to the dangerous tendency of the dispute, and to the unequal strength of the parties. The friends of the government held out the idea of the determination and power of the mother country to enforce the oppressive revenue acts, which had fallen into disuse, or rather had never been in operation. They represented that a strict enforcement of them would ruin the trade and fisheries of the colony; and that it would be better to submit, if by so doing, the duty could be reduced to a small amount, that would not be burthensome, rather than to hazard the consequences that would ensue from resistance. On these principles, Hutchinson would have acted zealously, and probably with more success than any other person; and if that course were to be taken, which was to alleviate the burthen on the country, and yet preserve the principle to the ministry, he was doubtless the most suitable agent.

Otis may be supposed to have been governed by considerations, both of a personal and public nature. A man, in his situation, might well pause in his career. His family was one of the most respectable in the colony; he himself was at the head of his profession, the pursuit of which was constantly interrupted by the thankless charge of public concerns. From the first moment that he took the side of his country against the administration, he saw himself denounced by it, and many persons in his accustomed circle of society estranged from him; he found himself covered with obloquy, ridiculed, and pursued with incessant misrepresentation. This was disheartening enough on the ground merely of private peace and enjoyment, but it was still more serious if considered with a view to interest and advancement, because he made immediate sacrifices of no trifling importance, and debarred himself from expectations for the future, that would have satisfied any reasonable ambition. There could be no selfish calculation in his breast of any equivalent for the losses, which he knowingly brought on himself. The cause he contended for, had no chance of ever being abetted by persons in authority, or of obtaining that favour with the throne, or the parliament, that should bring its adherents into power. With the most complete success, it could only derive a passive triumph for the rights of the colonists, without the probability of any reward to those who had maintained them.

As a question of public expediency, resistance to the parent country, in all reflecting minds, was replete with difficulty and danger. A contest with the British government, whose power in the colonies was thought to be irresistible, seemed downright madness to many. It was particularly repugnant to the feelings of the public at this period, though they were at the same time, so jealously alert against every encroachment on their rights. The Colonies had just come out of a war in which they had made great efforts, and by driving the French from Canada, had accomplished an object, which they had been labouring for above seventy years to achieve. They enjoyed a large share in this triumph, a high feeling of equality, and a closer sympathy with the nation to whom it was attributed. They felt under a youthful sovereign, " who gloried in the name of Briton," that hope and affection, which the beginning of a new reign is apt to inspire; and this epoch being attended with the conclusion of an advantageous peace, they were led more fully to indulge in those illusions about the dignity and beneficence of the monarch, which subjects, who are placed at a great distance from the throne, are always ready to entertain. All the public documents and the private traditions, respecting that period, shew these feelings to have been predominant; and that during the whole existence of the Northern Colonies especially, there never was a time when they were better affected towards the parent state, or could have been more heartily allied to its dominion and interests by a system of wise and liberal policy.*

The danger of opposition was also strongly felt by all thinking and honest minds, who saw its possible or probable termination in civil war. Such a

---

* An interesting passage from one of Governor Pownal's speeches, may be cited in confirmation of these opinions, and will serve to show how these people, who were so jealous and inflexible in resisting arbitrary measures, would have acted, if treated with justice and liberality. It is from a speech delivered May 8, 1770, in a debate " on the disturbances in America," when the ministry were trying the effect of their power on Massachusetts, by some new act of severity. Governor Pownal gave some historical proofs of the loyalty and services of Massachusetts; such as the taking of Nova Scotia, in 1711, the capture of Louisbourgh in 1745, their immense exertions in men and money, for the war that terminated with the peace of 1763, and then proceeded to say : " There is another service which though the occasion never called for it, yet was in intention, and from the weight and influence of those who were consulted and knew the spirit of the people, I may venture to say, would have been performed. *Haud incerta pro certa habeo.* I speak of what was plotted and set down. When it was apprehended that the French might invade England, and land a body of troops in it, there was a design amongst those who had an authority and lead with this people there, and who would have been able to have led them into the execution of it—there was a design, to propose the bringing over to this country, a body of men, to the assistance of the mother country, which they call their home; and if the French had actually landed any troops on English ground, this disaffected, this disloyal people, would have come to the assistance of their parent country, this their home, the native country of the colonists. But what is the case now and how are matters changed? Under an idea that this people cannot be recalled to a sense of lawful authority, we are sending troops there to insure their obedience, and to preserve their union with us."

struggle was contemplated with deep apprehension;
not so much in regard to the seeming disparity of
resources between the parties, as to the situation of
the colonies themselves, if successful against their
oppressors. It was feared they would be thrown
into a state of hopeless anarchy, and destructive
contests with each other; being without any system
of general government, any basis of harmony, or any
means of defence against foreign enemies.* These
colonies had been founded by men with different
views, and various principles, political and religious;
ignorance of each other, and their slight intercourse
still prevented the removal of early prejudices and

---

* The following passage is taken from Otis's answer to the "Halifax libel,"
page 16. "The supreme legislative, indeed, represents the whole society or
community, as well the dominions as the realm; and this is the true reason
why the dominions are justly bound by such acts of parliament as name them.
This is implied in the idea of a supreme, sovereign power; and if the parliament had not such authority, the colonies would be independent, which none
but rebels, fools, or madmen, will contend for. God forbid, these colonies,
should ever prove undutiful to their mother country! Whenever such a day
shall come, it will be the beginning of a terrible scene. Were these colonies
left to themselves, to-morrow, America would be a mere shambles of blood
and confusion, before little petty states could be settled. How many millions
must perish in building up great empires? How many must be ruined by
their fall? Let any man reflect on the revolutions of government, ancient
and modern, and he will think himself happy in being born here, in the infancy of these settlements, and from his soul deprecate their once entertaining
any sentiments, but those of loyalty, patience, meekness, and forbearance,
under any hardships that in the course of time, they may be subjected to.
These, as far as may be consistent with the character of men and christians,
must be submitted to." This language certainly proves, that he was contending for justice, not for a revolution; but even while looking only at the danger
on one side, and deprecating it with such enormous sacrifices, he still makes a
reserve in the words, "consistent with the character of men and Christians,"
for those rights of which he was the great champion, and which he afterwards
found were only to be maintained by assuming independence.

jealousies, which had been mutually formed. Only one abortive effort, had ever been attempted to organise a confederation and to combine their interests. Their present national union, established under the direction of wisdom, moderation, magnanimity, and virtue, rarely witnessed in the history of human affairs, could not have been expected by the most sanguine : that system of concession and compromise, of wide views and beneficent intentions, which in the brief period of a single generation, has formed so many separate and disjointed governments into one powerful and harmonious confederation; in which by a reciprocity of intercourse every portion is united to the rest, by the most powerful ties of interest, policy, and relationship; and the whole blended into one nation, more intimately allied, and with fewer diversities of character, language, habits and interests, than any empire of similar extent in the world : all this accumulation of happiness and strength, would have seemed only a splendid vision, beyond the conception of prophecy. The most ardent patriot could not have anticipated what has now become a glorious reality, which, from the suddenness and grandeur of its existence, will seem to future ages to have been created instantaneously ; and the origin of this nation may, in after times, be likened to the fable of Minerva, starting into being, all armed, wise and immortal.

A struggle that might terminate in the desperate results of civil war and intestine commotion, was regarded by the wisest men, with peculiar aversion. The leading patriots of that time, though stern republicans in their habits, practice, and many of their principles, were theoretically royalists; and were ready to obey their distant sovereign with alacrity, as long as he refrained from encroaching on their privileges. Otis in many places of his works, professes the strongest allegiance to the sovereign, and great admiration for the British Constitution. When he began his opposition, he believed he was only resisting the iniquitous and arbitrary measures of a ministry, which had deceived their king; and that a change of men and measures would restore harmony to the colonies, and place their rights in security. But, in proportion as circumstances unfolded the designs of the English ministry, and discovered the outlines of a systematic plan of taxation; the hope of any alleviation, by a change of men, was nearly destroyed, and the tremendous alternative of an armed resistance, became more distinctly shadowed out in the dark uncertainty of the future.

Those who were to lead in such a course as this, where fortune, life and honour, were all to be hazarded, might well pause before they advanced to positions, from which there was no retreat. Otis was at this time, the acknowledged head of opposition. Every measure was undertaken by his advice, and supported by his efforts. It behoved him especially, to make a calculation of consequences. The ministry showed the most determined resolution to enforce the acts of trade: and the feeling of the greater part of the nation, was in unison with this spirit.

Bernard and Hutchinson, who in the beginning, advised their superiors to be moderate in the burthens which they imposed, were anxious to make a compromise with the opposition. Although they shewed by their subsequent conduct, that their places and emoluments were to be preserved at all hazards, and that they would aid in prostrating the liberty and prosperity of all the colonies, rather than relinquish them; yet at first, they seemed anxious to prevent affairs from going to extremes. They held up therefore in the strongest light, the determination and the power of the government, and that the only safe course would be to submit to the principle, and endeavour to obtain a diminution of the duties named in the Revenue Acts: that by this means our trade would only be subjected to a light contribution, which otherwise would be annihilated by the excessive exactions proposed, and against which we could make no resistance.

Otis and his political friends in the legislature, seem to have despaired of being able to effect more for their constituents : and to have yielded their consent to making Hutchinson the agent, under the idea that his thorough knowledge of the interests of the colony, and his well-known attachment to the ministry, would enable him, better than any other individual, to shew the true character of the colonial trade, with a greater probability that his representations would be favourably received. In making this experiment,

Otis might have calculated on ascertaining two important facts: the first, how far the ministry were
flexible in their views, and willing to listen to reason in their colonial policy : the second, what was
the public feeling in the colony, in regard to a plan
of compromise, and how far it was disposed to go,
in contending for principle. This latter was all important to be ascertained; because he foresaw that
the plan of the ministry, if not submitted to, must
inevitable lead to absolute war at no very distant
period. He saw, that though his fellow citizens
were watchful and zealous against every encroachment, yet the largest portion of them could not anticipate the final consequences of this dispute ; and
except from their general character, there was no
mode of ascertaining how far they were prepared
to carry resistance. All the officers of government,
and their connexions, and several influential people
in various towns of the Province, were constantly ap-
pealing to the loyalty of the peaceable, and the fears
of the timid, against any collision with the mother
country ; and with this powerful influence to affect
the opinions of the inhabitants, the defenders of colonial privileges might feel some doubt, whether the
people would sacrifice immediate interests, in a
struggle with such fearful odds, for abstract rights
or remote contingencies.

If the motives of Otis for relaxing in his opposition, and assenting to a compromise, were such as
have been supposed; he was soon convinced that
there was no faltering in public sentiment, and that

his countrymen were not disposed to renounce any one of their rights. His conduct in keeping aloof from public meetings, and his disposition to unite and conciliate parties in the legislature, excited first surprise, next suspicion, and then obloquy. He was accused of treachery to the cause, and was in danger of terrible disgrace, when a most despicable but virulent lampoon, in a journal devoted to the government, proved to the public, that if he had relaxed from his opposition for a time, he had not changed sides. He saw what was the temper of his countrymen, that they were not disposed to yield, and that there was no middle course. At the first session of the legislature in 1765, he resumed his standing, and he, to use the language of President Adams, " on whose zeal, energy and exertions the whole great cause seemed to depend, returned to his duty, and gave entire satisfaction to the end of his political career."

This period in his life forms a very striking answer to the inveterate misrepresentations, which described him, as a factious intriguer and demagogue, who was the author of all the discontent; and alleged that the public would have been quiet and satisfied, if he and a few others had not kept agitation alive.*

---

* The following paragraphs from the London Gazeteer, and the London Public Advertiser, allude to the universal circulation of these calumnies. " If in criminal cases it is contrary to law to condemn a man unheard, surely in our political conversation and debates, it is both ungenerous and cruel, to abuse the absent, because they differ from us in our political opinions. I am led to make this remark, from the scurrility which is belched forth in most companies against Mr. Otis of Boston : a man of unblemished character, and the representative of a great people, whose liberty he thinks is invaded, and

He could neither recede, nor take a negative course;
he had no alternative but to be the leader in the
cause of his fellow citizens, or to be execrated for
abandoning it. While in all the public papers that
came from his hand, he made a manly and sincere
profession of loyalty and attachment to the government of his country; and in his private letters gave
warning of the consequences which he anxiously
deprecated; yet from the ardent enthusiasm which
he felt and inspired on all political subjects, it was
the aim of his enemies to represent him in England,
as a madman, who was inciting the colonists to insurrection and violence. But in fact, the character of

---

which in justice to himself, his country, and his constituents, he thinks he
ought legally and constitutionally to defend: This, in the opinion of his tra-
ducers, is a crime, and for which they bestow on him the names of incendiary,
firebrand, traitor, &c. of which he is no more deserving than Andrew Marvel,
Pym, Shippen and Sir John Barnard, which I think are the most illustrious
characters Old England has ever produced, and that of Mr. Otis the greatest
of New England."—*London Gazeteer, Nov.* 3, 1768.

" We are told sometimes that the people of America would generally be
quiet, if it were not for their factious demagogues, and that the whole mischief
is owing only to two or three restless spirits there; that the contest is really
between Messrs. *Otis, Cushing* and *Adams* on one part, and the whole people
of England on the other. This is merely to countenance the proposition of
sending for these men in order to hang them, which some seem to have much
at heart; though from the blood of these three would probably spring three
hundred more. But in truth, the parties are G. G., Lord H. and the Duke of
B. on the one side, and on the other, all our fellow subjects in America."

London Public Advertiser.

The remedy of executing these general disturbers was frequently suggested.
In a letter from London about the same date, Nov. 1768, there is the following passage: " We are told with a sneer that we shall soon have the company of Mr. Otis, &c. I do not believe it; 'tis impossible the Bostonians
should suffer it. It has been reported that you have delivered up your arms,
I have ventured to assert that you neither have, nor will; your friends would
forsake you for such an action."

his countrymen was too cautious and reflecting, either to be excited without sufficient motives, or to be easily lulled into unworthy submission. The alarm was universal respecting the arbitrary designs in contemplation, and the people could neither be terrified nor cajoled from the defence of their rights. They never would have submitted to imposition, and if one set of leaders had been faithless to their trust, others would have sprung up to take their places. However important and invaluable the services of particular individuals undoubtedly were, still the cause did not depend on any man or body of men; if it had, the issue might have been uncertain ; but its foundation was on the broad principles of justice, and its support in the virtue, intelligence and courage every where diffused among the citizens.

Chapter XIX.

Suggestions for a Representation of the Colonies in Parliament— Otis's Answer to the Halifax Libel—His Letter to a Noble Lord —Extracts from that Work.

THE idea of a representation of the colonies in parliament, was a favourite one with many writers at this period. Otis and others, who were willing to admit the supr˘˘˘cv of the British legislature, had this representation in view, as a preliminary measure, before any taxes could be equitably imposed: and without it, their acknowledgment of supremacy was only in words. In his answer to the "Halifax libel,"* as it was called, in which he admitted some things in relation to the power of parliament, that seemed not quite consistent with the principles which he had before assumed, he still maintains this inseparable condition, after allowing, "that the parliament of Great Britain hath a just, clear, equitable and constitutional right, power and authority, to bind the colonies in all acts wherein they are named:" and that it has also the same right, "to impose taxes on the colonies, internal and external, on lands as well as on trade;" he proceeds to render these ruinous concessions harmless, by the following explanation: "This" (the parliamentary right above mentioned) "is involved in the idea of a supreme legislative or sovereign power of a state. It will, however, by no means from thence follow, that 'tis always expedient, and in all circumstances equitable, for the supreme and sovereign legislative to tax the colonies; much less that 'tis reasonable this right should be practised upon, without allowing the colonies an actual representation. An equal representation of the whole state is, at least in theory, of the essence of a perfect parliament, or supreme legislative."

This scheme of a colonial representation in the

---

* Written by Martin Howard, Esq.

British parliament, and the numerous essays against taxation, were the occasion of a pamphlet entitled, "A letter from a gentleman in Halifax to his friend in Rhode Island," which was published in the latter part of 1764; in which the plan of representation was ridiculed, and the justice and expediency of taxation openly defended, and opposition to it considered factious, treasonable and unavailing. The doctrines inculcated by the author were those of non-resistance and passive obedience : and they were accompanied with that miserable sneering and insolence, which affected to consider the inhabitants of the colonies as an inferior race of men, who were and ought to be subordinate to England : that whatever the English parliament might do towards them, would be just and generous ; and should be received without murmuring or opposition, for fear of drawing upon themselves ill-will and punishment.

Otis wrote an answer* to this servile pamphlet, which was published early in 1765. The whole ar-

---

* The title is " A Vindication of the British Colonies against the aspersions of the Halifax gentleman, in his letter to a Rhode Island friend."

Sed fugite, ô miseri, fugite, atque ab litore funem
Rumpite !   *   *   *   *   *
Clamorem immensum tollit, quo pontus et omnes
Intremuere undæ, penitusque exterrita tellus
Italiæ, curvisque immugiit Ætna cavernis.

——Fluit æs rivis, aurique metallum
Volnificusque chalybs vasta fornace liquescit.
——Alii ventosis follibus auras
Accipiunt redduntque, alii stridentia tingunt
Aera lacu : gemit impositis incudibus antrum.
Illi inter sese multa vi brachia tollunt
In numerum, versantque tenaci forcipe massam.

Boston, Printed and sold by Edes and Gill, in Queen street, 1765.

gument of his work is directed to prove that the
colonies have a right to be represented, that the
idea of virtual representation is absurd, and the imperfect state of the representation in England itself,
is no reason against our rights and privileges. He
admits in express terms, that the parliament is supreme over all the dominions of the state. That
the " supreme legislature" is composed of three
branches, King, Lords, and Commons; but that this
" legislature" cannot be complete, and have an equitable right to tax the Colonies, until these are represented.

The author of the first pamphlet published another, entitled, " *A defence of the letter from a gentleman
at Halifax to his friend at Rhode Island*,"—in which
he attacks Otis's answer; and also the answer of
governor Hopkins, published in the Providence
Gazette. Governor H. replied to this in a pamphlet entitled, " *Brief remarks on the defence of the
Halifax libel on the British American Colonies.*" There
is a good deal of warmth exhibited in all these writings; but the dispute between Messrs. Howard and
Hopkins, was the most personal and acrimonious.
Otis indeed resents some of the impertinences of his
antagonist, towards the country at large, with suitable contempt, but he seems to use personal retort
only in the support of his second in the dispute.

In the course of the same year, 1765, Otis produced another work* on the same proposal, a par-

---

* The title is, " Considerations on behalf of the Colonists, in a letter to a
noble Lord. London, printed for J. Almon, 1765." The publisher says, that
this pamphlet was sent by an unknown person, from Boston in New England,

liamentary representation of the colonies. It is an answer to an English publication, and introduces the subject, in this way : " My Lord, I have read the *opusculum* of the celebrated Mr. J—s, called, ' Objections to the Taxation of the Colonies by the legislature of Great Britain briefly considered.' In obedience to your Lordship's commands, I have thrown a few thoughts on paper, all indeed that I have patience on this melancholy occasion to collect. The gentleman thinks it ' absurd and insolent' to question the expediency and utility of a public measure. He seems to be an utter enemy to the freedom of inquiry after truth, justice and equity. He is not only a zealous advocate for pusillanimous and passive obedience, but for the most implicit faith in the dictatorial mandates of power." He goes on to prove, that the principles of his opponent are erroneous, and slavish in their tendency. The chief topics which were then dwelt upon, in considering the questions of Taxation and Representation, are all glanced at in a rapid way. The letter is written with spirit and ability, and as it is the last work of Otis, a few extracts will be taken. The crisis too was so imminent, and the question of a representation of the Colonies was of such vast importance, by the consequences which it would have had, that the mind is readily led to amuse itself with speculations on the various contingences the subject involved.

---

with a request that it might be published immediately. After examination, finding nothing in it offensive to any body of men, he thought he should be inexcusable in withholding it from the public. It is dated, Boston, Sept. 4, 1765, and signed with the initials F. A.

The advocates for the measures of the ministry, always produced the trite and silly reason, that the Colonies should submit to being taxed without sending members to parliament, because many towns and districts in England were in that situation. The following extract contains a part of his remarks on this point :—" No good reason can, however, be given in any country, why every man of a sound mind, should not have his vote in the election of a representative. If a man has but little property to protect and defend, yet his life and liberty are things of some importance. Mr. J—s argues only from the vile abuses of power, to the continuance and increase of such abuses. This it must be confessed, is the common logic of modern politicians and vote-sellers. To what purpose is it to ring everlasting changes to the colonists on the cases of Manchester, Birmingham, and Sheffield, which return no members? If those, now so considerable, places are not represented, they ought to be. Besides, the counties in which those respectable abodes of tinkers, tinmen, and pedlars, lie, return members, so do all the neighbouring cities and boroughs. In the choice of the former, if they have no vote, they must naturally and necessarily have a great influence. I believe every gentleman of a landed estate, near a flourishing manufactory, will be careful enough of its interests. Though the great India company, as such, returns no members, yet many of the company are returned, and their interests have been ever very carefully attended to."

He is perhaps rather more cautious of admitting

the power of parliament, in this work, than in the
preceding one; as the exercise of it in the Stamp
Act grew more alarming.—Still, he does admit " that
from the nature of the British Constitution, and also
from the idea and nature of a supreme legislature, the
parliament represents the whole community or empire, and have an undoubted power, authority and jurisdiction over the whole." He proceeds to consider
this power in a light, that makes it merely theoretical, and that it will not be used, except in a case of
the last necessity, and then, with the greatest tenderness. In the course of his observations, to prove
that the colonies could not then be justly taxed, he
observes :—" Should the British empire one day be
extended round the whole world, would it be reasonable that all mankind should have their concerns
managed by the electors of Old Sarum, and the ' oc-
cupants of the Cornish barns and alehouses,' we
sometimes read of? We, who are in the colonies,
are by common law, and by act of parliament, declared entitled to all the privileges of the subjects
within the realm. Yet we are heavily taxed, without
being, in fact, represented.—In all trials here relating
to the revenue, the admiralty courts have jurisdiction given them, and the subject may, at the pleasure of the informer, be deprived of a trial by his
peers. To do as one would be done by, is a divine
rule. Remember, Britons, when you shall be taxed
without your consent, and tried without a jury, and
have an army quartered in private families, you will
have little to hope or to fear ! But I must not lose
sight of my man, who sagaciously asks, ' if the Co-

lonists are Englishmen when they solicit protection, but not Englishmen when taxes are required to enable *this country* to protect them ?' I ask in my turn; when did the Colonies solicit protection ? They have had no occasion to solicit for protection since the happy accession of our gracious sovereign's illustrious family to the British diadem. His majesty, the father of all his people, protects all his loyal subjects of every complexion and language, without any particular solicitation. But before the ever memorable revolution, the northern colonists were so far from receiving protection from Britain, that every thing was done from the throne to the footstool, to cramp, betray and ruin them : yet against the combined power of France, Indian savages, and the corrupt administration of those times, they carried on their settlements, and under a mild government for these eighty years past, have made them the wonder and envy of the world." In allusion to the distinction of " this country and that country," he afterwards says : " But if, according to Mr. J—s, Great Britain is a distinct country from the British colonies, what is that *country* in nature more than this country? the same sun warms the people of Great Britain and us ; the same summer cheers, and the same winter chills."

He adverts to the flippant use of the phrase "*our colonies,*" which was then so common, in the following observations. " But Mr. J—s will scribble about " *our American colonies.*" Whose colonies can the creature mean? The minister's colonies ? No, surely.

Whose then, his own ? I never heard he had any colonies. *Nec gladio, nec arcu, nec astu vicerunt.* He must
mean his majesty's American colonies. His majesty's
colonies they are, and I hope and trust ever will be,
and that the true native inhabitants, as they ever
have been, will continue to be his majesty's most
dutiful and loyal subjects. Every garretteer, from
the environs of Grub street to the purlieus of St.
James's, has lately talked of *his* and *my* and *our* colonies, and of the *rascally colonists*, and of *yoking*
and *curbing* the *cattle*, as they are by some politely
called, at ' this present now and very nascent crisis'—I cannot see why the American peasants may
not with as much propriety speak of their cities of
London and Westminster, of their isles of Britain,
Ireland, Jersey, Guernsey, Sark and the Orcades,
and of the ' rivulets and runlets thereof,' and consider them all, but as appendages to their sheepcots
and goosepens. But land is land, and men should be
men. The property of the former, God hath giv-
en to the possessor. ' These are either *sui juris*, or
slaves and vassals ; there neither is, nor can be any
medium.' "

One of the chief arguments brought forward for
taxing America, was the burthen of the national
debt, of which the colonies ought to pay a part.
On this topic, he observes :—" The national debt is
confessed on all hands, to be a terrible evil, and may,
in time, ruin the state.* But it should be remem-

---

* This is a matter in which prediction may naturally enough be received with
incredulity. Prophecy and declamation, in regard to the debt of England,

bered, that the colonists never occasioned its increase,
nor ever reaped any of the sweet fruits of involving
the finest kingdom in the world, in the sad calamity
of an enormous, overgrown mortgage, to state and
stock-jobbers.   No places, nor pensions, of thousands
and tens of thousands sterling, have been laid out to
purchase the votes and influence of the colonists.
They have gone on with their settlements in spite
of the most horrid difficulties and dangers; they
have ever supported, to the utmost of their ability,
his majesty's provincial government over them, and
I believe are, to a man, and ever will be, ready to
make grants for so valuable a purpose.   But we
cannot see the equity of our being obliged to pay off
a score, that has been much enhanced by bribes and
pensions, to keep those to their duty, who ought to
have been bound by honour and conscience.   We
have ever been from principle attached to his
majesty and his illustrious house.   We never asked
any pay : the heartfelt satisfaction of having served
our king and country, has been always enough for
us.   I cannot see why it would not be well enough to

---

have been falsified, year after year ; while the vitality of credit seems indes-
tructible, and the power of the nation in bearing, more and more, stupendous.
The late Mr. Sheridan said on this subject in a debate, that " he had grown
very cautious about prophecying in regard to the debt—he had years before
prophecied and believed that it could go no farther, and now there seemed to be
no limits to it.   He should therefore advise gentlemen to be prudent in their
predictions ; he could see no reason why they should not prove unfounded in
future, as they had been in the past."—The subject is a very portentous one ;
the danger is probably not to be apprehended from the violence and suddenness
of an acute disease, but from the deep seated and paralyzing effects of a chron-
ic disorder.

go a nabob hunting on this occasion. Why should not the great Mogul be obliged to contribute towards, if not to pay, the national debt, as some have proposed? He is a pagan, an East Indian, and of a dark complexion, which are full as good reasons for laying him under contribution, as any I have found abroad, in the pamphlets and coffee-house conferences, for taxing the colonists.

Though in favour of an American representation in parliament, he admits that the scheme was not popular.—" The gentleman has made himself quite merry with the modest proposal, some have made, though I find it generally much disliked in the colonies, and thought impracticable, namely, *an American representation in parliament.* But if he is now sober, I would humbly ask him, if there be really and naturally, any greater absurdity in this plan, than in a Welch and Scotch representation? I would by no means, at any time, be understood to intend by an American representation, the return of half a score, ignorant, worthless, persons, who like some colony agents, might be induced to sell their country and their God, for a golden calf. An American representation, in my sense of the terms. and as I ever used them, implies, a thorough beneficial union of these colonies to the realm, or mother country, so that all the parts of the empire may be compacted and consolidated, and the constitution flourish with new vigour, and the national strength, power and importance, shine with far greater splendour, than ever yet hath been seen by the sons of men.

An American representation implies every real advantage to the subject abroad, as well as at home.

"It may be a problem, what state will be of longest duration, greatest glory, and domestic happiness. I am not at leisure fully to consider this question at present. Time shall show. I can now only say, it will be that state, which like Great Britain, Heaven shall have favoured with every conceivable advantage, and given it wisdom and integrity enough to see and embrace an opportunity, which once lost, can never be regained. Every mountain must be removed, and every path be made smooth and straight. Every region, nation and people, must to all real intents and purposes, be united, knit and worked into the very bones and blood of the original system, as fast as subdued, settled or allied. Party views and short sighted politicians should be discarded with the ignominy and contempt they deserve.

"Mr. J—s seems to be seized with an immense panic, lest 'a sudden importation of American eloquence' should interfere with those, who are fond of monopolizing the place and pension *business.* He even insinuates that it would cost more to pay our orators, than a standing army *here.* I will ease him of this difficulty. There would not be many worth the high price of Britain. When trimmers, time-servers, scepticks, cockfighters, architects, fiddlers, and castle-builders, who commonly sell cheap, were bought off, there might not be more than three or four worth purchasing: and if they should sell as cheap in Britain, as I have known some of them in America, it would fall infinitely short of the blood and treasure, a standing army may one day cost."

He discusses very fully the meaning of the phrase, *virtual representation ;* he shews, there is no such expression in the laws or the constitution, that it is altogether a subtlety, an illusion, and as respects the colonies, wholly unfounded and absurd.   At the conclusion of his remarks, he observes : " The first parliament of James the first, ' upon the knees of their hearts,' (as they express it) agnize their most constant faith, obedience and loyalty to his majesty and his royal progeny, as in that high court of parliament, where all the whole body of the realm, and every particular member thereof, either in person, or, by representation upon their own free elections, are by the laws of this realm, deemed to be personally present.   But as much prone as those times were to mystic divinity, school philosophy, academic politics and other nonsense, they say not a word of the *virtual representation* of Ireland or the other dominions."

He concludes this letter with the two following paragraphs.   " It may perhaps sound strangely to some, but it is in my most humble opinion as good *law,* and as good *sense* too, to affirm that all the plebeians of Great Britain are in fact, or virtually represented in the assembly of the Tuskaroras, as that all the colonists are in fact or virtually represented in the honourable house of commons of Great Britain, separately considered as one branch of the supreme and universal legislature of the whole empire."

" These considerations, I hope, will in due time have weight enough to induce your lordship to use your great influence, for the repeal of the *stamp act.* I shall transmit your lordship, by the next mail, a simple, easy plan, for perpetuating the British empire in all parts of the world. A plan however, that cost me much thought before I had matured it. But for which I neither expect nor desire any reward in this world, but the satisfaction of reflecting that I have contributed my mite to the service of my king and country. The good of mankind is my ultimate wish."

The hints suggested in this little work, of a systematic consolidation of the British empire, by a regular plan of representation, from every part, were entertained by a few, and only a few persons on each side of the Atlantic. The views were too vast for the conception of ordinary minds, who, in the first instance, asserted it to be impracticable, and would then have proved it to be so, by the opposition of their own bigoted and sordid motives. There is something magnificent in the idea of a congress of such an empire, embracing some of the finest portions of the four quarters of the globe. If it had been realized, its power would have been so preponderant, that the visionary hope of a universal confederation among civilized nations, might have been possible. One consequence would in time have happened; a consequence, which Dr. Franklin was accused of meditating; that of transferring the seat of government.* There are some splendid visions that arise in the mind, while contemplating such a grand representative dominion, as this would have been; yet the good effects that might have resulted, will now be produced by the American revolution, in a more manageable, though, perhaps less imposing form, and the general advantage, not only to this country, but to the rest of the world, will be ultimately greater.

"The plan for perpetuating the British empire," if it were ever drawn, would have been an interesting document. He speaks of it so positively, that it was probably sketched, and remained among his papers, to share their fate at an after period. The anxiety respecting the stamp act was daily increasing, and the writer had too much to do, in opposing that measure, and the subsequent acts of the ministry for raising a revenue, to think of any general schemes of government, which the experience of every day proved to be more and more difficult. The English ministry, though fluctuating and change-

---

* Dr. Franklin, in writing to governor Franklin, from London, Nov. 25, 1767, giving some account of his plan for forming one settlement at the mouth of the Ohio, and another at Detroit, adds, " My lord, (Clare) told me one pleasant circumstance, viz. that he had shewn this paper to the Dean of Glouceste , Dr. Tucker) to hear his opinion of the matter ; who very sagaciously remarked, that he was sure that paper was drawn up by Dr. Franklin ; he saw him in every paragraph ; adding, that Dr. Franklin wanted to remove the seat of government to America : that, said he, is his constant plan." D . Franklin belonged to an order of minds, which according to a French expression, have a good deal of the future in them. The Portuguese experiment has shown that the transfer of a seat of government is not impossible.

able, still acted from the impulse, whether originating with themselves, or derived from others, of
taxing the colonies by the aid of their parliamentary
majority. This seemed to them a much more easy,
simple, and desirable method of ruling them, than
any other. Every day they engaged more deeply
in the design, and each successive warning of its danger, served only to throw a glare on their obstinacy,
without enlightening them as to the consequences
of their arrogant injustice.*

Chapter XIII.

*Origin of the Plan for Taxing America—Conduct of Parliament
—Influence of the King—Dr. Franklin's Opinions of Colonial
Grants—Agency of the Crown Officers.*

It is now perhaps impossible to ascertain with
perfect clearness, the origin of that system of colo-

---

* These consequences however, were perceived by some minds, and the immediate danger at least was apt to be exaggerated. In Mr. Pitt's speech for
the repeal of the stamp act in 1766, he says : " The gentleman (Mr. Grenville)
boasts of his bounties to America ! Are not these bounties intended finally
for the benefit of this kingdom? If they are not, he has misapplied the national
treasures. I am no courtier of America—I stand up for this kingdom. I maintain that the parliament has a right to bind, to restrain American. Our legislative power over the colonies is sovereign and supreme. When it ceases to
be sovereign and supreme, I would advise every gentleman, if he can, to sell
his lands, and embark for that country."

nial taxation, which led to the Independence of the
United States, and to the long train of consequences
which have been ever since in a course of develop-
ment. The share which the sovereign, the ministry, the parliament at large, or particular individuals had in maturing the design, is as obscure, as it
is notorious what part they took in the execution.
The credit of the scheme, every party is willing to
relinquish to others ; and as in the case of most unfortunate enterprises, to impute the blame to any
causes but their own mistakes.

With a policy as destitute of generosity, as it
was of wisdom, the English government actually
assigned as a reason for imposing new taxes, the
exertions and sacrifices made by the colonies, in the
war that secured the acquisition of Canada.* The
government and the nation began to be jealous of
the growing importance of their American possessions, and under a vague apprehension of their prospective independence, resolved to prepare timely
checks to this alarming prosperity, by a method
that should also replenish their own coffers. The
idea was popular with the great body of proprietors in England, who knew or cared very little
about their fellow subjects in America; until a lively interest was awakened by the expectation of

---

* " To render these proceedings more irritating to the colonies, the principal argument used, in favour of their ability to pay such duties, was the liberality of the grants of their assemblies, during the late war. Never could any
argument be more insulting, and mortifying to a people, habituated to the
granting of their own money."—Burke's Works, Vol. 1. p. 338.

being able to load them at will, with the burthens of the nation. The conduct of the great majority of the English landholders, who were steady advocates for American taxation, and for the American war, affords a striking lesson to shew, how men who may be highly estimable as individuals, will pursue, as a body, a blind and selfish career.

Burke in his speech on American taxation, which he proves had its origin at the epoch of the peace, in 1763, in shewing how the country gentlemen, were induced to vote for the increase of the army, says, " But hopes of another kind were held out to them, and in particular, I well remember, that Mr. Townshend, in a brilliant harangue upon this subject, did dazzle them, by playing before their eyes the image of a revenue to be raised in America." He goes on to remark that Mr. Grenville matured the new system, of which these hints of Mr. Townshend were the first glimmerings; he admits that with honest intentions he was the father of the fatal scheme ;* though he doubts whether it

---

* In the debate of the House of Commons, on the 15th of May, 1777, the following summary is given in the " Parliamentary Debates"—" Mr. Jenkinson lamenting the necessity of the war, the loss it was to the kingdom, but upholding the indispensable authority of parliament, and blaming the bad policy of some late ministers, reprobated in the strongest terms the Tea Act : he condemned the whole measure as impolitic, futile, childish, and paltry. Then turning to the Stamp Act, he said, that measure was not Mr. Grenville's ; if the act was a good one, the merit of it was not due to Mr. Grenville : if it was a bad one, the error or the ill policy of it did not belong to him ; the measure was not his." The authority of Mr. Jenkinson, on this matter, will be thought superior to any other, when it is recollected, that this gentleman, afterwards Earl of Liverpool, was brought forward by Lord Bute, to whom he was at first private secretary ; and that he succeeded that noble-

was entirely the result of his own speculation, but rather that his opinions, coincided with the instructions which he received. Lord Chatham and others attributed its origin to that "secret influence behind the throne," which formed a part of the "double cabinet," which there can be no doubt existed effectively, though not ostensibly, from the accession of George the third, till the termination of the American war.

How far the sovereign himself was responsible for the scheme of an American revenue, will perhaps never be known; unless some authentic, private memoirs should hereafter disclose the share, which each person had in the undertaking. History does not record many sovereigns, whose character was more estimable than that of George the third. He possessed firmness, integrity and good sense and his reign, one of the most remarkable for its length to be found in the annals of the world, was unquestionably the era of more momentous events, than ever before occurred in the life of a single monarch. The school in which he was educated, was not very favourable to sincerity, nor very friendly to constitutional maxims of government. The influence of his mother's court and disposition, though they fortunately left him a virtuous man in his private character, yet gave him an inclination towards some

---

man, in possessing the entire confidence of the king, in being entrusted with a knowledge of all his views, and being generally supposed to be the head, of that double cabinet, which whether imaginary or not, was so often denounced by Chatham, Burke, and others.

arbitrary ideas, and nourished an impatient pride, against parliamentary controul.*

The bias during almost half of his reign, kept alive a feeling of reserve with the acknowledged ministers of the Crown, and checked a thorough and frank cordiality towards his parliament. Though he was " born a Briton" and was far more naturalized than his predecessor and grandfather, who retained a good deal of the accent, idiom, and attachments of their German origin; yet his electorate was a possession very near his heart, and the pride of the absolute, German Prince, cherished his paternal domain of Hanover, the *mea paupera regna*, as a country where there was no interference with his wishes from the intractable or factious Lords and Commons who represented the wealth of Britain. His family, though they were transferred from a principality of moderate resources, to one of the most considerable thrones in the world, still felt for the former all the attachment arising from an exclusive possession, and less satisfaction with the latter, where constitutional usages prevailed to divide their

---

* "I have no hesitation or scruple to say, that the commencement of the reign of George the third, was the commencement of another Stuart's reign: and if it had not been checked by James Otis and others, first, and by the great Chatham and others afterwards, it would have been as arbitrary, as any of the four. I will not say it would have extinguished civil and religious liberty upon earth; but it would have gone great lengths towards it, and would have cost mankind even more than the French revolution to preserve it. The most sublime, profound and prophetic expression of Chatham's oratory, that he ever uttered was, ' I rejoice that America has resisted ; two millions of people reduced to servitude, would be fit instruments to make slaves of the rest.'" *President Adams' Letters.*

authority. His predecessors accustomed themselves with some difficulty, to the very different tenure of their power between their German and insular dominions, and after debarking, they seem never to " have burnt their ships." Though this feeling was diminished in the breast of George the third, yet it was not destroyed, and in the earlier parts of his reign, when counteracted by factions in parliament,* the idea of the royal yacht that might transport him to his continental refuge, readily presented itself. The pride and the personal feeling, attached to this family possession, prevented him from identifying himself with the British nation, and held in reserve an alternative, that did not make it necessary to stand or fall with his friends in that country.

This sovereign was not at all a projector, and was ever distinguished for his aversion to all innovation There is little or no reason to suppose, that the plan

---

* The king's dislike to Mr. Fox, and his indignation against the usurpation meditated by his famous India Bill, were well known. At that time he openly avowed his resolve to leave the country, rather than submit to the domination of a faction. The following note written to Mr. Pitt, during his memorable struggle against Mr. Fox, in 1784 exhibits his deep feeling on this subject.—" I trust the House of Lords will this day feel, that the hour is come, for which the wisdom of our ancestors established that respectable corps in the state, to prevent either the Crown or the Commons from encroaching on the rights of each other. Indeed, should not the Lords stand boldly forth, this constitution must soon be changed; for if the two only remaining privileges of the Crown are infringed, that of negativing bills, which have passed both houses of parliament, and that of naming the ministers to be employed, I cannot but feel, as far as regards my own person, that I can be no longer of utility to this country, nor can with honour continue in this island.'

Dr. Tomline's Life of Pitt, Vol. 1. p. 201.

of an American revenue originated with him; but
he was induced to sanction it from the persuasion
of his ministers. It is more probable that it was
devised by those secret advisers, who formed a kind
of domestic council, and determined on many measures without consulting the public ministers. Their
motive was to obtain a command of resources, whose
appropriation the parliament would not scrutinize
very closely, as they were not to be levied on their
constituents. They and their friends would have
had a wide field of patronage from colonial taxation; and the sovereign himself was persuaded, it
may be conjectured, that he might in this manner
command an ample revenue, that would make him
independent of his parliament: a boon too grateful
to be resisted by a youthful monarch, whose mind
had been strongly imbued with arbitrary principles
of reigning.

The following authentic anecdote on the origin of
American taxation, may be gratifying to persons
who are fond of tracing the current of events up to
their primitive sources, and who know how often
changes in human affairs are first put in motion by
very trifling causes. When President Adams was
Minister at the Court of St. James, he often saw
his countryman, Benjamin West, the late President
of the Royal Academy. Mr. West always retained
a strong and unyielding affection for his native land,
which, to borrow a term of his own art, was in fine
keeping with his elevated genius. The patronage
of the king was nobly bestowed upon him, and it

forms a fine trait in the character of both, that when a malicious courtier endeavoured to embarrass him, by asking his opinion on the news of some disastrous event to America, in the presence of the king, he replied, that he never could rejoice in any misfortune to his native country; for which answer the king immediately gave him his protecting approbation. Mr. West one day asked Mr. Adams, if he should like to take a walk with him, and see the cause of the American revolution. The minister having known something of this matter, smiled at the proposal, but told him that he should be glad to see the cause of that Revolution, and to take a walk with his friend West, any where. The next morning he called according to agreement, and took Mr. Adams into Hyde Park to a spot near the Serpentine River, where he gave him the following narrative. The King came to the throne a young man surrounded by flattering courtiers ; one of whose frequent topics it was, to declaim against the meanness of his palace, which was wholly unworthy a monarch of such a country as England. They said that there was not a sovereign in Europe who was lodged so poorly, that his sorry, dingy, old, brick palace of St. James, looked like a stable, and that he ought to build a palace suited to his kingdom. The king was fond of architecture,* and would therefore

---

* It is perhaps, fortunate that he had sufficient self controul to resist this inclination ; for if his taste may be judged from the anomalous, unfinished edifice at Kew, the whole merit of which, the architect resolutely attributed to the king's own designs, he would not have added any ornament to the country by his new palace.

more readily listen to suggestions, which were in fact all true. This spot that you see here, was selected for the site, between this and this point, which were marked out. The king applied to his ministers on the subject; they inquired what sum would be wanted by his majesty, who said, that he would begin with a million; they stated the expenses of the war, and the poverty of the treasury, but that his majesty's wishes should be taken into full consideration. Some time afterwards the king was informed, that the wants of the treasury were too urgent to admit of a supply from their present means, but that a revenue might be raised in America to supply all the king's wishes. This suggestion was followed up, and the king was in this way first led to consider, and then to consent, to the scheme for taxing the colonies. Mr. West always acquitted the king of all blame in the measures connected with the American war; but asserted, that he was from first to last kept in ignorance of the true state of the question, and of the situation of the colonies, and constantly deceived by the misrepresentations of those about him. Though it is unquestionably true, that the king was led unwarily into the dispute with the colonies, and that the design of taxing them was planned by others, yet he interested himself in it very deeply, and seemed to consider the struggle as a personal concern of his own. His character was naturally firm, in this case it became obstinate; and he yielded with the utmost reluctance his hold over the colonies.* The loss of this power however was soon found to be a mutual advantage to both countries; and perhaps served to cure him of any wish to imitate the arbitrary views of the Stuarts. The latter half of his reign, or, from the establishment of Mr. Pitt as minister, he became more truly and contentedly, a constitutional sovereign. The talents of that eminent statesman, the creation of new peers, the vast increase of patronage, and afterwards the droits of Admiralty, gave the king such abundant and substantial resources for the gratification of his personal views, that the subsequent policy of his reign became much more safe both for himself and the nation.

It might be a matter of curious speculation to consider what would have been the consequences, if the king, instead of taking the plan of his public or his secret cabinet, of raising his wished for revenue in America, through the agency of the English parliament; had asked for it, by direct application to the several colonial assemblies. There was indeed no anxiety in the colonists to pay taxes to any one;

* This personal feeling was natural to the pride of the sovereign, who made it more his own affair, than the king in a free government would do a common concern of the State. How a despotic monarch would have felt, may be seen in the Prince de Ligne's account of the familiar conversation of the Empress of Russia, and the Emperor of Germany: "Plutot que de signer la séparation de treize Provinces, comme mon frère George, dit Catherine II. avec douceur, je me serois tiré un coup de pistolet." The king of England, however, on this point acted with true dignity, when Mr. Adams, the first American ambassador was presented to him, he said, "Sir, I was the last man in my kingdom to consent to your independence, and I shall be the last to do any thing to infringe it."

but their whole opposition was founded on the attempt to assess them by a parliament, in which they
had no representatives.   It was this dangerous pretension that roused all their opposition ; a pretension
which had no equitable foundation whatever.   As a
matter of justice, the sovereign might as well have
laid a tax on the people of England by the instru-
mentality of one of his colonial assemblies, as by the
" giving and granting" of the English parliament,
have imposed a tax on the colonists : there was no
representation in either case.   The king was popular in America ; if he had brought himself more
closely into connexion with the various colonial assemblies ; and considered them as part of his dominions, over which the English parliament had no financial controul, the reception of his requests would
have been very different ; the blandishments of royalty in this more flattering and intimate, personal intercourse might at least for a time, have allured his
colonial subjects into liberal · contributions.*   Had
George the third taken Dr. Franklin for his adviser
and minister in American affairs, the separation of

---

* The reader will find in many passages of the very remarkable examination
of Dr. Franklin before the House of Commons, some striking hints on this topic ; which might be further elucidated by many opinions in his works.   It
would extend this note to an inconvenient length to take all the questions
and answers that bear upon this subject ; the following must suffice to give
an idea of the whole.

" Q. Suppose the King should require the Colonies to grant a revenue, and
the parliament should be against their doing it, do they think they can grant
a revenue to the King, without the consent of the parliament of Great Britain."

" A. That is a deep question.—As to my own opinion, I should think myself at liberty to do it, and should do it, if I liked the occasion."

the empire would have been postponed for some years: It was the benevolent dispensation of Providence for the welfare of mankind, that he did not pursue this course, for which no man would subsequently have been more devoutly thankful, than Dr. Franklin himself. There was a sort of fatality in the prejudice that the king had imbibed against Franklin; he had, it is true, the highest opinion of his abilities, but the greatest fear of them; and he never would listen to any thing that came from him. At the same time, there was no individual in his empire more desirous of maintaining it entire, more capable of suggesting the measures to effect this object, and more opposed to taking up arms, except against absolute, irremediable oppression. But taxation was resolved upon; the king placed his honour, his interest, and his pleasure in the prosecution of the system; and the nation at large, in all the intoxication of power, sought the gratification of a mercenary arrogance, in the taxation of " our colonies." Chatham and Burke in vain opposed the king and his parliament in their unjust career; but not in vain for their own glory, since to this opposition their country and the world are indebted for the most illustrious models of eloquence and wisdom, that legislative annals have produced.

The share which the Crown officers in the colonies had in producing this system of revenue, was altogether secondary; though the public at the time attributed a good deal of it to their agency. They even made some representations against it at first, but in a very feeble manner; and soon took care to shew by their alacrity to carry every measure into effect, that they were merely subaltern and servile agents, who thought only of their own fortune, and were ready to enforce any measures rather than resign their places. The blame to be imputed to them, was their want of manly and honest conduct, in lending themselves to the execution of an odious system, and placing their duty altogether in forwarding the views of the ministry, without regard to the interests of the people. Though they had no part in devising the plan, yet they had a very essential one in promoting it, and preventing its abandonment. They constantly misrepresented the state of the country and the feelings of the inhabitants; and in their eagerness to make their own fortunes, first deceived themselves, and then the ministry. They represented the opposition to be altogether instigated by a few factious demagogues. When the resistance, which was universal, became more open, and they saw beyond the possibility of delusion that the colonists never would submit to oppression; they then resorted for shelter to the power of Britain; they persuaded themselves, and sought to persuade others, that this power was irresistible. To maintain themselves and their cause, they induced the ministry at last to send a military force to their support; vainly supposing that a free people would be subdued by the appearance of a standing army; the only effect of which was, to hasten the crisis, and bring the question to a trial by arms.*

Chapter XIV.

The Stamp Act—Congress proposed—Riots in Boston—Liberty Tree.

THE remonstrances against the acts of trade, presented in 1764, were unavailing. Though they had been prepared after a concert between parties in the legislature, in a style, which the influence of the administration had made quite as submissive as the humblest petition could have used, yet they were not listened to. That no circumstance of conciliation might be wanting, and that they might reach the ministry in the manner least offensive to them, they were transmitted by the Governor and Lieutenant Governor, who supported them with their favourable opinion. Notwithstanding these precautions,

---

* The following extract from Dr. Franklin's examination before the House of Commons will prove how plainly the result of their measures was predicted.

" Q. Can any thing less than a military force carry the stamp Act into execution?

" A. I do not see how a military force can be applied to that purpose.

" Q. Why may it not?

" A. Suppose a military force sent into America ; they will find nobody in arms; what are they then to do? They cannot force a man to take stamps who chuses to do without them. They will not find a rebellion ; they may indeed make one."

they were disregarded by the ministers, who proceeded with alacrity, as if they had been encouraged
by the moderation and subdued tone of these representations, to take more decisive measures for re-
alizing their plan of an American revenue. Early
in February 1765,* the stamp act was passed with
an infatuated unanimity; an act, destined to obtain
very great celebrity. No legislative decree ever
occasioned a more remarkable and universal excitement. Its name was so strongly associated in men's
minds with oppression, injustice and danger, that the
very words became hateful, and a lasting odium in
this country was attached to a tax, which on some
occasions might be a useful measure of finance.†

When the information of the passage of this act,
which was not to go into operation till the following
November, reached the colonies, the assembly of
Virginia was the only one in session. They acted
with the energy and promptness suited to the occa-

---

* At the beginning o this year Mr. Otis received from Mr. Hollis a copy of
the beautiful 4to edition of Locke's Letters on Toleration, which he had pub-
lished. On a blank page, the donor wrote the following inscription:
" To an Asserter of *Liberty,* civil and religious,
James Otis, Esq.
of Boston, in New England,
An Englishman,
Citizen of the world :
In prato quod vocant *Runing* Med, inter Windlesor et Stanes; 1 Jan. 1765."

† An instance of this prejudice was shewn in the case of a moderate stamp
duty, that was laid during the first administration o the federal government.
The factious scribblers of that day, to excite opposition, appealed to the
ancient hatred against the " stamp act" with some success, though the name
was the only circumstance of resemblance.

sion. The memorable resolves introduced by Patrick Henry, assumed at once the lofty and open ground against taxation by any legislature, in which they were not represented. The Governor immediately dissolved them, but their resolves went abroad, and it was soon found that the public voice throughout the colonies, harmonized with the tone which they had taken.

When the account reached Boston in April, that the stamp act would be passed, there was a temporary suspension of public opinion, that led the administration into the most mistaken confidence; which, of itself, is sufficient to prove, that they were really ignorant of the state of public sentiment, and of the character of the people they governed. Hutchinson, with eager subserviency, wrote, " that they were waiting, not to know whether they must submit to a stamp duty, but when it was to take place, and under what regulations; and what further provision was to be made, if the duty should fall short of raising the sums that the colonies were to pay."*   This ominous silence, which was so strangely interpreted into passive submission, was merely the result of feelings that were too deep for superficial emotion. The public seemed, for a short period, absorbed in profound meditation, as to the mode of averting the menaced evils, and were preparing their minds, not to suffer, but to repel them.

---

* Minot, vol. 2. p. 202.

The Legislature did not meet till the last day of May, when the Governor addressed them in a speech that was principally occupied with suggestions relating to potash, lumber and hemp: towards the close of it, he informs them, that "the general settlement of the American provinces, which has been long ago proposed, and now probably will be prosecuted to its utmost completion, must necessarily produce some regulations, *which from their novelty only, will appear disagreeable*."—He concludes with this exquisite consolation for these "disagreeable novelties." " It is our happiness, that our supreme legislature, the parliament of Great Britain, is the sanctuary of liberty and justice, and that the Prince who presides over it, realizes the idea of a patriot King. Surely, then, we should submit our opinions to the determinations of so august a body: and acquiesce in a perfect confidence, that the rights of the members of the British empire will ever be safe in the hands of the conservators of the liberty of the whole." Doctrines like these, in due time, made Bernard a Baronet, and the colonies independent. Though Otis was on the committee to which was referred that part of the speech relating to the state of the province, no answer appears on the journals;* it is probable they thought that the measures proposed by them might be a sufficient answer.

Otis was one of the committee appointed by the house, consisting of members of different parties, to

---

* Massachusetts State Papers, p. 34.

consider what steps should be taken, " under the
many difficulties to which the colonies are, and must
be, reduced, by the operation of some late acts of
parliament ;" who reported the expediency of having
a general meeting of " committees" from the several
assemblies of the colonies, to be held at New York,
on the first Tuesday of October following. The
Speaker, Otis, and Mr. Lee, were then appointed to
prepare a letter to the speakers of the colonial legislatures. This was forthwith reported, and was
signed by Mr. White, the speaker, under date of
June 8th, 1765, and stated, that the opinion of the
legislature was unanimous in favour of the measure
of a general meeting of committees, " to consult together, and to consider of a general and united, dutiful and humble representation of their condition, to
his Majesty and the parliament, to implore relief."

This step, it appears by the letter, was taken
unanimously. The Governor and his friends, in
fact, dared not make any opposition. It was perfectly consistent with the previous petitions which
they had forwarded the preceding year : and they
also began to perceive, that the state of public opinion was not to be trifled with. It was their object
therefore, to get such a committee appointed as
would enter into their views ; and in that case, this
Congress might be the means of occupying public
attention, and diverting the people from more dangerous proceedings. They succeeded in part, in obtaining such a committee, and though Otis was upon
it, they opposed him with Brigadier Ruggles, who

with Mr. Partridge, also on the government side, made the delegates from Massachusetts.

This was the second attempt* at a general representation of the country, and is interesting in the preliminary history of their confederation, as must be every step towards a union of colonies, originally so distinct, and afterwards so closely united. The first was the Congress convened at Albany, on the suggestion of Governor Shirley, in 1754, aud which was held under the auspices of the British govern-

---

* There was indeed a partial confederation formed in 1643, under the name of " the United Colonies of New England." Chalmers, after describing this league, observes : " Such then, were the terms of the first confederacy to be met with in colonial story. The most inattentive must perceive the exact resemblance it bears to a similar junction of the colonies, more recent, extensive and powerful." (He alludes to the Congress of 1774.) " Both o iginated from Massachusetts, always fruitful in projects of independence. And wise men at the era of both, remarked, that those memorable associations established a complete system of absolute sovereignty : because the principles upon which it was erected, necessarily led to what it was not the policy of the principal agents at either period, to avow." p. 177.

Chalmers, in his animosity to Massachusetts, brings many charges against her as a colony, and is disposed to make her independence coeval with her existence. " Massachusetts" (he says) " in conformity to its accustomed principles, acted, during the civil wars, almost altogether as an independent state. It formed leagues, not only with the neighbouring colonies, but with foreign nations, without the consent or knowledge of the government of England——It permitted no appeals : it refused to exercise its jurisdiction in the name of the Commonwealth of England. It assumed the government of New Hampshire and Maine; It coined money : Thus evincing to all, what had been forseen by the wise ; that a people of such principles religious and political settling at so great a distance from control, would necessarily form an independent state." In further describing the transactions of this period, he says, " That colony not only thus gave the law to its confederates, but had the dexterity to foil the Long Parliament, so celebrated for its talents and power." He concludes as a kind of climax, " Not only did Massachusetts proudly dictate to its confederates, and artfully foil the parliament, but it outfawned and out-witted Cromwell."

ment. The design of a permanent union then failed, though several plans were proposed.   The
scheme drawn up by Dr. Franklin, which may be
found in his works, is a very curious document, and
discovers great ability in the first attempt to draw
order out of chaos. It was rejected however by the
king, because it took too much from the prerogative ;
and by the colonies, because it abridged their privileges ; whence Dr. Franklin concludes, not unreasona-
bly, that it probably preserved the true medium,
and was founded in justice.*

The question with regard to the Stamp Act, was
effectively settled before the Stamp Act Congress,
as it has been called, assembled. Its meeting was
to be so near the time when the act was to go into
operation, that the people probably thought it could
not convene in time to prepare a remedy ; and some
of the assemblies having been dissolved by the governors could not send delegates. The inhabitants
therefore throughout the colonies, with an energy
and unanimity that were irresistible, took the affair
into their own hands. Essays, sermons, and discourses of all kinds, meetings, committees, associations,

---

* Dr. Franklin's own remarks on this project, are too interesting to be omitted—" Its fate was singular, the assemblies did not accept it, as they thought
there was too much *prerogative* in it ; and in England it was judged to have
too much of the *democratic*. The different and contrary reasons of dislike to
my plan, makes me suspect that it was the true medium ; and I am still of
opinion it would have been happy for both sides, if it had been adopted—
Those who govern, having much business on their hands, do not generally like
to take the trouble of considering and carrying into execution new projects.
The best public measures are therefore seldom adopted from previous wisdom,
but forced by the occasion." *Franklin's Works*, V. 1. p. 201-203.

called the public to resistance. The people were taught, and most fortunately they perfectly understood the lesson, that the execution of this act would determine the question of freedom or slavery. Every where the most decided opposition was raised, and before the stamps themselves could reach the country, it was firmly resolved that they should not be used, and the officers, who had been appointed to distribute them, had all declined an employment, that was stigmatized with general abhorrence.

The effervescence was so great in Boston,* that some disorders took place, which formed an exception to the general character of the town. During a period of several years, the people at times, in relation to political affairs, may be said to have returned to the first form of government in the colony, which

---

* In a pamphlet entitled, " *The conduct of the late administration examined, with an appendix containing original and authentic documents; London,* 1767 ;" and reprinted in Boston, there are various extracts of letters addressed to different public offices. Otis is mentioned two or three times in this work ; and an opinion of his reported on hearsay, is given in the extract of a letter written probably by Governor Bernard. The letter was dated October 19th, 1765, and the following is the extract. " By this you may guess (writes a person of unshaken loyalty to England) what a state this government is in, and it is not likely to mend, till the power and authority of Great Britain come to our relief. For this I can quote a great politician of this town, who is now at New York. This gentleman (it is Mr. Otis of whom he speaks) has, I believe, contributed more than any one man whatever, to bring us into the state of outlawry and confusion we are now in, and now begins to be frightened at it : before he left this town for New York, he said to a gentleman, if the government at home don't very soon send forces to keep the province, they will be cutting one another's throats from one end to the other of it." No man was quoted and misquoted more than Otis, he might have expressed himself in his usual strong manner, respecting the agitation of public feeling ; the writer has attributed the remark to him, to justify sending a military force into the province.

was a simple democracy, and resumed their interference in a direct management of public concerns; yet this deviation was accompanied with very little turbulence, seldom with any destruction of property and never any of life. The conduct of these mobs, for such in truth they were, was remarkable for intelligence and moderation.

At this period there arose a practice which was occasionally repeated, of signifying public sentiment in a very effectual way, though without any responsible or even ostensible agent, unless an inanimate one, the *Liberty Tree*, can be so considered. This tree was one of those majestic elms, of the American species, that form one of the greatest ornaments in the landscape of this country. It stood in front of a house, opposite the Boylston Market, on the edge of the street, which its spreading branches overshadowed.*   On the 14th of August, 1765, an effigy representing Mr. Oliver, appointed to distribute the stamps, and a *boot* (the emblem of Lord Bute) with

---

* In a letter of Governor Bernard to Lord Hillsborough, dated Boston, June 16, 1768, a copy of which was afterwards communicated to the legislature, he gives a description of this tree, which is alluded to, in the Vindication of the Town, entitled *An Appeal to the World*, as follows : " Your lordship must know that Liberty tree is a large old Elm in the High Street, upon which the effigies were hung in the time of the Stamp Act, and from whence the mobs at that time made their parades. It has since been adorned with an inscription, and has obtained the name of Liberty Tree, as the ground under it has that of Liberty Hall. In August last, just before the commencement of the present troubles, they erected a flag staff, which went through the tree and a good deal above the top of the tree. Upon this they hoist a flag, as a signal for the Sons of Liberty, as they are called ; I gave my Lord Shelburne an account of this erection at the time it was made. This tree has often put me in mind of Jack Cade's Oak of Reformation."

the devil peeping out of it, with the Stamp Act in his hand, and various other satirical emblems, were suspended from its branches. Chief Justice Hutchinson, directed the sheriff to remove this pageantry, but his deputies, from the indications of popular feeling, declined the task ; and the Council of the Province thought if they did not interfere, that the affair would subside without disturbance. In the evening the figures were taken down, carried in procession through the streets, and through the Town House, to a small building in State-street, which Mr. Oliver had erected for a stamp office; this was entirely demolished, and the procession then moved to Fort Hill, where his house was situated, to make a bonfire of this pageantry. His family were alarmed, but some of his friends who were very obnoxious to popular ill will, remained with a shew of resistance. This provoked an attack, in which the windows were broken, and some injury done to the house and furniture.

The next day Mr. Oliver announced through his friends on the exchange, that he had declined the office of stamp distributor; but it being intimated to him, that it would conduce to the quiet of the public, if he would come to this tree and resign it, openly, he appeared there accordingly, and declared in the presence of a large concourse of spectators that he would not accept the place. It was thenceforward called Liberty Tree. In February of the preceding year, the tree was carefully pruned, and the following inscription placed upon it. " This tree

was planted in the year 1614, and pruned by order
of the sons of Liberty, Feb. 14th, 1766."*   On future
occasions there was seldom any excitement on political subjects, without some token of it appearing
on this tree : all popular processions paid a salute to
it. Whenever any obnoxious offices were to be resigned, or agreements for patriotic purposes entered
into, the parties received notice clandestinely, that
they would ·be expected at the Liberty Tree, at a
particular time, where they always found pens and
paper and a numerous crowd of witnesses, though
the genius of the tree was invisible. When the
British army took possession of the Town in 1774,
it fell a victim to their vengeance, or to that of the
individuals, to whom its shade had been disagreeable.†

The most striking instance of disorder occurred
in the latter part of the same month of August,
while the public exasperation against the stamp act
was at its height. A mob assembled in State-street
in the evening, and made an attack on the houses of
Mr. Story and Mr. Hallowell, two of the officers
connected with the customs, whose conduct had rendered them extremely unpopular. They entered

---

* See Boston Gazette, March 31, 1766.

† Every thing popular was contagious at that period. Similar trees were
consecrated in various places. In Providence, an inhabitant gave a deed to
the Town of a small piece of ground containing a large tree, to be used as a
" Liberty Tree" forever. In the early part of the French Revolution, this emblem was adopted, and for many years, at the entrance of every public building a liberty tree was planted ; the short-lived Lombardy poplar, which however survived what it was intended to be an emblem of, was used for this object,
and soon appeared in a shabby, decayed state.

these houses, breaking the windows, destroying the furniture, and almost demolishing them. At the house of Mr. Hallowell they penetrated to his cellar, and the liquors they found there inflamed them to madness. In this state they proceeded to the house of Lieutenant Governor Hutchinson, which they plundered of a considerable sum in money and plate, destroyed all the furniture, and left the house in the morning with nothing but the bare walls remaining. One part of the devastation was irreparable, they scattered a vast quantity of manuscripts relating to the history and various concerns of the colony, which Mr. Hutchinson had been collecting with great assiduity for many years, and of which a very few were recovered. Compensation was afterwards made to the sufferers for their losses; and the public indignation was so universal, that no similar outrage was ever afterwards perpetrated.

Chapter XV.

The Stamp Act Congress—Opposite Principles of the Massachusetts Delegates—Brigadier Ruggles—Message of Governor Bernard.

THE Committees from nine colonies, Masssachusetts, Rhode Island, Connecticut, New York, New

Jersey, Pennsylvania, Delaware, Maryland, and South Carolina, met in convention at New York, October 19th, 1765. The assemblies of the other colonies could not send delegates, being either dissolved or not in session. Mr. Alexander Wyly, the speaker of the assembly of Georgia, after consultation with a considerable majority of the legislature, which he had convened by expresses, wrote a letter to the Congress, fully approving its design, and pledging the most entire support to their proceedings by that colony. New Hampshire declined sending deputies, owing, " to the particular state of their affairs ;" but gave her approbation of the object, and offered to join in signing any suitable memorial. The Governor of New York, by repeatedly proroguing the assembly of the Province, prevented it from naming delegates; but a committee of five gentlemen, having been chosen at the last session, to consider the same subjects, they were admitted to take part in the Congress. Virginia and North Carolina were deprived of a representation by the dissolution of their assemblies.

The Congress on their first meeting chose Brigadier Ruggles chairman. They passed certain resolves, expressing their motives and principles, and then appointed three committees to prepare addresses to the King, Lords, and Commons. The first committee was composed of Robert R. Livingston, William Samuel Johnson, and William Murdoch : the second, John Rutledge, Edward Tilghman, and Philip Livingston: the third, Thomas

Lynch, James Otis, and Thomas Mc'Kean. On
Monday the 21st, they met according to adjournment, when the three committees reported. After
discussion and several amendments, the two first addresses, to his Majesty, and the house of Lords,
were accepted. On the next day, the petition to
the Commons was also discussed, amended and accepted. On the 24th, they met again, to sign the
addresses. They voted that copies of their proceedings should be sent to the several colonies, and
also, that " it be recommended by the Congress, to
the several colonies, to appoint special agents for
soliciting relief from their grievances, and to unite
their utmost interest and endeavours for that purpose." Copies were then immediately forwarded
to Mr. Jackson, the agent of Massachusetts in London. These petitions and memorials, were only signed by the committees of six of the colonies. Those
from South Carolina did not sign, because that colony, from " not rightly viewing the proposal of Massachusetts," had directed the addresses to be submitted for their approval before they were signed.
Connecticut also inserted a similar restriction in
her instructions; and the committee from New
York, not having been expressly authorised for the
purpose, could not regularly affix their signatures.
All these committees, however, entered zealously
into the measures, but Mr. Ruggles the chairman
dissented, and refused to sign the petitions.

These addresses were drawn up in a style of
great moderation and respect. The topics of all

were substantially the same, and prayed for the continuance of two privileges, the right of imposing their own taxes, and a trial by their peers. They said, in their address to the sovereign, " that to the English constitution these two principles are essential, the right of your faithful subjects freely to grant to your majesty, such aids as are required for the support of your government over them, and other public exigencies ; and trial by their peers. By the one they are secured from unreasonable impositions, and by the other, from arbitrary decisions of the executive power."

The following paragraphs are from the petition to the House of Commons.

" That the several late acts of Parliament, imposing divers duties and taxes on the colonies, and laying the trade and commerce thereof under very burthensome restrictions, but above all the act for granting and applying certain stamp duties, etc. in America, have filled them with the deepest concern and surprise ; and they humbly conceive the execution of them will be attended with consequences, very injurious to the commercial interest of Great Britain and her colonies, and must terminate in the eventual ruin of the latter.

" Your petitioners therefore most ardently implore the attention of the honourable house, to the united and dutiful representations of their circumstances, and to their earnest applications for relief from those regulations, which have already involved this continent in anxiety, confusion, and distress.

* * * * * *

" It gives us also great pain to see a manifold distinction made therein between the subjects of our mother country, and those in the colonies, in that the like penalties and forfeitures recoverable there only in his majesty's court of record, are made cognizable here by a court of admiralty ;* by these means, we seem to be, in effect unhappily deprived of two principles essential to freedom, and which all Englishmen have ever considered as their best birthrights, that of being free from all taxes but such as they have consented to in person, or by their representatives, and of trial by their peers.

* * * * * *

" That it is extremely improbable that the honourable house of commons should, at all times, be thoroughly acquainted with our condition, and all facts requisite to a just and equal taxation of the colonies.

" It is also humbly submitted, whether there be not a distinction, in reason and sound policy at least, between the necessary exercise of parliamentary jurisdiction in general acts, for the amend-

---

* The power given to the Court of Admiralty, was a great topic of complaint on the part of the Colonists. They had no Court of Exchequer as in England, and the jurisdiction exercised by that Court was given to that of the admiralty, in order to get rid of juries. This from habit was incorporated into the judicial system of the United States. A very learned and interesting account of the Admiralty Courts in this country, by Mr. Webster, may be found in Wheaton's Reports, Vol. 3. in the case of the U. S. v. Bevans.

ment of the common law, and the regulations of
trade and commerce through the whole empire,
and the exercise of that jurisdiction by imposing
taxes on the colonies.

*   *   *   *   *   *

" That the several subordinate provincial legislatures have been moulded into forms, as nearly
resembling that of their mother country, as by
his majesty's royal predecessors was thought con-
venient: and their legislatures seem to have been
wisely and graciously established, that the subjects
in the colonies might, under the due administration
thereof, enjoy the happy fruits of the British
government, which in their present circumstances
they cannot be so fully and clearly availed of in any
other way: under these forms of government,
we and our ancestors have been born or settled, and
have had our lives, liberties and property protected.
The people here, as every where else, retain a
great fondness for their old customs and usages,
and we trust that his majesty's service and the
interests of the nation, so far from being obstructed,
have been vastly promoted by the provincial legislatures."

The petition concludes with a request that they
may be heard by counsel in support of it, or in
such other manner as the honourable house may
decide. The conclusion of their address to the
sovereign, is as follows:—

" With hearts, therefore, impressed with the

most indelible characters of gratitude to your majesty, and to the memory of the kings of your illustrious house, whose reigns have been signally distinguished by their auspicious influence on the prosperity of the British dominions; and convinced, by the most affecting proofs of your majesty's paternal love to all your people, however distant, and your increasing and benevolent desires to promote their happiness, we most humbly beseech your majesty that you will be graciously pleased to take into your royal consideration, the distresses of your faithful subjects on this continent, and to lay the same before your majesty's parliament; and to afford them such relief, as in your royal wisdom, their unhappy circumstances shall be judged to require."

Arguments, facts, eloquence, anxiety, loyalty and respect, were of no avail. The king listened only to his courtiers and ministers; and they asserted that the Americans were able, and ought to bear the burthens imposed upon them. The parliament readily assumed the right to measure and distribute these impositions. What, indeed, could be expected from that body, when in the case of the stamp act, it absolutely refused to admit any address against the measure, because the rule of the house was not to receive any petition against a money bill, and under this poor pretence most arrogantly and unjustly precluding all discussion of a principle, against which a whole continent remonstrated.

The delegates from Massachusetts to this con-

vention, were James Otis, Oliver Partridge and
Timothy Ruggles.* The latter refused to sign
the petitions. The Governor had called the
legislature together in September, on account of
the opposition to the stamp act, and the riots
that had taken place in Boston. By the journal
of the House it appears, that " November 1st,
James Otis returned from New York, making his
appearance in the house, and laid on the table the
proceedings of the Convention." In the afternoon a vote of thanks was passed for their services.
At the succeeding session in February, 1766, the
House of Representatives passed a vote of censure
on Brigadier Ruggles, for his conduct at the Congress, and at the same time, a vote of approbation
to Messrs. Otis and Partridge, who signed the
petition. Ruggles was reprimanded in his place by
the speaker, and then obtained leave to enter his
reasons for the course he had taken, in the journal.
Afterwards when this statement was laid before
the House, the leave to insert it was withdrawn.

Brigadier Ruggles, son of the Reverend T. Ruggles, was born at Rochester in 1711, and took his
first degree at Cambridge in 1732. His father
intended him for his own profession, for which
however, he had no vocation. His first appearance
in public life, was as a representative for his native

---

* Governour Bernard, in an official letter on this subject, wrote—" Two
of three chosen" (meaning Ruggles and Partridge) " are fast friends to
government, prudent and discreet men, such as I am sure, will never consent
to any improper application to the government of Great Britain."

town, in 1736. He then moved to Sandwich, and
began the practice of the law. He there married
a widow and opened an Inn, and was remarkable
for his personal discharge of the various duties of
ostler, bar-keeper, &c. declaring, that he would not
shew himself to be above his business. He still however continued his practice as an attorney, and in attending the Courts in Barnstable County, was generally opposed to Colonel Otis, they being the most eminent men in the profession in that quarter. He
was a good scholar, with great natural strength of
mind : his manners were rude and misanthro-
pical : his wit was powerful, his language coarse.
In Mrs. Warren's dramatic piece of *The Group*,
he is described in the character of *Brigadier Hate-
all*. He was impressive as a pleader, and an able parliamentary debater. After a time, he removed from
Sandwich to Hardwick, in the county of Worcester.
In this latter place he received a commission in the
militia, and led a body of troops to join the army on
the frontier, under Sir William Johnstone, where he
distinguished himself in the action, in which the
French General, Baron de Dieskau, was wounded and taken. For his conduct in this affair, he received a lucrative place from George II. As the
leader of the government party in the house, he
was particularly opposed to Otis in every discussion. He was one of the most staunch and violent
supporters of all the measures of the administration,
and was named one of the *mandamus* counsellors in
1774. This appointment made him too unpopular

to remain at home, and he sheltered himself in Boston, while it was held by a British garrison. He adhered to the British side through the revolutionary contest, and passed the residue of his life in Nova Scotia.*

There were several individuals belonging to the stamp act congress, whose names are enrolled in the first class of American patriots. No member of it stood higher in the opinion of his colleagues, for energy and talents, than Otis. He was unfortuate in being associated with two others, in the committee from his province, whose views were so dissimilar to his own; one of whom, had no doubt, pledged himself to Governors Bernard and Hutchinson, to thwart every measure to the utmost of his power; and the other, was too "fast a friend to government," to engage heartily in the purpose of the meeting. Such being the character of the committee, the voice of Massachusetts was neutralized, and the tone of the addresses was rather more timid and submissive, than Otis would have chosen. He had here an opportunity to form a personal acquaintance with many distinguished men from different colonies, which was followed by a friendship and correspondence with several of them. Among these, were Mr. Rodney of Delaware, and Mr. Dickinson† of Pennsylvania,

---

* The facts in this account of Ruggles, are all taken from Mr. Knapp's Biographical Sketches.

† A kind of fatality seems to have attended all the manuscripts of Otis, and the attempt to recover them has been almost every where unsuccessful. The honourable C. A. Rodney, of Wilmington, had seen two letters from Otis

two of the most influential leaders of public opinion
in the provinces watered by the Delaware. He
corresponded with both of them, and especially with
Mr. Dickinson, who was in the habit of consulting
him on all his writings.*   The greatest advantage,

---

among the papers of his uncle, but they are irrecoverably mislaid. Mr.
Dickinson must have possessed many of his letters, but there are none now
remaining. Mr. Dickinson's house on the Delaware, was plundered by the
British troops, when they evacuated Philadelphia, his papers were carried off,
and afterwards scattered about the streets of New York; and as all his correspondence with Otis was previous to this misfortune, his letters were doubtless among the papers thus wantonly destroyed. These instances are mentioned, as specimens of the fruitless search that has been made after original
writings.

* The following letter from Mr. Dickinson to Mrs. Warren, the sister of
Otis, as it was written after an interval of forty years from their first acquaintance, and more than half that period after the death of his friend, has
all the advantage of a calm retrospect, and therefore more weight than a contemporary expression of regard. It is in answer to a letter accompanying a
copy of Mrs. Warren's History of the American Revolution

"Wilmington, 25th of the 9th month, 1805.

   " MY ESTEEMED FRIEND,
   " Thy letter with its enclosure came to my hand yesterday, for which I return many thanks. Thy approbation I consider as a real honour, and it is
greatly endeared to me by coming from a sister of my very deserving and
valued friend James Otis.
   " Our acquaintance with one another was formed at the first Congress held
at New York, in the year 1765, and it soon grew into friendship.—At this distant period, I have a pleasing recollection of his candour, spirit, patriotism and
philosophy.
   " In a longer continued existence on this earth, than was allotted to him,
I have endeavoured, as well as I could, to aid the cause in which his heart was
engaged, by asserting and maintaining the liberties for which he would have
been willing to share in all the distresses of our revolution, and if necessary,
to lay down his life.
   " It soothes my mind to bear this pure testimony to departed worth. May
divine goodness graciously bestow on his relations, a plentiful portion of consolation.
   " Thy generous exertions to inform thy fellow citizens and to present thy
country before the world, in a justly favorable light, will be, I believe, attended with the desired success. With every respectful consideration. I am thy
sincere friend,   JOHN DICKINSON.
MERCY WARREN, <i>Plymouth, Mass.</i>"

perhaps, that resulted from this short congress, was the occasion furnished to some of the principal characters in different colonies, to become personally known to each other, to compare their views and principles, and to give pledges of mutual support. There had been so little intercourse between the colonies, they were so separated by distance and by prejudice, that this chance of meeting for a common purpose, of combining their efforts, and of knowing the characters of those with whom they were to act, was invaluable. The foundation of political sympathy between distant provinces was laid, greater confidence was acquired in the defence of their rights, and a feeling of closer alliance was excited, which prepared the way for a more intimate and permanent confederation.

Just before the meeting of this congress, and while the Massachusetts legislature was in session, the unlucky stamps arrived in Boston, for that province; as also, those for Rhode Island and New Hampshire. Governor Bernard sent a message to the house, to ask their advice and assistance in regard to these papers, as the officers named to distribute them had all resigned, and there was no one to take charge of " the king's property of very considerable value." The answer was pithy and laconic enough : " The house having given all due attention to your excellency's message this day, beg leave to acquaint your excellency, that as the stamped papers mentioned in your message, are brought here without any directions to this government, it is the

sense of the house, that it may prove of ill consequence for them any ways to interest themselves in
this matter. We hope, therefore, your excellency
will excuse us if we cannot see our way clear to give
you any advice, or assistance therein."*

Chapter XIX.

*Angry Speech of Governor Bernard—Answer of the House—Viru-
lent attacks upon Otis—Messages and Answers respecting Counsellors
—Message and Answer on the repeal of the Stamp Act—Question
of compensation to the sufferers by the Riots—First opening of galleries for the public.*

THE Governor had pressed upon the house in his
opening speech, in September 1765, the duty of
submitting quietly to the stamp act, and also of
making compensation to the sufferers by the riots in
August. On this latter topic, he was so unguarded as to insinuate in a distant way, that the legislature might be thought to countenance those excesses.
In answer, they express unqualified disapprobation of
the stamp act, and warmly repel the implication,
that either they, or any respectable persons in the
community, could for a moment have countenanced
those outrages ; which in fact were repressed, not by

---

* Massachusetts State Papers, p. 49.

the government, but by the precautions and efforts
of the citizens. In closing the session he delivered a
very animated speech to both houses, reproaching
them with their altered tone towards him, denying
that he had any agency in producing the stamp act;
and hinting to them that they " may stand in such
need of advocates, as to make it not prudent to cast
off any of their natural and professed friends," of
whom he asserted himself to be one of the warmest.

At the beginning of the next session of the legislature, a committee was appointed, of which Otis
was chairman, to consider this speech of the governor. The answer bears strong marks of his manner.
It commences by saying, that its careful perusal had
been made the first business of the session, and they
would have been glad to have passed over it in
silence. They would not dispute his right to deliver a speech at whatever moment he pleased; at the
same time, when it contained sentiments that bear
hard on them, or their constituents, they add, " it
appears to us an undue exercise of the prerogative,
to lay us under the necessity, either of silence, or of
being thought out of season in making a reply."

The following paragraph will shew the feelings
of the legislature. " Your Excellency says, that
these times have been made more difficult than they
need have been; which is also the opinion of this
house. Those who have made them so, have reason to regret the injury they have done to a sincere
and honest people. We are glad, however, to find,

that the difficulty of the times is in a great measure removed; and we trust, that the province will be soon restored to its former tranquillity— your excellency is pleased to add, 'reputation.'—The custom-houses are now open, and the people are permitted to do their own business. The courts of justice must be open—open immediately, and the law, the the great rule of right, in every county in the province, executed.* The stopping the course of justice is a grievance which this house must enquire into. Justice must be fully administered through the province, by which the shocking effects which your excellency apprehended from the people's compliance with the stamp Act, will be prevented. Nothing now remains but to support the king's executive authority in this province, for which there is sufficient provision in the laws; and patiently to wait in hope, that the humble, dutiful, and loyal application, jointly made by the people of the continent, for the repeal of the act, will be successful. And though your excellency has told us, that you never thought it proper to express your sentiments against the act, we have reason to expect, that as it is 'a business in which you have no pretence to interpose' you have never taken any steps to prevent its repeal."

The Committee of grievances followed up the affair of the Courts very strenuously, and the House passed an imperative resolve, that the courts should

---

*" The courts had been suspended for some months, because they would not proceed to business without stamps, and the people declined using them."

Massachusetts State Papers, p. 61.

be opened. The Council non-concurred this resolve, giving as a reason, that they were convinced from information received, that the Supreme courts would be open at the commencement of the next term, and that all the others were preparing for the transaction of business. The administration had found, though the people had been remarkably orderly under this suspension of justice, that it would not be endured much longer, and that a very dangerous state of anarchy would ensue.

In the spring of this year, Otis was frequently assailed in the Boston Evening Post, a newspaper, that was devoted to the administration, as the Boston Gazette was to the patriotic cause. There was a considerable display of wit, with a full measure of acrimony in the direct personal attacks, that were made upon distinguished individuals, of the opposite parties: Bernard was the chief object on one side, and Otis on the other ; one of the series of papers, addressed to the former, was a kind of brief, sarcastic chronicle in latin : its writer could hardly be accused of inflaming the minds of the people at large. But of all these effusions, some of those, that were written against Otis, were the most outrageous ; they are really of a surpassing scurrility and brutal coarseness of language. Soon after one of these pieces had appeared, he mentioned it in a letter to his sister, Mrs. Warren, from which, the following extract is taken. It was dated April 11th, 1766. * * * " This country must soon be a * * * or may be engaged in contests that will require neither the tongue nor the pen of a lawyer. The enemies of our peace entertain hopes that we shall get no relief from home, but I am positive all appearances are against them. If we are to be slaves, the living have only to envy the dead; for without liberty I desire not to exist here. * * * Tell my Dear brother Warren to give himself no concern about the scurrilous piece in Tom Fleet's paper. It has served me as much as the song did last year. The tories are all ashamed of this, as they were of that, the author is not yet certainly known, though I think I am within a week of detecting him for certain. If I should, I shall try to cure him once for all, by stringing him up, not bodily, but in such a way, as shall gibbet his memory to all generations *in terrorem.* It lies between Bernard, Waterhouse, and Jonathan Sewall. The first, they say, has not wit enough to write any thing; the second swears off, and the third* must plead guilty

---

* It may oe safely affirmed, that neither Governor Bernard nor Mr. Sewall were the author of the libel in question, which was a kind of grotesque and now not very intelligible, history of his public career. It was more probably the work of *Samuel Waterhouse,* who is described in President Adams' letters, as " the most notorious scribbler, satyrist, and libeller, in the service of the conspirators against the liberties of America." The piece already mentioned was inserted in the Evening Post, March 31, 1766. In the same paper on the 3d of June, was an article signed *Cato,* the principal object of which was to comment upon the speech, imputed to him, but never proved, respecting " setting the Province in a flame." In the paper of the 9th of June, there is an excessively scurrilous piece, in language that would not now be tolerated, beginning each sentence with a pun on his name, the two first sentences, are, " O — tis you have poisoned the minds of the people to do and say absurd things to the prejudice of their country." " O – tis you that stepp'd forth at Faneuil Hall and offered yourself as a champion to decide the fate of America in single combat with George Grenville," &c. In the same journal on the 23d of the month, is a letter dated " in the shades from *Masaniello* to *James Bluster, Esq,*" imput-

or not guilty as soon as I see him * * * Till matters
are settled in England, I dare not leave this town, as
men's minds are in such a situation, that every nerve
is requisite to keep them from running to some irregularity and imprudence, and some are yet wishing
for an opportunity to hurt the country."

At the opening of the session, in May 1766, Governor Bernard congratulated them upon the repeal
of the Stamp Act, but in a manner that betrayed
chagrin, rather than satisfaction.   In the election of
counsellors, the House left out Hutchinson, the two
Olivers and Trowbridge, and chose Otis for their
speaker.   The Governor negatived Otis as speaker,
and also Colonel Otis, Gerrish, Saunders, Bowers,
Sparhawk and Dexter, who were chosen counsellors.
Otis no longer made himself a candidate for speaker, Mr. Cushing was chosen in his stead, and was
afterwards annually elected to the chair, till 1774.
The same course however, was pursued with regard
to counsellors, Colonel Otis was chosen every year
by the House, and as regularly negatived by Bernard, though when Hutchinson succeeded to the
chair, he approved him.

The loss of these staunch supporters of all his
measures in the council, exasperated the Governor
extremely.   He was thenceforward constantly representing to the ministry, the vicious constitution

---

ing to him several extravagant things, telling him that they expect him; that
Wat Tyler has already arrived, and when he comes, the triumvirate will be
complete.   These specimens may give some idea of the flood of abuse and
calumny, that was poured out upon him by the parasites of the administration.

of the Province, and that the Governor would never
have any power until the council was selected by
the crown. This was finally attempted in 1774,
when mandamus counsellors were appointed; who
never exercised their office. The Governor complained bitterly to the House that his particular
friends were not chosen, and though the repeal of
the Stamp Act was a fine occasion to have used
conciliatory language, the whole tenour of his speech
was irritating and angry.

Otis was on the committee, as usual, for preparing the answer, which met the Governor at all
points, and repelled his insinuations. In reply to his
allusions to the riots of the preceding summer, which
he imputes to the people at large, they say;
" There may, Sir, be a general, popular discontent
on good grounds. The people may sometimes have
just reason to complain; your Excellency must be
sensible, that in such a circumstance, evil minded
persons may take the advantage, and rise in tumult.
This has been too common in the best regulated,
and best disposed cities in Europe. Under cover of
the night a few villains may do much mischief. And
such, Sir, was the case here; but the virtue of the
people themselves finally suppressed the mob, and
we have reason to believe, that the unaffected concern which they discover at so tragical a scene,
their united detestation of it, their spirited measures
to prevent further disorders, and other circumstances well known to the honourable gentleman himself, (Hutchinson) have fully satisfied him, that

such an imputation was without reason. But for many months past there has been an undisturbed tranquillity in general, in this province, and for the greater part of the time, merely from a sense of good order in the people, while they have been in a great measure deprived of the public tribunals, and the administration of justice, and so far thrown into a state of nature." To his observations on the choice of counsellors, they say:—" But the manner in which you are pleased to explain the grounds of your testimony against the elections of the present year, seems to imply, that it is your opinion, that the two houses have been so far influenced by an inflammatory spirit in particular persons, as even to make an attack upon the government in form. The two houses proceeded in these elections with perfect good humour and good understanding; and as no other business had been transacted when we were favoured with your speech, it is astonishing to us, that you should think this a time to ' interrupt the general harmony.' We are wholly at a loss to conceive how a full, free, and fair election can be called ' an attack upon the government in form,' ' a professed intention to deprive it of its best and most able servants,' ' an ill-judged and ill-timed oppugnation of the king's authority.' These, may it please your Excellency, are high and grievous charges against the two houses, and such as we humbly conceive, no crowned head, since the revolution, has thought fit to bring against two houses of Parliament. It seems to us to be little short, if any thing, of a direct impeachment of the two houses, of high treason. Oppugnation to the king's authority is but a learned mode of expression, which reduced to plain English, is, fighting against the king's most excellent majesty. But, what, sir, is the oppugnation which we have been guilty of? We were summoned and convened here to give our free suffrages at the general election, directed to be annually made by the royal charter. We have given our suffrages according to the dictates of our consciences, and the best light of our understanding. It was certainly our right to choose, and as clearly a constitutional right in your Excellency to disapprove, without assigning a reason, either before or after your dissent. Your Excellency has thought proper to disapprove of some. We are far even from suggesting, that the country has by this means been deprived of its best and ablest servants. We have released those of the Judges of the Superior Court, who had the honour of a seat at the board, from the cares and perplexities of politics, and given them opportunity to make still farther advances in the knowledge of the law, and to administer right and justice within this jurisdiction. We have also left other gentlemen more at leisure to discharge the duties and functions of their important offices. This surely is not to deprive the government of its best and ablest servants, nor can it be called an oppugnation of any thing, but a dangerous union of legislative and executive power in the same persons; a grievance long complained of by our constituents, and the redress of

which, some of us had special instruction to endeavour at this very election to obtain."

A very few days after his speech at the opening
of the session, the Governor delivered another, on
the occasion of receiving Secretary Conway's letter
inclosing two acts of Parliament, one for the repeal
of the Stamp act, and the other "for securing the
dependence of the colonies on the mother country"
or, in other words, the act for losing the colonies.
This letter also contained the resolution of Parliament, that the colony should make compensation to
the sufferers in the late riots.   It was impossible to
deliver this information, which at best blended much
evil with its good, in a manner more ungracious, impolitic, and offensive, than that adopted by Bernard.
Indeed, the general tone of his speeches seems in
these times past endurance, when we are accustomed to an equality of courtesy and respect, between
the coordinate branches of government.   His speeches exemplify in full force the humiliating tenure of
colonial existence, where a mere vulgar placeman
apes the tone of the sovereign he represents; and
inflated with his transient favour, exercises his representative sovereignty with a mock dignity, that
is not relieved by the graceful consciousness of original power.   Such is too often the case in colonies,
where the inhabitants are condemned to witness the
fantastic tricks of a brief authority, and which
serves to prove, as in the case of some despotisms,
that it is much better to be near the centre, where
the power is generally the most tolerant and relaxed,

and where, if there is arrogance, it is the accompaniment of real majesty; while, in the distant provinces, a delegated authority becomes more rigid, more relentless and offensive, from being in the hands of subaltern and often servile agents. The governor in this speech, again returned, with singular indiscretion, to the subject of the counsellors who had been displaced; and again involved the whole community in blame for the riots, for which he demanded compensation in the most dictatorial manner. Though he knew the majority in the legislature was so great, as to come near unanimity, he indulges in the following irritating personal allusions, aimed chiefly at Otis, towards whom he maintained the most active enmity. " Gentlemen, both the business and the time are most critical; and let me intreat you to recollect yourselves, and consider well what you are about. When the fate of the province is put in a scale, which is to rise or fall, according to your present conduct; will you suffer yourselves to be influenced by party animosities, or domestic feuds? Shall this fine country be ruined, because every person in government has not been gratified with honour, or office, according to the full of his pretensions? Shall the private interests, passions or resentments of a few men, deprive this whole people of the great and manifold advantages, which the favour and indulgence of their sovereign and his parliament are even now providing for them ?"

After an apology for his ' openness,' ' earnestness,' ' sincerity,' and ' warmth'—he proceeds with a characteristical and absurd arrogance. "I have always been desirous of cultivating a good under-standing with you. And when I recollect the former happy times, when I scarce ever met the general court, without giving and receiving testimo-nies of mutual approbation, I cannot but regret the interruption of that pleasant intercourse, by the suc-cessful artifices of designing men, *enemies to the coun-try, as well as to me.* But now that my character for affection to the province, and attention to its interests, is confirmed by the most authentic testi-monials, I hope, that at the same time you renew your duty to the king, you will resume a confidence *in his representative.*"*

The answer of the council to this intemperate speech, is extremely able and dignified ; and by shewing how unreasonable and unfounded were the

---

* This vanity in the character of Bernard, met, on another occasion, with the powerful ridicule of Franklin, in one of those ludicrous parallels, which he seemed to have perpetually at command. In consequence of some article in the newspapers written by the Baronet, after his recall, Dr. Franklin pub-lished the folowing :—

TO THE EDITOR OF THE PUBLIC ADVERTISER.

"SIR,—D. E. Q , that is, Sir F. Bernard, in his long, laboured, and special dull answer to Q. E. D. endeavours to persuade the king, that as he was his majesty's representative, there was a great similitude in their characters and conduct ; and that Sir F.'s enemies, are *enemies of his majesty* and of all gov-ernment ! This puts one in mind of the chimney sweeper, condemned to be hanged for theft, who being charitably visited by a good clergyman for whom he had worked, said, *I hope your honour will take my part, and get a reprieve for me, and not let my enemies have their will ; because it is on your account, that they have prosecuted and sworn against me.*"—" On my account ! how can that be ?" "*Why, sir, because as how, ever since they knew I was employed by your honour, they resolved upon my ruin : for they are enemies to all religion, and they hate you and me, and every body in black.*"—Z.Z.

complaints, relating to the conduct of the people, in
regard to the disturbances, and of the legislature in
the choice of counsellors, places the imprudence of
those complaints in a very strong light. The answer of the house was made by a committee, composed of Mr. Cushing, the speaker, (of course, according to the practice of that day,) Otis, Major
Hawley, Mr. Samuel Adams, Mr. Saunders, Col. O.
Partridge and Col. Bowers. Generally speaking,
the first three gentlemen, after the speaker, were
on all political committees, and also Mr. Hancock.
Otis was the chairman, and his zeal, learning and
readiness, were all in requisition for draughting reports; these were afterwards a little moderated by
Cushing, revised and polished by Adams, and decided upon by Major Hawley, if necessary, whose opinion and influence were all-powerful in the legislature. Two or three extracts from this answer will
shew the feelings of the house. They notice his
remarks about the counsellors: " Your excellency
says, ' it is impossible to give any tolerable colouring to this proceeding.' The integrity and uprightness of our intentions and conduct is such, that no
colouring is requisite, and therefore we shall excuse
ourselves from attempting any. We hold ourselves
to be quite free in our suffrages; and provided we
observe the directions of our charter, and the laws
of the land, both which we have strictly adhered to,
we are by no means accountable, but to God and our
own consciences, for the manner in which we give
them—We believe your excellency is the first gov-

ernor of this province that ever formally called the
two houses of assembly to account for their suffrages,
and accused them of ingratitude and disaffection to
the crown, because they had bestowed them on such
persons, as in the opinion of the governor, were quite
necessary to the administration of government. Had
your excellency been pleased, in season, to have
favoured us with a list, and positive orders whom
to choose, we should, on your principles, have been
without excuse. But even the most abject slaves
are not to be blamed for disobeying their master's
will and pleasure, when it is wholly unknown to
them."

In further observations on this subject, they add,
" as to us, as our charter is, we should think it of
very little value, if it should be adjudged, that the
sense and spirit of it require the electors should be
under the absolute directions and control of the
chair, even in giving their suffrages. For, whatever
may be our ideas of the wisdom, prudence, mildness
and moderation of your administration, of your for-
giving spirit, yet we are not sure your successor will
possess those shining virtues."

With regard to the compensation for damages
done in the riot, they reserve that for future consideration; remarking in the " mean time, the recommendation is conceived in much higher and stronger
terms in the speech, than in the letter" of the secretary. They conclude with the following paragraphs,
after touching on the other topics of the speech, and
its angry, insolent tone. " In answer to the ques-

tions which your Excellency has proposed with so much seeming emotion, we beg leave to declare, that we will not suffer ourselves to be in the least influenced by party animosities or domestic feuds, let them exist where they may : that, if we can possibly prevent it, this fine country shall never be ruined by any persons : that it shall be through no default of ours, should this people be deprived of the great and manifest advantages, which the favour and indulgence of our most gracious sovereign and his Parliament are even now providing for them. On the contrary, that it shall be our highest ambition, as it is our duty, so to demean ourselves in public and private life, as shall most clearly demonstrate our loyalty and gratitude to the best of kings, and thereby recommend this people to further gracious marks of the royal clemency and favour."

" With regard to the rest of your Excellency's speech, we are sorry we are constrained to observe, that the general air and style of it savours much more of an act of free grace and pardon, than of a parliamentary address to the two houses of assembly ; and we most sincerely wish your Excellency had been pleased to reserve it, (if needful) for a proclamation."

After these answers to the Governor, a committee, of which Otis was chairman, reported an address of thanks to the king for the repeal of the stamp act, which glowed with the most affectionate loyalty ; thereby placing in a strong light the difference of their feelings towards the sovereign, or " his re-

presentative." The house also passed a vote of
thanks to several members of both houses of Parliament for their efforts in favour of the Colonies.
The subject of remuneration to Hutchinson and
others, was referred to a future session. They considered, that making compensation would be an act
of generosity, rather than justice, and therefore
wished to consult their constituents, before they
burthened them with the expense. They also in
expressing "their abhorrence of the madness and
barbarity" of the offenders, wished that they might
be brought to justice. The Governor sent a message in answer, that was perfectly consistent with
his former insinuations; alluding to their wish to
discover the offenders he said, "I dare say it will
be no difficult work to trace this matter to the bottom." The House immediately appointed a committee to wait on his Excellency, to ask him for any
information which he might possess, as to the individuals concerned in the riots. He told them he
had heard many hints, and some persons named, but
he had no minutes; that he would endeavour to
recollect what he had heard, and inform them. A
committee of secresy was appointed for this purpose, to sit in the recess; but when they called on
the Governor, he could give them no information.
The angry and implacable disposition of Bernard,
and the malignity of those about him, led him to
the most striking display of injustice and impolicy
in this affair. Bent on stigmatizing the patriotic
party, which, in fact, comprised the whole commu-

nity, he persevered in representing all the inhabitants of Boston as participating in the outrages that had taken place; although it was notorious, that they were universally grieved and indignant at those excesses, not only on account of the injury to the individuals whose property was destroyed, but because they truly foresaw, that their enemies would make it a pretence to calumniate them. If it was the object of the Governor and his adherents to prevent compensation being made; they took the most effectual measures for that purpose.

There was one occurrence at this session, that forms a remarkable event in the history of legislation. It laid the foundation of a most important change in their practice, which has since been adopted in the legislative assemblies of all free countries. Hitherto, in Massachusetts, as every where else, the sittings of the legislature had been close; no strangers were admitted to hear the debates. In England, a few persons were admitted by particular favour to listen to the debates in parliament, but were not allowed to report the speeches of the members, though some persons were occasionally employed, who repeated from memory what they had heard; and from these broken hints, speeches for the members were composed and published under feigned names, or only with initials, and purporting to have been delivered at a political club.* At this session on the 3d day of June, 1766,

* The anecdote of Dr. Samuel Johnson on this subject is well known. When certain celebrated speeches in parliament were praised, he said, "those speeches I wrote in a garret."

Otis brought forward a proposition, and was afterwards made chairman of a committee to carry it
into effect, " for opening a gallery for such as wished to hear the debates." This was the first instance of authorized publicity being given to legislative deliberations; an innovation that essentially
harmonized with the spirit of representative governments, and became one of the most powerful modes
of diffusing knowledge, and creating a watchfulness
of political affairs among the people.

Chapter XVII.

Joseph Hawley—John Hancock—Samuel Adams.

THE legislature of this year received an accession of three eminent members, who were returned
to it for the first time; Joseph Hawley, John Hancock, and Samuel Adams. Major Hawley, a representative from Northampton, acquired a very remarkable influence in the public councils. Perhaps
Massachusetts can boast of no citizen in all her
annals more estimable. He continued in the legislature till 1776, and during that period, it has been
said, that no vote on any public measure, either
was, or could have been carried, without his assent.

Joseph Hawley was born in 1724, educated at Yale College, and followed the profession of the law in Northampton, where he died in 1788, aged 64 years. As a lawyer he was possessed of great learning ; able as a reasoner, and a very manly, impressive speaker. He was at the head of the bar in the western counties of the Province. He had studied with diligence the principles of law, as connected with political institutions. This had prepared him for a clear perception of the effects, that would have resulted from the execution of the ministerial plans against the colonies; and caused him to take the most ardent and decisive part against the Stamp Act, and the whole series of arbitrary measures that followed it. The adherents of the administration dreaded him more than any individual in his part of the country, and, as usual, endeavoured, though most completely in vain, to injure his character. They succeeded, indeed, in their official persecution in throwing him over the bar, to which he was, however, soon restored.

The almost unexampled influence acquired by Major Hawley, was owing not only to his great talents, but still more perhaps to his high minded, unsullied, unimpeachable integrity. His enemies sought to undermine his reputation, by calumniating his motives, as was their manner towards every dis tinguished man on the patriotic side. They said, his conduct was factious and principles ruinous, and that the only object which he and his co-adjutors had in view, was, to bring themselves into power under a new order of things. The imputation of selfish, sordid views, was insupportable to a man of his character. He, therefore, at once, resolved, and pledged himself, never to accept of any promotion, office, or emolument under any government. This pledge he severely redeemed. He refused even all promotion in the militia, was several times chosen a counsellor, but declined ; and would accept of no other public trust, than the nearly gratuitous one of representing his town. A modest estate which descended to him from his father and uncle, was adequate to support his plain style of living, and he had no desire to accumulate wealth. His character was so noble and consistent, that his fellow citizens reposed unhesitating confidence in his integrity ; they believed that all the honours and wealth of the mother country would be insufficient to corrupt him, while they saw daily that he sought nothing from his own party. His talents, judgment and firmness, came in aid of this reputation for disinterestedness, and gave him, on all occasions, the power of an umpire. The weight of his character was sufficient to balance all the interest, which several gentlemen of great respectability in the western counties, exerted in favour of the administration. The country members, especially, followed his opinions implicitly, and the most powerful leaders in the legislature would probably have been unsuccessful, if they had attempted to carry any measure against his opinion.

The ascendancy which was allotted him by the deference of others, was a fortunate circumstance for his country. Never was influence exercised with more singleness of heart, with more intelligent, devoted and inflexible patriotism. He made up his mind earlier than most men, that the struggle against oppression would lead to war, and that our rights, at last must be secured by our arms. As the crisis approached, when some persons urged upon him the danger of a contest, so apparently unequal, his answer was, " We must put to sea; Providence will bring us into port !"*

---

* The following anecdote from one of President Adams' letters to Mr. Wirt, is highly characteristic of Hawley, and also contains some very interesting notices of other eminent individuals.

"When Congress had finished their business, as they thought, in the Autumn of 1774, I had, with Mr. Henry, before we took leave of each other, some familiar conversation, in which I expressed a full conviction, that our resolves, declarations of rights, enumeration of wrongs, petitions, remonstrances and addresses, associations and non-importation agreements, however they might be expected in America, and however necessary to cement the union of the colonies, would be but waste water in England. Mr. Henry said, they might make some impression among the people of England, but agreed with me that they would be totally lost upon the government. I had but just received a short and hasty letter, written to me by Major Joseph Hawley, of Northampton, containing ' a few broken hints,' as he called them of what he thought was proper to be done and concluding with these words, ' after all, we must fight.' This letter I read to Mr. Henry, who listened with great attention; and as soon as I had pronounced the words ' After all we must fight,' he raised his head and with an energy and vehemence that I can never forget, broke out with ' BY GOD, I AM OF THAT MAN'S MIND.' I put the letter into his hand, and when he had read it he returned it to me, with an equally solemn asseveration that he agreed entirely in opinion with the writer. I considered this a sacred oath, upon a very great occasion, (and would have sworn it as religiously as he did) and by no means inconsistent with what you say, in some part of your book, that he never took the sacred name in vain.

" As I knew the sentiments with which Mr. Henry left Congress in the Autumn of 1774, and knew the chapter and verse from which he had borrowed the sublime expression, ' We must fight,' I was not at all surprised at your history, in the 122d page, in the note, and in some of the preceding and following

Major Hawley did not appear in the legislature after the year 1776, but he never relaxed his zeal in the service of the country, and was always ready to contribute his efforts, to the public service. By his private exertions, he rendered assistance at some very critical and discouraging periods. At the season, when the prospects of the American army were the most gloomy, when the Jerseys were overrun, and the feelings of many were on the very verge of despondency, he exerted himself with great activity and success, to rally the spirits of his fellow citizens. At this time, when apathy appeared stealing upon the country, and the people were reluctant to march, on a seemingly desperate service, he addressed a body of militia, to urge them to volunteer as recruits. His manly eloquence, his powerful appeals to their pride, their patriotism, their duty, to every thing which they held dear and sacred, awakened their dormant feelings and excited them to enthusiasm.

---

pages. Mr. Henry only pursued in March 1775, the views and vows of November 1774.

" The other delegates from Virginia returned to their state in full confidence, that all our grievances would be redressed. The last words that Mr. Richard Henry Lee said to me when we parted, were, ' *we shall infallibly carry all our points. You will be completely relieved ; all the offensive acts will be repealed ;* the army and fleet will be recalled, and Britain will give up her foolish project.'

" Washington only was in doubt. He never spoke in public. In private he joined with those, who advocated a non-exportation, as well as a non-importation agreement. With both he thought we should prevail ; without either, he thought it doubtful. Henry was clear in one opinion, Richard Henry Lee in an opposite opinion, and Washington doubted between the two. Henry, however appeared in the end to be exactly in the right."

On another occasion, he rendered a service of much higher moment, and may be said not only to have prevented, but to have radically destroyed an incipient insurrection. At a time when the burthens and distresses of the war had produced great discontent, and even disaffection in some quarters, and Samuel Ely, a notorious demagogue, had, by his factious and treasonable efforts, gone far to organize in the western part of the state, an almost open resistance to the government, delegates from a large number of towns met in convention at Hatfield. The legislature sent Messrs. Samuel Adams, Stephen Gorham, and General Ward, as commissioners to meet them, and avert, if possible, the threatened danger. It was a moment of peril and anxiety. Major Hawley was a delegate from Northampton. At the opening of the meeting, the elements of mischief were visible in all their malignity, and seemed ready to burst into open fury. Hawley, with the deepest solicitude, which in great minds is the certain foundation of coolness and self possession, addressed this convention, consisting of two hundred. His spotless and lofty integrity, before which, even the most callous demagogues shrunk abashed, prepared the way to that triumph, which his masterly talents achieved. Arguments, satire, pleasantry, alternate appeals to their passions and to their reason, all managed with consummate address and irresistible energy; gradually subdued their inflamed, refractory humour, and finally moulded them entirely to his will. They not only renounced all their dangerous intentions, but agreed to sign a humble petition to the government, promising future obedience, and praying for an act of indemnity for the past, and to make the victory more complete, and to shew the danger was entirely destroyed, they were brought with the exception of five persons, to sign the petition, excluding Ely, the leader of all the disturbance, from the indemnity.

Major Hawley was a sincerely religious and pious man; but here, as in politics, he loathed all tyranny and fanatical usurpation. He was, near the close of his life, chosen into the senate of Massachusetts. Though he would not have taken the trust at any rate, he seized the opportunity to give his testimony against the test act, which till a recent period, was a stain in the constitution of that state. In a letter upon the subject, he asked if it was necessary that he should be called upon to renounce the authority of the king of Great Britain, and every foreign potentate? and whether it could be expected, that, having been a member of the church for forty years, he should submit to the insult of being called to swear that he believed in the truth of the christian religion, before he could take his seat?*

With all these powerful talents and noble feelings, he was not exempt from a misfortune, that occasionally threw its dark shadows over them. He was sub-

---

* This Test was copied almost verbatim from the English Test act, and its insertion in the liberal constitution of Massachusetts was a mortifying anomaly. At a late revision of that instrument, by a general convention, this remnant of superannuated bigotry was expunged by general consent.

ject at particular times, to an hypocondriac disorder, that would envelope him in gloom and despondency.   At these seasons he was oppressed with melancholy, and would lament every action and exertion
of his life.   When his mind recovered its tone, the
recollection of these sufferings was painful, and he
disliked to have them remembered.

Major Hawley was a patriot without personal
animosities, an orator without vanity, a lawyer without chicanery, a gentleman without ostentation, a
statesman without duplicity, and a christian without
bigotry.   As a man of commanding talents, his firm
renunciation and self denial of all ambitious views,
would have secured him that respect, which such
strength of mind inevitably inspires; while his voluntary and zealous devotion to the service of his
countrymen, established him in their affection.   His
uprightness and plainness, united to his ability and
disinterestedness, gave the most extensive influence
to his opinions, and in a period of doubt, divisions,
and danger, men sought relief from their perplexities
in his authority, and suffered their course to be guided by him, when they distrusted their own judgments, or the counsels of others.   He, in fine, formed one of those manly, public spirited, and generous
citizens, ready to share peril and decline reward,
who illustrate the idea of a commonwealth; and
who, through the obstructions of human passions and
infirmities, being of rare occurrence, will always be
the most admired, appropriate, and noble ornaments
of a free government.

The names of the two new members of the legislature elected from Boston, in 1766, were coupled together by a subsequent act of proscription, in a remarkable manner.   Samuel Adams and John Hancock, were chosen the colleagues of James Otis and Thomas Cushing, and these four gentlemen, who for several years composed the delegation of the capital exercised a wide influence in the affairs of the province, and are inseparably connected with all the events that led to the independence of the United States.   Otis and Cushing were only permitted to see the promise of American prosperity, but Adams and Hancock were destined to outlive the period of trial, during which their labours were never intermitted; they entered with the nation on the new grounds of the Federal Union, and by filling eminent stations in the government of their state, became associated with the administration, and the parties that grew up under the new confederation.

John Hancock, the son and grandson of eminent congregational clergymen, was born in Quincy near Boston, in 1737, and graduated at Harvard College in 1754.   His father died when he was a child, and he was then adopted by his uncle, Thomas Hancock, the most opulent merchant in Boston, a man of enlarged views and public spirit, who bequeathed some considerable legacies to different institutions. This benevolent uncle took the entire charge of his young relation, and received him into his counting house on the completion of his education at the university; and after a few years sent him to England, to see that country, and to become personally acquainted with his correspondents. He died of an apoplexy in 1764, leaving his nephew to succeed to his very extensive mercantile concerns, and heir to the largest estate in the province.

This sudden possession of wealth turned the eyes of the whole community towards him, his conduct under this trying prosperity secured universal esteem and good will. It made him neither giddy, arrogant, nor profligate ; he continued his course of regularity, industry, and moderation. Great numbers of people received employment at his hands, and in all his commercial transactions, he exhibited that fair and liberal character which commonly distinguishes the extensive and affluent merchant.

The natural influence which he acquired from his habits and his possessions, rendered him extremely popular, and he had been often called upon to act in the affairs of the town. At length he was placed in the legislature,* and this event decided his future career. The stake which he pledged in the large

---

* "I was one day walking in the mall, and accidentally met Samuel Adams. In taking a few turns together, we came in full view of Mr. Hancock's house. Mr. Adams, pointing to the stone building, said, 'This town has done a wise thing to day.' 'What?' 'They have made that young man's fortune their own.' His prophecy was literally fulfilled, for no man's property was ever more entirely devoted to the public. The town had that day chosen Mr. Hancock into the legislature of the province. The quivering anxiety of the public under the fearful looking for of the vengeance of king, ministry and parliament, compelled him to a constant attendance in the house, his mind was soon engrossed by public cares, alarms, and terrors ; his business was left to subalterns, his private affairs neglected, and continued to be so to the end of his life."

MS. letter from President Adams to the late W. Tudor, Esq,

fortune under his control, was a proof of his sincerity
in the principles which he professed, which had
great weight with minds of the common order, and
was quite obvious to even the meanest capacity.
He was gradually engrossed by political concerns,
and very early became highly obnoxious to the administration. Their enmity was shewn in several
attempts at insult and oppression, such as seizing his
vessels,* calling upon him for excessive bail, &c. all
of which only produced more decisive testimonies of
popular attachment to him, and a closer conviction
in his breast of the intolerable abuses with which
his country was menaced.

In the legislature Hancock was upon every important committee, so that all leading measures had his
sanction, though he seldom wrote any of the reports.
He had the full confidence of the patriotic party, as
they believed him to be unchangeably devoted to their
cause ; yet, on one occasion there was a difference of
opinion between him and Adams, on some propositions of Hutchinson, in regard to removing the
General Court to Boston, which created a temporary
schism in the party, and a long alienation of friendship between those eminent men. They were reconciled to each other, several years afterwards,
and filled the two first offices of the State together
during a considerable period.

General Gage issued a proclamation, in June 1775,

---

* The insolence of the Commissioners of the Customs led them to offer those
impolitic and vexatious offences, which were the immediate cause of much popular excitement.

a few days before the battle of Bunker Hill, offering a pardon to all rebels, excepting Samuel Adams
and John Hancock—" whose offences"—(said the
edict) " are of too flagitious a nature to admit of
any other consideration than that of condign punishment." This virulent proscription, which was
intended to ruin them, widely extended their fame.
A few others, it is well known, were secretly proscribed, and would doubtless have fallen victims to
ministerial vengeance,—but Adams and Hancock
were the only two expressly excepted from all hope
of pardon, and irrevocably denounced.*   The alter-

---

* Hancock and Adams, succeeded to a station which Otis had before held, in
being made the representatives of their countrymen, to bear all the denunciations and insults, which were directed in England against the American patriots. The instances of this substitution, are very numerous in all the writings
of that day. The two following are extracted from the speeches of Mr. Fox.
The first, occurred in a debate in 1779, on the Irish discontents, when he
assailed Mr. Dundas, and illustrated the present subject, by allusions to former
measures regarding America :—" What was the consequence of the sanguinary measures recommended in those bloody, inflammatory speeches?   Though
Boston was to be starved, though Hancock and Adams were proscribed—yet,
at the feet of these very men, the parliament of Great Britain were obliged to
kneel, to flatter and to cringe ; and as they had the cruelty at one time to de-
nounce vengeance against those men, so they had the meanness afterwards to
prostrate themselves before them, and implore their forgiveness.—Was he who
called the Americans ' Hancock and his crew,' to reprehend any set of men
for inflammatory speeches?"—In the debate on the address to the king, in 1781,
speaking of the American war, he said,—" They (the ministers) commenced
war against America after that country had offered the fairest propositions,
and extended her arms to receive us into the closest connexion. They did this
contrary to their own sentiments of what was right, but they were over-ruled
by that high and secret authority, which they durst not disobey, and from
which they derive their situations. They were ordered to go on with the
American war or quite their places. They preferred emolument to duty, and
kept their ostensible power at the expense of their country. To delude the
parliament and the people, they then described the contest to be a mere squab-
ble. It was not America with whom we had to contend, it was with " Han-

natives to which their fate was restricted, embraced the two extremes of human disgrace and glory ; they were either to be execrated and executed as traitors, or they were to aid in establishing a nation, and to be honoured as the benefactors of their country and mankind.

Hancock was President of the provincial Congress of Massachusetts, until he was sent as one of the delegation from that province to the Congress which met at Philadelphia, in 1775. In 1776, he had the honour to be President of that immortal assembly which signed the Declaration of Independence.* He continued in Congress till 1779, when ill health forced him to resign. He was annually chosen governor of Massachusetts, from 1780 to 1785, when he was succeeded by Mr. Bowdoin, for two years. In 1787, he was again elected to the same office. He was also made President of the Convention for the adoption of the federal constitution, and continu-

---

rock and his crew," a handful of men would march triumphantly from one end of the continent to the other. This was the language sounded in that house, and for this language a learned member of it (Lord Loughborough,) was exalted to the dignity of a peer, and enrolled among the hereditary council of the realm. He was thus rewarded for no other merit that he could discover, but that of vehemently abusing our fellow subjects in America, and calling their opposition the war " *of Hancock and his crew.*"

* Without reference to general views, a signature to that instrument, was to the individual, on personal considerations only, of the most momentous import. The only writing however, which appears trembling, is that of Mr. Hopkins, who had been afflicted with the palsy. Hancock seems to have had in mind an official proportion in the dimensions of his name ; and the force with which it is w,itten, shews that it was never intended to be erased. Those persons who are fond of relics, may be glad to know, that the pen with which these signatures were made, was preserved, and is now in the cabinet of the Massachusetts Historical Society.

ed to be chosen governor of the state till his death, which took place October 8th, 1793 –in the 56th year of his age.

Few persons have enjoyed greater or more invariable popularity than this distinguished patriot ; and there are not many men who have been so truly entitled to this kind of favour, which, unfortunately, is not always an unequivocal testimony of merit. His character and his fortune rendered his influence of great importance, and he threw the whole weight of both, without reserve, into the scale of his country. If he had kept aloof, and devoted himself to the care of his property, he might have accumulated a vast stock of wealth ; but he so disregarded his own affairs in his attention to public engagements, that had his estate not been very large, he would have died as poor as many of his colleagues. He was consulted, when it was contemplated to burn the town of Boston, in order to force the enemy to evacuate it. He answered, that although the greater part of his fortune consisted in buildings within the town, yet, if its destruction would be useful to the cause of the country, that this circumstance should be no impediment to its being set on fire immediately.

The greatest fault in his character, was a peevishness and irritability that often grieved his friends, but which was forgiven, on reflecting, that this failing was not owing to a bad heart, or a mean spirit, but to perpetual ill health. His constitution was naturally feeble, and he was for many years severely

afflicted with the gout. The greater portion of his
life, indeed, was passed in physical suffering—his
mind rose superior to this misfortune in the discharge of his public duties: and as he never relaxed
from these, while it was possible for him to continue
his efforts, his family, and his acquaintance, bore
with indulgence a natural consequence of infirmities,
under which a less powerful mind would have sunk
entirely.

In private life, he commanded the esteem, even
of those persons who differed from him in political
opinions. His beneficence never failed. In his exterior he exhibited the characteristics of a gentleman : dressing with elegance according to the fashion of the day, keeping a handsome equipage, and
being polite and affable in social intercourse. He
was renowned for his hospitality ; strangers who
were entitled to it, received a ready welcome, and
a large circle of acquaintance became frequent
guests at his parties, which were distinguished for all
the requisites, *material* as well as *personal*, which are
necessary to convivial enjoyments, among the refined classes of civilized society.

He possessed many valuable qualifications for
public life, a knowledge of business, and facility in
despatching it, and a ready insight into the characters of men. As an orator, he was not remarkable,
he seldom made an elaborate speech, and the only
discourse of his in print, is the oration on the 5th of
March, 1774. But as the president, moderator, or
speaker, of an assembly, whether it was a town

meeting, or a house of representatives, he was not surpassed by any person of his time. His voice was powerful, his acquaintance with parliamentary forms accurate, and his apprehension of questions quick; he was attentive, impartial, and dignified, and in these situations, inspired respect and confidence wherever he presided.

Towards the close of his career, as parties grew up under the new constitution, some respectable men were dissatisfied with his administration as Governor, but the amount of his popularity as signified by numbers, was not perceptibly diminished. In the adoption of the Federal constitution, though president of the state convention which discussed that instrument, he did not at the beginning take a very decided part; yet, towards the close of the session, he lent all his influence, which was very important, to procure the ratification of the new system. There were still, however, strong prejudices against him, arising rather from a dislike to particular individuals who surrounded him, than to his own proceedings. Men who were lukewarm, or inimical to the federal government, obtained an ascendancy over his mind, which was invidiously manifested at the last journey of Washington to Boston, in October 1789. The Governor was unfortunately persuaded to start some ill timed question of etiquette respecting his meeting with the president, which was wholly unexpected by the latter, and tended to mar the pleasure of his visit. At that moment of joyous enthusiasm, when infancy and age were exulting, the

one, that it had been born soon enough and the
other that it had lived long enough to see the beloved chief; when the people, and the magistrates,
both sexes, and every profession, poured forth in
processions with overflowing hearts to greet the
most venerated man in the nation, this coldness of
the Governor inspired universal dissatisfaction. He
himself regretted this mistake, and subsequently
endeavoured to remove its impression. In fine, his
talents may be estimated to have been rather useful than brilliant or profound, his habits and appearance were those of a gentleman, his feelings and
principles, those of a patriot, his morality and benevolence, those of a sincere professor of christianity;
he abandoned the care of private interest to devote
his time to the welfare of the public; his bodily infirmities could not subdue the energy of his mind,
and the part which he took, having been adopted
from a sense of duty, was inflexibly sustained: he
outlived the proscription of his enemies, to be
cherished and honoured by his fellow citizens, and
his name, which stands the leading signature in the
national charter, is conspicuously and indelibly
stamped in the history of his country.

Samuel Adams, the colleague of Hancock, was
destined to have a powerful agency in public affairs,
and to become one of the most remarkable men
connected with the American revolution. The famous proscription by General Gage, before mentioned, associated his name with that of Hancock,
though there was no personal cordiality between
hem, and even their public views were in some de-

gree modified by their individual and peculiar characters.

Mr. Adams, descended from a family that had
been among the early planters of New England,
was born in Boston, September 27th, 1722, was
educated at Harvard College, and received its honours in 1740. When he took the degree of Master in 1743, he proposed the following question,
" Whether it be lawful to resist the supreme magistrate, if the commonwealth cannot be otherwise
preserved ?" He maintained the affirmative, and
this collegiate exercise furnished a very significant
index to his subsequent political career. On leaving
the University, he engaged in the study of divinity,
with the intention of becoming a clergyman, but did
not pursue his design.

From his earliest youth, his attention was drawn
to political affairs, and he occupied himself both in
conversation and writing with the public concerns
of the day. He was opposed to Governor Shirley,
because he thought too much power was conferred
upon him, and was the friend of his successor, Pownal, as the latter assumed the popular side. He became so entirely a public man, and discovered such
a jealous, watchful, and unyielding regard for popular rights, that he excited the general attention of
the patriotic party, and they took the opportunity
in the year 1766, to place him in the legislature ;
from that period till the close of the revolutionary
war, he was one of the most unwearied, efficient,
and disinterested assertors of American freedom and
independence.

He grew conspicuous very soon after his admission into the House, of which he was chosen clerk ; it being then the practice to take that officer from among the members. He obtained the same kind of influence, and exercised the same indefatigable activity in the affairs of the Legislature, that he did in those of his town. He was upon every committee, had a hand in writing or revising every report, a share in the management of every political meeting, private or public, and a voice in all the measures that were proposed, to counteract the tyrannical plans of the administration. The people soon found him to be one of the steadiest of their supporters, and the government was convinced, that he was one of the most inveterate of their opponents.

When his character was known in England, and it was also understood that he was poor, the partizans of the ministry, who felt annoyed by the " disturbances in America," resorted to the usual practice when the clamorous grow too troublesome, and proposed that he should be quieted by a participation in some of the good things they were enjoying. Governor Hutchinson, in answering the inquiry of a friend, why he was not silenced in this manner, wrote with an expression of impatient vexation,— " Such is the obstinacy and inflexible disposition of the man, that he never can be conciliated by any office or gift whatever." This information was received with a ludicrous kind of incredulity, evidently occasioned by a confusion of ideas at the anomaly of such a disposition, compared with the personal and daily experience of all around them. But this circumstance ought to have caused the administration, to examine more accurately into the actual condition of the colonies. When so many leading individuals in this country, were not to be conciliated by the favours of government, when they spurned at places and pensions, and withstood the allurements of fortune; such conduct, which is not the natural temper of mankind, indicated that there was some deep and powerful cause for the dissatisfaction that prevailed. It is a portentous symptom in affairs, when men of strong character forego the common views of ambition, and disregard the acquisition of wealth, which in ordinary times, is as salutary to society in its general tendency, as it is advantageous to the individual. This state of things, which occurred in the colonies during the epoch of their resistance to the designs of England, required the most cautious treatment, and prompt alleviation : the existence of such enthusiasm is replete with danger to the ruling power, and wherever it is not effectually relieved, will bring about, as it did in America, the crisis of a revolution.

He continued in the legislature till 1774, when he was sent to the first congress of the old confederation. He had been previously chosen Secretary of Massachusetts, which office was performed by deputy during his absence. He was one of the signers to the declaration of 1776, which he laboured most indefatigably and unhesitatingly to bring forward.

He was an active member of the convention that
formed the constitution of Massachusetts; and after
it went into effect, he was placed in the Senate of
the State, and for several years presided over that
body.   In 1789, he was elected Lieutenant Governor, and held that office till 1794, when, after the
death of Hancock, he was chosen Governor, and
was annually re-elected till 1797.   He then retired
from public life, and died at his house in Winter
Street, Boston, October 2, 1803, in the eighty-se-
cond year of his age.

He was one of that class who saw very early,
that " after all, we must fight"—and having come
to that conclusion, there was no citizen more prepared for the extremity, or who would have been
more reluctant to enter into any kind of compromise.   After he had received warning at Lexington
in the night of the 18th of April, of the intended
British expedition, as he proceeded to make his escape
through the fields with some friends, soon after the
dawn of day he exclaimed, " this is a fine day!" " very
pleasant indeed," answered one of his companions supposing he alluded to the beauty of the sky and atmosphere—" I mean" he replied, " this day is a glorious
day for America!"   His situation at that moment
was full of peril and uncertainty, but throughout
the contest, no damage either to himself or his country ever discouraged or depressed him.

The very faults of his character tended, in some
degree, to render his services more useful, by con-
verging his exertions to one point, and preventing

their being weakened by indulgence or liberality towards different opinions. There was some tinge of bigotry and narrowness, both in his religion and politics. He was a strict calvinist; and probably, no individual of his day had so much of the feelings of the ancient puritans, as he possessed. In politics, he was so jealous of delegated power, that he would not have given our constitutions inherent force enough for their own preservation. He attached an exclusive value to the habits and principles in which he had been educated, and wished to adjust wide concerns too closely after a particular model. One of his colleagues, who knew him well, and estimated him highly, described him with good natured exaggeration in the following manner: "Samuel Adams would have the State of Massachusetts govern the Union, the Town of Boston govern Massachusetts, and that he should govern the Town of Boston, and then the whole would not be intentionally ill-governed."

It was a sad error of judgment that caused him to undervalue, for a period at least, the services of Washington during the revolutionary war, and to think that his popularity when President, might be dangerous. Still, these unfounded prejudices were honestly entertained, and sprang naturally from his disposition and doctrines. During the war, he was impatient for some more decisive action, than it was in the power of the commander in chief for a long time to bring about; and when the new Constitution went into operation, its leaning towards aristocracy, which was the absurd imputation of its enemies, and which his antifederal bias led him more readily to listen to, derived all its plausibility from the just, generous, and universal confidence, that was reposed in the chief magistrate. These things influenced his conduct in old age, when he was Governor of Massachusetts, and while the extreme heat of political feelings would have made it impossible, for even a much less positive character to administer any public concerns without one of the parties of that day being dissatisfied. But all these circumstances are to be disregarded, in making an estimate of his services. He, in fact, was born for the revolutionary epoch, he was trained and nurtured in it, and all his principles and views were deeply imbued with the dislikes and partialities which were created during that long struggle. He belonged to the revolution; all the power and peculiarity of his character were developed in that career, and his share in public life under a subsequent state of things, must be considered as subordinate and unimportant.

He possessed an energy of will that never faltered, in the purpose of counteracting the arbitrary plans of the English cabinet, and which gradually engaged him to strive for the independence of the country. Every part of his character conduced to this determination. His private habits, which were simple, frugal, and unostentatious, led him to despise the luxury and parade affected by the crown officers; his religious tenets, which made him loath the very name of the English church, preserved in his mind the memory of ancient persecutions, as vividly, as if they had happened yesterday, and as anxiously, as if they might be repeated to-morrow; his detestation of royalty, and privileged classes, which no man could have felt more deeply—all these circumstances stimulated him to perseverance in a course, which he conscientiously believed it to be his duty to pursue, for the welfare of his country.

He combined in a remarkable manner all the animosities and all the firmness, that could qualify a man to be the assertor of the rights of the people. Had he lived in any country or any epoch, when abuses of power were to be resisted, he would have been one of the reformers. He would have suffered excommunication rather than have bowed to papal infallibility, or paid the tribute to St. Peter; he would have gone to the stake, rather than submit to the prelatic ordinances of Laud; he would have mounted the scaffold, sooner than pay a shilling of illegal ship-money; he would have fled to a desert, rather than endure the profligate tyranny of a Stuart; he was proscribed, and would sooner have been condemned as a traitor, than assent to an illegal tax, if it had been only a six penny stamp or an insignificant duty on Tea, and there appeared to be no species of corruption by which this inflexibility could have been destroyed.

The motives by which he was actuated, were not a sudden ebullition of temper, nor a transient impulse of resentment, but they were deliberate, methodical and unyielding. There was no pause, no hesitation, no despondency; every day, and every

hour, was employed in some contribution towards the
main design, if not in action, in writing; if not with
the pen, in conversation; if not in talking, in meditation. The means he advised were persuasion, petition, remonstrance, resolutions, and when all failed,
defiance and extermination sooner than submission.
His measures for redress were all legitimate, and
where the extremity of the case, as in the destruction of the tea, absolutely required an irregularity,
a vigour beyond the law, he was desirous that it
might be redeemed by the discipline, good order,
and scrupulous integrity, with which it should be
effected.

With this unrelenting and austere spirit, there
was nothing ferocious, or gloomy, or arrogant in his
demeanour. His aspect was mild, dignified and
gentlemanly. In his own state, or in the congress of
the union, he was always the advocate of the strongest measures, and in the darkest hour he never
wavered or desponded. He engaged in the cause
with all the zeal of a reformer, the confidence of an
enthusiast, and the cheerfulness of a voluntary
martyr. It was not by brilliancy of talents, or pro-
foundness of learning, that he rendered such essential service to the cause of the revolution, but by
his resolute decision, his unceasing watchfulness, and
his heroic perseverance. In addition to these qualities, his efforts were consecrated by his entire superiority to pecuniary considerations; he, like most of
his colleagues, proved the nobleness of their cause,
by the virtue of their conduct: and Samuel Adams.

after being so many years in the public service, and
having filled so many eminent stations, must have
been buried at the public expense, if the afflicting
death of an only son had not remedied this honourable poverty.

Chapter XVIII.

*Question regarding compensation to the sufferers by the Riots—
Committee to inquire about Proclamations—Opposition to the
Lieutenant Governor's act in the Council—Arrival of a small
body of Troops.*

THE Committee of Secresy, which had been appointed to sit in the recess, with power to send for
persons and papers, and to receive any communications from the Governor respecting the actors in
the riots of the preceding year, obtained no information from him, as has been already mentioned.
In October, he convened the legislature expressly
for the purpose of granting compensation to the
sufferers. After much discussion, the House, by a
vote of 44 to 36, refused to make a remuneration.
A few days after, a motion to reconsider this motion was lost by the same majority, but with increased numbers; 51 to 43. November 5th, the question was modified by moving, that an account of the
losses should be prepared, and an estimate of what

each town would have to pay, if payment should be
made out of the public treasury : this also passed in
the negative.   November 6th, a committee was ordered to make out an estimate, to be printed; and
that the legislature should then have a recess, in
order to consult their constituents.   They assembled
again December 3d, and passed the bill for "granting
compensation to the sufferers, and general pardon,
indemnity, and oblivion, to the offenders."   The
numbers were 53 to 35; Otis, Adams, Hancock,
Hawley, &c. being in the affirmative.   The House
" ordered that Major Hawley, Mr. Otis, and Mr.
Adams, be a committee to prepare a resolve, setting forth the motives which induced this house to
pass the bill for granting compensation, &c. &c." who
reported thereon as follows :

   " Resolved, that this House, in passing the bill
for granting compensation to the sufferers, and of
free and general pardon, indemnity and oblivion,
to the offenders in the late times, were influenced
by a loyal and grateful regard to his majesty's
most mild and gracious recommendation ; by a
deference to the opinion of the illustrious patrons of
the colonies in Great Britain ; and for the sake of
internal peace and order, without regard to any
interpretation of his majesty's recommendation into a
requisition, precluding all debate and controversy :
and under a full persuasion, that the sufferers had
no just claim or demand on the Province ; and
that this compliance ought not hereafter to be
drawn into a precedent."   To this were added two

other resolves, one purporting that "it was the
indispensible duty of the sufferers to have applied
to the government here, rather than to the government at home," and another to remark, that by
the resolutions of the House of Commons it appeared, that the riots about the Stamp act were imputed to the resolves of certain assemblies in America,
which could not apply to them, as their resolves
were not passed till two months after the riots had
taken place.

The whole history of this transaction, in which
the parliament and the ministry took so much interest, is very instructive, and highly characteristic of
all the parties. The question was more than a year
in agitation, and was finally settled with great difficulty, and probably would not then have been decided, but for the reason assigned in the resolution, a
regard for the opinions of the distinguished friends
of the colonies in parliament. The Governor and
his adherents seized on the excesses committed by a
mob under the excitement of the Stamp act, as a
pretext for perpetual crimination of the people in
his government. He was constantly representing the
province as in a state of rebellion, in order to effect
his favourite object of obtaining a military force,
with the vain expectation of intimidating the patriotic party. The troops, indeed, came at last, and
proved the profound sagacity of Dr. Franklin's observation to the House of Commons, "they would
not find a rebellion; they might indeed make one."

Bernard, backed by the authority of parliament,

and the instructions of the ministry, went greatly
beyond the language of either, in his manner of de-
manding payment for the losses. The tone which
he assumed, and the expressions and insinuations
which he used, were so utterly offensive, that the
legislature were repelled from considering the question amicably. It seemed to be his design throughout, not so much to secure the compensation, as to
have it granted in an unconditional, humiliating manner; not as an act of deliberate justice and generosity, on the part of the colony, but of timid subserviency to the requisition, as he wished it to be considered, of Parliament, though the House of Commons
had been satisfied with the word " recommendation."
The parties themselves, who were to receive the
money, readily aided in this course of policy, because
it gratified their ill will and revenge : The delay
was of less consequence to them, since as it had been
a parliamentary concern, they were certain of being
ultimately paid, and, if the payment came from
that side, they would probably have gained by it, as
the accounts could not have been so closely scrutiniz-
ed. Perhaps a motive of this kind, joined to the
wish to make the most of these disturbances, for the
purpose of procuring the aid of military force, induced them to make their first application to the British Parliament ; which, in the language of the legislature, " it was their indispensible duty" to have
made to the government of the Province.

The character of the legislature and its leading
members, was also fully tried and manifested in these

transactions. They saw, from the first moment, the mischievous use that would be made of these excesses; which, trifling as they were, compared with many that had happened in the cities of Europe, and " even at the door of the royal palace," they regarded with heartfelt indignation. They would willingly, from generosity towards the sufferers, have indemnified them for their losses. But these individuals having insidiously applied to England for redress, the legislature was placed in a most difficult dilemma. The recommendation of parliament did not come very gratefully to them, while they were engaged in a most determined and scrupulous resistance to all attempts at disposing of their property, by a legislature, in which their constituents were not represented; and while animated by the most salutary jealousy of every measure that could lead to an encroachment on their rights. But the question was completely repugnant and intolerable, when the governor " interpreted the recommendation into a requisition," and seemed far more anxious to make the compliance a slavish precedent, than an act of healing mercy. They saw all the mischief that might result, and knew that many pestilent misrepresentations were made to their disadvantage, whilst the affair remained unsettled. This was one of the series of trials, which the patriots of that day had to undergo. The gratification of their own feelings, in the passage of an act in many respects expedient, was resolutely postponed, as long as it could be converted into an inference against the rights of the colonies. The moderate letter of Lord Shelburne,* and the tone which the Governor consequently adopted, prepared the way for a settlement. The anxiety which it gave to the advocates of the colonies in parliament, who were much annoyed by the advantage, which the administration derived from placing this transaction in an odious light, was a strong inducement to the passage of the act. Yet there was so much public feeling against the measure, that, after all the exertions and influence of the most distinguished patriots in the house, the majority in its favour was not very large.

During the same session, that this unpleasant business was settled, other proofs were given of the close attention that was paid† to every step of an encroaching administration.—Otis was made chairman of a committee, to examine if any acts of parliament had been inserted in the province law book, by order of the governor and council; and, also,

---

* Massachusetts State Papers, p. 99. In connexion with this letter also may be read on the next page, one from the agent, Mr. Deberdt, of August 6th, 1766, to the Speaker, who writes. " Since my last, I received a few lines from Lord Dartmouth, in which he says, ' I am sorry to hear that the Assembly of Boston has *refused* to make the indemnification *recommended* by Parliament. New York has complied." He goes on to observe, " Had you been here to be fully apprised of the long debate which your friends supported in the House to obtain the word ' recommend' as a term, entirely consistent with your liberty, it must have left a grateful impression on your mind," &c. &c. In this as in a subsequent letter, he urges compliance as a matter of conciliation, and due to the exertions in their behalf of their friends in Parliament.

† The act was afterwards negatived by the king in council. But the sufferers received their indemnification from the province. Governor Hutchinson appeared before the house to return them thanks personally for their liberality. The remuneration which he received was 3194*l*. 17*s*. 6*d*.

" to inquire, at large, into the practise of issuing proclamations from the governor and council, with promise of reward from the province treasury, for enforcing acts of Parliament." This committee reported a message on the subject; they answered, that it
had been done by the orders of his excellency by
the advice of council, and referred the house to him.
It was voted, that this answer was not satisfactory,
and Otis and others were appointed to consider the
matter during the recess. This is another proof of
the jealousy that was felt respecting the slightest
innovation, and that if the administration were seeking to invade the rights of the colony; the most
clear-sighted, vigilant and intrepid guardians were
stationed in their defence.

At the winter session in 1767, the governor's
speech consisted of only a short paragraph, in which
he recommends " the support of the authority of
the government, the maintenance of the honour of
the province, and the promotion of the welfare of
the people." But there was a witness to the speech,
that occasioned an answer of some length from the
house. This witness was the lieutenant governor,
who appeared among the counsellors at the delivery
of this speech. The governor, constantly angry and
impatient at the exclusion of his partisans from the
council, recurred to the expedient probably at the
suggestion of Hutchinson, of having the latter take
his seat as member of it. It had been decided on
former occasions, that the lieutenant governor could
not sit with the board, when the governor was pre-

sent. The house in their answer, object strongly to this intrusion, and conclude by saying, " If the honourable gentleman was introduced by your excellency, we apprehend that the happiest means of supporting the authority of the government, or maintaining the honour of the province, were not consulted therein. But if he came in and took his seat, of his own motion, we are constrained to say, that it affords a new and additional instance of ambition, and a lust of power, to what we have before observed." The governor afterwards requested that the question might subside for a time. He, meanwhile wrote to obtain instruction from the ministry in support of it.

The legislature now felt it to be their duty to watch over all the measures of government, and to resist every invasion of the principles of the charter, lest an infringement in one particular, should be made a precedent for another. Their well founded suspicion of the dangerous innovations meditated by governors Bernard and Hutchinson, made them more pertinaciously resist every unconstitutional step on their part, however slight it might appear. They therefore appointed a committee, Otis being chairman, to prepare a letter to the agent, that would enable him to meet the representations of the governor. After displaying fully the constitutional objections, and enumerating the precedents in support of them, they make the following personal objections. " We cannot but think this attempt of his honour the more unnatural, as he has so long enjoyed every honour and favour in the power of his

native country to confer upon him. Some of his
high offices are so incompatible with others of them,
that in all probability they never will hereafter be,
as they never were heretofore, thus accumulated by
any man. This gentleman was for years together,
lieutenant governor, counsellor, chief justice of the
province, and a judge of probate. Three of these
lucrative, as well as honorary places, he now enjoys,
and yet is not content. It is easy to conceive how
undue an influence the two first must give.—" The
office of a chief justice is most certainly incompatible
with that of a politician. The cool and impartial
administration of common justice, can never harmonize with the meanders and windings of a modern
politician. The integrity of the judge may sometimes embarrass the politician, but there is infinitely
more danger in the long run, of the politician's spoil-
ing the good and upright judge. This has often
been the case, and in the course of things may be
expected again."

At this same session a question arose respecting a
small body of troops that arrived in the harbour.
The house requested to know of the executive, if
any expenses had been incurred on account of the
province, and by whose orders, and if any more
troops were expected? He replied, that they had
been put into quarters at the castle and supplied
with fuel and candles by order of the governor and
council; and that he knew nothing of any other
troops coming here, except from private report.
The house remonstrated against this measure, as

appropriating the money of the province without its
consent, and obnoxious to the same objections that
operated againt the late stamp act. He, in answer
stated, that what he had done, was a matter of
course, and that within forty-eight hours, he had
communicated it to them, not being able to do it
sooner. It is easy to see that in other times, such
an affair as this would not have been noticed, but the
most rigid adherence to constitutional principles
was now sternly maintained. It was probably also
their intention to keep public sentiment alive to
the design of quartering a military force upon them,
with which they were threatened. Otis, Hawley,
Adams, &c. were on the committee, which sufficiently proves the importance attached to the subject by
the house.

At the session in May, after delivering his speech,
which was short, the Governor sent a message to
inform the house, that a small detachment consisting of a lieutenant and twenty-seven men, belonging to a regiment at Halifax, had arrived in the
harbour; and by advice of council, he wished the
house would make provision for them. This shewed the dispute of the former session was not without its use. It was in consequence resolved, " that
such provision be made for these men, while they
remain here, as has been *heretofore usually* made for
his majesty's regular troops, when *occasionally* in
this province; and that the commissary general
be, and he is hereby directed to see that this resolve be put in execution."

Chapter XXX.

*New Duties Imposed—Board of Commissioners Established—
Town-meetings on these Subjects—Committee of the Legislature
on Public Affairs—Extracts from their Report.*

In the year 1767, Parliament passed the act, laying a duty on certain articles imported into the colonies, and established a board for the management
of the customs, vested with the power of appointing
as many subordinate officers as they might think proper. This act excited great alarm, and the vexations and inconveniences that followed it, were very
truly anticipated. A town meeting was held in
Boston, in October, to consider the state of affairs.
Of this meeting, Otis was the moderator. He had
been gradually relinquishing his professional practice, and the care of his private concerns, to devote
himself almost exclusively to those of the public,
which grew rapidly more arduous and interesting.
Whether in the legislature or out of it, his name appears the first in every remonstrance and struggle
against arbitrary measures, that were almost daily
assuming more form and consistence. To assist
these new acts for raising a revenue, the people resolved in their primary meetings, to disuse the articles taxed. At this meeting in Boston, which is an
example of them all, resolves were passed, unanimously, against the consumption of the obnoxious

merchandise, in favour of economy, particularly in certain parts of dress, against expensive funerals and mourning; and to encourage as much as possible the use of domestic manufactures, such as woollen, linen, paper, glass, &c. Committees of the most respectable citizens were appointed to promote these views, and the foundation laid by voluntary agreements, for the subsequent non-importation acts. These measures created some alarm among the manufacturers in England, and gave rise to inquiries as to the expediency of sacrificing such a valuable trade as that with the colonies, for the sake of these new duties, and whether it was not risking the substance in trying to grasp its shadow. The agents of the government were constantly endeavouring to furnish the means of counteracting these inauspicious doubts; which were confidently used by the adherents of the ministry, both in parliament and in the newspapers, to satisfy the public that there was no danger. Governor Bernard represented some of these measures to be, " the last efforts of an expiring faction," at the very period, when the inhabitants of all the colonies were becoming more alarmed, irritated, and unanimous.*

---

* The following extract from a communication in the Boston Gazette, of May 3d, 1768, alludes to some of these representations, particularly in regard to the Boston town-meeting, of the preceding October. Alderman Trecothick mentioned in it, was a man of great wealth, and connected by marriage with some families in Boston. He was opposed in his election, by the ministerialists; and one prominent objection to him was, that he had been in this country, and would be partial to the Americans. A writer in one of the English papers at the time, seized hold of this circumstance, with masterly ad-

The acts of Parliament, establishing a board of customs and new imposts, produced a deep sensation in the colonies. Every fresh attack on colonial rights only extended the lines, and multiplied the ranks of defence. In Massachusetts, they were the cause of measures which increased the acrimonious feelings between the people, and the administration on both sides the ocean. Resistance, that had hitherto proceeded with cautious steps, now advanced

---

dress, and asks, what is to become of the doctrine, that the colonies ought to submit to taxes, because they were *virtually* represented, when Alderman T. was objected to and opposed, merely, because he had been for a short time in America!—"I find by the late London papers, that sundry complete blunderbusses, and among others, one whose signature is *Old England*, have thrown themselves into a pelting chafe, at the measures of this town and country. I know not if 'Old England,' be a near relation to *John Bull :* but certainly all these scribblers might as well rave and ba k at the moon. These measures either affect Great Britain, or they do not. By the scolding, she is affected. If so, the measures will be persisted in, till mother is brought to her senses. If she is not affected, why need the Jackasses bray? As to Mr. Alderman Trecothick's election, I feel very indifferent : First, because I observe he is a mighty dangler after Bishops, at society-meetings, &c. &c. Secondly, his pecuniary interest, which never yet lied, requires that he should prefer a sugarstick, a turtle, or guana, to the wheat fields, sheep folds, and fisheries of the north. It is however droll enough to perceive wretches endeavouring to persuade the people of England, that the votes of 3, sometimes 80 to 1 in the assembly, carried in the teeth, eyes and muns of power, are '*sure signs of the last efforts of an expiring faction*' But above all things picturesque, is the account of one of the wiseacres, received as it is evident from *another*, in Boston, that there was not a man at the meeting but Mr. Otis, 'the president, mouth and trumpeter, and alarm bell of all North American malevolence and fury.'—'That he insolently presumed to choose himself into office, and then sat as a chairman of a mob' (consisting only of his own proper person.) 'That by his ipse dixit he passed, and with his own hand recorded, and by his own authority published, the resolves against mustard, muffs, tippets, and French cambric. That he then declared said resolves, as unanimous,' (as well he might if there was no man to gainsay or contradict him,) 'Finally that there are no such persons existing, as he nominated and published, as committee-men and trustees to obtain subscriptions!'"

with rapid strides; the spirit of the people shewing itself equal to the difficulties that beset them, and rising as they were accumulated.

At the close of the year 1767, John Dickinson of Delaware, one of the most zealous patriots and able writers of that period, wrote that celebrated series of essays called the "*Farmer's Letters.*" Before committing them to the press, he sent them to Otis for his opinion, with a letter, of which the following passage is an extract: "5th, 12th month 1767.—In my gratitude to your Province in general, I do not forget the obligations which all Americans are under to you in particular, for the indefatigable zeal and undaunted courage, you have shewn in defending their rights. My opinion of your love for your country, induces me to commit to your hands the inclosed letters, to be disposed of as you think proper, not intending to give out any other copy—I have shewn them to three men of learning who are my friends. They think with me, that the most destructive consequences must follow, if these colonies do not instantly, vigorously, and unanimously unite themselves in the same manner they did against the Stamp Act. Perhaps they and I are mistaken. I therefore send the piece containing the reasons for this opinion to you, who I know can determine their worth." Otis of course was anxious that they should be immediately published. There were no papers, which engaged public opinion more strongly, than these interesting, argumentative, and animated letters. At Otis's suggestion, the town of

Boston passed a vote of thanks to the author, which example was followed by the town of Providence and many others.

The speech of the Governor, at the opening of the winter session in 1768, merely related to some boundary lines between this Province and some of the adjoining ones. The house soon appointed a committee, to take into consideration the situation of public affairs. The number and the names of this committee will shew, how much importance was attached to their deliberations. It consisted of the Speaker (Mr. Cushing,) Colonel Otis, Mr. Adams, Major Hawley, Mr. Otis, Mr. Hancock, Captain Sheaffe, Colonel Bowers, and Mr. Dexter.

This committee reported a petition to the king, a long letter to Mr. Deberdt, (the agent,) letters to Lord Shelburne, General Conway, the Marquis of Rockingham, Lord Camden, Lord Chatham, and the Lords of the Treasury, which were dated between the 12th, and the 20th, of January. They afterwards reported a circular letter to the several speakers of the houses of assembly in the other colonies. A copy of this memorable paper, was two days after laid before the Governor, in order, " that all effectual methods should be taken to cultivate harmony between the several branches of this government." At the same time this was done, the committee, of whom Otis was the chairman, were directed to request his Excellency, to communicate to the house the letter of Lord Shelburne, which he had read to them in his speech, and also copies of his own letters, to which it alluded. In answer, he referred them to the copy which he had left with the speaker, on condition that no other should be taken: with regard to " his own letters, he knew of none that could be of any use to them on this occasion." The house made a long reply, in which they inferred very justly from Lord Shelburne's despatches, that injurious misrepresentations of their proceedings in the choice of counsellors, had been made to his lordship, and therefore that these copies would have been important to them. They give their reasons, why they have a right to presume, that the misapprehensions of his lordship, in regard to their conduct, must have been founded on the statements made by the Governor. As a considerable part of the letter of the Secretary of State was inserted in one of their messages, and thus published in the newspapers, the Governor consented, though with evident reluctance, that the whole might appear. There were two reasons for his unwillingness; first, this official despatch proved, that he had made very angry representations against the legislature, and the other was that it contained a strong censure in the negative way, upon Bernard. Because it cautioned him against " the extremes even of legal right;" and the assurance, that his majesty would give him, " his countenance and protection in every constitutional measure," is accompanied with this proviso; " it will be your care and your duty to avail yourself of such protection, *in those cases only, where the honour and dignity* of his majesty's government is really, either mediately, or immediately concerned."

Toward the latter part of the session, the Governor communicated to the house, a scurrilous piece in the Boston Gazette, alluding to him, though without any name, as being a tyrant, seeking to introduce arbitrary power, &c. The house in reply, regret that his Excellency should have any apprehension of danger, to the being or dignity of his majesty's government, from any publication in the newspapers. That they have examined this piece, and find no one named in it, and do not think it worth attention. The liberty of the press, they call the great bulwark of the liberty of the people. The process for punishing offences of the press, they thought sufficient in the present emergency; but, they should, " at all times be ready to support the Executive power, whenever any extraordinary aid shall become needful."*—" The Governor the

---

* Governor Bernard in a letter to Lord Shelburne, of March 5th, 1768, gives a long account of this transaction, and attaches to it a very undue importance, as he was apt to do in most cases, where he was personally concerned. Speaking of the message of the house, he says, " the faction carried their points by small majorities ; upon the last question the numbers were 39 to 30, the greater of which is about one third part of the whole house ; upon this occasion Otis behaved like a madman ; he abused every one in authority, and especially the council in the grossest terms.—The next morning he came into the council chamber, before the board met, and having read the council's address, he with oaths and imprecations vowed vengeance upon the whole council at the next election, and told one counsellor who happened to be there, that he never should sit at that board after his year was out. This is the man who makes such a disturbance about my using my negative, in the appointment of counsellors; the annual election of whom is the cankerworm of the constitution of this government." Governor Bernard was perpetually complaining against, and misrepresenting Otis : a favourite topic for this lat-

next day delivered a speech, containing violent censures of the house, imputing all the troubles to a few factious men, to whom, " everlasting contention is necessary ;" and concluding with praising the council, whose merit he promised to represent to his majesty.

The several letters and addresses reported by the committee before mentioned, are among the most remarkable of those sincere and masterly state papers, which were produced during the period preceeding the epoch of the American revolution. There can be no preparatory study more useful for a statesman, in a free country at least, than the whole series of American documents. The interest which they excite is much enhanced, by the gradual change of feeling and of tone correspondent to it. When the colonies first began to complain of the arbitrary designs against them, they considered the system as founded in mistake and misapprehension, on the part of the ministers and the parliament; and they looked for redress from the sovereign, with an earnest and affectionate confidence. Their first addresses to him are filled with overflowing loyalty, and with evident anxiety to secure his regard and protection. When their resistance, aided by some fortunate accidents, had effected a repeal of the Stamp act, they gave free scope to the most ex-

---

ter purpose was to exaggerate his warmth and violence; and though in this respect he might perhaps have served for a mirror, yet the Governor who was remarkable for his vehemence and irritability, never saw in the conduct he reprobated, a reflection of himself.

travagant rejoicings; although the lowering aspect of the sky indicated, that the passing cloud which had overcast the land, was only the precursor of a lasting, malignant, desolating storm. When they saw the plan of raising a revenue was to be persisted in, they were disappointed, but not intimidated; they became less sanguine, and more resolute. Their expectation of redress was fainter, but their determination to ultimate resistance more apparent. Their indignation against the colonial officers, to whom, naturally enough indeed, they attributed a larger agency in the measures, than they were ever entrusted with,* was frank and cordial. The ministry they considered unfeeling oppressors; and their respect for the parliament was vastly lessened, when they saw a large majority of it contumeliously disregarding all their representations, and lending themselves without examination to the measures of the ministers, from a blind and selfish expectation of shifting their own burthens upon others. To the sovereign, also, they held an altered and more reserved tone, because their former enthusiastic confidence in his justice and affection towards them, would have seemed sarcastic; but their language was still respectful, loyal, and dignified. Those who look

---

* The Crown officers, in the colonies, were not the authors of American taxation, but they shewed themselves in almost every case the willing agents; their representations, especially in Massachusetts, suggested the means of executing it. They procured the assistance of a military force, which they considered an infallible remedy---such indeed it proved, for the disorder was thus brought to a crisis at once, which might else have lingered for years; the patient was cured, but the Doctor and the remedy were disgraced.

at these public documents, with a view to observe their indication of sentiment, will perceive, that after a period of encreasing distress, and stern remonstrance, when the moment of defiance approached and the scabbard was to be thrown away, while their hands were on the hilt and the sword was not yet drawn, that at this moment, the sentiments, though solemn, earnest, and energetic, were still persuasive, warning, and almost imploring. Eloquence, argument, with the most masculine plainness and sincerity, pervade and ennoble many of these compositions.

The petition to the king on this occasion, begins thus ; " Most gracious sovereign, your majesty's faithful subjects, the representatives of your province of the Massachusetts Bay, with the warmest sentiments of loyalty, duty and affection, beg leave to approach the throne, and to lay at your majesty's feet, their humble supplications in behalf of your distressed subjects, the people of this province."—This style was certainly submissive enough in these patriots. They go on to give a rapid and condensed summary of the origin of their settlements here, and the charters which ratified their rights, and appeal to him to maintain and preserve them. They thus allude to the revenue acts, of which they complain. " It is with the deepest concern, that your humble suppliants would represent to your majesty, that your parliament, the rectitude of whose intentions is never to be questioned, has thought proper to pass divers acts, imposing taxes on your majesty's subjects in America, with the sole and express purpose of raising a revenue. If your majesty's subjects here shall be deprived of the honour and privilege of voluntarily contributing their aid to your Majesty, in supporting your government and authority in the province, and defending and securing your rights and territories in America, which they have always hitherto done with the utmost cheerfulness; if these acts of parliament shall remain in force, and your majesty's Commons in Great Britain shall continue to exercise the power of granting the property of their fellow subjects in this province, your people must then regret their unhappy fate in having only the name left of free subjects."—They afterwards say, that they consider a representation of the province in parliament impracticable, and conclude with asking " relief in such a manner as in your majesty's great wisdom and clemency shall seem meet."

The letter to Lord Shelburne, occupies the same ground in some degree, but the constitutional arguments, suggestions as to the policy, as well as justice of the acts which they oppose, are more elaborately and freely explained. The following paragraph recounts their origin. " Your lordship is not insensible that our forefathers were, in an unhappy reign, driven into this wilderness by the hand of power. At their own expense they crossed an ocean of three thousand miles, and purchased an inheritance for themselves and their posterity, with the view of propagating the christian religion, and enlarging the English dominion in this distant part of the earth. Through

the indulgent smiles of heaven upon them, though
not without hardship and fatigue, unexperienced, and
perhaps hardly to be conceived by their brethren
and fellow subjects in their native land ; and with the
constant peril of their lives from a numerous race of
men, as barbarous and cruel, and yet as warlike, as
any people upon the face of the earth, they increased their numbers, and enlarged their settlement.
They obtained a charter from king Charles the
first, wherein his majesty was pleased to recognize
to them, a liberty to worship God according to the
dictates of their conscience ; a blessing which in
those unhappy times was denied to them in their
own country ; and the rights, liberties, privileges and
immunities of his natural born subjects within the
realm.   This charter they enjoyed, having punctual-
ly fulfilled the conditions of it, till it was vacated, as
we conceive arbitrarily, in the reign of king Charles
the second.   After the revolution, that grand era of
British liberty, when king William and queen Mary,
of glorious and blessed memory, were established on
the throne, the inhabitants of this province obtained
another charter, in which the most essential rights
and privileges, contained in the former, were restored to them.   Thus blessed with the liberties of Englishmen, they continued to increase and multiply, till
as your lordship knows, a dreary wilderness is become
a fruitful field, and a grand source of national wealth
and glory."

In the course of their letter, they express to him
very significantly, their fears that they have been

misrepresented, but rely on him to do them justice.
At the close of it, they introduce an appellation that
appears for the first time, at least, in the state papers
of Massachusetts—" They apply to you as a friend
to the rights of mankind, and of British subjects.
As *Americans*, they implore your lordship's patronage, and beseech you to represent their grievances
to the king, our sovereign, and to employ your happy influence for their relief.

In the letter to the marquis of Rockingham, they
allude to the question of independency which, at that
time they were without doubt perfectly sincere in
disclaiming, though they were equally so at last in
cherishing it when forced upon them.

" Your lordship is pleased to say, that you will
not adopt a system of arbitrary, rule over the colonies; nor do otherwise than strenuously resist, where
attempts shall be made to throw off that dependence, to which the colonies ought to submit.   And
your lordship, with great impartiality, adds, ' not only
for the advantage of Great Britain, but for their
own real happiness and safety.'

" This house, my lord, have the honour heartily to
join with you in sentiment ; and they speak the language of their constituents.   So sensible are they of
their happiness and safety, in their union with, and
dependence upon, the mother country, that they
would by no means be inclined to accept of an independency, if offered to them.   But, my lord, they
intreat your consideration, whether the colonies have
not reason to fear some danger of arbitrary rule over

them, when the supreme power of the nation has thought proper to impose taxes on his Majesty's American subjects, with the sole and express purpose of raising a revenue, and without their consent."

The letter to the agent, furnishes him with all the principles and arguments to be used in defence of their rights, and in reference to justice and reason only, are unanswerable. It was not, however, reason and justice, but ambition and avarice, that bore sway. The first of the following paragraphs will shew how extensive and well founded were their apprehensions; and the second was a favourite mode with Otis, to illustrate the topic of property, that he often used.

" When the parliament, soon after the repeal of the Stamp act, thought proper to pass another act. declaring the authority, power, and right of parliament, to make laws that should be binding on the colonies, in all cases whatever, it is probable that acts for levying taxes on the colonies, external and internal, were included; for the act made the last year, imposing duties on paper, glass, &c., as well as the sugar acts, and the stamp act, are, to all intents and purposes, in form as well as in substance, as much revenue acts, as those for the land tax, customs and excises in England. The necessity of establishing a revenue in America, is expressly mentioned in the preamble; they were originated in the honourable House of Commons, as all other money and revenue bills; and the property of the colonies, with the same form, ceremony, and expressions of loyalty and duty, is thereby given and granted to his majesty, as they usually give and grant their own. But we humbly conceive, that objections to acts of this kind may be safely, if decently made, if they are of dangerous tendency in point of commerce, policy, and the true and real interests of the whole empire. It may, and if it can, it ought to be made to appear, that such acts are grievous to the subject, burthensome to trade, ruinous to the nation, and tending on the whole, to injure the revenue of the crown. And surely, if such mighty inconveniences, evils, and mischiefs, can be pointed out with decency and perspicuity, there will be the highest reason, not only to hope for, but fully to expect, redress."

" It is observable, that though many have disregarded life, and contemned liberty, yet there are few who do not agree that property is a valuable acquisition, which ought to be held sacred. Many have fought, and bled, and died for this, who have been insensible to all other obligations. Those who ridicule the ideas of right and justice, faith and truth, among men, will put a high value upon money. Property is admitted to have an existence, even in the savage state of nature. The bow, the arrow, and the tomahawk ; the hunting and fishing ground, are species of property, important to an American savage, as pearls, rubies, and diamonds are to the Mogul, or a nabob in the East; or the lands, tenements, hereditaments, messuages, gold and silver of the Europeans. And if property is necessary for the support of savage life, it is by no means less so in

civil society. The Utopian schemes of levelling, and
a community of goods, are as visionary and impracticable, as those which vest all property in the crown,
are arbitrary, and despotic, and in our government
unconstitutional. Now, what property can the colonists be conceived to have, if their money may be
granted away by others, without their consent ?
This most certainly is the present case ; for they
were in no sense represented in parliament, when
this act for raising a revenue in America was made.
The Stamp act was grievously complained of by all
the colonies ; and is there any real difference between this act and the Stamp act ? They were
both designed to raise a revenue in America, and in
the same manner, viz. by duties on certain commodities. The payment of the duties imposed by the
Stamp act, might have been eluded by a total disuse
of the stamped paper ; and so may the payment of
these duties, by the total disuse of the articles on
which they are laid ; but in neither case, without
difficulty. Therefore, the subjects here, are reduced to the hard alternative, either of being obliged
totally to disuse articles of the greatest necessity in
common life, or to pay a tax without their consent."

" The security of right and property," they say,
" is the great end of government," and on this head,
after alluding to the flagitious acts of Andross under
James II. they observe, that in one respect, they
are in a worse situation than their ancestors, because,
when the latter were vexed by the tyranny of the
crown, the parliament interfered to protect them,

but now it is the parliament itself that does the injustice. " This, while the parliament continues to
tax us, will ever render our case in one respect,
more deplorable and remediless, under the best of
kings, than that of our ancestors was, under the
worst. They found relief by the interposition of
parliament. But by the intervention of that very
power, we are taxed, and can appeal for relief
from their final decision to no power on earth ; for
there is no power on earth above them."

After discussing the constitutional and legal provisions that secure their rights, and alluding to the
beneficial intercourse between the mother country
and the colonies, and asserting that they have always
borne their full proportion of the cost of securing and
extending his majesty's dominions in America, they
proceed to the consideration of the manner, in which
the revenue raised, is to be applied. This they consider no less injurious than the tax itself. The governor,
judges, and other crown officers were to receive
fixed stipends out of this revenue. The people,
therefore, would have no influence over the governors whatever, since they were not only appointed
by the crown, but were to receive such salaries as
the crown might direct. " Such a power, under a
corrupt administration, it is to be feared, would introduce an absolute government in America ; at best,
it would leave the people in a state of utter uncertainty of their security, which is far from being a
state of civil liberty. In the case of the judges the
operation would be worse. " The judges in the

several colonies do not hold their commissions, during good behaviour. If then they are to have salaries independent of the people, how easy will it be for a corrupt governor to have a sett of judges to his mind, to deprive a bench of justice of its glory, and the people of their security. If the judges of England have independent livings, it must be remembered, that the tenure of their commission is during good behaviour. And besides, they are near the throne, the fountain of right and justice, whereas American judges, as well as governors, are at a distance from it."

Their reasons are equally strong against the other appropriations of this revenue. " But the residue of these monies is to be applied by parliament, from time to time, for the defending, protecting and securing the colonies." This they consider unnecessary, and they say, if the government supposes they are backward in defending themselves, or securing his majesty's territories in America " it must have been egregiously misinformed." They proceed to speak against a standing army, which is particularly obnoxious and useless in the colonies ; even " if it be admitted that there may be some necessity for them in the conquered province of Canada, where the exercise of the Romish religion, so destructive to civil society, is allowed." They thus conclude their observations on this topic of a military force. " There is an *English* affection in the colonists towards the mother country, which will forever keep them connected with her, to every valuable purpose, unless it shall be erased by repeated unkind usage on her part. As Englishmen, as well as British subjects, they have an aversion to an unnecessary standing army, which they look upon as dangerous to their civil liberties; and considering the examples of ancient times, it seems a little surprising, that a mother state should trust large bodies of troops in her colonies, at so great a distance from her, lest in process of time, when the spirits of the people shall be depressed by the military power, another Cæsar should arise and usurp the authority of his master."

On the subject of the new officers of customs, they urge forcible objections. " In general, innovations are dangerous; the unnecessary increase of crown officers is most certainly so. These gentlemen are authorized to appoint as many as they shall think proper, without limitation. This will probably be attended with undesirable effects, an host of pensioners, by the arts they may use, may in time become as dangerous to the liberties of the people as an army of soldiers; for there is a way of subduing a people by art, as well as by arms."

They dwell with great earnestness on " the act for supending the legislative power of the assembly of New York on a certain condition." After several comments upon it, they ask : "What is the plain language of such a suspension ? We can discover no more or less in it than this : If the American assemblies refuse to grant as much of their own and their constituents' money, as shall from time to time be enjoined aud prescribed by the parliament, besides

what the parliament directly taxes them, they shall
no longer have any legislative authority; but if they
comply with what is prescribed, they may still be
allowed to legislate under their charter restrictions.
Does not political death and annihilation stare us in
the face as strongly on one supposition as the other?
Equally, in case of compliance, as of non-compli-
ance?"

Their religious prejudice against the catholics
was shewn in speaking of Canada, but the same feeling, when exhibited on the subject of the protestant
bishops, had substantial reasons for its excuse. In
enumerating the impending evils, a standing army,
commissioners of the customs, &c. they come to this
grievance. "The establishment of a protestant
episcopate, in America, is also very zealously contended for; and it is very alarming to a people,
whose fathers, from the hardships which they suffered under such an establishment, were obliged to fly
their native country, into a wilderness, in order peaceably to enjoy their privileges, civil and religious.
Their being threatened with the loss of both at
once, must throw them into a disagreeable situation.
We hope in God, such an establishment will never
take place in America, and we desire you would
strenuously oppose it. The revenue raised in America, for ought we can tell, may be as constitutionally
applied towards the support of prelacy, as of soldiers
and pensioners. If the property of the subject is
taken from him without his consent, it is immaterial
whether it be done by one man, or five hundred; or

whether it be applied for the support of ecclesiastic or military power, or both. It may be well worth the consideration of the best politicians in Great Britain or America, what the natural tendency is of a vigorous pursuit of these measures. We are not insensible that some eminent men, on both sides the water, are less friendly to American charters and assemblies, than could be wished. It seems to be growing fashionable to treat them in common conversation as well as in popular publications, with contempt. But if we look back a few reigns, we shall find that even the august assembly, the parliament, was, in every respect the object of a courtier's reproach. It was even an aphorism with king James the first, that the lords and commons were two very bad copartners with a monarch; and he and his successors broke the copartnership as fast as possible. It is certainly unnatural for a British politician to expect, that even the supreme executive of the nation can long exist, after the supreme legislative shall be depressed and destroyed, which may God forbid!" They proceed in a very powerful strain of argument, to infer the necessity of preserving the colonial legislatures and all their rights according to their charters.

The letter concludes with a suggestion " that the nation has been grossly misinformed, with respect to the temper and behaviour of the colonists; and it is to be feared that some men will not cease to sow the seeds of jealousy and discord, till they shall have done irreparable mischief." And they add, that he

" will do a singular service to both countries if he
can aid in detecting them." In the mean time, he
is desired " to make known to his majesty's ministers, the sentiments of this house contained in this
letter." The agent to whom this masterly composition was addressed, was a respectable merchant,
and a dissenter, which was one of his chief qualifications. He received, and delivered these despatches with fidelity, but he was utterly inadequate
to interfere between two such bodies, on subjects of
such transcendent interest. A striking exemplification of his incompetency is given in his brief answer,
acknowledging the receipt of these documents. After saying that he had delivered the several letters
as directed, he adds, " and at Lord Shelburne's desire, I sent him your *judicious observations on British liberty*, which sentiments are exactly my own:
but have not been admitted to converse with his
lordship on that head; nor has he returned me the
papers."

There is another paragraph, forming the chief
part of Mr. Deberdt's brief epistle, which affords
matter for reflection. " It is at present, a time of
great confusion; the heats and animosity of electing
new members of parliament are not yet subsided;
universal discontent on account of the dearness of
provisions, which spreads itself throughout the
kingdom, and will take up the whole attention of
the legislature, so that I do not apprehend any thing
will be done on American affairs. However, you
may rely on my watching the most favourable op-

portunity to throw in your petition, which, at present, will be by no means proper."

Can there be a more striking example of the injurious and degrading tenure of our colonial existence, than this letter? The absurdity of its continuance is not only apparent, but it seems almost impossible, that its dissolution should have been protracted eight years from that date. The common sympathy of mankind will even now bring home to our bosoms, a sensation, that may afford some idea of what was felt by those, to whom this letter was addressed. Consider these circumstances. Extensive colonies, an empire in themselves, full of life and the irresistible expansion of vigorous growth, had been roused unanimously against a financial imposition, that was abrogated by their invincible opposition. The same parliament in withdrawing this act, for which even in the remotest corner of the continent they could find no footing, resolved that they would effect their purpose by other devices. The colonists were every where anxious and alert. The new acts soon appeared, not only onerous as taxes, but accompanied with most alarming innovations in various branches of government. The colony that was affected in common with the others by all these acts, but more severely and peculiarly by a part of them, is thrown into a state of deep excitement by the impending evil. Its legislature, faithful to its trust, selects the most able, intrepid and virtuous of its members to consider what shall be the preventative and defence. They report a

series of petitions and remonstrances, friendly and
respectful indeed, but most earnest, urgent, and unanswerable. These documents, thus decisive and
weighty, are ratified by an overwhelming majority,
and transmitted, with deep anxiety for their effect.
Three months afterwards the agent informs them,
that he had delivered the letters to the minister,
who is pleased to consider " the observations judicious," but he has not been subsequently, " admitted
to converse with his lordship!" He gives however,
as his own opinion, that owing to the electioneering
squabbles of a new parliament, and to the higher
price of the quartern loaf, " nothing will be done
on American affairs."—He will still watch for the
most favourable opportunity to throw in the petition, " which at that time would be by no means
proper!"

The importance of elections under a free government will not be denied, any more than that of the
price of bread, under every form of dominion. But
the paramount interest of these local occurrences,
proves the inadequacy of parliament for the management of the colonies. They were assuming the
right to bind in all cases whatever, men, who would
not be bound at all ; they were giving and granting
the property of a people, who would stake fortune
and life itself, against the illegal exaction of a shilling,
and then would not even listen to their complaints,
till they had settled the more important questions,
whether this or that family should maintain its influence in a county, whether this or that venal mem-

ber should represent a rotten or a houseless borough. In looking back to this period, the blind
arrogance, indifference, or ignorance of the British
councils respecting American affairs, seem almost
incredible. What must have been the feelings of
such men as Otis, Hawley, Adams, Hancock, Cushing, Dexter, and others, on receiving, while in
breathless expectation, the assurance, that " the
time was not proper" to present their petition! the
gentlemen were too much heated by electioneering
disputes to, " pay attention to America," but he
would " watch for an opportunity to throw in their
petitions!" How must these men, absorbed in patriotic anxieties, standing on the portentous verge to
which they were driven, have read such a communication? with what bitter mortification, what ali-
enating disgust, must they have heard such pretences and excuses, for disregarding all their instant
appeals and intreaties? How must the inevitable
resort to independence for self preservation, have
rushed upon their minds? how vividly must they
have foreseen the alternative that after a few
more petitions, remonstrances and resolutions, " AF-
TER ALL, THEY MUST FIGHT!"

Chapter XX.

The " Circular Letter"—Requisition for the Ministry to rescind
it—Refusal of the Legislature—Dissolved in consequence by the
Governor—Passages from the Speeches of Otis.

THE most remarkable of the documents* reported
by the committee of the legislature, was the "Circular
Letter," addressed to the speakers of the several
colonies. This produced awakening consequences
every where. The ministry were alarmed, and
absurdly enough, wished the legislature of Massachusetts to recall the letter, which once sent, was
executed. This letter was a still stronger appeal,
than that proposing the congress of 1765. It was
a leading incentive to making a common cause, under common suffering. It created a sympathy between the colonies, and induced them to meditate
on the policy of confederation : and to feel, that
though singly they might be broken, they would
become strong when united.

This circular, dated "Province of Massachusetts
Bay, February 11th, 1768," begins by saying, that
the House of Representatives have taken into serious consideration, the late acts of Parliament, imposing
duties and taxes on the American colonies. They
then proceed,—" As it is a subject in which every

---

* All the principal letters and addresses here alluded to, will be found in
the Mass. State Papers, p. 121 to 144.

colony is deeply interested, they have no reason to
doubt but your House is deeply impressed with its
importance, and that such constitutional measures
will be come into, as are proper. It seems to be
necessary, that all possible care should be taken, that
the representatives of the several assemblies, upon
so delicate a point, should harmonize with each other.
The house, therefore, hope that this letter will be
candidly considered in no other light, than as expressing a disposition freely to communicate their
mind to a sister colony, upon a common concern, in
the same manner as they would be glad to receive
the sentiments of your, or any other House of assembly, on the continent."

They then describe the course which they have
pursued. They say, They have represented to the
ministry, that parliament is the supreme legislative
power over the whole empire : that the constitution
is fixed, and as the supreme legislature derive all
their power from it, they cannot overleap its bounds,
without destroying their own foundation. That the
constitution ascertains both sovereignty and allegiance,
and that his majesty's American subjects who owe
allegiance, have an equitable claim to a full enjoyment
of the fundamental rules of the constitution : " that
it is an essential, unalterable right in nature, engraft-
ed into the British constitution, as a fundamental law,
and ever held sacred and irrevocable by the subjects
within the realm, that what a man has honestly acquired, is absolutely his own ; which he may freely
give, but cannot be taken from him, without his con-

sent; that the American subjects may, therefore, exclusive of any consideration of charter rights, with a decent firmness, adapted to the character of freemen and subjects, assert this natural and constitutional right."

They state, that the acts raising a revenue, are an infringement on these natural rights; because, not being represented in parliament, their property is taken without their consent. They add, as it will be forever impracticable that they should be equally represented in that body, and consequently not at all—and considering this impracticability and other circumstances, they think "taxation, even without their consent, grievous as it is, would be preferable to any representation, that could be admitted for them there." Upon these principles, they have preferred humble and loyal petitions. They also mention in their representations, the evils that will arise from having Governors and Judges, with salaries independent of the colonists; over whom, in that case, they will then have no controul, either in pay or appointment. In addition to these subjects, they have represented to the ministry, the hardship of extending the mutiny act to them, and also the mischiefs that may be apprehended from the establishment of the Board of Customs, with their unlimited power of creating officers.

" These are the sentiments and proceedings of this house; and as they have reason to believe that the enemies of the colonies have represented them to his majesty's ministers, and to the parliament, as fac-

tious, disloyal, and having a disposition to make themselves independent of the mother country, they have
taken occasion, in the most humble terms, to assure
his majesty and his ministers, that with regard to the
people of this province, and as they doubt not, of all
the colonies, the charge is unjust. The house is
fully satisfied, that your assembly is too generous and
liberal in sentiment, to believe, that this letter proceeds from an ambition of taking the lead, or dictat-
ing to the other assemblies. They freely submit
their opinions to the judgment of others; and shal
take it kind in your house, to point out to them any
thing further, that may be thought necessary."

They conclude with expressing " the firm confidence in the king, our common head and father: that
the united and dutiful supplications of his distressed
American subjects, will meet with his royal and favourable acceptance."

The whole of these documents, from which a few
extracts have been taken, are some of the most able,
as they were by their consequences among the most
important of American State Papers. They were
drawn up by Otis and revised by Samuel Adams;
and though the style of the former is the most prevalent and obvious in their composition, yet traces of
the other may be perceived. This was the common
course of proceeding when these two gentlemen were
on a committee together. Otis, whose great learning, quickness, keen perception, bold and powerful
reasoning, made him the primary source of almost
every measure, generally gave the first draught;

Adams, who saw to every thing, and blended great caution with incessant watchfulness and exertion, revised, corrected, and polished where it might be requisite. The reports were then submitted in course, to the committee, for their sanction. This process is known to have taken place in regard to these documents. A friend of Otis' having met him while they were in preparation, inquired respecting them. His answer was " They are nearly ready. I have written them all, and handed them over to Sam, to *quisuvicue* them." By this term, which might puzzle the etymologist, he used to express this kind of revision, that he was too careless and impatient to undertake. In regard to this subject, it may be here remarked, as applicable throughout, that there was no jealousy repecting these political productions. They all contributed what they were most able to do in their composition; the reputation of fine writing was too unimportant compared with the magnitude of the cause in which they were engaged, to excite a moment's solicitude. The resolve has been cited, by which these proceedings were communicated to the Governor, at the time they were ratified by the house. He then took no notice of them; and at the first session of the next legislature in May 1768, the only topic of his speech was a settlement of the boundary line with New York. As usual, he negatived several counsellors, among whom were colonel Otis and Hancock. Towards the close of the session, he sent a message, containing a part of lord Hillsborough's letter, re-

quiring the house, " to rescind their circular letter."
The house in reply, request a copy of his majesty's
instructions alluded to in his message, copies of two
letters of lord Hillsborough, and also of the governor's letters to his lordship. He sent the whole of
the letter containing his instructions, which he would
have communicated at first, if he had not wished
that their "compliance with his majesty's requisition
might have had its fullest merit, by its appearing to
be entirely dicated by a sense of duty." In regard
to the other letter of the minister, he "reserves the
power of laying it before them when he shall deem
it expedient." Their request for copies of his own
letters, as it must have been made without any expectation of its being granted, was naturally calculated to produce a little warmth in his reply. With
regard to these copies, he tells them, "You may
assure yourselves, that I shall never make public my
letters to his majesty's ministers, but upon my own
motion, and for my own reasons."

The requisition from the ministry, was, that the
house should *rescind their circular letter;* and the
penalty for refusing, that they should be immediately dissolved. The house in answer gave a history
of the transaction, and remonstrated with the governor respecting the demand that was made upon
them ; pointing out its absurdity, and hinting very
intelligibly at the misrepresentations which must
have caused it. Respecting the feeling of the house
and his knowledge of it, they say ; " Your excellency
might have been very easily informed, if you was

not, that the measures of the late house, in regard
to sundry acts of the late parliament, for the sole
purpose of raising a North American revenue, were
generally carried by three to one; and we dare
appeal to your excellency for the truth of this assertion; namely, that there were many persons in the
majority, in all views, as respectable as the very
best of the minority; that so far from any sinister
views, were the committee of the late house, appointed and directed to take into their most serious
consideration the then present state of the province,
from going into any rash or precipitate measures,
that they, for some days actually delayed their first
report, which was a letter to Mr. Agent Deberdt,
on this candid and generous principle, that those
who were reasonably pre-supposed to be most warmly attached to all your excellency's measures, especially those for furthering, and by all means, enforcing the acts for levying the North American revenue, might be present, and a more equal contest
ensue. It would be incredible should any one assert
that your excellency wanted true information of all
these things, which were not done, or desired to be
hid, in a corner, but were notoriously transacted in
the open light, at noon day. It is to us, altogether incomprehensible, that we should be required on the peril of a dissolution of the great and general court or assembly of this province, to rescind a
resolution of a former house of representatives, when
it is evident that resolution has no existence, but
as a mere historical fact."

" Your excellency must know, that the resolution referred to, is, to speak in the language of the common law, not now ' executory,' but to all intents and purposes ' executed.' The circular letters have been sent, and many of them have been answered; those answers are now in the public papers; the public, the world, must and will, judge of the proposals, purposes, and answers. We could as well rescind those letters as the resolves; and both would be equally fruitless, if by rescinding, as the word properly imports, is meant a repeal and nullifying the resolution referred to. But, if, as most probable by the word, rescinding, is intended a passing a vote of this house, in direct and express disapprobation of the measure abovementioned, as " illegal, inflammatory, and tending to promote unjustifiable combinations against his majesty's peace, crown and dignity,*" we must take the liberty to testify, and publicly to declare, that we take it to be the native, inherent, and indefeasible right of the subject, jointly or severally, to petition the king for the redress of grievances; provided always, that the same be done in a decent, dutiful and constitutional way, without tumult, disorder or confusion." After some farther reasoning on this point, they impute to him unfriendly conduct towards the country, and believe, that the difficulties of the times are aggravated by his misrepresentations of the numbers, conduct and intentions of the majority in the legislature. Their de-

---

* Expressions in lord Hillsborough's letter.

termination respecting the requisition made to them, they announce as follows :

" We take this opportunity, faithfully to represent to your excellency, that the new revenue acts and measures are not only disagreeable, but, in every view, are deemed an insupportable burthen and grievance, with a very few exceptions, by all the freeholders and other inhabitants of this jurisdiction. And we beg leave, once for all, to assure your excellency, that those of this opinion are of no party, ' or expiring faction.' They have at all times been ready to devote their time and fortunes to his majesty's service. Of loyalty, this majority could as reasonably boast, as any who may happen to enjoy your excellency's smiles. Their reputation, rank and fortune, are at least, equal to those who may have been sometimes considered as the only friends to good government; while some of the best blood in the colony, even in the two houses of assembly, lawfully convened, and duly acting, have been openly charged with the crime of oppugnation against ' the royal authority.' We have, now, only to inform your excellency, that this house have voted not to rescind, as required, the resolution of the last house ; and that, upon a division on the question, there were ninety two nays, and seventeen yeas.* In all this we have been actuated by a conscientious, and finally, a clear and determined sense of duty to

---

* Several members who were absent, afterwards through the Gazettes gave in their ' adhesion' to the majority, making the numbers in all more than five to one.

God, to our king, our country, and our latest posterity: and we most ardently wish, and humbly pray, that in your future conduct, your excellency may be influenced by the same principles."*

Governor Bernard, on receipt of this message, immediately prorogued the General Court, and the next day by proclamation dissolved it. The house had previously prepared a long letter to Lord Hillsborough, in which they say, after mentioning his requisition;† " This house are humbly of opinion, that a requisition from the throne of this nature, to

---

* This decision of the house was received throughout the province, and in all the colonies, with enthusiasm. The number ninety-two became a favourite toast, and was a subject of frequent allusion. Mr. Dickinson, just after the event, wrote to Otis as follows :

"PHILADELPHIA, July 4th, 1768.

" DEAR SIR,—I inclose you a song for American freedom. I have long since renounced poetry. But as indifferent songs are frequently very powerful on certain occasions, I venture to invoke the deserted muses. I hope that my good intentions will procure pardon with those I wish to please, for the boldness of my numbers.

" My worthy friend, Dr. Arthur Lee, a gentleman of distinguished family, abilities and patriotism, in Virginia, composed eight lines of it.

" Cardinal de Retz always inforced his political operations by songs. I wish our attempt may be useful. I shall be glad to hear from you, if you have a moment's leisure to scribble a line to, dear sir, your most affectionate, most obedient servant,   JOHN DICKINSON."

A song thus composed, is curious from its parentage. It will be found in the Appendix.

† There was a regular *crescendo* in the tone adopted by the legislature year after year, as the ministerial menaces grew louder and more frequent. In an answer to Lieutenant Governor Hutchinson, in August, 1770, there is the following passage alluding to this requisition : " In June, 1768, the house, by an instruction, were ordered to rescind an excellent resolution of a former house, on pain of dissolution ; they refused to comply with so *impudent* a mandate, and were dissolved." The Lieutenant Governor in his reply, seems to have been deeply shocked at this epithet. See Mass. State Papers, p. 248.

a British house of commons, has been very unusual, perhaps there has been no such precedent since the revolution. If this be the case, some very aggravated representations of this measure must have been made to his majesty, to induce him to require of *this* house, to rescind a resolution of a former house, upon pain of forfeiting their existence." An accurate and minute account is given, of all the proceedings at the time the "circular letter" was written; they shew incontrovertibly, how large the majority was, and how faithfully they represented public sentiment. They entreat him in the most earnest manner, to examine into the true state of feeling in the colonies. They accuse the Governor of misrepresenting them and the whole colony, and warn the minister against his angry exaggerations.

Two letters from the agent, dated in July and August, 1768, speak of the strong sensation, with which the ministry received the news of the "circular letter." They considered it, "little better than an incentive to rebellion." Though he observes, he can see "nothing unjust or unreasonable in it," yet "the consequences may be serious." He continues, "you have already two regiments from New York quartered upon you, and my lord mentions another to be embarked," and says, "it has been resolved in council, that Governor Bernard have strict orders, to insist upon your revoking that letter; and if refused by the house, he was immediately to dissolve them. Upon their next choice, he was again to insist on it; and if then refused, he was to do the like ; and as often as the case should happen. My lord assured me of his great regard for America; nay, said if I did not represent it so, I should do him injustice. He wished nothing so much as a good understanding between the colonies and the mother country; and assured me, before the warm measures taken on your side had come to their knowledge, he had settled the repeal of those acts with Lord North, the chancellor; but the opposition you had made, rendered it absolutely necessary to support the authority of parliament, which the ministry at all events are determined to do." In his next letter he writes, " I was with him," (Lord Hillsborough) " a whole hour talking over American affairs." He says the whole ministry are united in the point of supporting the authority of parliament. He tells them, " I wish, in all your applications, you had left the matter of right out of the question, and only applied for a repeal of the laws, as prejudicial to the colonies and mother country. And my lord assured me, he should have obtained it, which now with him is a matter of doubt." His lordship is fully sensible of the mischiefs which will arise from a breach with the colonies, " but that the laws must be supported to prevent falling into a state of anarchy." He mentions the measure of sending troops to America, and says, " I expressed my fears that some arbitrary transactions of the military might be a means of inflaming the people." He seems however to have been quieted : " his lordship assured me, they had strict orders to preserve the peace, and act in concert with the civil magistrate."

There is nothing in Mr. Deberdt's letter to shew, that he was not the dupe of Lord Hillsborough's pretty protestations. Nothing, however, could be more insulting than this language, to those men, to whom these professions were transmitted, because it supposed a degree of credulity incompatible with only a moderate share of understanding. Mr. Deberdt was entirely out of his element in this agency, the habitual deference of most persons of his standing in England, to mere titled rank, prevents the due exercise of the faculties in their presence ; and the talking a *"whole hour with his lordship,"* seems to have prepared his mind for any belief whatever. With Hillsborough for a minister, and Bernard for a Governor, the affairs of the colonies would have been brought sooner to a crisis, which was retarded under the agency of Lords Shelburne and Dartmouth. The absurd and inconsistent statements of the Governor, that the whole country was on the eve of a rebellion, and yet there was no opposition, except what was caused by " a few dissatisfied leaders of an expiring faction," was acted upon in a kindred spirit, by this incompetent and blundering minister. A military force was the infallible remedy confided in by both. The proposition that one house should rescind the " executed" transactions of another, had something ludicrous in its very terms. The punishment for their contumacy, that they should be dissolved, was evidently

devised by some one wholly ignorant of the circumstances of the country, and who thought it would be
as serious an injury to the members, as such an operation would be to the members of the English
Parliament : when in fact, the only effect here
would have been, after two or three experiments,
to have procured a legislature unanimous in their
opposition.

Lord Hillsborough possessed a great deal of that
systematic duplicity,* and courtier-like flattery, which
have too often been mistaken by monarchs for the
substantial qualifications of statesmen. His measures, as secretary for the colonies, aggravated every
difficulty. Otis had seen so much of his mismanagement, that he felt a strong contempt for him, which
was expressed on several occasions. It has been
already regretted, that there are no reports of any
of his speeches; yet occasionally some contemporary,
the survivor of his generation, can recall some passage, that had made a strong impression from its
humour or peculiarity. One or two of these may
be cited, relating to Lord Hillsborough. At the
time the measures in regard to the circular letter
were under debate, and he was speaking in the most

---

* His power in this way must have been considerable, since he was
able to deceive even the sagacity of Franklin. When the latter was prosecut-
ing his favourite scheme of a great settlement on the Ohio, Hillsborough advised, with a warm appearance of friendship, to extend his demand for land.
' Ask for more,' said he, ' ask for enough for a province.'—This he did in order
to defeat his object by its extravagance. A very frank and amusing display of
Franklin's vexation on this subject, may be seen in the letter to his son giving
an account of it, as also of his paying him in his own coin, in an interchange
of flattery during an interview at Oxford.

animated manner of what was required of them by
the ministry; he asked with the most emphatic expression of contempt: " and who are these ministers? The very frippery and foppery of France,
the mere outsides of monkeys!"* On another occasion, after the legislature had been adjourned to

---

* These contemptuous expressions were related by the venerable Dr. Dan-
forth, who remembered them from their singularity. They probably occurred
in a speech, of which Governor Bernard gives the following account, in his
letter to the earl of Hillsborough, of June 25th, 1768. " In the afternoon,
when the messages, &c. (this was the message that communicated Lord Hillsborough s order to *rescind* the circular letter,) were read a second time. Otis
made a speech near two hours long, of the most violent and virulent nature.
He abused all persons in authority both here and at home ; he indeed excepted
the king's person, but traduced his government with all the bitterness of words.
He said that the king appointed none but boys for his ministers ; that they had
no education but travelling through France, from whence they returned full
of the slavish principles of that country ; that they knew nothing of business
when they came into their offices, and did not stay long enough in them to
acquire that little knowledge which is gained from experience ; that all business
was really done by the clerks, and even they were too frequently changed to
understand what they were about ; that the people in England did not know
what the rights of Englishmen were ; that there was not a person in England,
capable of composing so elegant, so pure, and so nervous a writing, as the
petition to the king, which passed the last session, &c.

" I give your lordship a specimen of this rhapsody ; and it was remarked
that in this general censure of the administration of the king's government, no
exception was made of the ministers who favoured America by the repeal of
the stamp act, and by other indulgences, by the abuse whereof this very faction has risen to this head : all were involved in one common obloquy. I quote
these sayings from the mouths of those who heard them delivered in the house,
which was laid quite open, both doors and gallery, upon this occasion, but
neither they nor I can pretend to exactness of words, but the substance, I dare
say, does not vary materially. In another part of his speech, he passed an
encomium on Oliver Cromwell, and extolled the times preceding his advancement, and particularly the murder of the king," Sir Francis, in repeating
these hearsays, is obliged to admit, that the orator spoke of the king with
respect ; but if he had not, he would have considered it little more reprehensi-
ble than the freedom with which he treated the minister and governor. The
speech of ' two hours' by Otis on this occasion was one of his most masterly
harangues.

Cambridge, as will be presently described, it was said in favour of some measure, that it was taken by advice of council. In noticing this justification, Otis exclaimed, " aye, by advice of council forsooth! and so it goes, and so we are to be ruined! The council are governed by his excellency, his excellency by lord Hillsborough, lord Hillsborough by his majesty, his majesty by lord Bute, and lord Bute by the Lord knows who. This recalls to mind what used to be said when I was a student in this place. It was observed at that time, that the president directed the scholars how they should act, madam directed the president, Titus their black servant governed madam, and the devil prompted Titus!"

Chapter XXX.

Seizures by the Commissioners—Town-meeting—Arrival of the Troops—Feelings of the people—Refusal of the inhabitants to join in amusements with the Crown officers—Meeting of the legislature in 1769—Proceedings relative to the army in Boston—Legislature adjourned to Cambridge—Protest—Answer to the Governor's requisitions—Recall of Governor Bernard—His administration.

On the 10th day of June, a vessel belonging to Mr. Hancock was seized by the commissioners of the customs, in a very violent and insulting manner.

Several barges from a ship of war took possession of the vessel, towed it from the wharf, and anchored it under cover of the guns of the Romney ship of war.   The inhabitants considered this act, as particularly designed to mortify the chief merchant, and one of the most distinguished patriots of the town. A mob assembled, assaulted some of the Custom-House officers, and burnt the collector's boat.   The next day, the officers retired to the castle, declaring that they did not consider their lives safe in the town.   This affair was doubtless concerted, that some disturbance might ensue, to justify the employment of the army that had been already ordered.   A Town-meeting was held at which Otis presided, when a committee of twenty-one, of which he was chairman, was appointed to draw up an accurate statement of the late occurrences, and transmit the same to the agent in England, to prevent misrepresentations from being listened to by the ministry. The council, whose conduct had always been studiously moderate, passed certain resolutions, censuring the Custom House officers; which the House could not act upon, before they were dissolved.   When the next legislature met in 1769, one of the first measures was to pass a resolve, thanking the council for their proceedings, which had involved them in a long altercation with Governor Bernard, and in which they had blamed the commissioners and justified the town.

After the letter of the agent, mentioning the intention of sending troops to Boston, was received at the close of the summer of 1768, and the Governor had also said in confirmation of common report, that some regiments were expected, the ferment in public opinion became general. A town-meeting was held Sept. 12th, which was opened with a prayer by Dr. Cooper. Otis was chosen moderator. The petition for calling the meeting requested, that enquiry should be made of his excellency, for " the grounds and reasons of sundry declarations made by him, that three regiments might be daily expected," &c. A committee was appointed to wait upon him, and it was also voted, that a petition should be presented, urging him in the present critical state of affairs to issue precepts for a general assembly of the Province, to take suitable measures for the preservation of their rights and privileges; and that he should be requested to favour the town with an immediate answer.* Another committee was chosen, to take

---

* Governor Bernard, in his letter to lord Hillsborough of June 16th, 1768, thus describes his interview with the committee :—" The same evening, the committee, which was in general very respectable, attended me in a train of eleven chaises : I received them with all possible civility, and having heard their petition, I talked very freely with them upon the subject, but postponed giving a formal answer till the next day, as it should be in writing. I then had wine handed round, and they left me, highly pleased with their reception ; especially that part which had not been used to an interview with me. The next day, Mr. Otis having received my answer in writing, reported the whole, took notice of the polite treatment they had received from me, and concluded, that he really believed I was a well wisher to the province : this from him was uncommon and extraordinary. The answer was universally approved, so that just at this time, I am popular : Whenever my duty obliges me to do any thing they don't like, there's an end of my popularity, and therefore I do not expect to enjoy it a week." There is a certain ingenuousness, in the remark that those of the committee were most pleased with him, who were unaccustomed to seeing him ; and in the suggestion that his popu-

the state of affairs into consideration, and report at the adjournment the next day.*

At the adjourned meeting, the Governor's reply was read. It stated, that his " apprehensions that some of his majesty's troops were to be expected in Boston, arose from information of a private nature :" he had no public letters on the subject : if quarters were wanted for the troops, he should apply to the Council. On the other point he answered, " The business of calling another assembly for this year, is before the king ; and I can now do nothing in it, till I receive his majesty's commands." The committee appointed to consider the state of affairs, reported several resolves, tracing their rights to the provisions of the charter, and several acts of parliament since the revolution of 1688, and that they could not be called on to pay taxes, which they had not voted. They also, after citing an act of Parliament of

---

larity depended on his not doing any thing which they would dislike, and therefore it would not last a week. The latter part of his remarks shew, that with a man of Bernard's temper, a restoration of " the ancient good nature and good humour," was impossible, under any circumstances.

* In a letter to the Commissioners from one of their spies, written on the day of this Town meeting, to give them an account of what passed, the inforer tells them, that the people met in Faneuil Hall ; that Mr. Otis was chosen moderator, and was received with a universal clapping of hands ; that the hall not being large enough to contain them, they adjourned to Dr. Sewall's meeting house ; that several motions, and the appointing a deputation to wait on his Excellency, they agreed to adjourn to the next afternoon ; " the moderator first making a speech to the inhabitants, strongly recommending peace and good order, and the grievances the people laboured under might be in time removed ; if not, and we were called on to defend our liberties and privileges, he hoped and believed we should one and all resist even unt bolood ; but at the same time, prayed Almighty God it might never so happen."

William and Mary, and shewing that its provisions were applicable to them, voted that " the raising or keeping a standing army, without their consent in person, or by their own free election, would be an infringement of their natural, constitutional and charter rights, and the employing such army for the enforcing of laws made without the consent of the people in person, or by their representatives, would be a grievance." They referred to the same acts for the declaration, that parliaments should be held frequently, and as the Governor had declared himself unable to call a General Court, in the present emergency, they voted, that the town should then make choice of a committee, to meet with the committees of other towns in a convention, to be held in Faneuil Hall on the 22d of the month. Otis, Cushing, Adams and Hancock were chosen the committee. All these votes passed unanimously. The next motion is stated to have passed by a very great majority. It was in the following form. " Whereas by an act of parliament, of the first of king William and queen Mary, it is declared, that the subjects, being Protestants, may have arms for their defence : it is the opinion of this town, that the said declaration is founded in nature,* reason, and sound policy, and is well adapted for the necessary defence of the

---

* It will be perceived, that by the authority they quoted, it was only *"protestants,"* that could be justified by *" nature, reason and policy,"* for having arms. There lurks in this resolve, as well as in that of the legislature, in the observation, that " an army brought among them without their consent, was an *unlawful assemblage* of the worst and most alarming nature," a kind of grave humour, which does not disparage the soundness of the reasoning.

community :" It proceeds to say, that by a good and wholesome law of the province, it was ordered that every man should be armed, " and as there is at this time a prevailing apprehension in the minds of many, of an approaching war with France," it was voted, that all the inhabitants should observe the injunctions of the law. It was then voted, that the selectmen should wait upon the several ministers of the gospel, to request them to observe the next Tuesday as a day of fasting and prayer. After which, and ordering their proceedings to be published, the meeting was dissolved. They here proceeded according to the ancient habits of the colony ; first declared their rights, and resolved to maintain them ; armed themselves, and then invoked the sanction of Heaven.

Committees from sixty-six towns met in convention at Faneuil Hall, at the day named. They considered themselves as a body of private citizens, assembled from different parts of the province, and as such, petitioned Governor Bernard to call a General Court. In his answer, he warned them of the dangerous nature of their meeting, and repeated, that it was out of his power to grant their request, till he had received instructions from England. The convention then made a report, detailing their grievances, declaring their rights, deprecating the employment of a standing army, but recommending to the inhabitants of the province to persevere in the most prudent and peaceable conduct, to discourage all violence, and to wait with patience, till the justice and clemency of the sovereign should afford them relief.

Every effort was made to avert the evil of having an army quartered in the Province. General Gage, commanding in chief, was besought in the most pressing manner, to countermand it; the inutility of this force and the mischievous consequences that might ensue, were stated in vain. The regiments, with several vessels of war, arrived in October. The ships were stationed in a position, as if to blockade the town; and during various disputes about quarters for the troops, after the barracks at the Castle were filled, they were lodged in the town house, in Faneuil Hall, and partly encamped on the Common :* and the town was afflicted with all the appearance and inconveniences of a garrisoned place. Though the troops were well disciplined, and kept under as much control as possible; vexations and quarrels soon multiplied. The citizens were more and more irritated and alienated; while the insolence and indiscretion of some of the subaltern officers, increased by the ill-will, which they saw every where entertained against them, were constantly galling the feelings of the sensitive and high minded, and inflaming a wound, that was soon rendered incurable.

The intrusion of this military force was a capital error, and shewed a truly profound ignorance of the

---

* Dr. Byles walking in the Mall, and looking at the troops, observed sarcastically to some of the citizens, in a pun upon the colour of their uniform, and a phrase in frequent use : " Well gentlemen, you have been exerting yourselves for some time, and I congratulate you now, that your grievances are red-ressed."

character of the people, among whom it was sent.
There was no possibility of employing it advantageously, in furtherance of the object of the ministry.
The people were not intimidated at its aspect, and
man to man were always ready to meet it. But it
was not on mere animal force and courage they
relied. They knew there were certain principles of political and civil liberty, to which they
were habitually attached, that would support their
cause. Unless therefore, the British ministry meant
to decimate the inhabitants, and subject them to the
absolute supremacy and brutal action of military
law, the force sent here, must have been at once
odious and inert, as in fact it proved. The colonists, besides their own intrinsic strength and energy,
had an echo to their voice in England, which distant as they were from it, was yet distinctly respon-
sive. When they resisted oppression, there where
those, who " thanked God, they had resisted ; two
millions of people reduced to servitude, would be fit
instruments to make slaves of all the rest :" these
persons to be sure, might be out voted, but they
could not be disregarded. The cupidity of the
crown officers here made them believe, that the
people would be awed into servility by the aspect
of a military power, which only exasperated them
into defiance. But by a strange incoherence of purpose, and the means to enforce it, the ministry sent
soldiers, whom they dared not suffer to use their
arms. As soon as they came to that extremity, war
was at once kindled, and the issue, it may now be

said, could not be doubtful. There was no one circumstance that made a military force available, unless it was intended to produce what followed, a civil war. The people, on whom it was quartered, were neither ignorant, turbulent nor cowardly enough, to make it applicable. They were neither to be seduced from their principles, nor frightened from their duties; nor were they cruel and ferocious in maintaining their rights. They adhered steadily to their cause, and were capable of following and acting intelligibly with skilful leaders, well versed in all points of law, who took no step that did not put their enemies in the wrong.* The

---

* An extract from Burke's speech on conciliating the colonies, and General Gage's letter, will illustrate this topic. " Permit me, Sir, to add another circumstance in our colonies, which contributes no mean part towards the growth and effect of this untractable spirit. I mean their education. In no country perhaps in the world, is the law so general a study. The profession itself is numerous and powerful; and in most provinces it takes the lead. The greater number of the deputies sent to the congress were lawyers. But all who read, and most do read, endeavour to obtain some smattering in that science. I have been told by an eminent bookseller, that in no branch of his business, after tracts of popular devotion, were so many books as those on the law exported to the plantations. The colonists have now fallen into the way of printing them for their own use. I hear that they have sold nearly as many of Blackstone's Commentaries in America, as in England. General Gage marks out this disposition very particularly in a letter on your table. He states, that all the people in his government are lawyers, or smatterers in law; and that in Boston, they have been enabled by successful chicane, wholly to evade many parts of one of your capital penal constitutions. The smartness of debate will say, that this knowledge ought to teach them more clearly the rights of legislature, their obligations to obedience and the penalties of rebellion. All this is mighty well. But my honourable and learned friend on the floor, (the Attorney General) who condescends to mark what I say for animadversion, will disdain that ground. He has heard, as well as I, that when great honours and great emoluments do not win over this knowledge to the service of the state, it is a formidable adversary to government,

army, in their absurd employment, was made first
odious, then ludicrous, and eventually captive. Even
from the very moment of their arrival, the strong
language used at a subsequent period by General
Lee, to his friend General Gage, was perfectly true,
" they stood on such cursed bad ground, that it was
washing from under them every minute."

The sentiments of respect and good will, which
had existed but a very few years before, towards
the British army, the ardour and cheerfulness, with
which they had been received, and the fellow feeling that led the colonists to share all their dangers,
and exult in all their triumphs, was now forever
gone. Personal civility was still shewn to individuals among them, but with the exception of the
crown officers, who had been so solicitous for their
introduction, they were, as a body, regarded with

If the spirit be not tamed and broken by these happy methods, it is stubborn
and litigious. *Abeunt studia in mores.* This study renders men acute, in-
quisitive, dexterous, prompt in attack, ready in defence, full of resources."

General Gage wrote to the ministry ; " When the houses were ready to receive the troops, the officers were threatened with the clause of the mutiny
act against officers, who presume to take upon themselves to quarter troops,
&c. and to prevent their being put to any trouble on that account by pervert-
ing the act in that particular, as had been done in so many others, Governor
Bernard gave a particular warrant to a commissary, against whom no action
could lie, to quarter the soldiers in the houses fitted for their reception. I
would take the liberty, my lord, to represent, that the clause in question is
by no means calculated for the circumstances of this country, where every
man studies law, and interprets the laws as suits his purposes, and where the
measures of government are opposed by every evasion and chicane, that can
be devised. An officer of rank and long experience, may be cashiered by the
management of two Justices of the peace, the best of them the keeper of a
paltry tavern, who shall find evasions to disobey the clauses of the mutiny
act, which they dislike, and to pervert the sense and meaning of others, to
serve their designs against him."

universal detestation. An example of this feeling was
given by Otis, on the following occasion. The superior court met by adjournment in November, at the
town house, in the council chamber. The main
guard was opposite, cannon were planted before the
building, and a body of troops quartered in the representatives chamber. After the court was opened,
Otis rose, and moved that the court should adjourn
to Faneuil Hall. With a significant expression of
loathing and scorn, he observed, " that the stench
occasioned by the troops in the representatives
chamber, might prove infectious, and that it was
utterly derogatory to the court, to administer justice, at the points of bayonets, and mouths of cannon."

The tyrannical and vindictive purposes, which had
oppressed the capital of the province, by quartering
upon it this military force, placed in a bright and
thrilling contrast the pure and exalting influence
that pervaded society. If the opposition to the
measures of the government had been only " the last
efforts of an expiring faction," the imposing appearance of these disciplined regiments; the blandishments
of an accomplished military retinue; accompanied
with all that was most agreeable in the ' pomp and
circumstance of war,' would have dissipated the
frowns and ill-will of the inhabitants, and won them
over, to a cheerful interchange of civility. But the
state of public feeling was demonstrated, as well by
the common aspect and movements of society, as by
official protests and remonstrances. A virtuous.

brave and enlightened people, saw the chains that
were prepared for them, and neither snares nor
threats, neither force nor seduction, could make
them waver for a moment in their design of resistance. An union of sentiment, founded on the purest
and noblest qualities of human nature, blended all
classes of society in one common disposition. While
the country was in danger, while its defenders were
in deep anxiety, amusements, that would have been
at other times innocent and congenial, were fore-
gone; especially, if they were to be partaken
with those, who were held to be the instruments of
despotism. A striking example of the prevalence of
these principles was given the winter after the
British troops arrived. Some of the crown officers,
who thought the public gloom disloyal, circulated a
proposal for a regular series of dancing assemblies,
with the insidious design of engaging the higher
classes in fashionable festivity, to falsify the asser-
tions of the prevailing distress; and also, to undermine
the stern reserve that was maintained towards the
army, and thereby allay the indignation against the
system which they were sent to enforce. But out
of the contracted limits of their own circle, they
could not obtain the presence of any ladies. Elegant
manners, gay uniforms, animating bands of music,
the natural impulse of youth, all were resisted. The
women of Boston, on this occasion, refused to join in
ostentatious gaiety, while their country was in mourning.*

---

* The following extracts are taken from the American Gazette, published
periodically in London, which contains a regular journal of occurrences in

How finely does this circumstance illustrate the
character of those heroic times! On how many
occasions did the noble minded women of America,
shew themselves worthy of being respected and
cherished! Their sex indeed, is not called upon to
take an active part in public affairs. In ordinary
times, their voluntary interference in political concerns
is very rarely acceptable, and always liable to be
misconstrued. Their exclusion from the irritating
cares of common politics has the fortunate tendency,
to prevent the bitterness of party spirit from invading and overwhelming the scenes of domestic quiet,
and of social intercourse. But in eras of great national trial, when the whole fabric of liberty, prosperity, and honour, is in danger; if women, either
through ignorance or corruption, then hesitate in

Boston. *December* 10*th*, 1768. While the friends of the country are recommending and countenancing by their example, the strictest economy, commissioner Paxton and company are endeavouring to establish a weekly and brilliant assembly at Concert Hall ; where the board is again held in the day time,
and a centinel placed for their guard : one of their livery boatmen has waited
upon the gentlemen and ladies of the town, with proposals and a subscription
paper ; which, to use a courtly phrase, has been almost universally treated
with the contempt it deserves.

December 23.—It may now be said, that the governor and commissioners
have the last night had a sort of assembly at Concert Hall. Never were the
gentlemen concerned more liberal in their invitations ; even the ladies who declined subscribing had their cards ; the neighbouring towns were reconnoitred
for females, and the good-natured solicitor for the Board of Commissioners,
was so complaisant as to offer to go as far as Salem, to bring two damsels
from thence : their efforts were finally so successful as to procure from among
themselves and their connections, about ten or twelve unmarried ladies, whose
quality and merits have since been related, with the sprightly humour of a
military gallant. There was indeed a numerous and blazing appearance of
men, but the ladies of all ages and conditions so few, that the most precise
puritan could not find his heart to charge the assembly with being guilty of the
crime of mixed dancing."

their predilections; if they will smile on the feathered, embroidered, foreign aggressor, in preference
to the plain and manly defender of his country, that
country is, or will be soon, enslaved, or else possessed by men little superior to a reckless banditti. It
is at epochs like that of the American revolution,
when the opinions of women, secluded as they are
from the struggle of political life, become of importance to a cause; when they help to animate and sustain men through every perilous chance of fortune.
Such was the virtuous course, such the benign influence of American women, at this momentous period.
Their conduct shewed, that their country and themselves were worth defending; their national sympathy gave a glow to all the charities of kindred,
stimulated patriotism by its applause, and rewarded
it with their affection.

After the legislature was dissolved, in the summer
of 1768, the governor declined calling another, and
the regular winter session therefore did not take
place. A new legislature was summoned in 1769,
and met at the usual time, the last Wednesday of
May. As soon as the house was organized, Otis was
made chairman of a committee to remonstrate against
the armed force that occupied the town, and immediately surrounded the place of their meeting; and
to request the governor to give prompt orders
for the removal of this force " by sea and land, out
of this port, and the gates of this city, during the
session." The same committee reported a protest
and resolutions against this armament, declaring that

they took their part in the elections of the day from necessity—and their having done so, while an armed force remained in the town, "was not to be considered a precedent, or construed as a voluntary receding of the house from their constitutional claim." The answer of the governor was laconic: "Gentlemen, I have no authority over his majesty's ships in this port, or his troops in this town; nor can I give any orders for the removal of the same."

Otis, and his father, who had been again negatived as a counsellor, together with Hawley, Hancock, Adams, Preble and Warren, were the committee for answering this speech. They began by declaring their opinion, that his excellency is the king's lieutenant and captain general, and commander in chief within the province, and in as ample a manner, as his lieutenant in Ireland or any other dominion appertaining to the realm. It thence follows that all officers, civil and military, are under his controul, at least, so far as is necessary to the security of the privileges of the house. They admitted the king's prerogative to order his forces whither he pleased. That to destine the fleets and march the armies of the state to any part of the world, where they may be necessary for the defence and preservation of the society, belongs to the crown; yet it is impossible to believe, that a military power, or a standing army, procured and stationed here, in consequence of misrepresentations of the duty and loyalty of his majesty's subjects of the province, and suddenly quartered, not only contrary to act of par-

liament, and to every principle of reason, justice and
equity, but accompanied with every mark of contempt, reproach and insult, to as brave and loyal a
people as ever served a prince, can be uncontrolable by the Supreme Executive of the Province;
which, within the limits of the same, is the full and
just representative of the supreme executive of the
whole empire.

"It is well known, that it is no uncommon thing
for disturbances to happen in populous cities; and
such as have unfortunately taken place in this Province have been greatly misrepresented. We have
not only been told of, but all parts of the empire
have been alarmed with apprehensions of danger to
his majesty's government in North America in general, and this Province in particular, by reason of the
most exaggerated accounts of certain disturbances;
which however, have in every instance, been far,
very far, from being carried to that atrocious and
alarming length to which many have been in Britain, at the very gates of the palace, and even in
the royal presence."

They conclude by saying: "we think we can
infer, from your Excellency's declaration, that this
military force is uncontrolable by any authority in
the Province. It is then a power without any
check here; and therefore so far absolute. An
absolute power, which has the sword constantly in
its hand, may exercise a vigorous severity whenever
it pleases. What privilege, what security is then
left to this house, whose very existence, to any pur-

pose, depends on its privilege and security? Nothing remains in such a state, if no redress can be had from the king's lieutenant in the Province, but that the oppressed people unite in laying their fervent and humble petition before their gracious sovereign." This answer placed the Governor in a very awkward dilemma, the positions assumed were incontrovertible, and if he could not command the military forces, it was a degradation that no other Governor had known. He doubtless might have ordered them away, at least to a short distance, yet this would have been a still greater humiliation, as he had been chiefly instrumental in procuring them to be sent. The legislature adjourned from day to day, transacting no business; when the Governor, after a fortnight, sent them a message, re-asserting that he could not command the troops to remove. He lamented that they should have passed a fortnight doing nothing, and at the expence of " five hundred pounds lawful." The attempt to shake their popularity by the mention of this waste of five hundred pounds, bordered on the ludicrous; when, at the same time, he had mischievously occasioned an expenditure of tens of thousands, by bringing this armament upon the inhabitants. He said, " I cannot sit still and see such a waste of time and treasure to no purpose," and as they would not proceed to business where they were; he should remove the court to Cambridge; and it was accordingly adjourned to that place. The house, when assembled at Cambridge, sent an answer to this message, in which they begin by observing, that, as his Excellency had not attempted to invalidate the principles, which they had laid down with regard to his authority, they had reason to presume them to be well grounded. But, instead of the least abatement of the military parade, he had preferred to remove the assembly from its ancient seat, where the business could be transacted with the greatest convenience and dispatch. They add, " It is with pain, that we are obliged here to observe, that the very night after this adjournment was made, the cannon were removed from the court house, as though it had been designed, that so small a circumstance of regard should not be paid to the assembly, when convened by the royal authority and for his majesty's service in the colony." They conclude by noticing his allusion to the cost of time and expense in this session ; justify their conduct with dignified moderation, and assure him, that they and their constituents will consider the expence he mentions, wholly insignificant, in comparison " with *their* rights and liberties, and the privileges of the house," which they had been called upon to defend.

Two days after this answer, the house passed certain resolutions, declaring, that in proceeding to transact any business at Cambridge, which was not the proper place for the assembly to be held, they acted from *necessity*, and protested against its being considered as a precedent. The Governor, on the same day, sent a message, urging them to proceed to business, and specifying particularly, certain public acts, that were necessary to be passed. On the 28th of June, he informed them of his recall, in the following terms : " Gentlemen, I think it proper to inform you, that his majesty has been pleased by his sign manual, to signify to me his will and pleasure, that I repair to Great Britain, to lay before him the state of the Province." He adds, that he understands he is to be continued in the office of Governor; that during his absence, one half the salary and emoluments of the office will be paid to the Lieutenant Governor, and desires them to proceed to grant his salary, before attending to any other business.

The next day, a large committee of the house, Otis being one, reported a long series of resolutions, accusing Governor Bernard of having given, " false and highly injurious representations of the conduct of his majesty's truly loyal and faithful council of this colony, and of the magistrates and inhabitants of the town of Boston." They dwell with indignation on the standing army that has been quartered on the colony, and the numerous mischiefs that have resulted from it. They repel the calumnies that have been cast on the Province, deny that any resistance has been made to the execution of the laws, or any act of violence committed to interrupt the course of justice, except by the officers of the customs. They also enumerate several serious grievances, connected with various innovations, in judicial processes.

A week after the house received the message, an-

nouncing the Governor's recall, they sent an answer;
in which, after reciting his expressions in communicating it, they add :—" We are bound in duty, at all
times, and we do, more especially at this time, cheerfully acquiesce in the lawful command of our sovereign. It is a particular satisfaction to us, that his
majesty has been pleased to order a true state of
this province to be laid before him; for we have
abundant reason to be assured, that when his majesty shall be fully acquainted with the great and alarming grievances which his loyal subjects here have
suffered, through your administration, and the injury
they have sustained in their reputation, he will, in
his great clemency and justice, frown upon, and forever remove from his trust, all those, who by wick-
edly informing his ministers, have attempted to deceive even his majesty himself. Your excellency is
best acquainted with the part you have acted : your
letters have enabled this house and the public, in
some measure, to form a judgment. And while you
will necessarily be employed, as this house conceives,
in setting your own conduct in the most favourable
light before his majesty, we are persuaded, we shall
be able to answer for ourselves and our constituents,
to the satisfaction of our sovereign, whenever we shall
be called to it."

With respect to the salary, they say, he must be
sensible, that the people of the province have never
failed in their duty to make ample support for the
government. They remind him, that he is " fully
paid up to the 2d of August next—before the expi-

ration of which time, you will embark for Great
Britain. We shall then make the necessary provision 'for the support of the dignity of government.'"
They observe, that his majesty's 49th instruction,
which he has communicated, is a rule for him, but
was never intended for them. They are glad however to perceive by it, that he will not be prevented from signing any bills, that the public service may
require. This attempt of the Governor to anticipate the grant of a salary, and to obtain payment for
a sinecure, was a striking instance of impolicy; and
served only at the moment of separation, during a
state of strong collision, to shew in a stronger light,
his avaricious spirit, which had already excited so
much disgust among the people.

On the 6th of July, he sent a message, containing
an extract of a letter from General Gage, wishing
funds to be provided to discharge the expense of
quartering the troops in Boston; and also some further communications from other officers, relating to
the quarters of the troops. The house not having
replied, he sent a second message on the 12th, re-
questing an answer to these requisitions, and that
it should be explicit and distinct. In reply, they remark upon his impatience and urgency, when he had
not sooner imparted to them any knowledge of General Gage's letter, though it had been in his possession
for six weeks. They then go into a very " distinct
and explicit" examination of these requisitions, and
the clauses of the mutiny act, on which they are
founded. The committee who gave this answer.

was composed of nearly the same individuals, as
many previous ones that have been mentioned.
Colonel Otis, Major Hawley, Col. Williams, Mr. Adams, Mr. Otis, Col. Ward and Mr. Hancock. The
conclusion of this message, the last which the house
sent to Governor Bernard, is both for style and matter, such as might be expected from the men who
prepared it.

" We shall now, with your Excellency's leave,
take a nearer view of the act of Parliament above
mentioned. The whole continent has, for some
years past, been distressed with what are called
acts for imposing taxes on the colonists, for the express purpose of raising a revenue; and that without their consent in person, or by representatives.
This subject has been so fully handled by the several assemblies, and in the publications that have
been made, that we shall be as brief as possible
upon that head; but we take leave to observe, that
in strictness, all those acts may be rather called acts
for raising a tribute in America, for the further purpose of dissipation among place-men and pensioners.
And, if the present system of measures should be
much further pursued, it will soon be very difficult,
if possible, to distinguish the case of widows and
orphans in America, plundered by infamous informers, from those who suffered under the administration of the most oppressive of the governors of
the Roman provinces, at a period, when that once
proud and haughty republic, after having subjugated
the finest kingdoms in the world, and drawn all the

treasures of the east to imperial Rome, fell a sacrifice to the unbounded corruption and venality of its grandees. But of all the new regulations, the Stamp Act not excepted, this under consideration is the most excessively unreasonable. For, in effect, the yet free representatives of the free assemblies of North America, are called upon to repay, of their own and their constituents' money, such sum or sums, as persons, over whom they can have no check or control, may be pleased to expend! As Representatives, we are deputed by the people, agreeable to the royal charter and laws of this province. By that charter and the nature of our trust, we are only empowered to ' grant such aids,' and ' levy such taxes for his majesty's service, as are reasonable;' of which, if ' we are not free and independent judges, we can no longer be free representatives, nor our constituents free subjects. If we are free judges, we are at liberty to follow the dictates of our own understanding, without regard to the mandates of another; much less can we be free judges, if we are but blindly to give as much of our own and of our constituents substance, as may be commanded, or thought fit to be expended, by those we know not.'

" Your Excellency must, therefore, excuse us, in this express declaration, that as we cannot, consistently with our honour, or interest, and much less with the duty we owe our constituents, so we never shall, make provision for the purposes in your several messages above mentioned."

The house had previously, on the 27th of June, voted a petition to the king for the removal of Sir Francis Bernard, Baronet, from the government, and making a long list of accusations against him, founded in part on the letters he had written to the ministry, copies of which were obtained and forwarded by Mr. Bollan, and which entirely unmasked him. This petition was drawn up by a committee, composed like the one that answered the preceding message. On the same day, July 15th, that the Governor received that answer, he sent them a message, accusing them of factious opposition, of trifling away their time, and neglecting the transaction of public business. He tells them, that "to his majesty and to his parliament, must be referred your invasion of the rights of imperial sovereignty. By your own acts you will be judged. You need not be apprehensive of any misrepresentations, as it is not in the power of your enemies, if you have any, to add to your publications; they are plain and explicit, and need no comment." He then informs them that he shall prorogue them, to the usual period of meeting in the winter. Governor Bernard soon afterwards returned to England.

Thus terminated the disastrous administration of Sir Francis Bernard. This gentleman was educated at Oxford, and was a solicitor practising in Doctor's Commons, when he received in 1758, the appointment of Governor of New Jersey. In 1760, he was removed to Massachusetts. No Governor was ever better received, or more liberally rewarded, than he was, in the beginning of his career. If he had fallen on ordinary times, he might have run his course, without being remarkable, or exciting either very strong complaints, or regrets. He had a sufficient share of legal knowledge to qualify him for his station. He was a good scholar, and fond of literature; he had read much, had a powerful memory, and boasted that he could repeat the whole of Shakspeare. He was a friend to Harvard College, and when one of the college edifices, with the library, was burnt, he exerted all his influence to repair the misfortune. The building now called Harvard Hall, was erected by legislative aid; the plan was given by him, and he took great interest in its execution, giving a part of his library to assist the formation of a new one.

In his administration, he soon began to commit mistakes, but public opinion was not rashly turned against him. He entered by his natural disposition, and his arbitrary principles of government, into all the views of the ministry, whom he stimulated to continue their system of taxation, by representing, that they could infallibly obtain every point they wished. He was blinded by his bad temper, to believe, that the opposition in the colony, which daily grew more extensive and resolute, could be easily subdued. His personal animosity towards particular individuals led him to think, that all the discontent was owing to their efforts, and that, if they were out of the way, the people would submit. When he could not doubt that the ministerial scheme of revenue was unpopular, and could not be carried into effect while the government continued on its ancient principles, he did not advise that the system should be abandoned, but occupied himself incessantly to destroy the charter, in order to subvert the rights it protected. He was arrogant, irritable and implacable; and one of the chief promoters of the policy which brought a military force upon the country. He was grasping in the pursuit of fortune,* and excessively parsimonious : of which disposition, many ridiculous stories were circulated by his own household, that served to draw upon him the contempt of the public. His character was not of a kind to procure him private friends, who might console him for public ill-will. He found the people of his government, free, loyal, prosperous, and attached to the mother country ; he left them, discontented, oppressed, and on the brink of irrevocable alienation. After a residence of ten years, he quitted a country, where he had been originally received with great cordiality, decorated with the fa-

---

* The day preceding the termination of the last session, of the legislature under his administration, after the house had refused his request to pay the salary in advance, for a place he was not to occupy, they passed a resolve, with the obvious intention of placing his sordid disposition in a strong light : "July 14th, the house resolved that Henry Hutton, William Burch, John Robinson, and Charles Paxton, Esquires, commissioners, should be called on to pay the Province, 54l. 4s. as rent for the use of the rooms at the castle, occupied by them 4 1-2 months ; it being the sum of two dollars per month for each room, and half as much as Governor Bernard demanded for each of said rooms, of the inhabitants of this Province, who had the small-pox in them." As Captain of the castle, he had in a moment of public distress exacted this unworthy perquisite from the inhabitants, for the use of barracks, that had been built at the expence of the Province.

vour, and pensioned by the bounty of his sovereign,
and followed by public hatred and derision.

Chapter XXII.

*Speeches of Otis—Anecdote of him and fragment of a Letter—Cal-
umnies against him by the Crown Officers—Advertisement—Assault upon him—Consequences of his wounds—Gives up the damages—Town-Meeting and Vindication of the Town of Boston.*

WHEN the new legislature assembled in Boston,
at the close of May 1769, and found the building
surrounded with cannon and military guards, Otis
rose immediately after they were organized, and in
a brief address of deep energy and impassioned eloquence, declared how unworthy it was of a free
legislature, to attempt any deliberations in the presence of a military force; and moved the appointment of a committee, to make immediately the protests and remonstrances, that have been already mentioned, and which were followed after some days
delay, by their being transferred to Cambridge.
When they had assembled in the college chapel,
Otis again addressed them, before proceeding to
business.   Besides the members, deeply affected,
mortified and indignant at the insult which they had
received from a standing army, and revolving in

their minds the growing tyranny and the gloomy
prospects before them; the students were attracted
by the novelty, as well as by a sympathy, that was
felt with all the ardour of youth for a patriotic legislature, placed under a kind of proscription and
driven from their own halls. These youths were
clustered round the walls in listening groups, to witness the opening of their deliberations. He spoke
of the indignity that had been offered them, on the
sad situation of the capital, oppressed by a military
force, on their rights and duties, and the necessity
of persevering in their principles to obtain redress
for all these wrongs, which the vile calumnies and
misrepresentations of treacherous individuals had
brought upon them. He harangued them with the
resistless energy and glowing enthusiasm that he
could command at will; and in the course of his
speech took the liberty, justified by his successful
use of it, as well as by the peculiarity of the occasion, to apostrophize the ingenuous young men, who
were then spectators of their persecution. He told
them the times were dark and trying, that they
might be soon called upon in turn, to act or suffer—
he made some rapid, vivid allusions to the classic
models of ancient patriotism, which it now formed
their duty to study, as it would be hereafter to imitate. Their country might one day look to them
for support, and they would recollect that the first
and noblest of all duties, was to serve that country,
and if necessary, to devote their lives in her cause.
Dulce et decorum est pro patria mori. They listened

with breathless eagerness, every eye filled with
tears, and their souls raised with such high emotion,
that they might have been led at once, to wrest
from their enemies the cannon, which had been
pointed against the legislature.

A speech of a different kind was made while the
court were in session at Cambridge, which was at
once brief, strange and inexplicable. On some question in dispute between the legislature and the governor, Brigadier Ruggles, the staunch friend of the
latter, had delivered a very powerful and ingenious
argument, which seemed to make a strong impression on the members. Otis rose after him, and with
the fullest tone and most impassioned manner, that
seemed to arrest the very breathing of the house,
began, " Mr. Speaker, the liberty of this country is
gone forever ! and I'll go after it." He immediately turned round, and walked out of the chamber.
The house were thrown into a ludicrous kind of
amazement, some smiled, and their thoughts were
shaken from their reflections on the speech of Ruggles. Whether this was his object, and that feeling a disinclination to answer his antagonist, he resorted to this burlesque mode of interrupting its
effect, no one appeared to know.

A fragment of his correspondence in this year,
has been preserved in print. A nobleman had written him a letter, dated April 13th, 1769, a few paragraphs of which were inserted in the Boston Gazette
in July, as being part of a letter " from a peer of
the best blood in Britain, to his friend in North

America," but the name of the writer is not given. It is in rather a studied, though elegant style ; imbued however, with that querulous and desponding tone, in speaking of public affairs, that is apt to be found among statesmen who are out of office. It concludes thus : " Farewell sir, be of good courage, and remember, that even in these last times, you had the comfort to receive such praises, and such sympathetic expressions of emotion, from a despised remnant of a despised and unfortunate, yet a bold and generous race of patriots—tell Mr. Cushing and those other gentlemen whose regard I possess and value, that I remember them with honour and with pleasure : tell them, tell all who deserve to be told so, that there is a peer in Britain, who is a true friend to injured innocence and to America ; one who loves liberty and virtuous exertions for their own sakes, and not for the popular applauses which often accompany them. That he withdraws himself from his reward, and is preparing himself diligently for a better country. I am with high consideration and sir, your obedient," &c.

The following extract from his answer is preserved in Dr. Eliot's Biographical Dictionary, Boston July 18th, 1769.

" I embrace the opportunity with all humility and gratitude, to acknowledge the honour I have received in a letter from your lordship. At a time when so heavy a cloud seems to be impending over North America, it gives singular pleasure to find a nobleman of your lordship's rank, genius and learning, so clearly avowing the cause of liberty and injured innocence.   Your lordship's sentiments are a full proof, that the love of virtue and truth is the best and securest basis of nobility.

" The cause of America is, in my humble opinion, the cause of the whole British empire.   An empire, which from my earliest youth, I have been taught to love and revere, as founded in the principles of natural reason and justice ; and upon the whole, best calculated for general happiness of any, yet risen to view, in the world.   In this view of the British empire, my lord, I sincerely pray for its prosperity and sincerely lament all adverse circumstances.

" The Honourable Thomas Cushing, speaker of the House of Representatives, Mr. Samuel Adams, John Hancock, Esq. and the Hon. James Otis of Barnstable, desire to present their respectful thanks to your Lordship, for putting it in my power, to gratify those you have distinguished, as of the same principles and sentiments of civil and religious liberty with yourself.

" Situated as we are, my lord, in the wilderness of America, a thousand leagues distant from the fountains of honour and justice, in all our distresses we pride ourselves in loyalty to the king, and our affection to the mother country."

Expressions like these in a letter to a peer in opposition, as well as those, which there is unquestionable proof he was in the habit of using in all the sincerity of private correspondence, as may be seen in the small portion of it yet remaining, together with all

his public testimonies to the same effect, demonstrate
how sincerely he deprecated a separation, which he
most zealously laboured to prevent. His warnings
were given in vain, and contributed to his own destruction. The angry effusions of Bernard, the personal ambition of Hutchinson, and the despicable designs of a few Custom-House officers, to fill their
own pockets by exactions and seizures, were the
ground work of representations, which were alone '
heeded by an infatuated ministry, while the preservation of an Empire was in immediate question. The
absurd and malignant reports of a few greedy place-
men were implicitly believed. Otis, and his fellow
patriots hurled their javelins in vain; the soldiers
were introduced, and their presence very soon placed the dispute in a way, to be acted upon by them
professionally. The result was fortunate for all the
world : but it is due to the character of those American statesmen, who first engaged in this dispute, to
shew, that they endeavoured with equal earnestness
and honesty to vindicate the rights of their countrymen, and to prevent a civil war. It is necessary to
their integrity and consistency to prove, that, in the
outset, their object was to resist oppression, not to produce a separation ; but this integrity and consistency
were completely tried and proved, when the alternative of independence was forced upon them, by the
glorious constancy with which it was asserted and
maintained.

Otis had long been so conspicuous as a leader of the
patriotic party, his power of exciting public feeling

was so irresistible, his opposition to the administration was so bold and vehement, his detestation against those who were bringing ruin on the country, was so open and mortifying, that secret representations had long been making to render him particularly obnoxious to the ministry, and to stimulate them to arrest and try him for treason.   At length, in the course of this summer, copies of several of the letters of Governor Bernard, and of the commissioners, filled with insinuations, and even charges of a treasonable nature, were procured at the public offices in England, and transmitted to him; leaving no doubt, that if these persons had ventured on such a crimination in official letters, they had gone much further in their private correspondence.

He was stung to madness, by the discovery and proofs of these malignant calumnies, and this secret treachery.   Agitated as he was by the actual and impending evils, that threatened the whole country, and that were more especially directed, at this period, against his own province, and his own town; penetrated with anxious responsibility for the expediency of those measures of opposition, of which he was one of the chief advisers, and had long been the ostensible leader; these attempts to destroy his character, if not his life, excited the deepest indignation. In defending the cause of the colonies, he had looked forward to the time when justice would be done them, and when he should derive advantage and honour for all his exertions and sacrifices.   He was not acting as a demagogue, nor as a revolutionist.   He was proud of his rank in society; and in opposing the ministerial schemes, he still felt loyalty towards the sovereign, and affection for England; and longed for the period, when he might give proofs of both, not in opposing, but in supporting the views of government. While at this very time, he found that the crown officers had been assiduously labouring to blast his reputation, and endeavouring to have him torn from his home, to undergo imprisonment and persecution in the mother country. With the proofs of their conduct in his possession, he could no longer restrain himself, but hurled his defiance and contempt in the following notice.*

" Advertisement. Whereas I have full evidence, that *Henry Hutton, Charles Paxton, William Burch,* and *John Robinson,*† Esquires, have frequently and lately, treated the characters of all true North Americans in a manner that is not to be endured, by *privately* and publicly representing them as *traitors* and *rebels,* and in a general combination to revolt from Great Britain; and whereas the said *Henry, Charles, William* and *John,* without the least provocation or colour, have represented me by name, as inimical to the rights of the crown, and disaffected to his majesty, to whom I annually swear, and am determined at all events to bear true, and faithful allegiance : for all which general, as well as personal abuse and insult, satisfaction has been personally demanded,

---

* Boston Gazette, September 4th, 1769.

† These were the commissioners of the customs.

due warning given, but no sufficient answer obtained ; these are humbly to desire the lords commissioners of his majesty's treasury, his principal Secretaries of State, particularly my lord Hillsborough, the Board of Trade, and all others whom it may concern, or who may condescend to read this, to pay no kind of regard to any of the abusive representations of me or my country, that may be transmitted by the said *Henry*, *Charles, William* and *John*, or their confederates ; for they are no more worthy of credit, than those of sir Francis Bernard, of Nettleham, Bart., or any of his cabal ; which cabal may be well known, from the papers in the house of commons, and at every great office in England."   JAMES OTIS.

There were some further documents inserted in the same Gazette, such as a correspondence with the collector, and some extracts from the letters of these officers to the treasury and board of trade in England.*

The next evening, about seven o'clock, Mr. Otis went to the British coffee-house† where Mr. Robinson, one of the commissioners, was sitting, as also a number of army, navy, and revenue officers. As soon as he came in, an altercation took place, which soon terminated in Robinson's striking him with a cane, which was returned with a weapon of the same kind. Great confusion then ensued. The lights

---

* For these and other papers relating to this dispute, see Appendix.

† The British coffee-house was on the spot where the Massachusetts Bank now stands in State street.

were extinguished, and Otis without a friend, was surrounded by the adherents of Robinson. A young man by the name of Gridley passing by, very boldly entered the coffee-house to take the part of Otis, against so many foes; but he was also assaulted, beaten, and turned out of the house. After some time the combatants were separated, Robinson retreated by a back passage, and Otis was led home wounded and bleeding.

This affair naturally excited much attention. Various and contradictory statements were given in the newspapers respecting it. It was said, that this intentional assault was the result of a meditated plan of assassination. Five or six bludgeons and one scabbard were found on the floor after the struggle. Otis received a deep wound on the head, which the surgeons, Doctors Perkins and Lloyd, testified must have been given by a sharp instrument. The accusation of a preconcerted intention to murder, is doubtless unfounded; but from all the evidence in the case, it is plain, that it was a brutal and cowardly assault, in which several persons took part, with a disposition, that in the fury of the moment, sought to disable this great patriot, whom they so rancorously hated. If such was their purpose, it to a considerable degree succeeded.

The natural indignation that was roused against the authors of this ruffian-like attack, the animosity that existed towards the revenue officers, for their insolent and oppressive conduct; the keen feelings natural to a state of violent political excitement, the

sympathy and admiration that were cherished for
the liberal character, powerful talents and efficient
services of the leading patriot of his day, all con-
spired to make the public give this transaction,
the odium of a scheme of assassination. Pity for the
sufferer made them also impute the impairment of
his reason to this event exclusively. It is not however, necessary to believe, that an assassination had
been planned, in order to cover the perpetrators in
this barbarous assault, with ignominy. Nor can the
mental alienation which afterwards afflicted him,
and deprived the world of his great talents, in the
vigour of manhood, for he was at this time only in
his forty-sixth year, be wholly attributed to the
wound he received. His disposition was so ardent,
and his mind so excitable, that its natural tendency,
under aggravating circumstances, was to insanity.
Had he lived in ordinary times, in the usual exercise of professional or political duties, undisturbed
by adverse events, he might have escaped the misfortune that befel him. His generous and social
humour, his wit and ready talent, would have rendered his career, easy and tranquil. But he was
called upon to act in public affairs at a most arduous epoch : he had to maintain a continual struggle
against insidious placemen, and insolent oppressors :
he himself was denounced, proscribed and frequently insulted. The feelings of his own injuries joined
to those for his country, kept his mind in constant
action, anxiety and irritation. Having espoused the
cause of his fellow citizens, with all his strength

and all his mind, at a time when new wrongs and new difficulties were incessantly recurring: he knew no repose. His faculties were perpetually agitated, and he did not sufficiently master and subdue his indignation against subaltern agents, though prime movers in this mischief, yet who were in reality deserving only of his contempt. It was an unfortunate yielding to his anger, the placing himself, as he did in some degree, on a level with the commissioners of the customs, whom he ought merely to have unmasked and left to public scorn, without degrading himself to a personal rencounter. The injuries he sustained in it, impaired his power of self control, and contributed essentially to his subsequent derangement.

He instituted an action against Robinson, who shortly after this transaction, was married to the daughter of Mr. Boutineau, a respectable merchant, and left the country, bonds having been given to answer to the suit. The Jury awarded two thousand pounds sterling damages. This sum, a very considerable one, in those times at least, he nobly gave up, on a written apology being made, in which the defendant acknowledged his fault and begged his pardon. Otis appears not to have understood that process of calculation, by which money can be assessed, as an equivalent for a given amount of injury to sentiment, affection or reputation. In one of his notes published at the time in the newspapers, in which he gave several reasons for being opposed to actions of damages for defamation, he concludes with this one, " It is absolutely impossible that I should take a penny from a man in this way, after an acknowledgment of his error." The cause was not decided, owing to various delays obtained by the defendant, till August 1772. When Mr. Boutineau appeared in court, signed the acknowledgment, paid the costs, and received a discharge, drawn up by Otis at the time, and which with the other papers was ordered by the court to be recorded.*

After the letters of Governor Bernard and other officers, which represented the conduct of the people of Boston in a very injurious manner, had been obtained from England and published; a town-meeting was called on the 4th, of October, 1769, and continued by adjournment till the 18th. The subject of these misrepresentations was given to a committee to consider and report an answer. The committee consisted of Thomas Cushing, Samuel Adams, John Adams, James Otis, Joseph Warren, Richard Dana, Joshua Henshaw, Joseph Jackson, and Benjamin Kent. Their report was ordered to be printed, and several copies of it sent to different persons in England. This document† which was a joint production of Otis and Samuel Adams, contains state-

---

* See Appendix.

† The title is "An appeal to the World; or a Vindication of the town of Boston, from many false and malicious aspersions contained in certain letters and memorials, written by Governor Bernard, General Gage, Commodore Hood, the commissioners of the board of customs and others, and by them respectively transmitted to the British ministry. Published by order of the town. Reprinted, London 1770."

ments of the occurrences which had excited attention, as they actually happened, and a very close and severe examination of the false colouring that had been given to them, by the civil and military officers. It is a masterly investigation of the real conduct and feelings of the citizens, and of the insidious reports, exaggerated fears, studied perversions, and unfounded inferences of the complainants. It throws great light on the character and history of the times, and ably vindicates the reputation of the town. The following paragraph will shew, that the citizens were resolved to make no compromise in regard to the tyrannical Acts of Parliament, and that they would never cease their opposition till the whole system was abandoned.

" Notwithstanding the town have been obliged in justice to themselves, to say thus much in their own vindication, we should yet be glad, that the ancient and happy union between Great Britain and this country, which Governor Bernard has laboured so industriously to interrupt, might be restored. Some have indeed flattered themselves with the prospect of it ; as intelligence is said to have been received from administration, that *all* the revenue acts would be repealed: but as it since appears by lord Hillsborough's own account, that nothing more is intended than the taking off the duties on paper, glass and painter's colours, upon commercial principles only ; if that is all, it will not give satisfaction ; it will not even relieve the trade from the burdens it labours under ; much less will it remove the grounds of dis-

content, which runs through the continent, upon
much higher principles. Their rights are invaded
by these acts; therefore until they are *all* repealed,
the *cause* of their just complaints cannot be removed. In short, the grievances which lie heavily upon
us, we shall never think redressed, till *every act,*
passed by the British Parliament for the express
purpose of raising a revenue upon us without our
consent, is repealed; till the American board of
commissioners of the customs is dissolved, the troops
recalled, and things are restored to the state they
were in before the late extraordinary measures of
administration took place."—p. 52.

Chapter XXIII.

*The Legislature again assembled at Cambridge in 1770—Protest
—Remonstrance against the army in Boston—Massacre of 5th of
March—Conduct of the Citizens—Troops removed to the Castle—
Captain Preston acquitted—Vote of thanks of the Town of Boston to Otis in 1770—James Bowdoin chosen in his place—Otis
elected for the last time in 1771—He withdraws from his profession—Anecdote of him.*

THE legislature, instead of assembling at the usual
time in the winter, were prorogued by the Lieutenant
Governor, till the 15th of March 1770, when they
again met at Cambridge. In his speech at the

opening of the session, he informed them that the
delay was owing to instructions he had received to
convene them at that time and place, and that he
soon expected something in special command from
his majesty relative to the state of the province to
lay before them. The style of his address to them
was courteous, and without the offensive arrogance,
that had marked the speeches of his predecessor.
Otis was one of the committee for making the answer, which was short, but in which this new method
of infringing their rights by " instructions," meets
with strong animadversion. They said, " The house
of Representatives of this his majesty's colony, observing in your proclamation for proroguing the general
assembly, that you were pleased to assign as the *only*
reason, ' that you had received instructions to meet
the said assembly at Cambridge,' think it their indispensible duty to remonstrate to your honour,
against any such reason for proroguing this court,
as being an infraction of our essential rights as men
and citizens, as well as those derived to us by the
British constitution, and the charter of this colony."

They further remonstrate against the legislature
continuing to sit in Harvard College, as repugnant to
the interests of that seminary; as being inconvenient
to the members, from the want of requisite accom-
modation for them in Cambridge, and from the delay of public business, in their being at a distance
from their archives.

This subject occasioned several other messages
during the session, and at every succeeding one, it

gave rise to remonstrances on the part of the house. Some of these papers are extremely able, and far more interesting than the narrowness of the question would seem to admit. But the measure in itself involved consequences of some magnitude, and various other topics were blended with it. The real motives of the administration, were to remove the legislature from the resources which the capital afforded; which was also mortified by this removal, and prevented from that immediate observation and sympathy, which existed while it was convened within its walls; but the principal reason undoubtedly was, that the army might still be retained to overawe the town, and they knew that it was too flagrant an outrage against all the principles of the government, to maintain it there, during the sessions of the legislature, against the will of that body. Otis was prevented by indisposition from taking his usual active part in affairs. He was, however, one of a committee towards the close of the session, to answer a message of the lieutenant governor, in which he called their attention to a disturbance, that had taken place in the town of Gloucester. The answer is written with great animation and force. The legislature considered the occurrence he mentioned, as not requiring their intervention. The following extract will shew their language respecting the troops that oppressed them.*

---

* This answer will be found in the Massachusetts State Papers, p. 203. The committee were Col. Otis, Mr. Williams, of Taunton, Maj. Hawley. Mr. S. Adams, Mr. Otis, Mr. Hancock and Mr. Saunders of Gloucester.

"A military force, if posted among the people, without their express consent, is itself one of the greatest grievances, and threatens the total subversion of a free constitution; much more, if designed to execute a system of corrupt and arbitrary power, and even to exterminate the liberties of the country. The bill of rights, passed immediately after the revolution, expressly declares, that ' the raising and keeping a standing army within the kingdom, in a time of peace, without the consent of parliament, is against law.' And we take this occasion to say, with freedom, that the raising and keeping a standing army within this province, in a time of peace, without the consent of the general assembly, is equally against law. Yet we have seen a standing army procured, posted, and kept within this province, in a time of profound peace, not only without the consent of the people, but against the remonstrance of both houses of assembly. Such a standing army must be designed to subjugate the people to arbitrary measures. It is a most violent infraction of their natural and constitutional rights. It is an unlawful assembly of all others the most dangerous and alarming; and every instance of its actually restraining the liberty of any individual, is a crime, which infinitely exceeds what the law intends by a riot. Surely then, your honour cannot think this house can descend to the consideration of matters, comparatively trifling, while the capital of the province has so lately been in a state of actual imprisonment, and the government itself is under duress.

"The fatal effects which will forever attend the keeping a standing army within a civil government, have been severely felt by this Province. They landed in a hostile manner, and with all the ensigns of triumph; and your Honour must well remember that they early invested the manufactory house in Boston; a capacious building, occupied by a number of families, whom they besieged and imprisoned. The extraordinary endeavours of the Chief Justice* of the Province, to procure the admission of troops into that house, in a manner plainly against law, will not easily be erased from the minds of the people. Surely your Honour could not be so fond of military establishments, as willingly to interpose in a matter, which might come before you as a judge. To what else can such astonishing conduct be imputed, unless to a sudden surprise, and the terror of military power in the Chief Justice of the Province, which evidently appeared to have also arrested the inferior magistrates.

"We shall not enlarge on the multiplied outrages committed by this unlawful assembly; in frequently assaulting his majesty's peaceable and loyal subjects; in beating and wounding the magistrate, when in the execution of his office; in rescuing prisoners out of

---

* To feel the full force of this remarkable passage, the reader will recollect, that the Lieutenant Governor whom they were addressing, was also the Chief Justice, whose "astonishing conduct" is imputed to "the terror of military power;" and who certainly acted under the miserable delusion, that a military force would awe his countrymen into submission. The manufactory house mentioned, was an extensive building, erected for the purpose of a linen manufacture; it stood on the site of what is now called Hamilton Place.

the hands of justice ; and finally in perpetrating the most horrible slaughter of a number of inhabitants,* but a few days before the sitting of this Assembly, which your Honour must undoubtedly have heard of. But not the least notice of these outrageous offences has been taken; nor can we find the most distant hint of the late inhuman and barbarous transaction, either in your speech at the opening of the session, or even in the message to both Houses. These violences, so frequently committed, added to the most rigorous and oppressive prosecutions, carried on by the crown against the subject, grounded upon unconstitutional acts, and in the Court of Admiralty, uncontroled by the Courts of common law, have been justly alarming to the people. The disorder which your Honour so earnestly recommends to the consideration of the Assembly, very probably took its rise from such provocations. The use, therefore, which we shall make of the information in your message, shall be to inquire into the grounds of the people's uneasiness, and to seek a radical redress of their grievances. Indeed, it is natural to expect, that while the terror of arms continues in the province, the laws will be in some degree silent. But when the channels of justice shall be again opened, and the law can be heard, the person who has complained to your Honour, if he has truly represented his case, will have his remedy. We yet entertain hopes, that the military power, so grievous to the

---

* " The massacre of the 5th of March."

people, will be removed from the province to stations where it may better answer the design for which it was originally raised. Till then, we have nothing to expect, but that tyranny and confusion will prevail in defiance of the laws of the land, and the just and constitutional authority of government.

" We cannot avoid, before we conclude, to express the deepest concern, that while the people are loudly complaining of intolerable grievances, the General Assembly, itself, has just reason to remonstrate against a violent and repeated infringement of their constitutional right. In order to avoid the flagrant impropriety of its being kept in a garrison town, it was the last session, as it were, driven from its ancient and legal seat; and even now, it is held in this place, at a distance from its offices and records, and subject to the greatest inconveniences, without any necessity which we can conceive, or the least apparent reason. These alarming considerations have awakened and fixed our attention; and your Honour cannot think we can very particularly attend to things of less moment, within the jurisdiction of the Executive Court, at a time, when in faithfulness to our constituents, our minds are necessarily employed in matters which concern the very being of the constitution."

The allusions in this message to the sad occurrence on the 5th of March, are a powerful reproach to Hutchinson, for having omitted all mention of that event.

The presence of the troops in Boston had now

produced one of the effects, which had been fore-
told by those persons, who had deprecated their
being sent to the country. The feelings of reserve
and ill-will towards the army, which pervaded the
whole community, often led to quarrels and fighting
between the soldiers and some of the labouring
classes. The troops behaved well generally, though
in many instances individuals were insulted by them,
and some few cases of outrage and wounding unarmed persons occurred. Yet in looking at the chroni-
cles of those days, where no event of this kind was
either omitted or palliated, they seem to have been
under good discipline, and to have demeaned themselves as well as could have been expected, when it
is remembered, that they were quartered among a
people who always met them with aversion. At
length a quarrel arose, from an insulting answer given
by a black man to a soldier. A battle ensued, in
which the soldier after beating the negro, was, for
an insolent answer to the fellow's master, beaten himself in turn. Afterwards, when several of his com-
rades engaged in the dispute, they were also worsted,
and being bent on revenge, they reinforced their
numbers to renew the struggle on another day,
which was promptly followed by the people, till the
whole town became agitated by the disturbance. In
this state of things, a dispute occurred between the
guards stationed in State-street,* and some men and
boys to the number of eighty or a hundred, who

---

* Then called King-street.

had assembled in that street. A sergeant's guard, in passing to relieve a centinel at the custom house, pushed or struck some of the people with their muskets, and immediately they began to pelt them with snow balls, stones, or any missiles they could find. Captain Preston was in command of the guard, and he directed the soldiers to fire in self defence. About eighteen or twenty were killed and wounded,* and the town was thrown into the most violent commotion. Captain Preston was arrested, and committed to prison. The British troops were all ordered to be on the alert. The volunteer corps of the town were instantly called together, and remained on duty night and day. All the leading patriots and respectable inhabitants exerted their influence to the utmost, to prevail on the people to be quiet, pledging themselves, that the troops should be absolutely removed from the town. They succeeded in persuading a

---

* Among the persons wounded was Edward Payne, Esq. a respectable merchant, who having been attracted by the noise in the street, was standing as a spectator at his own door, at the corner of Congress street when he received two balls through his arm, that afterwards lodged in the door-post. This gentleman's mild manner of expressing his vexation, when he found himself wounded, excited a smile among his friends, "I declare," he said with emphasis, "I think those soldiers ought to be talked to." These balls are now in the possession of his son William Payne, Esquire, and may be considered an interesting *relic* of the revolution. On this topic it may be remarked, that the vestiges of that event are much fewer in number, than might be expected to exist in a town where some of its first scenes were laid. Two marks of it, however, may still be found on the church in Brattle street. One of these, is the defacement of the name of *John Hancock*, on a corner stone of the church, in the building of which, he assisted as one of the leading members of the congregation; the other, is in the wall of the tower, an indentation made by a cannon ball, fired from one of the American batteries during the seige of Boston.

brave and irritated,* but orderly and humane people,
to forbearance ; thus preventing a scene of dreadful
tumult and bloodshed; and effectually shewing the
falsehood of the calumnies of their enemies, that
they wished to produce riot and rebellion. If such
had been their purpose, this was the moment to
have accomplished it, for every man was ready and
eager for action. The matches were all lighted, it
was their efforts and firmness alone that prevented
an explosion.

The Lieutenant Governor convened the council;
a town-meeting was held, and adjourned to the Old
South Church, because the hall could contain only
a part of the multitude that assembled. The British soldiers were all kept in readiness at their
quarters, and all the militia of the town were called
out. Every brow was anxious, every heart resolute.
A vote of the town was passed, that " it should
be evacuated by the soldiers at all hazards." A
committee was appointed to wait on the Lieutenant
Governor, to make this demand. Samuel Adams
was the chairman of this committee, and discharged
its duties with an ability commensurate to the occasion. Colonel Dalrymple was by the side of
Hutchinson, who, at the head of the council, received
the delegation. He at first, denied that he had

---

* In an account of this event, while speaking of the imposing appearance
of the soldiers, and the aspect of the people, it is said : " But so little intimidated were they, notwithstanding their being within a few yards of the main
guard, and seeing the 29th regiment under arms, that they kept their station
and appeared, as an officer of rank expressed it, ' ready to run upon the
very muzzles of their muskets.'"

power to grant the request. Adams plainly in few words proved to him that he had the power by the charter. Hutchinson then consulted with Dalrymple in a whisper, the result of which, was an offer to remove *one* of the regiments. At this critical moment Adams shewed the most noble presence of mind. The officers civil and military were in reality, abashed before this plain committee of a democratic assembly. They knew the imminent danger that impended; the very air was filled with the breathings of compressed indignation. They shrunk, fortunately shrunk, from all the arrogance which they had hitherto maintained. Their reliance on a standing army faltered before the undaunted, irresistible resolution of free unarmed citizens; and when the orator, seeming not to represent, but to personify, the universal feeling and opinion, with unhesitating promptness and dignified firmness, replied; "If the Lieutenant Governor or Colonel Dalrymple, or both together, have authority to remove one regiment, they have authority to remove two; and nothing short of the total evacuation of the town by all the regular troops, will satisfy the public mind, or preserve the peace of the Province," the desired effect was produced. The commanding officer pledged his honour, that the troops should leave the town, and it was immediately afterwards evacuated.*

---

* A most impressive and animated description of this scene, is given by President Adams, in the printed correspondence, which has been referred to several times in this volume.

The excellent conduct of the inhabitants through all these transactions, was completed in the trial and acquittal of Captain Preston. Notwithstanding the deep excitement of the moment, the hatred towards the army, and the recollection of those who had suffered in the affray; still justice held its course through this conflict of passions, and Captain Preston was absolved by a jury, taken from among the citizens. He was defended with masterly ability by John Adams, who in so doing, gave a proof of that elevated, genuine courage, which ennobles human nature. To a leader on the patriotic side, the attempt, while the public were in a state of such high exasperation, to defend an officer who was accused of murdering his fellow citizens, required an effort of no ordinary mind; it was made successfully, and will ever hold a distinguished rank among those causes that adorn the profession of the law; in which a magnanimous, fearless advocate boldly espouses the side of the unfortunate, against the passions of the people, and hazards his own safety or fortune in the exertion.*

To return to the proceedings of the legislature.

---

* Josiah Quincy was associated with him as junior counsel, and acquired much reputation from his able services in this cause. When it is recollected, that these gentlemen were then rising statesmen, how just, how strong the public prejudices were against the army, and that all their ability and zeal would be useless without popularity, the value of this effort may be appreciated. The impression which it gave to many minds at the time, may be imagined from the fact, that thirty years afterwards, when Mr. Adams was President of the United States, a factious writer in one of the newspapers, tried to evoke a spirit of jealousy against him, for being under " British influence," of which his conduct on this occasion was cited as a proof.

The committee, from whose answer to the Lieutenant Governor's message some extracts have been given, seems by the journals to have been one of the last of which Otis was a member. His name, from this period, gradually disappears from public life, and though it left a wide space to be filled, yet this was soon after occupied by his pupil and friend, Mr. Adams, and whoever consults the remaining part of the volume of State Papers from which the preceding extracts have been taken, will perceive no diminution of ability, and perhaps an increase of interest, as the great crisis of separation approached. Although Otis, ever since his unfortunate quarrel and the wound which he had received, had remitted his exertions in public affairs, yet he still held the leading rank in opinion abroad.* When he had entirely withdrawn from the scene, others succeeded to his station, and if these succes-

---

* The following extract from the debates in Parliament, on the answer to the king's speech, January 23d, 1769, will shew how his name predominated in the minds of those members who were interested in the ministerial plans against America. " Lord Clare urged the danger of the colonies, hearing there was any doubt in that assembly of their guilt, or any appearance of dis-union, wished his noble friend to consider, whether the alterations would not be such as Mr. Otis himself would have proposed, and whether what was agreeable to Mr. Otis, would be properly approved by that house?" Much more was said by others, when Mr. Burke delivered himself as follows :

"It may appear an effect of the highest presumption in me, to offer my poor sentiments on this most important crisis in the affairs of this kingdom ; but I feel myself so strongly affected, that I am unable to keep silence ; America is indeed near my heart ; and if this house will indulge me with their patience while I submit my opinion to them, I shall little regard whether that opinion will be approved by Mr. Otis or not ; nor am I so narrow minded as not to be equally indifferent as to the sentiments of Mr. Otis, or those of the noble lord."

sors had failed, they would have been replaced : so
unanimously was the country excited to oppose the
designs of the mother country, and so useless would
the pious wish have proved, if it could have been
accomplished, that if " Otis and two or three more
factious leaders could be removed, the people of
America, would then generally be quiet." He retired about this time into the country for the benefit of his health, and though the papers early in
May, announced that he was convalescent, it appears
that he was not in a state to be chosen a representative for that year.   At a town-meeting held in Boston, on the 8th of May, 1770, for the choice of representatives, the following vote was passed.   " The
Honourable James Otis, having by the advice of his
physician retired into the country for the recovery
of his health—*Voted ;* that the thanks of the town
be given to the Hon. James Otis, for the great and
important services which as a representative in the
general assembly through a course of years, he has
rendered to this town and Province ; particularly
for his undaunted exertions in the common cause of
the colonies, from the beginning of the present
glorious struggle for the rights of the British constitution.   At the same time, the town cannot but
express their ardent wishes for the recovery of his
health, and the continuance of those public services,
that must long be remembered with gratitude, and
distinguish his name among the patriots of America.
Voted, that the gentlemen, the selectmen, be a

committee to transmit to the Honourable James
Otis an attested copy of the foregoing vote.

Attest,   William Cooper, *Town Clerk."*

Cushing, S. Adams and Hancock, who had been
for several years the colleagues with Otis, were
again chosen, and James Bowdoin was substituted
in place of the latter to complete the Boston delegation.   Mr. Bowdoin was descended from a French
protestant family, that left France on the revoca-
tion of the edict of Nantz; going first to Ireland,
and afterwards coming to this country in 1688.   He
was born in Boston, 1727, and took his degree at
Harvard College in 1745.   He inherited from his
father a large estate, to which he did honour, by
his talents, his sound principles, and generous views.
He was first elected into the legislature in 1756, and
was subsequently chosen every year into the council,
till negatived by Governor Bernard, in 1769.   He
was afterwards approved by Hutchinson, in 1771,
because he said, that his influence was more prejudicial in the house, than in the council.   His patriotism
was enlightened and steady, and he always enjoyed the
esteem and confidence of his fellow citizens.   Under
the provincial congress, he was one of the committee, which, on the principles of the charter, represented the executive.   He was president of the convention that formed the constitution of Massachusetts, in 1780; and was Governor of the State, during the years 1785 and 1786.   Mr. Bowdoin was a
liberal friend of learning, and cultivated himself se-

veral branches of science with success. He was one
of the founders, and first president of the American
Academy, to which institution he bequeathed his
valuable library. He was a correspondent of Dr.
Franklin, on scientific subjects ; communicated many
papers to the transactions of the American Academy; was a member of the Royal Society of London,
and several other foreign societies. He was a patron of Harvard College, and for his talents, public
spirit and usefulness, must be enrolled among the most
eminent citizens of his native state. He died Nov.
6th, 1790, at the age of 64.

At the election in 1771, Otis was again chosen a
representative; and at the first session of the legislature, he was chairman of some committees on political affairs. In the subsequent sessions of that year,
his name does not appear in the journals. His infirmities had now increased so much, that he could no
longer give a close and continued attention to business. He withdrew almost entirely from the practice of his profession. This was the last year that
he took a part in public concerns, except occasionally
to appear in a town-meeting. In his lucid intervals,
he was the delight of his friends, and his wit and talents still made him an oracle in social life. The
following anecdote, which belongs to this period, is
so well told by President Adams, that it throws
great light on his character, and brings him before
the reader in a very lively manner.*

---

* This is extracted from a letter of President Adams, in the collection which
has been so frequently cited.

'Otis belonged to a club who met on evenings; of which club William Molineux,* whose character you know very well, was a member. Molineux had a petition before the legislature, which did not succeed to his wishes, and he became for several evenings sour, and wearied the company with his complaints of services, losses, sacrifices, &c., and said;— "That a man who has behaved as I have, should be treated as I am, is intolerable!" &c. Otis had said nothing; but the company were disgusted and out of patience, when Otis rose from his seat, and said, " Come, come, Will, quit this subject, and let us enjoy ourselves: I also have a list of grievances; will you hear it?" The club expected some fun, and all cried out, "aye! aye! let us hear your list."

"Well then, Will: in the first place, I resigned the office of Advocate General, which I held from the crown, that produced me—how much do you think?" "A great deal, no doubt," said Molineux. "Shall we say two hundred sterling a year?" "Aye, more, I believe," said Molineux. "Well, let it be two hundred,—that for ten years, is two thousand. In the next place, I have been obliged to relinquish the greatest part of my business at the bar: Will you set that at 200 more?" "Oh! I believe it much

---

* Mr. Molineux was a merchant, but much more of a sportsman and a *bon rivant*, than a man of business. His sentiments were warmly in favour of his country; and though often a companion of the English officers, yet an intimate acquaintance of the leading patriots of the day. He is mentioned by President Adams in another letter, as *protecting* "Sam Adams' two regiments," as lord North sarcastically called them, when they left the town in March 1770, on the requisition of the inhabitants.

more than that." "Well, let it be 200; this for ten years, is 2000. You allow, then, I have lost £4000 sterling." "Aye, and much more too," said Molineux.

"In the next place, I have lost an hundred friends; among whom, were the men of the first rank, fortune, and power in the province: at what price will you estimate them?" "D—n them," said Molineux, "at nothing: you are better without them, than with them." A loud laugh. "Be it so," said Otis.

"In the next place, I have made a thousand enemies; among whom are the government of the province and the nation. What do you think of this item?" "That is as it may happen," said Molineux.

"In the next place, you know I love pleasure: but I have renounced all amusement for ten years. What is that worth to a man of pleasure?" "No great matter," said Molineux, "you have made politics your amusement." A hearty laugh.

"In the next place, I have ruined as fine health, and as good a constitution of body, as nature ever gave to man." "This is melancholy indeed," said Molineux "there is nothing to be said on that point."

"Once more," said Otis, holding his head down before Molineux, "look upon this head!" (where was a scar in which a man might bury his finger) "what do you think of this? and what is worse, my friends think I have a monstrous crack in my scull."

This made all the company very grave, and look very solemn. But Otis setting up a laugh, and with a gay countenance, said to Molineux; "now, Willy,

my advice to you is, to say no more about your grievances; for you and I had better put up our accounts
of profit and loss in our pockets, and say no more
about them, lest the world should laugh at us."

This whimsical dialogue put all the company, and
Molineux himself, into good humour, and they passed the rest of the evening in joyous conviviality.'

Chapter XXIV.

*Dr. Franklin chosen Agent—Remarks on certain Points of his
Character.*

The different intrigues and interests, that had, during an important period, prevented the choice of a
suitable agent, to take charge of the arduous affairs
of the province in England, at length yielded, as the
pressure of difficulties increased; and, in the year
1770, Dr. Franklin was entrusted with the agency.
The next year, a jealousy of this eminent man, which
prevailed among different classes from various causes,
shewed itself by the appointment of a colleague, a
friend of Dr. Franklin, but selected from another
province. Arthur Lee, of Virginia, who had made
a visit to Boston, was appointed a joint agent. He
was very warm and zealous in all the opinions of the
patriotic party, and therefore possessed their entire
confidence. The common adage, that no man is a

prophet in his own country was curiously verified in the case of Franklin, and there may be some interest in considering, what were the reasons that prevented the people of Massachusetts, from having an unlimited reliance on the great talents, and advantageous experience, of one of the most distinguished and the most widely known of all her citizens.

There were three causes of distrust, that operated on the minds of many people in Massachusetts to the disadvantage of Franklin. These were, his religion, his politics, and taken in connection with one or the other of these subjects, according as they prevailed in the minds of the observer, his worldly shrewdness and thrift. His deep sagacity, diversified experience, ingenious wit, punctuality, industry, economical views, disciplined temper, tolerant philosophy, extensive knowledge of men and things, and practical philanthropy, though they commanded a large share of respect and admiration, yet could not wholly overcome the prejudices against him, which originated in a difference of theological or political opinion. In addition to his other qualifications for the public service, he possessed the very useful one of a personal acquaintance with various parts of his own country and of England;* and on

---

* Benjamin Franklin was born in Boston, January 6th, 1705-6, in a house that stood in Milk-street, opposite the old South Church. He passed the first seventeen years of his life in Boston, whence he migrated to Philadelphia. He went first to England, in 1724, returning in 1726. A second time in 1757, and came back in 1762. He made a third visit in 1764, and returned in 1775. He was sent to France, in 1776, and took a final leave of Europe in 1785. He died in 1790, aged 85. It appears therefore, that he lived seventeen years in Boston, twenty-seven in Europe, and forty-one in Pennsylvania.

the subjects he was particularly called to discuss, he had that superiority, which is given to the person who has actually traversed, examined and measured a region, over another who has only beheld it on a map, or merely pictured it in his mind from description.

Dr. Franklin was born at a period, when the religious feelings that gave rise to the settlement of the colony, still existed with little abatement. His father was an honest, hard working, puritan tradesman, in whose family the son was accustomed to close labour, long prayers,* rigid tenets, and a severe abstinence from all cheerfulness and indulgence. His lively, strong, and active faculties were excited against irksome austerities, that appeared to him either hateful or ludicrous. He, like many other young men, injudiciously treated, revolted against what was taught by the narrow-minded and tyrannical, and easily fell into the error of associating the tenets of religion, with the practice of some of its professors. The restiveness of a powerful intellect, with the rashness of youthful inexperience, was repulsed by the exaction made by inferior minds, of implicit submission to their dictates. In this way, religion was rendered odious to him, not in itself,

---

* Wit was an early characteristic of Franklin, and traits of it, that should have been considered mere marks of a sprightly mind, were regarded by many as the evidence of a perverse heart. The instance of his suggesting to his father, when engaged in packing a barrel of beef for winter's use, that *it would be a great saving of time, if instead of a long grace every day, over each piece he should ask a blessing over the whole at once*, was one of those graceless effusions, among others, that left a strong tinge of prejudice against him in the minds of his austere connections.

but in the conduct of its professors. Those were the days of creeds and platforms, intolerance bore sway, human teachers assumed infallibility in expounding what was mysterious and divine, and he who did not submit in every point, was reprobated entirely. The opinions which he perhaps might have embraced, or under which he might, at least, have sheltered himself from obloquy, were not then introduced. The irreligious impressions which were given him by the bigotry and intolerance of those about him, were unfortunately confirmed by the companions of his youthful career. Some of his fellow workmen and associates were without religion, and though one of the most effectual modes of disgusting a refined free-thinker with his opinions, would be to hear them from the lips of a low and vulgar infidel; yet he was not sufficiently above them in habits and manners, however superior in talents, to be thus affected. He pursued, not with bad intentions, but with misguided efforts, his speculations against religion, and thereby rivetted a prejudice in the minds of many persons, who, if they escaped his theoretical delusions, were never capable of imitating, or even appreciating, his long and able discharge of the great practical duties that are most useful to society.

His reputation for scepticism constantly followed him, and infected the minds of the clergy and the more rigid members of their congregations, with suspicions of Franklin's integrity, and fear of his principles; which were gradually weakened by his regular life, his benevolent exertions, and his great

public services, without however being entirely
effaced. It will always be remembered to the honour of Franklin, that his sound sense and good feeling, led him, in his maturer years, to discourage all dis-
respect for religion, and to aid every thing that tended to enlarge its influence. No man more consistently discountenanced the two extremes of fanaticism and
infidelity, of which lasting proofs remain, in his two
letters, one addressed to Whitefield, and the other
to some person, who had consulted him in regard to
publishing a work against Christianity. His early
bias seems still to have left his mind in an unsettled
state, and it was a strange vagary, that appears from
some passages in his writings to have occasionally
passed through it, of establishing a new sect. In
his answer to Dr. Stiles, who had questioned him on
his faith 'in Jesus of Nazareth,' though he goes
little further than to say, that he thinks 'the system
of morals and religion which he left us, the best the
world ever saw, or is likely to see' yet religious
men who might wish that he had borne a stronger
testimony to the truth, will in candour recollect the
disadvantages of his early life; and if no person be
allowed to quote his doubts in justification, until they
have done as much good to their fellow men, as he
accomplished, the world will not see more than
one sceptick in at least a century.

To the reasons here alleged for the sentiments of
the religious part of the community, must be added
the doubts respecting his political views, which were
entertained by many of the strenuous politicians of

the patriotic party. Dr. Franklin was steadily and
earnestly opposed to the revolution. His favourite
object was to keep the British Empire together,
which he frequently compared to a magnificent china
bowl, that would be ruined if a single piece were
broken out. He had conceived vast ideas of the
country watered by the Mississippi and its tributa-
ries, at a time when few men, even in thought,
had crossed the Alleghany ridges. He looked forward to a prodigious developement of the intrinsic
resources of America, and thought that at no very
distant period, this portion of the dominions would
preponderate, and that the seat of government
might be transferred to it. He also thought the
contest, on our part, would be rash and premature,
that the disproportion between the strength of the
parent country and the colonies, was too excessive
against the latter, to admit of their engaging in it
with any probability of success. War, which he
detested so cordially as to say, " that he almost believed there never had been a good war or a bad
peace" was an alternative, that he perhaps would
never have resorted to in any extremity ; and to the
latest period he was opposed to adopting it. He
still hoped by patience, by compromise, by yielding
a little at the time, that we might, when we gained
strength, retrieve what had been lost. After several
leading members of opposition in Massachusetts, as
well as in other provinces, had made up their own
minds, and were gradually leading those of their
countrymen, to the assumption of independence,

Franklin was writing to his correspondents to persuade them to moderation, and censuring the policy
that led to violent resistance.* These counsels were

---

* Several passages from his correspondence would illustrate these remarks.
The following extracts, between the dates of two of which there is a considerable interval, may suffice. From a letter to Governor Franklin, dated
"London, November 25th, 1767.—I think the New Yorkers have been very
discreet in forbearing to write and publish against the late act of Parliament.
I wish the Boston people had been as quiet, since Governor Bernard has sent
over all their violent papers to the ministry, and wrote them word that he
daily expected a rebellion. He did, indeed, afterwards correct this extravagance by writing again, that he now understood those papers were approved
but by few, and disliked by all the sober sensible people of the province. A
certain noble lord expressed himself to me with some disgust and contempt of
Bernard on this occasion ; saying, he ought to have known his people better,
than to impute to the whole country, sentiments, that are perhaps only scrib-
bled by some madman in a garret, that he appeared to be too fond of contention, and mistook the matter greatly in supposing that such letters as he wrote
were acceptable to the ministry."

From a letter marked "*private*," to the " Hon. T. Cushing. London, Jan.
5, 1773. But our great security lies, I think, in our growing strength, both in
numbers and wealth, that creates an increasing ability of assisting this nation
in its wars, which will make us more respectable, our friendship more valued,
and our enmity feared ; thence it will soon be thought proper to treat us not
with justice only, but with kindness, and thence we may expect in a few years
a total change of measures with regard to us ; unless by a neglect of military
discipline we should lose all martial spirit, and our western people become
as tame as those in the eastern dominions of Britain, when we may expect the
same oppressions, for there is much truth in the Italian saying, *Make yourselves
sheep and the wolves will eat you.* In confidence of this coming change in
our favour, I think our prudence is meanwhile, to be quiet, only holding up our
rights and claims on all occasions, in resolutions, memorials, remonstrances,
but bearing patiently the little present notice that is taken of them. They
will all have their weight in time, and that time is at no great distance."

The same ideas are repeated to this gentleman in subsequent letters of that
year, but especially in one of July 7th, in which the policy of forbearance is
very earnestly and elaborately displayed.

From a letter to Mr. Winthrop, dated " July 25th, 1773."

"I am glad to see that you are elected into the Council, and are about to
take part in our public affairs. Your abilities, integrity, and sober attachment to the liberties of our country, will be of great use in this tempestuous

very unwelcome to men, who felt the stern necessity of maintaining the position which they had taken, without being at all blind to the dangers in which it would inevitably involve them. While they were, therefore, endeavouring to stimulate their fellow citizens to firmness and perseverance, these distracting opinions of Franklin were extremely irritating, and they occasioned a deep, though unfounded suspicion of his want of heartiness in the cause of his country.

Dr. Franklin, however, was perfectly honest and consistent in the course which he pursued. He was opposed to all the ministerial measures, and only differed as to the mode and extent of resistance that should be made to them. He yielded his own opinion to the determination of his countrymen, which he perceived was almost unanimous, and signed the

time, in conducting our little bark into safe harbour. By the Boston newspapers, there seems to be among us some violent spirits who are for an immediate rupture. But I trust the general prudence of our countrymen will see, that by our growing strength we advance fast to a situation, in which our claims must be allowed ; that by a premature struggle we may be crippled and kept down another age : that as between friends, every affront is not worth a duel, between nations every injury is not worth a war, so between the governed and governing every mistake in government, every encroachment on right, is not worth a rebellion. 'Tis in my opinion sufficient for the present, that we hold them forth on all occasions, not giving up any of them, using every means at the same time to make them generally understood and valued by the people, cultivating a harmony among the colonies, that their union in the same sentiments may give them greater weight : remembering withal, tnat this Protestant country (our mother, though of late an unkind one) is worth preserving, and that her weight in the scale of Europe, and her safety in a great degree, may depend on our union with her. Thus conducting, I am confident we may in a few years, obtain every allowance of, and every security for our inestimable privileges that we can wish or desire."

Declaration of Independence, while his colleague Mr. Dickinson, one of the most distinguished patriots of the day, opposed it. Still, the knowledge of his former views and his known dislike of war, created a fear in many persons, that he would not inflexibly adhere to the lofty ground which was taken by Congress in 1776, and that he might yet be willing to renew the union with the mother country, on the spirit of compromise. There is nothing to justify this jealousy in his writings; and he seems throughout his correspondence, to consider the measure as irrevocable,* and he was prepared to sustain it with all his efforts, and share the result, whatever it might be, with his country.

These jealousies on the score of religion and politics, were rather aided in the minds of those who

---

* A man with far less intelligence than Franklin, would readily perceive that this was one of the cases to assume the motto, *nulla vestigia retrorsum :* that there was no middle ground, that the choice lay between taking " a stand among the nations of the earth," or acquiescing in the most hopeless, degrading subserviency. The following extracts from letters will shew what he thought of a federal union with England. From a letter to Dr. Ingenhouz, dated " Passy, June 21st, 1782. England at length sees the difficulty of conquering us, and no longer demands submission, but asks for peace. She would now think herself happy to obtain a federal union with us, and will endeavour it : but perhaps will be disappointed, as it is for the interest of all Europe to prevent it." On the 28th of the same month, he wrote to Mr. Livingston, " *The king hates us most cordially.* If he is ever admitted to any degree of power or government amongst us, *however limited,* it will soon be extended by corruption, artifice, and force, till we are reduced to absolute subjection ; and the more easily, as by receiving him again for our king, we shall draw upon ourselves the contempt of all Europe, who now admire and respect us ; and we shall never again find a kind friend to assist us." There is something in the air of these sentences, that look as if they had been written after a representation of the French ministry against such a scheme, which indeed at that period, no person could seriously have expected to realize.

harboured either the one or the other, by his great shrewdness and success in worldly affairs, and his personal relations with the British government. He, himself, held for many years the office of post-master general in the colonies, which was in the gift of the crown. His son was the Governor of New Jersey, and a zealous promoter of the views of the ministry.

The place of distributors of stamps, in Pennsylvania and New Jersey, though he had opposed the act, yet had been given on his recommendation, when his countrymen thought its very touch pollution. He had also solicited some extensive favours in the project for settling the Ohio territory. The skill and industry which he had discovered in acquiring a fortune, amidst all his engagements in politics and scientific pursuits, were reasons with many persons to suspect that his connexions with, and expectations from the British government, might be obstacles in the way of his supporting the interests of his constituents against their designs. Yet in England they complained, that notwithstanding all these favours, he was inveterately opposing all the measures of the ministers.*

---

* He turned these complaints into ridicule, just before he left England in 1774, by one of his ingenious apologues, in the following communication; " To the printer of the Public Advertiser; Sir, your correspondent Brittanicus inveighs violently against Dr. Franklin, for his ingratitude to the ministry of this nation, who have conferred upon him so many favours. They gave him the post office of America; they made his son a governor; and they offered him a post of five hundred a year in the salt office, if he would relinquish the interests of his country; but he has had the wickedness to continue true to it,

Franklin long endeavoured to conciliate the king, and to persuade him to give his cordial protection to the colonies, and to govern them by the aid of their local parliaments, as he governed Britain through the intervention of the English parliament. He sought to convince the sovereign,* that in this way he might receive all the supplies he wanted; that the colonial legislatures would grant his applications with cheerful liberality, while they never would submit to have their property voted away by a body,

---

and is as much an American as ever. As it is a settled point in government here, that every man has his price, 'tis plain they are bunglers in their business, and have not given him enough. Their master has as much reason to be angry with them, as Rodriguez in the play, with his apothecary, for not effectually poisoning Pandolpho, and they most probably make use of the apothecary's justification, viz.

SCENE 4TH.

" Rodriguez, and Fell the Apothecary.

" Rodriguez. You promised to have this Pandolpho upon his bier in less than a week; 'tis more than a month since, and he still walks about and stares me in the face.

" Fell. True; and yet I have done my best endeavours. In various ways I have given this miscreant as much poison as would have killed an elephant. He has swallowed dose after dose; far from hurting him, he seems to be the better for it. He hath a wonderfully strong constitution. I find I cannot kill him, but by cutting his throat, and that, as I take it, is not my business.

" Rodriguez. Then it must be mine."

* He esteemed the king in the early part of his reign. Writing to Mr. Ross, from London, May 14th, 1765, after speaking of the troubles that then agitated London, he says;—" What the event will be, God only knows. But some punishment seems preparing for a people, who are ungratefully abusing the best constitution and the best king any nation was ever blessed with ; intent on nothing but luxury, licentiousness, power, places, pensions and plunder; while the ministry, divided in their councils, with little regard for each other, worried by perpetual oppositions, in continual apprehension of change, intent on securing popularity in case they should lose favour, have for some years past had little time or inclination to attend to our small affairs, whose remoteness makes them appear still smaller."

in which they were not represented. But all his suggestions were in vain. If the sovereign had taken him for an adviser instead of Mr. Grenville or lord Hillsborough, the course of events might have been very different. The king seems originally to have had a strong prejudice against Franklin ; he admired and feared his talents,* and by a singular though fortunate fatality, he considered that individual as his greatest enemy, who for a long period was perhaps more earnestly opposed than any of his subjects to a separation, and who could have exerted a very powerful influence in its prevention.

Dr. Franklin was the able and faithful agent of his native province during the remainder of his stay in England, yet he does not seem to have given entire satisfaction to the legislature, and it may perhaps be imputed in part to some lingering prejudices, that they censured him for neglect, in not giving them notice of the act for paying Judges salaries by the crown, and a clause in another act, that interfered

---

* The king often cautioned his ministers to beware of Dr. Franklin, or that he would obtain the advantage over them. The royal dislike was shewn on one occasion in a whimsical way. A Mr. Wilson had enlisted many of the political opponents of Franklin, in an absurd attempt to prove, that *blunt conductors* were better than *pointed* ones, and a lightning rod of the former description was erected on the queen's house, which gave rise to many sarcasms. When Dr. Franklin was informed of it, he replied to his correspondent with characteristic humour, from " Passy, Oct. 14th, 1777. I have no private interest in the reception of my inventions by the world, having never made, nor proposed to make, the least profit by any of them. The king's changing his *pointed* conductors for *blunt* ones, is therefore a matter of small moment to me. If I had a wish about it, it would be that he had rejected them altogether, as ineffectual. For it is only since he thought himself and family safe from the thunder of Heaven, that he dared to use his own thunder in destroying his innocent subjects."

with their shipping. He submitted without reply to this reproof, though in a private letter to their Speaker, he justifies himself with great moderation from the negligence laid to his charge.* In fact his zeal in their service brought upon him some of the most troublesome scenes, that he met with in the course of his life. The transmission of the letters of governor Hutchinson and other officers, that were considered of so much importance, may be esteemed the fulfilment of an extra duty, which exposed him to a variety of vexations and insults, that he felt much more deeply than he expressed; and which exhibited to great advantage many of the most estimable traits of his character.

In the spring of 1773, Dr. Franklin, was put in possession of a number of letters of governor Hutch-

---

* Dr. Franklin understood and practised very successfully, on one of the principles necessary to be observed by every candidate for popular favour in a republic, to treat with deference that intangible but omnipresent body, the public, in spite of all its caprices and injustice : and he well understood, that of all sovereigns there is none more susceptible of flattery than the sovereign people. He, like most others who have served the state, experienced occasional ingratitude, and, what perhaps *he* could less complain of, an unpleasant reaction of those penurious maxims, to which he gave an extensive currency, and which, notwithstanding their general good tendency, have some injurious effects in the management of national affairs. There is a degree of bitterness in the contemptuous expressions of the following extract on this subject, which is rarely to be found in his works. It is from a letter to the honourable Robert Morris, dated "Passy, July 26th, 1781—You are wise in estimating beforehand, as the principal advantage you can expect, the consciousness of having done service to your country. For the business you have undertaken is of so complex a nature, and must engross so much of your time and attention, as necessarily to hurt your private interests; and the public is often niggardly even of its thanks; resembling those little, dirty, stinking insects, that attack us only in the dark, disturb our repose, molesting and wounding us, while our sweat and blood are contributing to their subsistence."

inson, lieutenant governor Oliver, commissioner Paxton, &c. which he forwarded to Mr. Cushing, with an injunction, that no copies should be allowed to be taken of them, but that they might be communicated to the legislature, to whom a knowledge of their contents would be sufficient to display the political intrigues of the writers in a true light. But this correspondence had too direct a bearing on the transactions of that time to be kept from the public, and under some plausible pretence it was published, concealing however the means by which it was obtained. When the report of this disclosure reached England, a duel took place between Mr. Temple and Mr. Whately, growing out of this subject. Dr. Franklin then generously came forward to prevent any farther ill consequences, and declared in the public papers that he transmitted the letters. His enemies seized with avidity this pretext to turn their ill will towards him, and insinuated that he had purloined these letters; and they tried to convert an act of public duty into a mean effort of clandestine mischief. When he came, in pursuance of orders from the legislature, to support their charges against the governor, he was the person who was put to a severe trial. Mr. Wedderburne assailed him in the most provoking style, in a speech which may be considered truly coarse and impudent, while the lords of council were chuckling and enjoying all the abuse and indignities that were heaped upon him. This indeed formed a pitiable exhibition of human meanness and insolence ; these lords of council, who stripped of the livery of office, would have felt themselves naked pigmies before the gigantic power of Franklin's intellect, participated with safe and unmanly exultation in the effort to overwhelm him with obloquy. He bore it all without a remark or a murmur, or any attempt to exonerate himself from the insinuations and charges of the crown advocate, though they might have been easily repelled.* Before the privy council he appeared

---

* Dr. Franklin kept the secret respecting these letters till his death, as did all the other parties. Mr. Hartley, M. P. and Sir John Temple, had perhaps some agency in this matter ; but the gentleman to whom they were actually delivered, was the late Dr. Hugh Williamson of Pennsylvania, in whose life by Dr. Hosack, there is an interesting account of the transaction, which is there for the first time divulged. Mr. Chalmers, in his Annals, who is prompted by his political feelings to make particular allusions to recent events, in his narrative of former occurrences, glances more than once at the affair of these letters, which, though they may now be considered of little interest, yet at the time, both in England and America, attracted great attention from circumstances connected with them. In speaking of the letters which were intercepted from the persons, who were expelled from the colony in 1630, he remarks; " Thus early was introduced into the politics of Massachusetts, the dishonourable practice of appropriating the communications of private friendship wrongfully obtained, to the malevolent purposes of party ; It then rooted in her system and in after times produced abundantly."—p. 146. In a note to this passage he says ; " The memorials and other public papers which were presented to the committee of the colonies, during the disputes with Massachusetts, in the reign of Charles II. were constantly obtained by ' indirect means,' and transmitted by the colonial agents ; whereby, said the complainants on this subject, not only the king's councils have been discovered, but there has been laid a scene of ruin to those suspected of loyalty." He concludes the note with the following extract of a letter from Col. Nicholls, Governor of New York, dated in October 1666. " I think it my duty to inform you, that a copy of his majesty's signification to the Massachusetts, was surreptitiously conveyed over to them by some unknown hand, before the original came to Boston ; and formerly the very original of Mr. Maverick's petition to the king in council, (concerning Massachusetts) was stolen out of Lord Arlington's office by Captain John Scott, and delivered to the Governor and council at Boston. This I affirm positively to be true,

with silent, concentrated firmness and pride; but the
deep impression of the injurious treatment which he
had received, was afterwards shewn by a trifling
circumstance, in a most significant way. During this
examination he was dressed in a particular suit of
velvet, which he never subsequently wore, till the
day when he signed the treaty of alliance with
France, as the minister of the United States.

Before his return to America in 1775, he talked
of his right to retire from public life, in consideration of his age and long services; but wherever this
kind of language is not mere cant, it is most generally the result of self deception, which is dissipated
as soon as the wish for retirement is gratified. After signing the declaration of Independence, he
was sent on a joint mission to France. His residence of nearly nine years in that country, though
it was accompanied with some of the infirmities of
age, was doubtless the most agreeable portion of his

---

though Scott, when I questioned him upon the matter, said a clerk of *Mr.
Williamson's* gave it to him."—p. 149.

The coincidence of the above name would not fail to be remarked by Mr.
Chalmers, if Dr Hosack's life of *Dr. Williamson* should fall under his eye.
He adverts to this topic in another place, as follows : " During the reign of
Charles II. the General court maintained no standing agents in England ; but
it enjoyed the advantages arising from the services of emissaries zealous and
intelligent, Collins, Knowles, Thompson, and others from the public offices,
who intrigued, who distributed money, though to no great amount." Lord
Anglesey he thinks was bribed by them ; Rushworth was employed at a small
salary to procure papers' from the public offices ; some of the clerks of the
council were bribed ; considerable sums were voted by the General court, in
1682, to go to the agents to secure their charter, " There is no evidence in
history, in records, or papers, to shew that any of the other colonies enjoyed
similar means to gain their ends in England."—p. 461.

life. He was indeed introduced to the brilliant
court and polished society of that nation, under a
concurrence of favourable circumstances. It was a
period when ancient abuses and modern illumina-
tion were in strange contrast. The learned and the
polite were eager in the pursuit of improvement.
Wise and good men were even then lighting the
torches, which, afterwards, in the hands of the bad
and the ignorant, consumed the whole fabric of the
monarchy, and all the institutions of society. The
great reputation of Franklin had preceded him.
His age his wisdom, his philosophy, and his wit, all
contributed to excite personal respect. Even his
simple dress* was advantageous to him, in a
community, where satiety was sighing after novelty,
and where a large share of frivolity was mingled
with much intelligence and the highest refinement.
The young and ardent were impatient for a crusade
in favour of liberty ; while the enterprising and ambitious statesmen were meditating on the opportunity of gratifying national animosity, in the destruction of a rival power.

The admiration and celebrity which he obtained
in Paris, were in some degree reflected on his coun-

---

* Persons who are unacquainted with the state of manners in Paris, at that
period, can hardly imagine the importance that was attached to this subject.
The question as to his costume at court was much discussed, and his fur cap
and spectacles procured him many admirers. He is more than once mentioned in Madame du Deffand's letters to Horace Walpole, and the observations of that remarkable woman, particularly when it is remembered that she
was blind, will give some idea of the attention that was bestowed on this
topic. See the letters of December 31, 1776, and March 22, 1778.

try, and this perhaps may be considered one of the greatest services he rendered it, though his influence as a minister, on many occasions, was advantageously exerted. But in the definitive treaty, when the French government wished to deprive the United States of the fisheries, his conduct was an additional motive for the prejudices that existed respecting him in his native state. The preservation of that great source of wealth and maritime strength, was thought to be owing to the firmness of his colleagues in the negotiation; when he would have yielded to the insidious designs of the French cabinet. The venerable philosopher was partially overcome by the cajolleries of the Parisians. He had been treated with such unbounded kindness and deference, he was so followed, cited and admired, not only by the learned and the noble, but by the young, the gay, and the fashionable; he was so truly regarded as an oracle equally by fine women and eminent philosophers, that it must have been extremely difficult for him to separate the claims of his country from his personal obligations. To have enforced her rights rigidly, would have seemed in him discourteous and ungrateful. He was by these means in a degree disqualified for resisting the pretensions of that power; and it was fortunate, that others were associated with him in a negotiation, in which he, himself would have been unwilling to assume the whole responsibility.

Though from the causes that have been enumerated, Franklin never received many testimonials of kind-

ness from his native town; yet he was not estranged from its welfare by his long separation. At the
close of his life, early associations were remembered, and he gave proofs of that affecting and enno-
bling disposition, that recalls to us on the brink of a
distant grave, the cradle of our infancy; *Et dulces
moriens reminiscitur Argos.* He made some be-
quests to the town for public purposes;* among
them one that revives his memory in the most
grateful manner. He directed, that a certain number of medals should be annually distributed to the
children, who distinguished themselves in the public
schools. The recollection therefore of the benevolent philosopher and of the enterprising citizen, who
achieved his own prosperity and fame, is associated
with the quick pulsation of the first enkindling reward received by youthful merit, which may thus
be excited to further emulation by the useful hope
that his example inspires.

It would be a superfluous task to give a summary of
Dr. Franklin's character, which has so often been
done by accurate observers. He was not a man of
profound learning. His discoveries and his writings
were the expansive results of a vigorous mind, which
were thrown off without pretension, and seemed as

---

* One of these he extended prospectively to a very distant period, while it
is remarkable, that a man who was so clear-sighted and so well acquainted
with the many contingencies to which the soundest calculations are subjected,
should have left these funds in a manner that renders them peculiarly
liable to accidents, and that will never suffer his ultimate views to be realized.

if designed rather for a pastime, than for fame. He was no orator, and yet his power of instructing and carrying a point by means of some striking apologue, was almost irresistible. He cannot rank high as a constitutional statesman, since he was in favour of the most radical and fatal error in a constitution, that of making a legislature to consist of one body. His theoretical deficiencies in religion may obtain forgiveness, through the number and extent of his beneficent efforts. His wit, his indulgent humour, and his intuitive discernment, made him the delight of society. His industry, his moderation, his love of peace and his public spirit, established his merits as a citizen. His writings will ever preserve his name with his countrymen, while his discoveries will make its fame no less sure in the annals of philosophy. His connexion with the American revolution will place his statue in the temple of universal memory: but his most lasting claims to the gratitude of mankind, were his powerful efforts against war, oppression and inhumanity of every species. He was in truth, a real philanthropist; and his views tended to promote the welfare of his race, under all governments, and in every clime.

Chapter XXV.

*Governor Hutchinson's me-sages in favour of Parliamentary supre-
macy—Answers of the Legislature—Arrival of the Tea—Proceedings of the Inhabitants of Boston—Destruction of the Tea.*

THE dispute between the Governor and the legislature, respecting the place where they should assemble, continued through 1771, and a part of the
first session in June, 1772. On the 16th of that
month, the Governor adjourned the court to meet
at their regular place in Boston. One motive for
doing so, was probably, to remove a part of their
dissatisfaction; that they might receive in a better
humour the information, which he communicated to
them at the same time; that in future, his salary
would be paid by the crown, and not by the vote of
the colony. This essential violation of the charter
produced a long series of resolutions, protesting
against the measure. It was followed in a few
months, by an act in the same spirit, for paying the
salaries of the judges by the crown; which was resisted, by declaring any judge, who should accept of
such compensation, to be an enemy to the constitution, and seeking to introduce arbitrary government.
These acts were part of that course of surreptitious
measures, by which the ministry sought to undermine and destroy the charter of this, and some other
provinces: which system of innovation and disorder,

they afterwards consummated by measures of open violence and cruelty.

Though Otis was not a member of the legislature after 1771, and the motive for giving a sketch of legislative proceedings connected with him has ceased, yet there was one occurrence in 1773, that was of too much consequence to be passed over without at least a slight notice, as it furnishes materials of the highest value and interest to the historian, and to every civilian who wishes to investigate the original relations of the English and colonial governments.

At the winter session in 1773, Governor Hutchinson in his speech to the legislature, began by observing, that he had nothing in special command from his majesty to communicate to them, but as it was his general duty to recommend peace and order, and as the country was in a very disturbed state, he thought he could point out the cause of it, and if he could make this appear clearly to them, he had no doubt, that they would unite with him in endeavouring to remove it. After this introduction, he went back to the origin of the colonies, and attempted to shew that they were completely dependent on parliament, which had the supremacy over them ; that the denial of this supremacy and the resistance to parliamentary regulations, were the causes of the prevailing evils. He asked them to consider with calmness what he had disclosed without reserve. That if they would adhere to his principles, they might yet be happy; that the people will be influenced by them to desist from their unconstitutional proceedings, they will be convinced that every thing that is valuable to them depends upon their connexion with the parent state ; that this connexion cannot exist without a dependence on parliament, and that notwithstanding this dependence, " they will enjoy as great a proportion of those rights to which they have a claim by nature, or as Englishmen, as can be enjoyed by a plantation or colony." Hutchinson seems to have been intoxicated by power, or infatuated by vanity, when he was led to the flagrant impolicy of making this speech. He invited them to discuss the subject, and challenged them to overthrow the principles that he laid down, to which he thought they must accede, or else claim "independence, which," he said, " I cannot allow myself to think you have in contemplation." The answer of the council is able and perspicuous, both in the style and argument, and was probably written by Mr. Bowdoin, who was chairman of the committee.

The answer of the house is a profoundly learned and elaborate exposition of the rights of the colonists, under the constitution and the charter, and confutes the whole argument of the Governor. It claims for the colony an independence of parliament, with an acknowledgment of full allegiance to the king. They take care to expose his impolicy, in provoking the discussion, as follows : " To conclude, these are great and profound questions. It is the grief of this house, that by the ill policy of a late injudicious administration, America has been driven into the consideration of them. And we cannot but express our con-

cern, that your excellency by your speech, has reduced us to the unhappy alternative, either of appearing by our silence to acquiesce in your excellency's
sentiments, or of thus freely discussing this point."

Three weeks afterwards, the Governor delivered
a long rejoinder, and proved " that he could argue
still." To this speech the council made a short answer; but the house, notwithstanding the regrets
which they expressed at the consideration of these
questions, shewed themselves not loth to continue
their refutation. Their reply is even more extended than the former one, descending into some minute
details, and proceeding with a more emphatic tone
to deny the supremacy of parliament. The first
plain avowal of independence by any legislative body
in the colonies, is to be found in these answers of the
house of representatives. There are many portions of
them which are admirable for the eloquence of their
style, as well as the closeness of their reasoning and
the sound learning which they display ; the concluding section of the second reply, will afford a
short specimen of the whole.

" We cannot help, before we conclude, expressing
our great concern, that your excellency has thus repeatedly, in a manner, insisted upon our sentiments on matters of so delicate a nature and importance. The question appears to us, to be no other,
than whether we are the subjects of absolute unlimited power, or of a free government, formed on the
principles of the English constitution. If your excellency's doctrine be true, the people of this province

hold their lands of the crown and people of England ; and their lives, liberties and properties are at their disposal, and that, even by compact and their own consent. They were subject to the king, as the head *alterius populi*, of another people, in whose legislative* they have no voice or interest. They are, indeed, said to have a constitution and a legislative of their own, but your Excellency has explained it into a mere phantom, limited, controlled, superseded, and nullified at the will of another. Is this the constitution which so charmed our ancestors, that, as your excellency informed us, they kept a day of solemn thanksgiving to Almighty God when they received it ? and were they men of so little discernment, such children in understanding, as to please themselves with the imagination, that they were blessed with the same rights and liberties which natural born subjects in England enjoyed, when, at the same time, they had fully consented to be ruled and ordered by a legislative, a thousand leagues distant from them, which cannot be supposed to be sufficiently acquainted with their circumstances, if concerned for their interest, and in which they cannot be in any sense represented ?†

---

* This word, now used only as an adjective, was in common use by the writers and speakers of that day as a substantive. Otis in most of his writings so employs it. The fact might be inferred even from this unsettled phraseology, that legislatures had not the paramount importance they have since obtained. Parliaments, assemblies, &c. had been the synonyms in use ; but the more modern and classic word became necessary, when the constitutions of the United States, jointly and severally, were construed and defined with severe accuracy and precision.

† The speeches and answers that have been alluded to, will be found in the

It was an unfortunate moment of overweening confidence, that led Governor Hutchinson to this ill-timed contest. It could produce no possible good to the government, while it gave an opportunity to the legislature, to issue a manifesto on the whole subject of the dispute between the colonies and the mother country, and to exhibit still more openly and decisively than had yet been done, the claim of the former to absolute independence of the British Parliament. By the superiority of learning and argument which the answers displayed, the pretensions of the administration were disgraced, while the rights of the colonies were exhibited in brighter and bolder relief. The ministry were excessively vexed and disconcerted at a step, which aggravated all the difficulties between the two countries, and rendered the assumption of independence a much more probable and nearer event. Hutchinson, who had meditated a triumph, only lessened his consideration with the cabinet, and thereby materially injured his ambitious expectations.*

Massachusetts State papers from p. 336 and 399. These answers were written by President Adams, though his name does not appear among the committee, as he was not a member of the legislature. This circumstance was owing to Major Hawley, who proposed to his colleagues that Mr. Adams should be called to join in their conferences ; because, as Hutchinson had thrown the gauntlet in a very laboured production, it was necessary to use great precautions in answering him. The draught prepared by President A. was accepted by the committee unanimously.

* There is a very interesting letter of Dr. Franklin's in his works relating to these answers, which as soon as he received them, he had printed and distributed. In a letter to Mr. Cushing, dated May 6th, 1773, he said, speaking of Hutchinson, " the administration are chagrined with his officiousness." " Some

At the first session of the next legislature in May, the establishment of a committee of correspondence was voted, 100 to 4, in conformity to a proposal made by the house of burgesses of Virginia. These committees were a most efficient instrument in forwarding the revolution. They were originally suggested, as has been before mentioned, by General Warren at Plymouth to Samuel Adams, who immediately perceived their utility, and occupied himself in having them carried into effect, which was soon afterwards done throughout the Province. The proposal was privately made to some of the leading patriots of Virginia, to have the system adopted by the several colonies, as it was deemed expedient, that the first public intimation should come from that province, lest Massachusetts should appear too active and assuming; as the ministry were directing some of their most offensive measures against them in the first instance, the opposition which they were obliged to make, might give them the reputation of being the only colony disaffected to the course

---

say he must be a fool, others that though misinformation he really supposed Lord Hillsborough to be again in office." Lord Dartmouth said, " What difficulties that gentleman has brought us all into by his imprudence ! Though I suppose he meant well; but what can now be done? It is impossible that Parliament can suffer such a declaration of the General Assembly, asserting its independence, to pass unnoticed." The whole letter is filled with this matter.

On the same subject, he thus speaks in a letter to Dr. Cooper of July 7th, 1773. " The Governor was certainly out in his politics, if he hoped to recommend himself here by entering upon that dispute with the Assembly. His imprudence in bringing it at all upon the tapis, and his bad management of it, are almost equally censured. The Council and Assembly on the other hand, have by their coolness, clearness and force of their answers, gained great reputation.

pursued by the British government, while in reality, the majority in every part of the country harmonized with them entirely. One of the first good effects of this committee, resulted from the union of sentiment in regard to the duty on tea, and the unanimous resolution through the continent, that it should not be landed. The history of the tea, sent by the East India company to America, in the autumn of 1773, has often been either partially narrated, or misrepresented. The whole procedure constitutes one of the most remarkable, and to the inhabitants of the colonies, one of the most honourable events, in the revolutionary annals.

After the act laying a duty on paper, glass, tea, &c. was repealed, with the exception of tea, on which the duty was continued, associations were entered into in all the colonies, to discourage the use of it. The consumption was of course greatly diminished, and the tea accumulated in the English warehouses. The East India Company sought relief from government, and urged them to take off the duty on importation in America, and double the duty on exportation in England. This proposal, which would have produced nearly the same result as to the amount of revenue received, and have obviated one serious cause of dispute, was declined. The ministry bent on levying their American duty, thought this tea the most useful article for the experiment. They calculated that this luxury, which from long habit and extensive use had become almost a necessary of life, would inevitably find purchasers in spite of all private associations or patriotic agreements. In this case, as in many others, they reposed a false confidence in their estimate of human character; and forgot that some general maxims, however just in ordinary times, may be inapplicable in great emergencies, even among a people more corrupt and effeminate, than those whom they were now endeavouring to subdue. But to meet the wishes of the company, a drawback was given in England, equal to the duty which they had asked to have removed, and a guarantee against loss, in the experiment of making shipments of tea to the colonies.*

---

* The following passage from " The Life of the Rt. Honourable William Pitt, Earl of Chatham," affords some curious particulars of the secret history of the Tea business, if they are authentic. " When the duties to be paid in America on paper, paint and glass, were repealed, it was pretended, that the Tea duty (which had been imposed by the same act of Parliament) was left standing to *serve* the Company. But this was not the fact. The tax was left unrepealed to preserve the *right*, as it was called, to tax the colonies. That was the *true* motive. The service of the East India Company made no part of the consideration. The tea sent to Boston was that sort called *Bohea*, which was conferring no favour on the Company, but the reverse ; for that sort of tea was no burden to the Company. It was the sort called *Singlo* which lay heavy on their hands, and of which all their warehouses were full. But the resolution was agreed to in a *private* committee, when only *three* persons were present. Mr. Bolton was chairman. A matter of such importance ought to have been agitated in a full committee, which consists of eleven. The truth is, the Bohea was more saleable than the Singlo ; it was, therefore, the resolution of the cabinet, to send the most saleable ; presuming that the temptation to purchase being greater, by the offer of good tea, than by the offer of an inferior sort, some of the Americans might be thereby induced to barter liberty for luxury, and perhaps a schism might be created among them. Had the question of determining the kind of tea to be sent to America been agitated in a full committee ; it is more than probable, that the interests of the Company would have prevailed over the views of the Cabinet of St. James's. When the directors were informed of the conduct of the committee, they explained this distinction of the tea to the ministry, and wished to have the Singlo substituted. But the ministry would not consent. It was again

Large shipments of tea were made to the principal ports of the continent, and a general ferment prevailed over every part of the country. It was not only determined that the tea itself should not be received; but whoever made use of this (ministerially) obnoxious herb, was regarded as an enemy to the country. The utmost vigilance was employed to prevent its being consumed by those persons, whose innocent daily comforts were thus involved in the vortex of national contention; a rigid inquisition was every where enforced for this purpose, that on other grounds would have been both odious and absurd, but was justified by the necessity of combating in this familiar shape, a principle, which was shortly after to be resisted by open war.

Long before the ships arrived with the tea, arrangements were made to avert the threatened mischief. In many cases the consignees were induced to decline accepting the charge of it. Very spirited resolutions were entered into at a public meeting of the citizens in Philadelphia, with which the consignees complied by resigning their appointment. From that city and from New York it was sent back to England in the same ships that brought it. In

---

objected to at the minister's house. To the last application, Lord North being perhaps wearied with representations on the subject, said, "It was to no purpose making objections, for the king would have it so." These were his lordship's words; and he added, "that the king meant *to try the question* with America," vol. 2. This account seems equally precise and positive, but some doubt may be thrown upon it, if the reader recurs to what was said by Mr. Jenkinson on the tea act, see p. 202, of which, he would hardly have spoken in the terms he used, if the king's share in it had been so immediate.

Charleston it was landed, and stored expressly in damp warehouses, where it was destroyed by the humidity. In Boston it was destined to a more violent destruction.

Two of the vessels with the tea arrived on Saturday November 27th. A town-meeting was held on the Monday following, and resolutions were passed similar to those of Philadelphia, calling on the consignees, among whom were two sons of Governor Hutchinson, to decline the charge of it.

A vote was then passed with acclamations, " that the tea shall not be landed, that no duty shall be paid, and that it shall be sent back in the same bottoms." After this vote, Mr. Quincy* a young and eloquent advocate, and ardent patriot, with a strong perception of the events that would follow from the measures now in contemplation; and wishing to try

* Josiah Quincy, descended from one of the most respectable families in Massachusetts, was born in Boston in 1743, educated at Cambridge and received his first degree 1763. He qualified himself for the bar, and in his short career shewed himself to be an eloquent advocate. He was employed with President Adams, as counsel in the defence of Captain Preston. He entered with great fervour into the arduous politics of his times, and by his talents and zeal in his speeches and writings, was one of the patriots who excited the brightest expectations, which were prematurely blasted. His intense application and anxiety impaired his health, and he was induced to take a voyage to England, with the hope of restoring it, and also to procure accurate information respecting the views of parties in the perilous state of things then existing. He left Boston in September 1774, and died on his return in April 1775, on the same day that the vessel in which he was passenger reached Cape Ann. He had, therefore, no opportunity of communicating to his countrymen the result of his observations, which was eagerly expected. The regret on this account, was however, merged in the universal sorrow for the untimely loss of a virtuous and gifted patriot, who was cut off in his 31st year. from the service of his country in the very crisis of her affairs.

the spirit and to increase the energy of his fellow citizens, by setting before them in a strong light, the
consequences that might be expected from their resolves, addressed the meeting in the following terms.

" It is not, Mr. Moderator, the spirit that vapours
within these walls that must stand us in stead.   The
exertions of this day will call forth events, which
will make a very different spirit necessary for our
own salvation.   Whoever supposes that shouts and
hosannas will terminate the trials of the day, enter-
tains a childish fancy.   We must be grossly ignorant of the importance and value of the prize for
which we contend; we must be equally ignorant of
the power of those combined against us ; we must
be blind to that malice, inveteracy, and insatiable
revenge, which actuate our enemies public and private, abroad and in our bosom, to hope that we
shall end this controversy without the sharpest conflicts ; to flatter ourselves that popular resolves,
popular harangues, popular acclamations, and popular vapour, will vanquish our foes.   Let us consider
the issue.   Let us look to the end.   Let us weigh
and consider, before we advance to those measures,
which must bring on the most trying and terrible
struggle this country every saw."

The vote was again submitted to the meeting,
and was again passed unanimously.   A guard for
the protection of the vessels was appointed, which
protection, included the protection of the public
against the landing of the tea.   This guard of twenty five men were respectable citizens, volunteers,

and acting under the direction of the committee of correspondence.

The meeting was then adjourned to the next day, when the town were again assembled, the answer of the consignees was read: they refused the proposition to send it back, but offered to store it. The sheriff came in and read a proclamation from the Governor, ordering the meeting to disperse, which was received with one universal hiss. Votes were passed ordering the owners and captains of the vessels not to suffer the tea to be landed. Attempts were made in the mean time to negotiate, and induce the merchants and the custom-house to clear out the tea, and send it back. All was in vain. At length the time was expiring when the tea could remain any longer in this situation; the patience of the inhabitants was exhausted, the anxiety and watching were too troublesome to be further endured. A body meeting* was held on

---

* A *body-meeting* was an assembly after public notification, at which any citizen might attend, and at which many of the principal inhabitants of the neighbouring towns attended. Town-meetings were confined to the people of the town, and were called by order of the municipal authority. These body meetings were in fact, only an orderly, well regulated mob; their irregular action was salutary and indispensable at the time, but the habit of interfering in this manner with public affairs was a dangerous one, and it proves the virtue of the people that it did not produce permanent evils. During the partial *interregnum* of government, that existed in the transition from British authority to the establishment of state government, popular interference had been so frequently exercised, that some persons were reluctant to resign it, and slight traces of its effects might be perceived long afterwards. Mr. Ames in a letter to the late W. Tudor, Esq. dated at New York, July 12th, 1789, remarks : " A mob is despotic *per se*, and it tends to destroy all liberty. One Abner Fowler, it is said in 1787, would have the town instruct their members to vote against the constitution, for he observed, it would destroy their liber-

the 15th of December at the Old South Church, when Mr. Rotch, the owner of the vessel which had the largest parcel of the tea, attended, and after much difficulty he was persuaded to apply to the custom-house for a clearance, and the meeting adjourned to hear the result till the next morning. Ten gentlemen accompanied him to the custom-house, and the clearance was refused in a peremptory manner. A vote of the meeting was then passed, ordering him to protest against this refusal, and a deputation was sent with him to Governor Hutchinson, who was at his country house on Milton hill, seven miles from Boston, to intreat him to grant a pass that the vessels might leave the harbour.

In the mean time various speeches were made in the meeting, to keep the people together, which were said to amount to six or seven thousand persons. Mr. John Rowe, an eminent merchant and patriotic citizen, who was doubtless in the secret of the measures that were to be taken in the last resort, hinted in the form of inquiry, " Who knows how tea will mix with salt water ?" which was received with applause. At length, about sun-down, the deputation returned from the governor, with his refusal to grant the pass. A few minutes after, a band of eighteen or twenty young men, who had been prepared for the event, went by the meeting house, giving a shout.* It was echoed by some

---

ties, they never could have another mob ! I wish that his judgment may be verified." Mass. His. Soc. vol. 8. p. 319.

* This fact is from a gentleman now living, who was one of the number. No one of his party was in any disguise.

within; others exclaimed, the mohawks are come! The assembly broke up, and a part of it followed this body of young men to Griffins'-wharf, (now called Liverpool wharf,) on the south side of the town.

Three different parties,* composed of trust-worthy persons, many of whom in after life were among the most respectable citizens of the town, had been prepared in conformity to the secret resolves of the political leaders, to act as circumstances should require. They were seventy or eighty in all, and when every attempt had failed to have the tea returned, and the final refusal of the governor to interfere was received, it was immediately made known to them, and they proceeded at once to throw the obnoxious merchandize into the water. This was done with as much good order and regularity, as if the tea had been discharged in the ordinary way. The chests were hoisted upon the decks, broken open, and their contents emptied over the side of the ship into the channel. A large crowd of people was collected, who were quiet spectators of the operation, which was completed in the course of the evening. Three hundred and forty two chests of tea were thus destroyed, and not the slightest injury was done to any individual, or to any property

---

* One, if not two, of these parties, wore a kind of Indian disguise. Two of these persons in passing over Fort-hill, to the scene of operations, met with a British Officer, who on oberving them, naturally enough, drew his sword. As they came nearer, one of the *Indians* drew a pistol, and said to the officer : " The path is wide enough for us all ; we have nothing to do with you and intend you no harm—if you keep your own way peaceably, we shall keep ours."

on board the vessels, except the unlucky* tea, and, after the work was finished, the actors and spectators calmly retired to their several homes.

Of all this tea, the whole quantity saved, is contained in a small phial still in existence. One of the operators on his return home, found his shoes filled with it; this he put into a bottle and sealed up. Not a pound of the tea was purloined. One of the persons engaged in the business, who wished to preserve too large a specimen, was observed by some

---

* It merited this appellation for various reasons, and it was unfortunate for every one who had any connexion with it. There was in Boston, at that time, a shopkeeper by the name of *Jolley Allen*, whose advertisements have a very shewy appearance in all the newspapers of that day. He could accommodate his customers with almost every article " cheap for cash." He drove a very thriving trade, and in addition to his other dealings boarded many of the British officers in his house, and also kept " horses and chaises to let." He seems to have been a person of very exuberant loyalty, with a strong mixture of cockney simplicity and trading shrewdness. He had accumulated a considerable property, and was a staunch government man, mistaking in common with some abler men, the extent of the British power, which he and they thought unlimited. Having sided with the English altogether, he was obliged to share their fate, and left the town, with the evacuating army, and the unhappy fugitives, that accompanied it, in a moment of great confusion and distress. He hired a vessel to transport his family and property to Halifax : the man who made the bargain with him, was a knave, utterly ignorant of the management of a vessel, and the day after they sailed, being separated from the fleet, they arrived, not at Halifax, but at Cape Cod, where the property was confiscated and all hands imprisoned. Jolley Allen after many troubles reached England, and wrote a narrative to support his claims for relief. This journal still remains in manuscript, and is called, " an account of part of the sufferings and losses of Jolley Allen, a native of London." It begins thus ; " sometime I think in the month of October 1772, I bought two chests of tea of *gover* *ner* Hutchinson's two sons, Thomas and Elisha, about eleven o'clock in the forenoon," &c. This purchase was the prime cause of all his misfortunes. There is a strong tinge of the ludicrous in the distresses of this individual ; though he undoubtedly suffered much, after making allowance for exaggeration. His bad spelling, his cunning and his ignorance, all contribute to make the narrative characteristic.

of his companions to have the pockets of his coat a
little distended. This was treated as an accident,
which was remedied however, in a good natured
way, without resistance, by the application of a
knife across the waist of the coat, which left it a
kind of garment, that has in later times been called
a *Spencer*, and the part separated was thrown over-
board to accompany its kindred tea. The most
scrupulous care was taken that none of it should be
secreted. The shores of the harbour at high water
mark, were lined with it the next day, as with other
worthless weeds. A chest containing a few pounds,
floated into a creek in Dorchester, where it was discovered, brought into town, and publicly committed
to the flames.

The motives of Hutchinson on this occasion were
pitiful, and his conduct very deficient in foresight.
A large part of the tea was consigned to his sons, and
their small gain was a prevailing consideration in his
mind. Though the public attention was alive on this
subject throughout the colonies; though he knew the
inhabitants of Boston had been watchful and anxious
for near three weeks, and had determined with as
much unanimity as energy, that the tea should not
be landed; though the question of receiving this tea,
had become the pivot, on which the whole great dispute about taxation turned at that moment; though
a civil war might depend upon it, and did actually
ensue, the commissions that would accrue to his sons
preponderated against all other considerations. He
thought himself safe. The Custom-house refused a

clearance, unless the tea was landed, the naval commanders refused to let the ships pass without a clearance, therefore it must be landed. He forgot, or never indeed seemed to understand, that he was acting against men, who, if they could not untie a knot, would cut it. The same difficulties did not occur in other places. At New-York and Philadelphia, the officers yielded to the force of public opinion, and prudently assisted in having the tea returned. The Admiral commanding in Boston, offered to receive it under his protection;* but the Governor determined that it should go into his sons' warehouses, and the people of Boston then resolved, that it should go into the sea. Every exertion was made by them to avoid the destruction of property, by this necessary act of violence. When nothing would avail, when neither remonstrances nor intreaties could move the Governor, they had no alternative but to destroy the ministerial and royal grocery, or abandon all the principles which they had been eight years contending for, and which, in a brief period after, they shed their blood to maintain.

---

* Admiral Montague then commanded on the Boston station. He had offered to receive the tea, which was refused. He probably anticipated its fate. On the evening of its destruction, he was visiting at a house in Atkinson street, which terminates near the spot where the tea ships laid. His secretary perceiving a great movement in the neighbourhood, came in a hurry to tell him, that something was in agitation. In reply, he was asked "to sit down and keep himself quiet, and not meddle with other people's business." When this officer returned to England, he gave such answers respecting the character of the people and their Governors, as prevented the ministry from ever consulting him farther, as they listened to no one who did not encourage them to persevere in their infatuated scheme.

Chapter XXVI.

The intercepted letters of the Governor and others—His recall—Character of Governor Hutchinson.

IN the summer preceding this affair of the tea, the famous letters already mentioned as transmitted by Dr. Franklin, which had been written by Governor Hutchinson and other officers, were published by order of the General Court, and it may be truly said, rendered his situation no longer tenable. These letters, written five or six years before, laid bare his hypocrisy, and exposed the odious counsels which he had given against the rights of his countrymen. His obstinacy in preventing the tea from being safely returned, and the mischievous consequences that might follow from its destruction, completed the exasperation of the public against him. When the legislature were in their winter session, he received his recall, of which he informed the Court, and soon after prorogued them. He was succeeded in the command of the province by General Gage, and sailed for England on the first of June, 1774.

There was, perhaps, no single officer of the British government in America, who contributed more to produce the separation of the two countries, than Governor Hutchinson. It is therefore a matter of some difficulty and delicacy, to delineate his character and administration; because those who sided with him, will object to the impolicy of some of his measures, and the final result of them all; while an American who disapproves of his political course, will be softened in the disposition to blame, by the recollection of the glorious fortunes of his country, which the advice and conduct of this eminent person, did very considerably, though most unintentionally, serve to originate.

Thomas Hutchinson, of a distinguished family in the annals of New-England, was born in Boston in 1711. He was sent to Harvard College at a very early age, and received his first degree at that seminary in 1727. After leaving college, instead of pursuing a learned profession, he chose a mercantile life. As a merchant, he was more esteemed for his probity than his skill, and rather lessened than increased his patrimony. His friends advised him to engage in the study of law and politics, and qualify himself for public life. His first office was that of a Selectman of Boston, and he was sent to London to transact some business for the town, which charge he executed satisfactorily, and on his return was elected a representative. He was after a few years chosen speaker of the house, and in 1752, succeeded his uncle as Judge of Probate. He was placed in the council, and was appointed Lieutenant Governor in 1758, and Chief Justice in 1760; all of which offices he held simultaneously for several years, without inspiring a general distrust of his designs, by this inordinate and indecent accumulation.

It was owing to his intrigues, that the colony was

so long without a suitable agent in England; his favourite object for a considerable period, was to obtain that station; and when finally disappointed, he used all his influence to keep inferior men in the place, that the representations of the legislature might be rather weakened than enforced, in passing through their hands. The regularity of his life, the plausibility of his manner and his extreme assiduity, tended to preserve his influence with the community, and even with many persons who differed from him in politics.

He was a fluent and graceful speaker, with great capacity for business, possessing a command of temper, and courteous in his demeanour. His efforts were incessant to obtain influence and to secure support to his views. Every young man who came into life with any promise of distinction, was regularly assailed, and several were won over to embrace his politics, who naturally belonged to the patriotic party. These he served, while it could promote his own ambitious designs; but all gratitude ceased, for past exertions, the moment the individual declined any thing he required of him.

Being a native of the province, and not a member of the Episcopal church, were both advantages to him over most other crown officers in the attainment of popularity. He took every advantage of religious prejudices to secure influence, and resorted to the modes of hypocrisy in use at that day. He was a promoter of all those irksome and irritating restraints on the most innocent movements of the citizens.

which the narrow bigotry of the Sabbatists were
eager to impose, and which in former times produced
a species of oppression, that was hateful in some
cases, in others ridiculous. Yet in his private letters
at the same time, he treated this austere spirit with
contemptuous sneers,* when it interfered with his
wish to averawe the country, by maintaining a standing army in it.

In his politics he was originally thought to have
been, and on many occasions really was, the advocate
of the rights of his countrymen. But his ambition
led him step by step, to sacrifice his knowledge
and his principles, in order to abet every arbitrary
regulation, and to suggest the most odious means of
enforcing them. He deceived many persons by his
assurances, that he had written against several of the
measures that were taken, and induced them to believe, that, though his situation made it necessary for
him to support all the orders of the administration,
he was still a devoted friend to the province ; yet
at the same period he advised to innovations on its
charter, and plainly asserted, that in regard to the
colonies " there must be an abridgement of English
liberties."

His anxiety to enrich and aggrandize himself, appeared to have entirely blinded his judgment, and

---

* The military parade on Sundays was considered a profanation by many
persons, and tending to destroy the solemnity of the day. On this subject, he
wrote, that " five or six men of war, and three or four regiments disturb nobody, but some of our grave people, who do not love assemblies and concerts,
and cannot bear the noise of drums upon a Sunday."

losing sight altogether of the character of his countrymen, he thought they possessed neither the intelligence, the inclination, nor the courage to defend
their rights. He believed the power of England
absolutely irresistible,* and that the quartering of a
few regiments in Boston would control the country.
He looked to the ministry for his whole reward, and
that he might not be disappointed of it, was willing
to sacrifice all the privileges of the colonies, and to
renounce the example and political inheritance of his
ancestors, though no man was better versed in their
history and character, which were most entirely
opposed to such a recreant policy.

His conduct, as a judge, was irreproachable, except that in some cases, political considerations may
have influenced him in the management of proceedings, though not in the judgments which he rendered. His ability on the bench might be held to be
remarkable, when it is remembered, that he was not
originally bred to the profession of the law. In the
probate office he was greatly esteemed, as his manners were adapted to soothe the feelings of the large

---

* Dr. Eliot in his biography of him, introduced the opinions of three different governors upon the question of going to war with America, which are curious and authentic. " Hutchinson said that the people would not resist with
their armies the power and authority of Great Britain; that a few troops
would be sufficient to quell them if they did make opposition. General Carle-
ton thought, that America might easily be conquered, but they would want a
considerable army for that purpose. That he would not pretend to march to
New York or Boston (from Canada) without 10,000 men. Tryon said it
would take large armies and much time to bring America to their feet. The
power of Great Britain was equal to any thing, but all that power must be
exerted before they put the monster in chains."

portion of clients, which comes into that court in a
state of bereavement and affliction.

As a writer he is more valuable for his facts than
his style. Besides occasional essays, and a pamphlet
on colonial claims in 1764, his only work was the
History of Massachusetts Bay, in two volumes, with
a third volume of state papers.* He was most assiduously engaged for many years in collecting manuscripts of all kinds, relating to the colonies, and the
number which he had obtained was very extensive.
They were unfortunately destroyed in part, during
the riot, when his house was nearly demolished.
Many of the most essential documents he had fortunately preserved in print, and a few others were
saved; but the loss of original papers on this occasion
was irreparable.

When he was appointed governor, as his manners
and temper were more conciliating, than those of
his predecessor, he might have been on better terms
with the legislature; but he had deeply pledged
himself in a course of measures, that rendered it impossible for him to give satisfaction to the country.
He grew more intoxicated with his elevation, till at
last he challenged the legislature to a discussion of
the whole basis and superstructure of colonial rights,
which, in the height of vanity or simplicity, he believed he could convince them by argument, that

---

* This history was brought down to the year 1750. He left a continuation
of it, which has remained in MS. since his death. Some measures have been
taken by the Massachusetts Historical Society to get it printed, which it may
be hoped will be attended with success.

they did not understand, and ought to abandon. The impolicy of this discussion and the discomfiture which he met with in the undertaking, were no recommendation to him in England.

When he was accused before the privy council of mal-conduct, by order of the legislature, it was, perhaps a fortunate circumstance for him, that Dr. Franklin was the organ of the accusers; since the government seemed so anxious to humble the agent, that they were quite ready to support the Governor. When the whole vengeance of parliament was directed against the town of Boston, after the destruction of the tea, and the two countries were rapidly approaching to the beginning of a civil war, the extraordinary delusion of Hutchinson as to the disposition of his countrymen, and the degree of resistance that might be expected from them, were too congenial to the obstinate purpose of the ministry not to be received with cordiality, and to procure him their countenance. He was rewarded for his services by a pension; and he stimulated the government to perseverance by his advice and information, which for a time had great weight.

After the first events of the war had shewn that the Americans were not to be easily overcome, and its further progress increased the probability of their eventual success, he began to be disregarded by the ministry; and treated with neglect at Court.*

* " When I agreed with you in your opinion of Mr. Hutchinson's repentance, I should have added, he had very great reason for repentance. Fled in his old age from the detestation of a country where he had been beloved,

He now saw all his ambitious dreams dissolved, his country mercilessly ravaged, and himself an exile forever. Although he used, as other Americans did, the term *home*, in speaking of England, yet the home of his affection was in Massachusetts. He had there obtained a degree of consideration and influence, which his devotion to the arbitrary designs of the administration, and zeal to bring his country under the yoke, had not entirely destroyed. He had been gradually enticed by his avidity for rank and fortune, to aid in destroying the rights of the colonies, and making them completely subordinate to the usurpation of parliament. Still, his attachments were local, and it was only in his native land that he could have enjoyed the distinction and power, which he so ruinously sought, had he succeeded in their attainment. As it resulted, he saw himself and his adherents irreversibly banished, his country on the road to triumph over his counsels, and the cause which he had supported too deeply disgraced,

---

esteemed, admired and applauded with exaggeration, in short, where he had been every thing from his infancy, to a country where he was nothing : pinched by a pension, which, though ample in Boston, would barely keep a house in London ; throwing round his baleful eyes on the exiled companions of his folly, hearing daily of the slaughter of his countrymen and conflagration of their cities, abhorred by the greatest men and soundest part of the nation, and neglected if not despised by the rest : hardened as had been my heart against him, I assure you, I was melted at the accounts I heard of his condition. Lord Townsend told me that he put an end to his own life. Though I did not believe this, I knew he was ridiculed by the courtiers. They laughed at his manners at the levee, at his perpetual quotation of his brother Foster, (Foster Hutchinson brother of Governor H. was a Judge of the Supreme Court in Massachusetts,) searching his pockets for letters to read to the King, and the King's turning away from him with his nose up, &c. &c."—Extract of a MS. letter of President Adams to the late W. Tudor, Esq.

to leave him any hope of reward for having promoted it. To these political reverses and withered expectations, were added domestic afflictions. He lost a most amiable daughter before leaving America, whose death occasioned him a deep and lasting regret; and in February 1780, his youngest son died of a pulmonary complaint. He was himself attacked early in the spring of that year, by the illness of which he died on the 3d of June, at Brompton, in his 69th year.

Governor Hutchinson was dazzled by the vast patronage in the power of the crown. Imposing titles and unbounded wealth might be the prize of successful service. The hopes inspired by these, corrupted his principles; and to secure his own fortune, he was willing to impair that of his country. The only excuse that can be offered for his political errors was, his thorough conviction, that the power of England was overwhelming. He and many others appeared stupified at the aspect of that power, and always treated the idea of the colonists defending themselves by an appeal to arms, as the suggestion of ignorance or insanity. He thought, as the colonies must be prostrated by the first blow of the parent country, that the only safe course to be pursued was to yield to its will, and endeavour by petitions to make its regulations as little onerous as possible. In this way he reconciled himself to the course which he adopted. In the progress of it, he omitted no exertion. Argument, persuasion, flattery, threats, perpetual watchfulness and intrigues, all were brought into action. If he had succeeded in placing the country in the power of the British parliament, it would not have been worth inhabiting. He and his arrogant superiors were utterly confounded by the event, and the colonies which they intended to crush, expanded from that very compression into a prosperous nation.

Apart from politics, the character of Hutchinson was highly estimable. He was temperate, industrious, indefatigable, affable and polite in his intercourse with society, a friend to literature, and rendering invaluable service in that branch of it connected with American history. He was upright in his private transactions, and condescending to those below him. Without being possessed of what is called genius, his incessant application and steady perseverance usefully supplied its deficiency. His natural position, and many of his inclinations, called him to the side of his native land, where he would have reached very high distinction; his ambition led him astray, and he died a pensioned, broken hearted exile.

Chapter XXVII.

*Termination of the British authority in Massachusetts in May
1774—Vindictive Measures against that Province—Mandamus
Counsellors—Boston Port Bill and Acts in Connection with it—
State of Public Feeling at this Epoch.*

THE termination of the British government in
Massachusetts, was very distinct and abrupt. .Gene-
ral Gage, the commander of the military forces, met
the new legislature on the 26th, of May 1774, and
delivered them a short speech, in which he announced his appointment as governor, and added
that he had the king's particular commands to hold
the general court at Salem, from the first of June.
After the court was adjourned to that place, the
council presented an answer to the speech, which
began with congratulating him on his appointment,
and offering their assurance of a cheerful co-opera-
tion in every thing, that could tend to restore harmony, and extricate, the province from its present em-
barrassments. They proceeded to say " we wish
your excellency every felicity. The greatest, of a
political nature, both to yourself and the province,
is, that your administration, in the principles and
general conduct of it, may be a happy contrast to
that of your two immediate predecessors." The
governor here interrupted the chairman, and desired
him to proceed no further, as he could not receive
an address which reflected so highly on his predeces-

sors, but that he would assign his reasons to the council in writing. On the 14th of June, he sent them the following message. " I cannot consent to receive an address which contains indecent reflections on my predecessors, who have been tried and honourably acquitted by the lords of the privy council, and their conduct approved by the king. I consider the address as an insult upon his majesty, and the lords of the privy council, and an affront to myself."

The legislature foreseeing they should be dissolved, chose members to join the first congress, which assembled at Philadelphia, in September of the same year, and also agreed to have a provincial congress to supply the place of the general court. On the 17th of June, while they were occupied in these transactions, the governor sent the secretary to dissolve them. When he came to the stairs, he found the door of the representatives chamber locked. The messenger was sent in, who gave notice to the speaker, that the secretary was in waiting. He informed the house, and they ordered the doors to be kept fast. The proclamation for dissolving them, was then published on the stairs, in presence of several of the members and of other persons. Thus expired, in fact, the political authority of the British government in Massachusetts.

That part of the charter, allowing the representatives to elect counsellors, was revoked in June, and mandamus counsellors were appointed in August, but their existence was only nominal. The administration of justice was continued in the king's name till July 1776. General Gage, employed himself in fortifying Boston in the summer, and the robes of civil government were changed for the uniform of military rule. The provincial Congress met at Salem, October 7th, and immediately adjourned to Concord. They chose John Hancock, speaker, and Benjamin Lincoln, clerk. They sent a message to General Gage, in which they informed him, that owing to the dissolution of the legislature, they had been chosen to "concert some adequate remedy for preventing impending ruin, and providing for the public safety." They remonstrated against his fortification of Boston, which, they said, had uselessly occasioned great uneasiness and resentment. They mentioned the severe measures then in execution against the province, and asked him, if it would not be insanity in a people tenacious of their rights, to neglect taking precautions for their security in such an alarming and menacing state of things. They issued an address to the inhabitants of the province in December, reminding them of the arduous situation in which they were placed, and that the eyes of their country and all Europe were upon them, and recommended firmness, moderation and perseverance. They exhorted them to do nothing "unbecoming their character as Americans, as citizens, and as christians." They advised them to look to their arms, and get them in readiness, as the worst might be apprehended, while the British ministry was suffered to tyrannize over America in the manner they then did. They hoped that the wisdom of the general congress might be able to extricate them from their present difficulties, and assured them " with the utmost cheerfulness" of their determination " to stand or fall with the liberties of America."

In the spring of this year, parliament, exasperated by the destruction of the tea, and many of the circumstances of that event having been grossly misrepresented, passed the Boston Port Bill without a division and almost unanimously ; a measure of equal rashness and cruelty. This was followed by that series of well known acts, which destroyed the most valuable privileges of the charter.

The shutting up the port of Boston, which took away the entire means of subsistence from several thousand persons, was an act of indiscriminate vengeance, that should not have been exercised till a most thorough investigation had been made, and the most atrocious guilt substantiated. Neither of these preliminaries had been undertaken, and the transaction offers a striking example, that even a parliament may through misapprehension and anger, deliberately pass an act, that might be expected only from the petulant and barbarous violence of an ignorant despot.* To the Boston Port Bill succeeded, " an act

---

* The debate on the " Boston Port Bill" exemplifies in a remarkable manner, the injustice which a legislative body may commit under an impulse of anger. Lord North observed, " that Boston had been the ringleader in all the riots, and had, at times, shewn a desire of seeing the laws of Great Britain attempted in vain, in the colony of Massachusetts Bay. That the act of the mob in destroying the tea, and other proceedings, belonged to the act of the public meeting, and that though other colonies were well and peaceably

for regulating the government of Massachusetts
Bay," which subverted the charter from its foundation. Two other bills were also passed, one for
" the trial of treason committed in America," reviving an obsolete statute of Henry VIII., the spirit of
whose reign was truly congenial to that, which then
dominated in parliament; and the other, " for the
impartial administration of justice" in the same province. This act was termed in the message of the
provincial congress, an act " to license murder." It
provided, " that in case any person should be indicted in that province for murder or any other capital
offence, and it should appear by information given
on oath to the governor, that the fact was committed

---

inclined towards the trade of the country, and the tea would have been landed
at New York without opposition, yet when the news came from Boston, that
the tea was destroyed, Governor Tryon, from the advice of the people, thought
that the face of things being changed since that account was sent, it would be
more prudent to send the tea back to England than to risk the landing of it.
His lordship observed, that Boston alone was to blame for having set this example, and therefore Boston ought to be the principal object of our attention
for punishment."

Even Colonel Barré, who was generally the friend of America, and had
corresponded with some of the leading patriots of Massachusetts, abandoned
his ground on this question. Colonel Barré said, " he was urged to rise to
discharge his duty in not giving a silent vote upon the occasion. The proposition before the house he could not help giving his hearty affirmation to : that
he liked it, harsh as it was ; he liked it for its moderation, and argued that the
noble Lord's (North) conduct would be of the same stamp throughout. He
said, I think Boston ought to be punished. *She* is your eldest *son* (here the
house laughed.")

But the most extraordinary speaker in these debates, was a member of the
name of Van. Mr. Van said, " he agreed to the flagitiousness of the offence
of the Americans, and therefore was of opinion that the town of Boston ought
to be knocked about their ears, and destroyed. *Delenda est Carthago*," said
he, "I am of opinion you will never meet with that proper obedience to the
laws of this country, until you have destroyed that nest of locusts."

in the exercise or aid of magistracy in suppressing
riots, and that a fair trial could not be had in the
province, he should send the person so indicted to
any other colony, or to Great Britain, to be tried."*

---

* In the debate on this bill, April 15th, 1774, Colonel Barré made some
atonement by his opposition to it, for his credulity and inconsistency in voting
for the Boston Port Bill. The following passage is extracted from his speech.

"It is proposed to stigmatize a whole people as persecutors of innocence,
and men incapable of doing justice ; yet you have not a single fact on which
to ground that imputation. I expected the noble lord would have supported
this motion, by producing instances of the officers of government in America
having been prosecuted with unremitting vengeance, and brought to cruel and
dishonourable deaths by the violence and injustice of American juries. But
he has not produced one such instance ; and I will tell you more, sir, he cannot produce one. The instances which have happened are directly in the
teeth of his proposition. Captain Preston and the soldiers who shed the blood
of the people, were fairly tried and fully acquitted. It was an American jury,
a New England jury, a Boston jury, which tried and acquitted them. Captain Preston has under his hand, publicly declared, that the inhabitants of the
very town in which their fellow citizens had been sacrificed, were his advocates and defenders. Is this the return you make them ? Is this the encouragement you give them to persevere in so laudable a spirit of justice and moderation ? When a commissioner of the customs, aided by a number of ruffians, assaulted the celebrated Mr. Otis in the midst of the town of Boston, and with the
most barbarous violence almost murdered him, did the mob, which is said to rule
that town, take vengeance on the perpetrators of this inhuman outrage agains
a person who is supposed to be their demagogue ? No, sir, the law tried them,
the law gave heavy damages against them, which the irreparably injured Mr.
Otis most generously forgave upon an acknowledgment of the offence. Can
you expect any more such instances of magnanimity, under the principle of
the Bill now proposed ?"

In this discussion, the same Mr. Van before cited, again signalized himself,
It is difficult to imagine what idea he had formed of the country, but he dis-
plays an ignorance that would be ludicrous, if his malevolence did not excite
more serious emotion. Every parliamentary body is liable to the evil of having such members ; it might perhaps be a useful lesson to give them for perusal, a few similar effusions of their compeers. Mr. Van said, "if they oppose
the measures of our government that are now sent out, I would do as was
done of old, in the time of the ancient Britons, I would burn and set fire to all
their woods, and leave their country open, to prevent that protection they now
have ; and if we are likely to lose that country, I think it better lost by our
own soldiers, than wrested from us by rebellious children."

These statutes tended to enslave and outlaw all the inhabitants of the colony.

These tyrannical and oppressive statutes, called into action among those whom they were intended to alarm and subdue, some of the noblest qualities of human character; courage, perseverance, generosity and fidelity. The people of Boston assembled after they were promulgated, and pledging themselves to abide by the principles which they had avowed, re-asserted their rights in still more energetic language. The town of Salem spurned the idea of raising their port on the ruins of its neighbour. The merchants of that place and of Marblehead, offered those of Boston the free use of their wharves and warehouses, till their harbour should be re-opened. In every town of the province, meetings were held to give the people of the capital assurances of sympathy and support. Contributions were every where made in money, clothing, and provisions for the use of the labouring classes, who were deprived of their customary means of living. The same enthusiastic feeling pervaded all the colonies. The cause of Boston was made the cause of the country. Her sufferings were pitied, her firmness admired, her constancy stimulated others. The ministry believed that by making an example of Boston, they should either force its inhabitants into submission, or if they continued refractory, that the province would be divided, and the other colonies deterred from taking its part. Never were mean and cruel calculations more signally confounded. The period was one of high and generous emotion. All the common rivalries and local competitions, which in ordinary times may be laudable and necessary, were suspended. Distances seemed lessened, and places remote from each other were brought into close friendship and communion. No one sought for safety by abandoning the sufferer, but the inflictions of ministerial vengeance made all the colonies volunteer, to defend the cause of those on whom the arm of power first fell, and as they had assumed the same principles, so in the hour of trial, they solemnly pledged themselves to partake the same fate.

Chapter XXVIII.

Character and Peculiar Circumstances of the People of Boston.

Though the ministerial designs were directed equally against all the colonies, yet a variety of circumstances concurred to make them bear more heavily on the New-England provinces, in the first instance, and more especially on Massachusetts, against whose capital they were concentrated. This was owing partly to these provinces being the most commercial, and their occupations were therefore more immediately injured by the parliamentary innovations; in part also, to the vigorous and unmixed character and denser population of the district, and still further to some peculiarities in the charter, and greater activity in the intrigues and enmity of the crown officers; to which may be added, their origin from the puritans and commonwealth's men of England, and the institutions and habits they had established; which although much enfeebled by time, were still to be seen through the transparent surface of society, like the veins and arteries carrying pulsation and life to every portion of the body.

As Boston was the capital where the army was collected, and the seat of the council that was to direct it, and as this city by its resistance, was doomed to be subdued in the first instance, to serve both as an example to others, and a point of departure for the forces of government; the circumstances are worthy of examination, which enabled that town to engage and finally triumph in a contest, so apparently unequal and so fraught with peril.

Boston possessed, at that period, an importance relatively, compared with the several cities of the continent, which as respects commerce and population, has since been transferred to other cities by the natural progress of events. The number of its inhabitants was about seventeen thousand. As they had shewn themselves extremely refractory against the new system, the government resolved, as the minister expressed it, " to try the question with them," and reduce them to unqualified submission. The forces employed seemed sufficient for the occasion, and the conduct of these citizens in maintaining the struggle for several years without yielding, affords a memorable example of virtue and courage. In a mighty battle it has happened that one party, out-numbered by the other, has been obliged to form its battalions into solid squares, and remain on the defensive against the desperate assaults of a superior force; and the world have admired the discipline and firmness that sustained such a struggle, and eventually achieved the victory; but, to every friend to human rights, how much greater interest does such a spectacle present, when unarmed citizens, surrounded, intersected, out-numbered, insulted by mercenary soldiers, yet still remaining vigilant, resolute, undismayed, are at last triumphant!

Many of the traits to be remarked in the character of the people of the capital, were equally to be found in the inhabitants of the province at large, as well as in those that bordered on it. Among the first may be stated the sobriety and prudence, the pertinacity and independence, which characterized their puritan ancestors, and which descended to them, modified, rather than impaired. The prevailing sect in the country, known by the name of independents or congregationalists, was the one, which of all the forms of protestantism, was the most averse to the domination of a hierarchy. This disposition in that sect, was called into fresh vigor, at this epoch, from the alarm about the establishment of an American episcopate : the men who opposed it were the lineal descendants, and in several cases the direct inheritors in unbroken succession, of hatred against Laud and the English Church, for the persecution of their ancestors. The people at large were much influenced by the clergy, as all their pastors were of their own choice, and were emphatically their fellow citizens, and readily imbibed their jealousies; which was rendered so much the easier, as most of the Crown-officers belonged to the obnoxious church, and sometimes with an offensive ostentation preferred its forms, and sneered at the austere simplicity of the congregational worship.

Next to religion, and still more active in its influence, was the civil organization of the community. The people were the subjects of a distant monarch, but royalty was merely in theory with them. They were not only republican, but democratic, and that in the simplest form. Originally, "the freemen in person," constituted a part of the government of the whole colony, but when they had so far spread, that they could no longer assemble together, they altered the charter to suit their convenience, and sent representatives to the general court,* but retained in the organization of all the towns, the principle of a simple democracy. All the officers were annually chosen; and all town affairs were decided upon in general meetings of the citizens, convened at stated peri-

---

* Chalmers, speaking of this change from a democracy to representative government, which took place in 1634, while he admits the necessity of it, adds, " the legality of those measures, however, cannot easily be supported by fair discussion, or by any other than those principles of independence, which naturally sprang up among such a people, during such a season, and have at all times governed their actions." p. 158.

ods, or whenever a dozen of the inhabitants thought it proper that the town should be called together. In this manner, not only measures of finance and regulations of police were considered and established, but also political subjects were openly discussed and decided according to the will of the majority. Every separate *town*, or incorporated district, therefore, formed a small republic of itself, which chose its own officers and managed its own concerns. Education, of the common kind at least, and moral and religious instruction, were universal, and enabled the people to transact their public business, and to act with moderation and intelligence under a form of government, of which they were individually component parts. Such is the effect of habit and education, that this unqualified democracy was as much the government of Boston,* as it was of the smallest district in the commonwealth; and in the capital as elsewhere, the numerous meetings of the citizens were held without guards, and without disturbance or confusion. The shew of hands determined every vote, and the hard hand of the day labourer, counted the same, as that which could give an order for tens of thousands. One salutary consequence that resulted from their town meetings, was the knowledge that the citizens attained of each other, and their mutual dependence and mutual restraint. Age and public services were always treated with suitable, though voluntary de-

---

* The *town* of Boston was made a *city* in 1822. The change in many respects is merely nominal.

ference, and this apparent equality in the decision of
questions, taught every man practically, the greatest principle of a republic, that the majority must
govern ; and also gave him a pride in maintaining its
decisions, as he was thereby paying respect to his
own agency.*

To the extensive influence of these religious and
civil institutions, enforced and explained by a common system of education, may be added other circumstances, which were accidental, but which especially distinguished the state of society in Boston at
the epoch of the revolution. The first was, the
little diversity that existed in the religious opinions
of the people, and which tended very much to their
acting harmoniously together. The variety of denominations that have established themselves in the town,
did not then exist : in fact, it may be said that there
were then only two, episcopalians and congregationalists, the latter being three or four times the most
numerous. There were no catholics, quakers, jews,

---

* " Their governments are popular in a high degree ; some are merely popular, in all the popular representative is the most weighty ; and this share of
the people in their ordinary government, never fails to inspire them with lofty sentiments, and with a strong aversion for whatever tends to deprive them
of their chief importance."—*Burke.*

In the " Vindication of the Town of Boston," the character of their public
meetings is defended, in noticing Governor Bernard's misrepresentations. " The
Governor has often been observed to discover an aversion to free assemblies :
no wonder then that he should be so particularly disgusted at a legal meeting
of the town of Boston, where a noble freedom of speech is ever expected and
maintained : an assembly of which it may be justly said, to borrow the language of the ancient Roman, with a little variation, *sentire quæ velint, et quæ
sentiunt dicere licet;* they think as they please and speak as they think : such
an assembly has ever been the dread, and often the scourge of tyrants." p. 29.

nor any regular churches at least, of several kinds of protestants.* The second peculiarity was the identity of its population. There were very few foreigners of any description, not even English, Irish, or Scotch ; much less those from continental Europe. Several very respectable families of French protestant descent, having lost their original language were completely blended with the rest of the inhabitants, who were almost wholly of English extraction, and had gradually increased from their own stock, with few additions from abroad, for the century preceding.

Besides the real equality of political and religious rights, there was no great disparity in the fortunes, or diversity in the style of living among the inhabitants. No hopeless inevitable poverty existed, and in the few instances of great wealth that were to be found, the absence of all daring display prevented any very obvious distinction between its possessors and their less opulent fellow citizens. The children were all educated at the same schools, where they were placed exactly on a level; and when their age entitled them to take a part in public concerns, they met on one floor, with an equal right to vote as they pleased on every question. The greater portion of the citizens were in a state of decent competence, which was created by their frugality and industry. They were tranquil and

---

* There were many quakers and some baptists in different parts of Massachusetts, there was also a quaker meeting-house in the capital, which has been for a very long period unoccupied.

virtuous in their habits; hardy, intelligent and enter-
prizing.* Their boyish associations, or their civic
meetings, brought them all to a personal acquaintance with each other. Every man's conduct was
known, and no person could be independent of popular opinion. No profession was entrenched in privileges, nor separated in interests from those of the
community. Men of all professions mingled in private social meetings as well as in public assemblies:
Even the clergy, who possessed great influence,
were in the habit of constant intercourse with their
fellow citizens, and shared in their pains, their plea-
sures, and opinions. It may be imagined, how easily
and rapidly every question and feeling of general
concern, circulated through the whole body of the
people, and with their habits, information, energy
and similarity of interests, what facilities existed for
an union of sentiment and action. Such was the
character and situation of the town,† against which

---

* In addition to the number of individuals who distinguished themselves in
different departments of the public service in their native land ; some inferences as to the general character of the inhabitants, may be drawn from the fortunes of those who took the part of the mother country. There were at one
time, seven natives of Boston and its vicinity, who were generals or admirals
in the British service, some of whom had other distinctions conferred upon
them ; and nearly as many more who attained very high rank in the civil service. Most of these gentlemen are now living, and there is probably no portion of the British dominions of an equal population, that has furnished such
a list of persons belonging to one generation, who have reached the same
eminence, without the aid of hereditary rank.

† To this brief sketch of the character and situation of the inhabitants of
Boston, one shade may be added, particularly as it regards a class, that has
long ceased to exist. There were before the revolution four or five thousand
slaves in the province, of which about one thousand were in the capital.

the British government directed this their first efforts, with an avowed intention of bringing it to submission, or to ruin.

Slavery was formally abolished in Massachusetts, at the formation of the constitution in 1780, and virtually so, some years before. A decision like that of Lord Mansfield's in the Somerset case, so much and so justly vaunted in England, had been previously made in this country; a particular account of which, will be found in an interesting report made to the legislature of Massachusetts by T. Lyman, Jr. Esq. in 1821. In Boston, the slaves were generally house servants, who led rather an easy life. They did only the slave's share of work, and were humanely treated. They were a careless, laughing race, faithful, subservient, impudent, and affectionate, and under the pretence of being slaves, often took great liberties. Many of them obtained their freedom by enlisting as soldiers, or sailors, previously to 1763, and several of them fought bravely in the battles of the revolution. Their dialect and their blunders in language, have a peculiar character, which has often been employed in ridicule. Though the majority of these people exhibited that hebetude, which is the usual concomitant of ignorance, yet there were many among them who possessed much natural shrewdness and humour. A large collection of anecdotes might be made on this subject, but the following must suffice for examples in this way.

If some previous remarks on Doctors Cooper and Chauncy are recollected, they will render the following story more intelligible. Dr. Cooper, who was a man of accomplished manners and fond of society, was able, by the aid of his fine talents, to dispense with some of the severe study that others engaged in. This, however, did not escape the envy and malice of the world, and it was said in a kind of petulant and absurd exaggeration, that he used to walk to the south-end of a Saturday, and if he saw a man riding into town in a black coat, would stop, and ask him to preach the next day. Dr. Chauncy was a close student, very absent and irritable. On these traits in the character of the two clergymen, a servant of Dr. Chauncy's laid his scheme to obtain a particular object from his master. Scipio went into his master's study one morning to receive some directions, which the Doctor having given, resumed his writing, but the servant still remained. The master, looking up a few minutes afterwards, and supposing he had just come in, said, "Scipio, what do you want?" "I want a new coat, massa." "Well, go to Mrs. Chauncy, and tell her to give you one of my old coats;" and was again absorbed in his studies. The servant remained fixed. After a while, the doctor, turning his eyes that way, saw him again, as if for the first time, and said, "What do you want, Scip?" "I want a new coat, massa." "Well, go to my wife, and ask her to give you one of my old coats," and fell to writing once more. Scipio remained in the same posture. After a few minutes, the doctor looked

Whatever may be the reputation of Boston in history, there is one circumstance at least, to be remarked through the whole revolutionary ferment, for which it is perhaps in vain to seek a parallel in the annals of any other country; and which, wherever cruelty shall be execrated as the greatest of crimes, and mercy and humanity honoured, as the highest marks of civilization, will be admired and remembered. The struggle against oppression, while the hand of the British government was immediately upon the town, may be said to have begun with the stamp act, in 1765, and continued till the evacuation by the English army in 1776. During this peri-

---

towards him, and repeated the former question, "Scipio, what do you want?" "I want a new coat, massa." It now flashed over the doctor's mind, that there was something of repetition in this dialogue. "Why, have I not told you before, to ask Mrs. Chauncy to give you a coat? get away." "Yes, massa, but I no want a black coat." "Not want a black coat! and why not?" "Why, massa, I 'fraid to tell you, but I don't want a black coat." "What's the reason you don't want a black coat? tell me directly." "O! massa, I don't want a black coat, but I 'fraid to tell the reason, you so passionate!" "You rascal! will you tell me the reason?" "O! massa, I'm sure you be angry." "If I had my cane, you villain, I'd break your bones: will you tell me what you mean?" "I 'fraid to tell you, massa, I know you be angry." The doctor's impatience was now highly irritated, and Scipio perceiving, by his glance at the tongs, that he might find a substitute for the cane, and that he was sufficiently excited, said, "Well, massa, you make me tell, but I know you be angry.---I 'fraid, massa, if I wear another black coat, Dr. Cooper ask me to preach for him!" This unexpected termination realized the negro's calculation; his irritated master burst into a laugh: "Go, you rascal, get my hat and cane, and tell Mrs. Chauncy, she may give you a coat of any colour; a red one, if you choose." Away went the negro to his mistress, and the doctor to tell the story to his friend, Dr. Cooper.

A negro whose principles were in favour of the administration, met one day with Edes, the printer of the Boston Gazette, which was entirely devoted to the patriotic cause, and enquired of him, what was the news? the printer told him there was nothing new. "Well, if you've nothing new, massa Edes. I s'pose you print the same dam old lie over again."

od, there happened many occasions of great excitement; the vexations on commerce were numerous and irritating; a military force stationed within the walls, at one time consisting of only a few companies, increased at others, till it out numbered the male inhabitants of the city; the most obnoxious and violent of the ministerial partizans, whether natives or others, collected on this spot, against which they were covertly soliciting and stimulating the vengeance of the mother country; the civil and military officers frequently goading the citizens with menaces and insults, and the soldiers, in one case, firing upon and killing several persons; yet notwithstanding all these circumstances, in spite of all the exasperation of the times, and all the rashness that may be supposed incidental to a populous democracy; throughout this whole period of ferment and revolution, not a single human life was taken by the inhabitants either by assassination, popular tumult, or public execution.*

---

* See Appendix.

Chapter XXIX.

Proceedings of General Gage—History of the two pieces of artillery called the " Hancock and Adams"—Approach of hostilities— Anecdotes—General Warren—Battle of Bunker Hill—Colonel Prescott.

AFTER General Gage assumed the government of the province, the military aspect of the administration grew daily more predominant ; and he, more accustomed to the duties of military than of civil life, occupied himself more particularly with cares of the former description, while the people had, by their proceedings in self-defence, nearly divested him of all agency in the latter department. At the close of 1774, and in the early part of 1775, he began to take into his possession, all the arms and military stores belonging to individuals and the public. These measures, which led to the commencement of hostilities, occasioned a transaction in Boston, which is worthy of being recorded.

In November, 1766, the General Court ordered four brass cannon to be purchased for the use of the artillery companies in Boston. Two of these guns, which were three-pounders, were kept in a gun house that stood opposite the Mall, at the corner of West street. A school house was the next building, and a yard inclosed with a high fence was common to both. Major Paddock* who then commanded

---

* Major Adino Paddock was a coach maker, a reputable citizen and decided loyalist : he left Boston with the British army, and was subsequently rewarded

the company, having been heard to express his intention of surrendering these guns to the British army, a few individuals resolved to secure for the country a property which belonged to it, and which, in the present emergency, had an importance very disproportionate to its intrinsic value.

Having concerted their plan, the party passed through the school house into the gun house, and were able to open the doors which were upon the yard, by a small crevice, through which they raised the bar that secured them. The moment for the execution of the project was that of the roll call, when the sentinel who was stationed at one door of the building, would be less likely to hear their operations. The guns were taken off their carriages. carried into the school room, and placed in a large box under the master's desk, in which wood was kept. Immediately after the roll call, a lieutenant and sergeant came into the gun house to look at the cannon, previously to removing them. A young man* who had assisted in their removal, remained by the building, and followed the officer in, as an *innocent* spectator. When the carriages were found without the guns, the sergeant exclaimed " By G—, they 're

---

by the government of Guernsey. There is one circumstance that may cause him to be remembered in Boston, when his share in the politics of the day will be forgotten. The row of elm trees in front of the Granary burying ground, was planted by him.

* Samuel Gore, Esq., from whom this narration was received. The persons who aided, were Messrs. Balch, Gridley, Whiston, and two or three more. The schoolmaster, who of course knew the whole transaction, was *Master* Holbrook.

gone! I'll be d——d if these fellows won't steal the
teeth out of your head, while you're keeping guard."
They then began to search the building for them,
and afterwards the yard; and when they came to
the gate that opened into the street, the officer observed, that they could not have passed that way,
because a cobweb across the opening was not broken.
They went next into the school house, which they
examined all over, except the box, on which the
master placed his foot, which was lame; and the officer, with true courtesy, on that account excused him
from rising. Some boys were present, but not one
lisped a word. The officers went back to the gun
room, when their volunteer attendant, in kind sympathy for their embarrassment, suggested to them,
that perhaps they had been carried into Mr. Green-
leaf's (now the Washington) garden, opposite. On
this, the sergeant took him by the collar, gave him
a push, and said " it was very likely that he was one
of the d——d rebels who helped to get them off, and
that he had better make himself scarce!" This was
too near a guess to make it worth while to wait for
a second hint, and he left them. They soon after
retired in vexation.

The guns remained in that box for a fortnight, and
many of the boys were acquainted with the fact, but
not one of them betrayed the secret. At the end of
that time, the persons who had withdrawn them,
came in the evening with a large trunk on a wheel-
barrow; the guns were put into it and carried up to
Whiston's blacksmith's shop at the South-end, and

there deposited under the coal. After lying there for a while, they were put into a boat in the night, and safely transported within the American lines. Under the circumstances of almost utter destitution of all military stores, in which the American army was about to commence a long contest with a nation, which covered the sea and the land with her cannon, this acquisition was far from being insignificant.*

The guns were in actual service through the whole war. After the peace, the State of Massachusetts applied to congress for their restoration, which was granted according to the following resolve ;

"MONDAY MAY 19TH, 1788.

" Congress assembled. Present, New Hampshire, Massachusetts, Pennsylvania, Delaware, Maryland, Virginia, and South Carolina, and from Rhode Island, Mr. Arnold, from New York, Mr. Hamilton, from North Carolina, Mr. Williamson, and from Georgia, Mr. Baldwin. The Secretary at war having represented to congress ; That there are in the arsenals of the United States, two brass cannon,

---

* When it is remembered that America, trusting in Providence, entered the field with only a sling and a few pebbles, the fortunate and skilful undertaking to remove these cannon from the very midst of the British army, becomes peculiarly interesting. A very prompt and essential service in this way, was rendered by the late patriotic Governor Langdon and General John Sullivan, of New Hampshire, who seized and transported to a place of safety, a quantity of gunpowder and fifteen light cannon from the fort at Portsmouth, only the day before a frigate and sloop of war arrived with a detachment of troops, that were sent to protect these military stores. An account of this well executed affair may be found in Belknap's New Hampshire, Vol. 2. p. 376.

which constituted one moiety of the field artillery, with which the last war was commenced on the part of America, and which were constantly on service throughout the war; that the said cannon are the property of the Commonwealth of Massachusetts, and that the Governor thereof hath requested that they be returned." Therefore,

Resolved, That the Secretary at war cause a suitable inscription to be placed on the said cannon; and that he deliver the same to the order of his Excellency the Governor of the Commonwealth of Massachusetts."

General Knox, then secretary at war, who had commanded the artillery of the American army during the revolution, one of the most gallant, generous, high minded men whom that army contained, well knew the history of these cannon, as they were his *fellow townsmen* from the beginning. In pursuance of the orders of congress, he caused the arms of Massachusetts and the following inscription to be chiseled upon them in bold relief. These two cannon are now in charge of " the Ancient and Honourable Artillery Company," and called the *Hancock* and *Adams*, after the two patriots proscribed by General Gage, from whose grasp they were rescued.

" The
ADAMS.
Sacred to Liberty.
This is one of four cannon,
which constituted the whole train

of Field Artillery,
possessed by the British colonies of
North America,
at the commencement of the war.
on the 19th of April 1775.
This cannon
and its fellow
belonging to a number of citizens of
Boston,
were used in many engagements
during the war.
The other two, the property of the
Government of Massachusetts
were taken by the enemy.
By order of the United States
in Congress assembled
May 19th, 1788."

The other cannon referred to, were concealed in the stable of the second house west from the court house, on the south side of Court Street. Mr. Williams, a respectable farmer of Roxbury, drove in his own team with a load of hay, which was taken into that stable; the cannon were then put in the bottom of the cart, which was loaded with manure, and in this way they were taken out of town without opposition. The British officers heard on the same day, that the cannon were concealed in that street, and were to be removed in the evening, and in consequence, many of them patrolled the street for several hours, but the guns were already safe within the American lines.

These offensive measures of precaution by the

Governor of the Province, induced preparations for defence on the part of the people ; for it may be truly said, that the people universally had made the dispute their chief concern.

The patriotic leaders who remained in Boston, whose communications with the country became gradually more embarrassed and restricted, watched with sleepless vigilance all the movements of the British army. Dr. Warren, having ascertained that the British General was preparing an expedition to destroy the stores at Concord, sent Mr. Revere* as an express to give Messrs. Adams and Hancock notice of the movement. The British officers were patrolling the roads, and the messenger was arrested on his way, but the alarm was spread in all directions. The troops embarked that night from the westerly side of the town, landed at Lechmere point, and met a small body of militia at Lexington. The memorable skirmish of the 19th of April began at that place, and the declaration of American rights was then for the first time written in blood.

---

* Colonel Paul Revere afterwards commanded a regiment of artillery in the militia of Massachusetts. His original profession was that of a goldsmith, but, subsequently, he established a considerable foundry of cannon and bells, which is continued. He was one of the most influential citizens of the town, and entirely in the confidence of the leading patriots. He kept himself in readiness to go as an express at any moment. He had a small canoe concealed in a dock at the north part of the town, and a riding dress always in order to be put on at a moment's warning. Warren came to him as soon as he heard of the intended expedition, and Col. Revere silently rowed himself by the ships of war and landed in Charlestown. He wrote an account of this expedition, which may be found in the Fifth volume of the Mass. His. Soc. Coll. Mr. Revere was through life an upright, useful, respectable citizen. He died in 1818, in his 84th year.

The events of this period, and the innumerable demonstrations of public feeling, render the delusion by which the British government was then bewildered, with regard to the temper and character of the country, almost marvellous. The alarm of this attack seemed to spread with the velocity of sound, and armed men rushed in from every quarter, with the quickness of an echo. A fine collection of anecdotes might be made, to illustrate the determined resolution and ardent enthusiasm, that pervaded the country. The instance of General Putnam is well known, who, hearing of the Lexington engagement while he was ploughing on his farm, more than an hundred miles distant, unyoked his cattle, left his plough in the unfinished furrow, and without changing his dress, mounted his horse and rode off to Cambridge, to learn the state of things. He then returned to Connecticut and brought a regiment in the course of a few weeks. Among other examples that might be related, the following is from a living witness. The day that the report of this affair reached Barnstable, a company of militia immediately assembled and marched off to Cambridge. In the front rank, there was a young man, the son of a respectable farmer, and his only child. In marching from the village, as they passed his house, he came out to meet them. There was a momentary halt. The drum and fife paused for an instant. The father, suppressing a strong and evident emotion, said, " God be with you all, my friends! and John, if you, my son, are called into battle, take care that you behave like a man, or else let me never see your face again!" A tear started into every eye, and the march was resumed.

General Warren left the town on the morning of the 19th of April, after being informed by an express that the British troops had fired on the militia at Lexington. He arrived in time to take a part in the engagement with the enemy on their return, in the course of which his temple was grazed by a ball. In the absence of Mr. Hancock he was chosen president of the Provincial Congress, which assembled at Cambridge on the 22d of April. There are few names in the annals of American patriotism more dearly cherished by the brave and good; few that will shine with more increasing lustre, as the obscurity of time grows darker, than that of General Warren. He will be the personal representative of those brave citizens, who with arms hastily collected, sprang from their peaceable homes to resist aggression, and on the plains of Lexington and the heights of Charlestown, cemented with their blood the foundation of American liberty.

He was born in Roxbury, a town which bounds Boston on the south, was educated at Harvard College, and received his first degree in 1759. He studied medicine and exercised his profession in Boston. As a physician, he was possessed of great skill. His practice was extensive among the richer classes of society, while his gratuitous visits to the poor, which were never withheld, procured for him that high degree of respect and affection, which an able and humane physician is always sure to obtain. Had he lived in ordinary times, he might have continued this useful career, and in alleviating human suffering and prolonging human life have secured the gratitude of society, and placed his name among the distinguished individuals of a most respectable profession. But another and a loftier destiny was alotted to him.

The disputes with the mother country, regarding taxation, began about the same time that he was entering the world. His attention was early drawn to political affairs, and he soon engaged in them with the whole ardour of his soul. He realized very fully, that this dispute respecting a tax, comparatively insignificant, involved the question of liberty or slavery, of respect or degradation; and he was soon prepared to bring it to a decision. He was one of those persons who saw very early, " *that we must fight*," and the impetuosity of a young and gallant spirit made him always ready for the alternative. He wrote many essays in the newspapers of those times, and never fell below the tone of the day. Yet, with very great decision, and great frankness of manner, he possessed circumspection, prudence, and judgment in the management of political concerns.

General Warren belonged to a secret committee or association, composed of some of the leading patriots and a number of the principal mechanics, who met originally at the north part of the town, and afterwards at the Green Dragon tavern. At these meetings, which first gave rise to the term *caucus*,* many

---

* This word may be found in Mr. Pickering's Vocabulary. Although of such recent origin, it is difficult to settle its derivation; it is pretty well understood, however, in every part of the United States.

measures were concerted that afterwards were proposed in town meetings. They also fixed on the candidates who should be supported for various public offices. A respectable mechanic commonly presided, and propositions were often made by men of that class, which had been prepared by others. Many persons were instrumental in the adoption of resolutions by these assemblies, who were not conspicuous before the public; and a determination made by the caucus, seldom failed of being carried into effect. Warren and S. Adams were two of the principal advisers of this assembly.

As the times grew more difficult, he took a larger part in public business, was on all the important committees of the town, and was twice requested to deliver public orations. His profession had not called upon him to be profoundly learned in matters of law and legislation, but every department was filled, and he supported those who possessed these acquirements. His style, imbued with a classic love of liberty was vehement, declamatory, eloquent, and flowed naturally from his disposition.

When he delivered his second oration on the 5th of March 1775, he exhibited marked proofs of the energy and firmness of his character. This was the fifth anniversary* of " the Boston Massacre ;" a name that would seem very pompous in countries more

---

* This commemoration was kept up till the year 1783; after which period there being no longer any danger of standing armies, it was on many accounts expedient to change the subject of the oration, and after that year the 4th of July was substituted.

accustomed to such scenes, but which indicated the rarity of bloodshed, and the horror which it created among the people, no less than their hatred of a standing army as an instrument of governing. The ceremony was far from being an agreeable one to the army then quartered in the town, and many threats had been thrown out, that the oration would be interrupted if the orator cast any reflections on standing armies. After these endeavours to intimidate were known, Warren volunteered through his friends, to deliver the address. The regular authorities of the town were present, and the form of an adjourned town meeting, as is still the case for the annual oration, was observed, and like that it was delivered in the Old South Church.*

The circumstances on this occasion were of a very trying kind, and even a brave man might have been embarrassed. The building was crowded to excess, and even the aisles and pulpit stairs were so completely filled, that he was obliged to enter the desk by a ladder placed against the window, as the famous Whitefield had once done before him for the same reason. Many British officers were present with their side arms, and an air of menace was as-

---

* During the siege of Boston this church was turned into a riding school for a regiment of cavalry, and the retainers of the army kept a dram shop in one of its galleries. This was an exhibition of resentment that was neither dignified nor manly, but it can hardly be called "sacrilege," as has been sometimes done. The dissenting sects do not attach any superstitious sanctity to the walls of a meeting house, which is used occasionally for temporal concerns. The church in question was particularly obnoxious, from having been the scene of so many public meetings for political purposes.

sumed by many in rather an ostentatious manner.
The various excitement of an immense audience was
apparent in every countenance, and seemed flushing
and panting for an explosion. Warren was perfectly unruffled, and proceeded with deliberation to deliver a most animated discourse. •On the subject of
the mischief of standing armies, the most zealous
patriot could have wished for no stronger language.
He adverted to the case of ancient Rome, and
shewed how she had fallen from her height of glory
and power, by the means of her mercenary soldiers,
until she became the scorn of mankind. From this
he passed to the employment of soldiers in modern
times; that they were necessarily the enemies of
freedom and justice, because the first principle that
was taught them, is to obey their officers without
reference to the laws of the land. That every nation which suffered them must finally be corrupted
and enslaved. He described the event they were celebrating, in the most vivid manner, pictured the actual
crime which the military had committed, and the
scenes of horror they had almost produced, but that
the firmness of the inhabitants had prevented the
dreadful scenes that were so near taking place, that
they had procured their dismissal from the town;
and if it had not been for their humanity, that the
whole body of troops would have been destroyed.
Stronger language could not have been used, if no
threats had been uttered, or no English officer been
present. There was, however, no disturbance, and
the oration was delivered without interruption to an
admiring and applauding audience.

As the crisis approached, Warren who had long determined to abandon all his professional views, and to enter the foremost ranks of the American army, devoted some time every day to regular practice of the manual exercise. His duties often led him into circles frequented by the English officers, and though they avoided affronting him personally, he could not escape hearing much of that insolence which was too prevalent among them. He felt these insults to his country as if they had been directed against himself. A gentleman* who was a student with him in 1774, relates, that in returning one evening to his house situated in Hanover-street, he passed in Court-street a number of British officers; among them Colonel Wolcot, who afterwards made himself remarkable for a paltry insult in addressing General Washington, as " Mr. Washington," in a letter on the subject of prisoners; and as Warren's friends were then constantly expecting, that some attempt would be made to seize him by the British, he mentioned the circumstance, and advised him not to go out. He replied, " I have a visit to make to Mrs. ——— in Cornhill this evening, and I will go at once; come with me." He then put his pistols in his pocket, and they went out. They passed the officers without molestation from them. It was found the next day, that they were watching for the cannon which had been safely removed that same morning, as before mentioned. Warren said one day to this student,

---

* Hon. William Eustis.

having his spirit fretted by some of the taunts that the British officers were frequently uttering, "These fellows say we won't fight; by heavens, I hope I shall die up to my knees in blood!" This was spoken but a few weeks previous to his death.*

General Warren received his commission, as Major General, only four days before the battle of Bunker Hill. But after the affair at Lexington, when the militia began to collect, and an army to be formed, he was incessantly engaged with a few officers who had obtained experience in former wars, in endeavouring to introduce some regular organization among men, who where enthusiastic and brave, but unarmed, undisciplined, and with none of the habits or knowledge of soldiers. He was, at the same time, President of the provincial congress, which place he held till his death. He had no opportunity to assume an actual military command.

---

* How much fatal animosity has been created between nations, by the despicable insolence of sneering at others' courage. Reflections of this kind, though they may sometimes be uttered by men of honour, from thoughtlessness, are commonly the effusions of bullies and cowards. The British officers had before the commencement of the contest some excuse for giving way to this feeling. Confident in their own discipline, their abundant preparation and their brilliant appearance, they thought there was nothing to oppose them but a rabble which might be easily dispersed, and which they were eager to effect. A few of the officers felt an esteem for the people, and were reluctant to engage in a civil war, which they knew would bring great misfortunes upon the country, and as they supposed, overwhelm it. There was so much folly and disgusting arrogance in many of the subalterns, and careless ignorance about the whole subject of dispute, that one of their superior officers published a small pamphlet, entitled, "A letter from a Veteran to the Officers of the army encamped at Boston." It is remarkably well written, and while it justifies his own government, reproves the frivolity and rashness that treated the Americans with contempt. It was attributed to General Prescott.

The battle of Bunker Hill has been too often and too well described, to require any repetition of the attempt.* In itself, it was in many respects, one of the most remarkable conflicts that has moistened the earth with human blood. No spirit of prophecy is required to foretel, that from the consequences with which it is connected, and which it may be said to have guaranteed, after ages will consider it one of the most interesting of all battles, and that it will be hallowed by the gratitude of mankind, as among the most precious and beneficent contests, ever waged in behalf of human rights and human happiness. The American force on that day was commanded by the brave colonel Prescott. General Warren went to the ground as a volunteer, not to take any command, but to encourage his fellow citizens, for they were not yet soldiers, in the hour of danger. He fell in the redoubt, towards the close of the action, and when his death was known, the enemy consoled themselves in believing, that his single life was nearly an equivalent for the heavy loss, which they had experienced.

The exultation of his enemies could not, however, exceed the grief of his friends. Distinguished by great comeliness of face and figure, his countenance exhibited rather the air of the youthful period he

---

* General Burgoyne wrote a brilliant description of this battle. In the seventh volume of the North American Review, there is a sketch in which the *moral* circumstances attending it are alluded to, with masterly discrimination, and the writer has really rendered any further effort superfluous. A recent account of it with a plan, has been published by Colonel Swett, who has preserved many interesting anecdotes that would soon have been lost.

was leaving, than of the mature age on which he had entered.* Intrepid, generous and high minded, gifted with fine talents and an ardent soul, his loss seemed irreparable and was bitterly deplored. If fame, however, be the noblest object of human pursuit, he was early crowned with success; and who would not exchange all the years of a lingering existence for his premature fate! Perhaps his fall was as useful to his country, as it was glorious to himself. His death served to adorn the cause for which he contended, excited emulation, and gave a pledge of perseverance and ultimate success. In the grand sacrifice, of which a new nation was that day to celebrate in the face of the world, to prove their sincerity to Heaven, whose Providence they had invoked, the noblest victim was the most suitable offering.

The American troops in this battle were commanded by Colonel William Prescott, of Pepperel, an officer distinguished by the most determined bravery. He was the son of the Hon. B. Prescott of Groton, who was for many years an influential member of the colonial legislature, and who was once chosen agent for the province in England. William Prescott was born in 1726, and was a lieutenant of the provincial troops at the capture of Cape Breton, in 1758. The British General was so much pleased with his conduct in that campaign, that he offered him a com-

---

* His very youthful expression will be remarked by every one in Colonel Trumbull's picture of the battle of Bunker Hill.

mission in the regular army, which he declined, to return home with his countrymen. . From this time till the approach of the American war, he remained on his farm in Pepperel, filling various municipal offices, and enjoying the esteem and affection of his fellow citizens. As the difficulties between the mother country and the colonies grew more serious, he took a deeper and more decided part in public affairs.

In 1774 he was appointed to command a regiment of *minute men*, organized by the provincial congress. He marched his regiment to Lexington, immediately on receiving notice of the intended operations of General Gage against Concord, but the British detachment had retreated before he had time to meet it. He then proceeded to Cambridge, and entered the army that was ordered to be raised; and the greater part of his officers and privates volunteered to serve with him for the first campaign.

On the 16th of June, three regiments were placed under him, and he was ordered to Charlestown in the evening, to take possession of Bunker Hill and throw up works in its defence. When they reached the ground, it was perceived that Breed's hill, which is a few rods south of Bunker's hill, was the most suitable station. The troops under the direction of Colonel Gridley, an able engineer, were busily engaged in throwing up a small redoubt and breast-work, which latter was formed by placing two rail fences near together, and filling the interval with the new mown hay, lying on the ground. There was something in the rustic materials of these defences, hastily made, in a short summer's night, within gun-shot of a powerful enemy, that was particularly apposite to a body of armed husbandmen, who had rushed to the field at the first sound of alarm.

As soon as these frail works were discovered the next morning, the British commander made preparations to get possession of them. General Howe with various detachments amounting to near 5000 men, was ordered to dislodge the " rebels." The force which Colonel Prescott could command for the defence of the redoubt and breast-work, was about 1200 men. Very few of these had ever seen an action. They had been labouring all night in creating these defences; and the redoubt, if it could be so called, was open on two sides. Instead of being relieved by fresh troops, as they had expected, they were left without supplies of ammunition or refreshment, and thus fatigued and destitute, they had to bear the repeated assaults of a numerous, well appointed, veteran army. They destroyed nearly as many of their assailants, as the whole of their own number engaged ; and they did not retreat till their ammunition was exhausted, and the enemy supplied with fresh troops and cannon completely overpowered them.

Colonel Prescott lost nearly one quarter of his own regiment in the action. When General Warren came upon the hill, Colonel Prescott asked him if he had any orders to give ; he answered, " no,

colonel, I am only a volunteer, the command is yours."
When he was at length forced to tell his men to
retreat, as well as they could, he was one of the last
who left the intrenchment. He was so satisfied with
the bravery of his companions, and convinced that
the enemy were disheartened 'by the severe and unexpected loss which they had sustained, that he
requested the commander in chief to give him two
regiments, and he would retake the position the
same night.

He continued in the service till the beginning of
1777, when he resigned and returned to his home.
But in the autumn of that year he went as a volunteer to the northern army under General Gates, and
assisted in the capture of General Burgoyne. This
was his last military service. He was subsequently
for several years a member of the legislature, and
died in 1795, in the 70th year of his age.

Colonel Prescott* was a genuine specimen of an
energetic, brave, and patriotic citizen, who was
ready in the hour of danger to place himself in the
van, and partake in all the perils of his country,
feeling anxious for its prosperity, without caring to
share in its emoluments ; and maintaining beneath a
plain exterior and simple habits, a dignified pride in
his native land, and a high minded love of freedcm.

The immediate results of this engagement were

---

* In Colonel Trumbull's painting of the battle of Bunker hill, Colonel Prescott is represented in a dress which is characteristic of the force he commanded ;
though he does not occupy so prominent a station in the picture, as he did in
the action.

great and various. Though the Americans were obliged to yield the ground for want of ammunition, yet their defeat was substantially a triumph.* The actual loss of the British army was severe, and was deeply felt by themselves and their friends. The charm of their invincibility was broken. The hopes of the whole continent were raised. It was demonstrated, that although they might burn towns, or overwhelm raw troops by superior discipline and numbers, yet the conquest at least would not be an easy one. Those patriots, who under the most arduous responsibility, at the peril of every thing which men of sense and virtue can value, hazarded in the support of public principles present ruin and future disgrace, though they felt this onset to be only the beginning of a civil war, yet were invigorat-

---

* The anxiety and various emotions of the people of Boston, on this occasion, had a highly dramatic kind of interest. Those who sided with the British troops began to see even in the duration of this battle, the possibility that they had taken the wrong side, and that they might become exiles from their country. While those whose whole soul was with their countrymen, were in dreadful apprehension for their friends, in a contest, the severity of which was shewn by the destruction of so many of their enemies. After the battle had continued for some time, a young person living in Boston, possessed of very keen and generous feelings, bordering a little perhaps on the romantic, as was natural to her age, sex, and lively imagination, finding that many of the wounded troops brought over from the field of action were carried by her residence, mixed a quantity of refreshing beverage, and with a female domestic by her side, stood at the door and offered it to the sufferers as they were borne along, burning with fever and parched with thirst. Several of them grateful for the kindness, gave her, as they thought, consolation, by assuring her of the destruction of her countrymen. One young officer said, " never mind it my brave young lady, we have peppered 'em well, depend upon it." Her dearest feelings, deeply interested in the opposite camp, were thus unintentionally lacerated, while she was pouring oil and wine into their wounds.

ed by its result, which cleared away some painful un-
certainties, while the bravery and firmness that had
been displayed by their countrymen, inspired a more
positive expectation of being ultimately triumphant.*

* When Americans wish to estimate the merits of the leading patriots, who
obtained the independence of their country, it is not sufficient to consider the
good that has resulted from their efforts, vast as it may be, but to do them
full justice, the circumstances in which they acted and the chances which
they were liable to, must be examined. The concluding paragraphs of the
essays of *Massachusettensis*, the most able papers that were produced on the
government side during the dispute, will throw some light on this subject. The
author was evidently sincere in his opinions, and they were urged with great
earnestness and eloquence ; yet mild and humane as he was, it may be inferred from his hints, that the fate of the patriots, if they had been unsuccessful,
would have been an ignominious death. This last letter, addressed "to the
inhabitants of the Province of Massachusetts Bay," was published April 3d, a
fortnight only before the battle of Lexington.

" Do you expect to conquer in war? War is no longer a simple, but an intricate science, not to be learned from books, or two or three campaigns, but
from long experience. You need not be told that his majesty's generals, Gage
and Haldimand, are possesed of every talent requisite to great commanders,
matured by long experience in many parts of the world, and stand high in
military fame : that many of the officers have been bred to arms from their
infancy, and a large proportion of the army *now* here, have already reaped
immortal honours in the iron harvest of the field. Alas, my friends, you have
nothing to oppose to this force, but a militia unused to service, impatient of
command, and destitute of resources. Can your officers depend on the privates, or the privates upon the officers? Your war can be but little more than
mere tumultuary rage ; and besides there is an awful disparity between
troops that fight the battles of their sovereign, and those that follow the standard of rebellion. These reflections may arrest you in an hour that you think
not of, and come too late to serve you. Nothing short of a miracle could gain
you one battle, but could you destroy all the British troops that are now here,
and burn the men of war that command our coast, it would be but the beginning of sorrow ; and yet without a decisive battle one campaign would ruin
you. This province does not produce its necessary provision, when the husbandman can pursue his calling without molestation ; what then must be your
condition when the demand shall be increased and the resource in a manner
cut off? Figure to yourselves what must be your distress, should your wives
and children be driven from such places, as the king's troops shall occupy, into
the interior parts of the province, and they as well as you, be destitute of sup-

Chapter XXX.

*Anecdotes of Otis after the close of his public career—His residence
in Andover—Last visit to Boston—Return to Andover—Remarkable death—His character.*

THE public career of Otis, may be said to have
ended in 1769, for though in 1771 he was again in the
legislature, his exertions were less arduous ; and after
that period, notwithstanding his occasional appearance in the courts of justice and in town meetings,
yet he was little more than a majestic ruin. In his
lucid intervals he was still powerful, but as these
were liable to be interrupted, it was impossible to
confide important business to him. During the remaining years of his life, he was sometimes in a fren-
zied state, at others, exhibited rather the eccentricity of a humourist than absolute derangement. The
wound which he had received rendered him ex-

·port. I take no pleasure in painting these scenes of distress. The whigs affect
to divert you from them by ridicule ; but should war commence, you can expect nothing but its severities. Might I hazard an opinion, but few of your
leaders ever intended to engage in hostilities, but they may have rendered
inevitable what they only intended for intimidation. Those that unsheath the
sword of rebellion may throw away the scabbard, they cannot be treated with
while in arms, and if they lay them down they are in no other predicament
than conquered rebels. The conquered in other wars do not forfeit the rights
of men, nor all the rights of citizens, even their bravery is rewarded by a generous victor ; far different is the case of a routed rebel host. My dear countrymen, you have before you at your election, peace or war, happiness or
misery. May the God of our forefathers direct you in the way that leads to
peace and happiness, before your feet stumble on the dark mountains, before
the evil days come, wherein you shall say, we have no pleasure in them."

tremely susceptible of excitement, and deep thinking
would easily inflame him : it operated too, as it often
does in similar cases, inducing delirium from any
stimulant.   Even a glass or two of wine had an immediate effect, and created a feverish action on the
brain, that prevented self-control, and tended to re-
produce itself.

There are many sayings and actions of his, in this
last and clouded part of his life, that are remembered for their singularity or extravagance.   The number of his contemporaries who can recollect him in
the vigour of his powers, has become almost extinct ;
but there are many yet remaining who knew him
when his reason had been shaken.   He passed two
entire days in destroying all his correspondence and
other writings, and thus annihilated many records of
his public services, and some literary productions that
would have furnished rich materials for his own
history and that of his times ; while many traits of
his ardent mind after its derangement are still preserved.   If he, in happier moments, or his friends,
could have decided, these circumstances would have
been reversed; they would have saved the documents of the first portion of his life, and obliterated
all the latter.   As neither alternative can now be
adopted, it may be excusable to cite a few occurrences that took place during this afflicting period,
which may serve, like a caricature, when no faithful portrait can be obtained, to aid in forming a judgment of his character.

His contempt for lord Hillsborough, with whose

blunders in the management of colonial affairs he was completely disgusted, was often shewn, and has been already alluded to. The following short epistle was written by him, in the first fit of insanity after his wound. It advises a perusal of the bible.

"MILTON MANUFACTORY, BOSTON, JANUARY 13TH, 1770.

"MY LORD,—I take the liberty most humbly to recommend to your lordship's perusal, the great book of God, of nature, of arts and sciences. My humble North American word of honour for it, my lord, these volumes will hurt neither thee, nor thy master, nor in this world, nor in that which is to come.

"I am, my lord, his majesty's liege, true and faithful subject: no man's enemy, ergo, your lordship's friend.

JAMES OTIS.
"*Rt. Hon.* LORD HILLSBOROUGH."

In the records of the legislature, there is a petition for the payment of interest on some state notes, which he held. Though extremely brief and pithy, it marks a disordered mind, particularly in the caprice of writing his name differently from the manner which he and his family had always used, and according to the common mode of spelling it in England.

"To the assembly of the colony of Massachusetts-bay, sheweth James Oates, that there was due to him, the 20th of June last, two thousand and thirty-nine pounds lawful money, with two years interest:

that said James wants the interest of said sum, and *demands* payment.

JAMES OATES.

JULY 1776."

This petition was referred and granted. Two years afterwards there was another memorial to the same effect, in which his name on the record appears in the usual manner; the petition itself is not in the files.

During a period that he resided with his father at Great Marshes, a small privateer, with one gun, belonging to New London, was chased into Barnstable harbour, by a British sloop of war, and was obliged to seek for safety, by going far up a shallow creek, where the enemy's vessel could not follow. John Otis, a brother of James, was a magistrate, and had a command in the militia, whom he kept in readiness to oppose any attempt of the English to destroy the privateer with their boats. Two or three gentlemen of respectability were present at Col. Otis's, where the master of the privateer had gone to obtain a protection. This commander had previously studied, if not practised law, and was a vapouring coxcomb. He gave himself many airs, and while seeking for protection for his vessel, paid no regard to the gentlemen who were present. Otis saw this conduct, and resented the want of respect to his father by mortifying the offender. With his hair powdered, and a dress as disordered as his mind, he came up to the captain and said,—" my brother, I am glad to see you: we are brethren, I take it, in three respects. In the first place, you are my brother, as being one of the human race; secondly, as you have studied law, we are brother lawyers; and, being both unwillingly detained here, we are brethren in distress, so long as you continue lord high admiral of these narrow seas."

His love of literature was always predominant, and his stores of it almost unbounded. Even while suffering under the sad derangement of reason, he seized with avidity every occasion for the discussion of literary topics, the strength of his memory enabled him to display his copious acquisitions, which his wit and animation always rendered interesting. A gentleman visited him one day at Barnstable, at a time when the violence of his mental malady made it necessary to subject him to severe restraint. He arrived at the house about sunset, intending merely to make a friendly call. Otis, whose feelings were highly social, was delighted to see him, and engaged at once eagerly in conversation. Every subject was started, politics, law, history, poetry, the fine arts, &c. &c. and though there was sometimes a slight incoherence in his transitions, yet he talked with so much brilliancy and force, that the visit was insensibly prolonged till after midnight.

While residing at Barnstable, he was seldom absent from public worship. In those days, when the present rapidity of the mails and wide circulation of newspapers did not exist, the government, in order to make known important intelligence, sent letters and proclamations to the clergymen, who read them

to their congregations after the service was over.
Otis was always most eagerly attentive, and when
fortunate events were announced, his involuntary
exclamations, as it were thinking aloud, would be
heard almost throughout the church.

After he had given up the practice of his profession, he sometimes went into the courts as a spectator, and often gave useful advice to his friends.
Mr. Thomas in his " History of Printing," has given
an instance which happened to himself.   When
threatened with a prosecution for a libel, on account
of certain political essays which he had published,
he received an unexpected visit from Otis, who examined the case, and promised him, if a suit was instituted, to appear gratuitously in his defence.*
The following example occurred of his giving an
opinion in court, which was rendered more striking,
as the case involved the proceedings of an individual
who was insane.†

An action was brought in Boston at the supreme
judicial court, for the recovery of a tenement and
its appurtenances.   After evidence had been given
of the plaintiff's right and seizin, the defendant's
counsel introduced the plaintiff's own deed of sale,
duly acknowledged and recorded.   Upon this the
plaintiff's counsel moved the court for permission to
shew to the jury, that at the time of making and

---

* See Thomas's History of Printing, Vol. I. p. 476.

† This curious cause was communicated by the venerable Judge Sewall of
York, and is copied without any essential variation from his manuscript.

executing the deed, the plaintiff was insane or *non compos mentis*. To this, the opposite party objected, that it was a settled rule of law, that no man should be permitted to *stultify* himself, and introduced several authorities to establish the rule, although they seemed to allow that the heir might do it, after the decease of his ancestor. It was argued on the part of the plaintiff, that the truth of the fact was more likely to be obtained in the life time of the party, than at a more remote period, after his death, &c. After a considerable time occupied in the debate, Otis stepped forward and said : that he was not of counsel for the plaintiff or defendant in this suit, but requested, as *Amicus Curiæ*, to be heard a few words on the occasion. The court assented. He began by observing, that since the declaration of Independence we had become a new nation, whose judicial decisions, he hoped and wished, might be founded in sound reason; and that no decisions from the books, however long and complete they might appear from respectable and established authorities, ought to prevail against the dictates of reason and common sense. He added, that this would be for the honour of the nation upon its emancipation from Great Britain; with some other concise and pertinent remarks.

The motion for admitting the evidence, prevailed by the opinion of two, out of three of the Judges. It appeared by the evidence, that the plaintiff was a widower, advanced in years, having several grown up children. A woman from another state had agreed to marry him, after he had given her a deed of the estate which was the cause of the action. When she had obtained the property, she refused to perform her engagement. The plaintiff's counsel on these premises argued, that he must have been insane in this transaction, for no money appeared to have been paid, although the same was acknowledged by the deed, under the plaintiff's hand and seal. The jury, to the satisfaction of the court and a crowded audience, found a verdict for the plaintiff.

The two last years of his life, a short interval excepted, were passed at Andover. He lodged with Mr. Osgood, a respectable inhabitant of that town, who resided on a pleasant farm in a retired part of the south parish. After being there about two years, his friends thought he was entirely restored, and advised him to return to Boston. He came back and undertook some professional engagements. He pleaded a cause in the Court of Common Pleas, in which he was heard with eager attention and curiosity: he displayed considerable power in the case, but far less than he would once have done.

One of the few fragments in his hand writing, now extant, is a memorandum on a slip of paper, made at this period, on a Sunday, after returning from public worship. It is as follows, " I have this day attended divine service, and heard a sensible discourse, and thanks be to God I now enjoy the greatest of all blessings, *mens sana in corpore sano.*"

All his old friends shewed him great attention.

and among others Governor Hancock, who, after frequent invitations, at last persuaded him to dine with him. Even before he went to this dinner, he was observed to have, at times, a melancholy expression, but after it, he shewed evident marks of unsettled reason. The excitement resulting from such a party to a character so ardent, and a mind so shattered, might well have been feared. What various and conflicting emotions must it have awakened! The meeting with many old friends, the warm welcome, the festive hilarity, the recollection of the past, the confused and crowded images of twenty eventful years; imagination carrying him back to those trying times, when with some of that circle he had began the first, almost desperate, opposition to usurpation; the long contest that had followed, then verging to a triumphant termination; the memory of active friends and foes, who had alike disappeared from these stormy scenes; his own broken intellect and long mental eclipse, the hazards and changes, the passions and illusions, the triumph and inanity of human affairs; all must have hurried through his mind in quick and painful succession.

His brother advised him soon after, to return to Andover, which he did voluntarily, and with perfect gentleness.* While on this last visit to Boston, he

---

* The following extract of a letter from his nephew the Hon. H. G. Otis, relates some circumstances of his last visit to Boston.—"I brought him in a gig from Andover to Boston in the year 1782, at a period when my father and his friends thought he was recovered. Nothing could be more delightfully instructive than his conversation on this journey, but it was in reference chiefly to the study of my profession, which it was intended I should pursue under his

made his will, which began thus. " In the name of God, Amen.—I James Otis, being in no kind of fear of death, though by some called the king of terrors, and by old Bannister in his will a sergeant, I make this my last will and testament." He then speaks of his eldest daughter, who married a British officer, in a manner that shews how deeply that alliance had offended him, bequeaths her five shillings, and gives the remainder of his property to his wife and second daughter. This instrument is dated the " 31st day of March, in the year of Jesus Christ one thousand seven hundred and eighty three and of the assumption or declaration of the Independence of the thirteen United States of North America, the seventh year."

The day after his return to Andover he exhibited some marks of agitation. He took a hatchet in the morning and went to a copse of pines standing on a rising ground a few yards from the house, and passed all the forenoon in trimming away the lower

patronage.—But I went back to college—He remained at home for a few weeks, and was induced to go into the Court of Common Pleas, where it is said he displayed great powers in a very pathetic case, but as I have learnt from those who heard him, he appeared a sun shorn of his beams. His house however became the resort of much company calling to visit and converse with him. Governor Hancock was particularly attentive, and forced him to dine with him in a very large party. He was observed before this time to become thoughtful and sad, lying in bed until a very late hour; but immediately after this dinner, there was a visible oscillation of his intellect—He was overwhelmed by the recollection of past days, impressed probably with greater force, by the presence of Hancock and others of the *convives* and by the scene altogether. There was however no frenzy—A hint was given him by my father that he had better return to Andover, and he went like a lamb, where in a very short period he was struck with lightning."

branches of the wood. When Mr. Osgood came to call him to dinner, he said with great earnestness; " Osgood, if I die while I am in your house, I charge you to have me buried under these trees :" and then added with a little touch of humour, that shone forth like a bright gleam in a tempestuous sky ; " you know my grave would overlook all your fields, and I could have an eye upon the boys and see if they minded their work."

During the whole of his residence in Mr. Osgood's family, except in the instance just mentioned, he never went fifty yards from the house. He shewed neither violence nor restlessness. He lived very temperately, and his principal sustenance was bread and milk. He passed his time in reading, lying much in bed, and in consequence of this life of tranquillity and indolence he grew very corpulent. He was always kind and good humoured to the family, and delighted them with his wit, his stories and knowledge on every subject. Those who were then young, are now old, and after the lapse of forty years can recall few particulars of his conversation, though the general impression of its great power and richness is indelible. The following instance is recollected as an example of his readiness. Mr. Kendall Osgood, who had been a surgeon in the army, was at home on a visit, when a distant relation died in a neighbouring town. Most of the family went to the funeral, and one of them inquiring if he was going, he answered, " O no, let the dead bury their dead." Otis immediately asked him, if he knew the meaning of that

THE OSGOOD FARM—ANDOVER.

Published by Wells & Lilly 98 Court St. Boston

text, and on his confessing that he did not, he entered at once on a learned commentary and explanation
of it.

Six weeks exactly after his return, on Friday afternoon the 23d day of May 1783, a heavy cloud suddenly arose, and the greater part of the family were
collected in one of the rooms to wait till the shower
should have past. Otis, with his cane in one hand,
stood against the post of the door which opened
from this apartment into the front entry.* He was
in the act of telling the assembled group a story,
when an explosion took place which seemed to shake
the solid earth, and he fell without a struggle, or a
word, instantaneously dead, into the arms of Mr. Osgood, who seeing him falling, sprang forward to receive him. This flash of lightning was the first that
came from the cloud, and was not followed by any
others that were remarkable. There were seven or
eight persons in the room, but no other was injured.
No mark of any kind could be found on Otis, nor was
there the slightest change or convulsion in his features.

It is a singular coincidence, that he often expressed a wish for such a fate. He told his sister, Mrs.
Warren, after his reason was impaired, " my dear
sister, I hope when God Almighty in his righteous
providence shall take me out of time into eternity,

---

* His own room was on the left hand side of the front door, when looking
at the plate ; and at his death, he was standing.in the door way of the room
to the right. The lightning struck the chimney, followed a rafter of the roof
which rested upon one of the upright timbers, to which the door post was
contiguous. The casing of this door was split, and several of the nails torn
out all which marks still remain as they were at the time.

that it will be by a flash of lightning," and this idea he often repeated.

There is a degree of consolation blended with awe in the manner of his death, and a soothing fitness in the sublime accident which occasioned it. The end of his life was ennobled, when the ruins of a great mind, instead of being undermined by loathsome and obscure disease, were demolished at once by a bright bolt from Heaven.

His body was brought to Boston, and his funeral was attended with every mark of respect, and exhibited one of the most numerous processions ever seen in the town. Among the tributes to his memory the following verses are the most conspicuous, and besides the interest of their subject, possess an intrinsic merit that will preserve them.

===

ON THE DEATH OF JAMES OTIS,

KILLED BY LIGHTNING, AT ANDOVER, SOON AFTER THE PEACE OF 1783. BY THE HON. THOMAS DAWES, WRITTEN AT THE TIME.

When flushed with conquest and elate with pride,
Britannia's monarch Heaven's high will defied;
And bent on blood, by lust of rule inclined,
With odious chains to vex the freeborn mind;
On these young shores set up unjust command,
And spread the slaves of office round the land;
Then Otis rose, and great in patriot fame,
To listening crowds resistance dared proclaim.
From soul to soul the bright idea ran,

The fire of freedom flew from man to man :
His pen like Sydney's, made the doctrine known,
His tongue like Tully's, shook a tyrant's throne ;
Then men grew bold—and in the public eye,
The right divine of monarchs dared to try ;
Light shone on all, despotic darkness fled—
And for a *sentiment* a nation bled.

From men like Otis, Independence grew;
From such beginnings empire rose to view.
Born for the world, his comprehensive mind
Scanned the wide politics of human kind :
Blessed with a native strength and fire of thought,
With Greek and Roman learning richly fraught,
Up to the fountain head he pushed his view,
And from first principles his maxims drew.
Spite of the times, this truth he blaz'd abroad,
" The people's safety is the law of God."—*

For this he suffered ; hireling slaves combined
To dress in shades the brightest of mankind.
And see they come, a dark designing band,
With murder's heart, and execution's hand.—
Hold, villains ! Those polluted hands restrain ;
Nor that exalted head with blows profane !
A nobler end awaits his patriot head ;
In other sort he'll join the illustrious dead.
Yes ! When the glorious work which he begun,
Shall stand the most complete beneath the sun ;
When peace shall come to crown the grand design,
His eyes shall live to see the work divine—
The Heavens shall then his generous " spirit claim,
" In storms as loud as his immortal fame."—†
Hark, the deep thunders echo round the skies !
On wings of flame the eternal errand flies.

---

* Salus populi, &c. was the motto of one of his essays.
† Waller on the death of Cromwell.

One chosen charitable bolt is sped—
And Otis mingles with the glorious dead.

When God in anger saw the spot,
On earth to Otis given,
In thunder as from Sinai's Mount,
He snatch'd him back to Heaven.—*Anonymous*

Such is the imperfect relation that can now be given of the life of JAMES OTIS, derived from the frail recollections of tottering, expiring tradition, the scanty gleanings of forgotten journals, and the formal entries of neglected records. Disconnected and imperfect as are these materials, they have been unskilfully managed, if the reader be not convinced, that he was one of the most able and high minded men that this country has produced. He was, in truth, one of the master spirits who began and conducted an opposition, which at first, was only designed to counteract and defeat an arbitrary administration; but which ended in a revolution, emancipated a continent, and established by the example of its effects, a lasting influence on all the governments of the civilized world.

The chief fault of Otis was his irascibility, that grew naturally in such a character, and was almost inseparable from his frankness and ardour. It often led him to be too vehement and unguarded in his expressions; and in his zeal for the security of fundamental principles, to be too impatient at obstacles; and while he was labouring under deep anxiety and responsibility for the state of public affairs, he was

apt to brush away little men and things that interrupted his course, without sufficient regard or consideration.

It would have been better for him if his great
spirit had been less easily chafed, if it had been subjected to more moderation and forbearance with
what was inferior, perverse, or servile. Yet if this
spirit had been thus subdued, perhaps his power of
rousing popular sentiment, of infusing life, soul, and
energy into that many bodied mass, the public, would
have been enfeebled or lost.

In forming an estimate of every man's character,
the circumstances in which he is placed, and the persons with whom he is called to act, should be considered. Otis possessed talents, a grasp of thought and
elevation of mind, which would have qualified him
to move at the head quarters of human affairs, to direct the measures of a cabinet, and contend with the
highest and noblest opposition. Instead of this situation, he was placed in collision with the secondary
agents of a remote, and to him, intangible ministry.
In resisting the sinister, or corrupt designs of a distant administration, his efforts could not be directed
against them face to face, but the struggle was necessarily maintained with subaltern agents, whom he
had a right to despise for their venality, and their
subserviency. While such were the men, who were
made the willing instruments of the design to enslave his country, it was difficult for a powerful or a
virtuous mind to restrain its indignation.

The side too which he adopted, was not always to

be defended with the more cultivated forms of legal pleading, or parliamentary debate, but it required continually the interference of popular agency. Public sentiment was to be kept alive by intercourse and argument with all kinds of people, public assemblies were to be addressed, whose very numbers precluded the idea of refinement; and who were to be affected, not by the closeness of argument and the polish of delicate wit, but by such tones as could be heard amidst the murmurs of the sea shore, by ideas that were plain and direct, by allusions that would be obvious, coarse even, and cutting. The timid were to be encouraged, the ignorant awakened, the lukewarm stimulated, the ardent directed, and the profligate overawed. In all these duties, at all times and opportunities, in the *caucus* and the town meeting, as well as in the halls of justice and legislation, he was to be found presiding, proposing, animating, and controlling. Such incessant exertions on such different theatres, left him little time to study the minor courtesies of life, and although good humoured and placable, he sometimes prostrated an opponent by a vehement sally or sarcasm, whom at another moment he would have disregarded, or set aside with gentleness and caution.

He espoused the cause of his country, not merely because it was popular, but because he saw that its prosperity, freedom and honour, would be all diminished, if the usurpation of the British parliament was successful. His enemies constantly represented him as a demagogue, yet no man was less so. His character was too liberal, proud and honest to play that part. He led public opinion by the energy which conscious strength, elevated views and quick feelings inspire, and was followed with that deference and reliance, which great talents instinctively command. These were the qualifications, that made him for many years the oracle and guide of the patriotic party. It was not by supple and obscure intrigues, by unworthy flatteries and compliances, by a degrading adoption of plebeian dress, manners, or language, that he obtained the suffrages of the people,* but by their opinion of his uprightness, their knowledge of his disinterestedness, and their conviction of his ability. He vindicated the rights of his countrymen, not in the spirit of a factious tribune, aiming to subvert established authority, but as a Roman senator, who became the voluntary advocate of an injured province. He valued his own standing and that of his family in society, and did not wish a change or a revolution. He acknowledged a common interest with his countrymen, and sacrificed in their support all his hopes of personal aggrandizement. Had he taken part with the administration, he might have commanded every favour in their power to bestow; in sustaining that of his native land, he well knew that his only reward would be the good will of its

---

* He had a great contempt for those shallow, obtrusive, noisy, agents, who are the appropriate evil of popular governments, as the arrogant, servile, profligate minion is of monarchies. Going one evening to attend a meeting for some political purpose, and seeing that some ordinary demagogues were the most prominent persons, he exclaimed to those who accompanied him, " Zounds ! what have we here ? the world butt end foremost."

inhabitants, and the sweet consciousness of performing his duty; and that he must be satisfied with the common lot of great patriotism in all ages, present poverty and future fame.

Persons who were annoyed by his opposition or mortified by his superiority, revenged themselves by citing and exaggerating his strong or unguarded remarks. With much warmth and goodness of disposition, unyielding activity of mind, a strong perception of humour, a great vivacity of thought and facility of expression, it was to be expected, that intensely engaged, as he was, in the litigious politics of his time, and deeply anxious on points whose consequences were vast, and many of them prospective, he should have disdained to occupy himself with verbal scruples, or in weighing the probability of misrepresentation. Hence arose a thousand calumnies and false reports,* hence all the scandal that was attempted to be heaped upon him for his natural ebullition of resentment, at the injury done to his father, by the appointment of Hutchinson, which busy malice absurdly represented, as the sole impulse of his whole political course. In like manner, hundreds of others were imputed to him, which

---

* One of these is alluded to in an article in the Boston Gazette of July 25th, 1768, in a dialogue between " a Pensioner and a Divine," of which the following is an extract ; " *Pensioner*. It seems to me that the clergy interest themselves too much in the political disputes of the day. The gentlemen in crape have no right to intermeddle in such things. But Otis says, he could not carry his points without the aid of the black regiment. *Divine*. If Mr. Otis expressed himself in that manner, (which I question) he might have expressed himself rather more decently ; but surely you will allow this to be a day of darkness and difficulty, and you will also allow us to pray for light and direction."

however, being not so deeply connected with prophecy, as the speech on the former occasion, sank
successively into oblivion. A man like Otis, would
throw off in every conversation sparks that might
illuminate and kindle the hearer; and which, in a
more phlegmatic or cautious disposition, would have
lain smouldering invisibly through a long existence.

As in every case of public or private oppression,
he was willing to volunteer in the cause of the sufferer, and as in many instances where he thought
the occasion would justify it, he employed his talents gratuitously, his enemies were forced to acknowledge his liberality. As he relinquished and
withstood the patronage of the crown, and renounced the highest and most lucrative professional pursuits, to employ all the vigour of his mind in an un-
requited and fearless defence of his country, not for
a brief period merely, but through a succession of
anxious and momentous years, his friends and fellow
citizens admired and honoured his generous devotion. Yet, it is worthy of observation, that with all
his superiority to mercenary calculations as an individual, in the great question at issue between the
colonies and the British parliament, respecting taxation, he watched with the utmost narrowness every
expenditure, and contended against the smallest fis-
cal imposition, as strongly, as if it involved total con-
fiscation. In his writings and his arguments he perpetually recurred to the topic of property, to the
maxim, that what was a man's own, should not be
assessed without his consent. The most timid miser

in calculating the minutest fraction of interest, could not discover a more anxious solicitude at any deficiency, than he did at scrutinizing every effort to place in the coffers of the king, a single penny, that was not granted from the subjects by whom it was paid. This contrast furnishes one of the striking traits in his character, that the man who was disdainful of pecuniary temptations, and liberal to excess of his own property, should have been of all others the most jealous, watchful, and unyielding, in contending for the principles, which consecrated the wealth of the community against the touch of arbitrary power.

In fine, he was a man of powerful genius, and ardent temper, with wit and humour that never failed: as an orator, he was bold, argumentative, impetuous and commanding, with an eloquence that made his own excitement irresistibly contagious; as a lawyer, his knowledge and ability placed him at the head of his profession; as a scholar, he was rich in acquisition and governed by a classic taste; as a statesman and civilian, he was sound and just in his views; as a patriot, he resisted all allurements that might weaken the cause of that country, to which he devoted his life, and for which he sacrificed it. The future historian of the United States, in considering the foundations of American independence, will find that one of the corner stones must be inscribed with the name of JAMES OTIS.

Appendix.

A.

EXPLANATION OF THE ENGRAVINGS.

The likeness of Mr. Otis, engraved for this work, by Mr. A. B. Durand, of New-York, one of the most eminent engravers in this country, is from a portrait painted by Blackburn, in 1755, an artist who succeeded Smibert, and preceded Copley, in that line of art in Boston. The painting possesses only moderate merit; the expression of the countenance gives little idea of the energy of his character. It rather answers to his own description of himself in page 384, when he says, that he was naturally fond of pleasure and amusement. A presumptive proof however, of its resemblance at the period when it was painted, is the fact, of the family likeness that may be perceived in it to some of his living relations.

The vignette prefixed to the first chapter, was taken from the *Allyne House* at Plymouth. It was originally intended to take a drawing of the house in which he was born, at Great Marshes, Barnstable, which is still standing, but with the loss of its wings, and rather in a decayed state. This house at Plymouth, in which his mother was born, was built a few years earlier, and serves to shew the style of building of respectable families in the latter part of the seventeenth century. This house was pulled down two or three years since, and very few dwellings in that style now remain. The spot has been purchased by the Pilgrim Society, with an intention to erect on it a building, to commemorate the landing of the forefathers. It stood in the first street in Plymouth, and in the back ground is seen the outline of the harbour of Plymouth, and the ship marks the spot where the *May Flower* anchored in December, 1622.

The plate representing the Osgood farm at Andover, is from a very neat and accurate drawing, taken by Mr. Penniman, on the spot, the present summer. The house and objects about it, are the same as they were in 1783, excepting the poplars in front. Mr. Otis was standing in the door of the room, to the spectator's right of the front door, and close to it. The lightning struck the chimney, and shattered the posts of these doors. The picture presents a pleasing specimen of a New England farm house.

The fac simile is from a fragment copied from a letter book, containing some letters to his clients; a few of which were copied by himself.

B. page 5.

ORIGIN OF THE OTIS FAMILY.

The following minutes relating to the first generations of this family, may have some interest for those readers who have a taste for tracing genealogies. John Otis with his family came from Hingham, in Norfolk, England, June 1635, in company with the Rev. Peter Hobart, and took the freeman's oath the 3d of March following. He was probably a substantial yeoman, who left his country, partly to accompany his pastor, a staunch non-conforming clergyman; his will, dated May 3d 1657, and proved 28th of July in the same year, is recorded in the first volume of the Suffolk Registry of Probate, and as it bears his mark in place of signature, it appears he was unable to write, a deficiency not so singular at that time, as it would at present. Of his children there is little known : John Otis is mentioned in the records of Hingham, as being a landholder there in 1668-9, and Richard Otis, another son went to some part of Maine ; from thence he was taken by a band of Indians in one of their incursions, and carried captive with the greater part of his family into Canada, where the name is still to be found among his descendants. The MS. journal of the Rev. Mr. Hobart contains two or three entries relating to this family, which are here transcribed. He writes the name in various ways, Oats, Oattis, Ottis, in England it is often written Oates, " May 1, 1653, Mary Otis" (the grandchild of John) " was baptized May 28th, John Oattis wife died, July 9th, 1654. Tabitha Lyon being scalded in a kettle of water, at John Oattisses house, died in a few hours after, March 31st, 1657. John Otis died at Waimouth." Mr. Otis by the mother's side was connected with the founders of the Old Colony who arrived in the first ship, the *May Flower*, in 1620. By the records of Plymouth it appears, that in 1699 Mr. Joseph Allyne married Mary Doten, daughter of Edward, and grand-daughter of Edward Doten, who came in the *May Flower*. Mr. Allyne's children, recorded as born at Plymouth, (in the house represented in the vignette at the head of the first chapter) were Elizabeth in 1700, Mary in 1702, who was the mother of James Otis, and a woman of very superior character. A good portrait of her in the costume of that time, is now in the possession of the Hon. H. G. Otis. Mr. Allyne removed with his family from Plymouth to Wethersfield in Connecticut.

The Rev. Mr. Hobart above mentioned, was educated at Cambridge and left England for non-conformity ; he began the settlement, and was the first minister of Hingham, and a very rigid puritan. His journal begins thus : " June 8th 1635, I with my wife and four children came safely to New-England : forever praised be the God of heaven, my God and king !" He was the ancestor of the late Judge Hobart of New York, and of the Rev. Dr. Hobart the present bishop of the episcopal church in that state. Lechford, a lawyer, came over in 1641, but getting into some difficulties on religious matters, remained only a year, and in a book which he published after his return, he found naturally enough, from the disputes he had been engaged in, a good deal to blame in the conduct of the infant colony. In giving a list of the ministers of the different towns, and mentioning at Hingham " Mr. Hubbard," as he writes the name, " Pastor, and Mr. Pecke, Teacher," he adds, " They refuse to baptize old Otis's grandchildren though he was a member of their church." As twelve years after a minute of the baptism of Mary Otis is made in Hobart's journal, the difficulty whatever it was, had been removed. It is probable that the only copy of this tract of Lechford's, existing in America, (excepting an incomplete MS. copy in the library of the Massachusetts Historical Society) is one in the Ebeling collection, in the library of Harvard University : the title is, " *Plain dealing, or news from New-England : a short view of New-England's present government both ecclesiastical and civil, compared with the anciently received and established government of England, in some material points fit for the gravest consideration in these times. By Thomas Lechford of Clement's Inn, in the county of Middlesex, Gent. London, printed by W. E. & I. G. for Nat. Butler at the sign of the Pyde Bull near St. Austin's gate,* 1642."

C.   page 139.

A notice of this work was given by the late Rev. J. S. Buckminster, in the Monthly Anthology, under the head of retrospective reviews. The following extract is from an answer of the late Rev. Dr. Bentley of Salem, to a letter of inquiry respecting Mr. Otis. It communicates in the peculiar style of that learned antiquarian, some of Otis's literary opinions. It was dated February 4th, 1819. " I knew Mr. Otis from my youth, but my acquaintance began with him in 1777, when I took part in the instruction of the Grammar school in Boston. He was often at the house in which the grammar masters lived, and often turned the conversation on the book which he wrote upon Latin Prosody. Not thinking of the future value of these interviews, you may suppose a youth would recover but a little of the desultory conversation, which his lucid intervals could continue. Of his rudiments published in 1760, and just before his political career, he used to observe, that he had contented himself with a view of the best writers, and had combined what he found in them so as to give the most comprehensive view of them ; doing for Prosody, what Cheever had done for grammar in his Accidence, that the one book might accompany the other. It was from him I gained the knowledge of Brinsley's

Accidence, which was taught before Cheever's Accidence, and differs from it chiefly in being in question and answer. I have Master John Swinnerton's copy of John Brinsley's Accidence, with Master Swinnerton's name and date 1652. The manner in which Cheever has simplified it, is admirable, and suggested to Mr. Otis the work he has performed successfully. To Otis's Latin Prosody, succeeds his work on Letters, in which he has given the power and the organs employed on them: and his views of pronunciation and of adjusting the quantity and accents, well deserve the attention at this time, when some notice has been taken of Greek pronunciation. Mr. Otis felt all the difficulty. He pronounces no part of Grammar so defective as pronunciation; and contrary to an opinion now openly defended, he says : ' It seems to be now generally agreed among the learned, that the present marks for the Greek accents, instead of helping the reader, only serve to mislead and perplex him, and that with the ancient Greeks, the true accent always followed the quantity.' "

D. page 139.

The following minutes derived from Chalmers' " opinions of eminent lawyers," will perhaps serve to shew what results might have been expected, if the English hierarchy had been extended to this country. In 1705 the bishop of London brought before the ministry, the question of the Roman Catholic clergy in Maryland : this colony was founded by a catholic nobleman, expressly for the purpose of offering an asylum to catholics, with an entire toleration of other forms ; yet the Attorney General Northey gave his written opinion, that any priest or jesuit, who should exercise any function of the catholic church, might under a certain statute of William, be condemned to perpetual imprisonment if a native, and if an alien, be banished the realm.

In 1725 the bishop of London, who is diocesan of all the British colonies, brought before the lords of the council, the subject of a synod proposed by a convention of the clergy at Boston, and which the general court authorised to be composed of all the congregational churches in the Province, for the express purpose of remedying the decay of piety and promoting the growth of religion. The episcopal clergymen Cutler, and Myles, rectors of Trinity and Christ churches, brought this to the attention of the bishop; and on his application, the Attorney and Solicitor Generals, *Yorke* and *Wearg*, gave their opinion that no synods could be holden without royal license. That the applying to the Governor and Council and House of Representatives, to authorise the synod, is a violation of the king's prerogative, as the application ought to have been to the Governor alone, who represented his Majesty. That the meeting might be separated if held, by the authority of the Governor, and the principal actors therein prosecuted for a misdemeanor. They however consider that if this meeting only pass an address without any authoritative act, that it will not be any infringement, provided the subject matter of such address be lawful.

In 1702 the Attorney General, Northey, gave it as his opinion, that the Governor had the advowson of the churches, and the parishioners could not eject nor refuse support to the incumbent; and in 1719 Mr. West, a crown lawyer, gave his opinion that the king's prerogative of collating to any vacant benefices, remained entire, notwithstanding any acts of the provincial assembly.

E. page 171.

The following is the title page of this work : " The Rights of the *British colonies asserted and proved.* By James Otis, Esq.

> Hæc omnis regio, et celsi plaga pinea montis,
> Cedat amicitiae Teucrorum : et fœderis æquas
> Dicamus leges, sociosque in regna vocemus ;
> Considant, si tantus amor, et mœnia condant.

Boston, printed. London re-printed for J. Almon, 1764.

This work which attracted much attention at the time, is a pamphlet of 120 pages. It contains a learned, and at the same time, a very lively dissertation on the origin of government. It is written with great energy, and with evident rapidity and carelessness. There is a degree of incoherence in the reasoning, which grew out of contradictory principles, that were irreconcileable, the entire rights of the colonies, and the absolute supremacy of parliament. A copious analysis of that interesting work was prepared for this appendix; but the size of the volume has made it necessary to omit it.

F. page 322.

A SONG NOW MUCH IN VOGUE IN NORTH AMERICA.

Tune, *Hearts of Oak.*

Come join hand in hand, brave AMERICANS all,
And rouse your bold hearts at fair LIBERTY's call;
No *tyrannous acts* shall suppress your *just claim*,
Or stain with *dishonour* AMERICA's name.

    In FREEDOM we're born, and in freedom we'll live
    Our purses are ready,
    Steady, friends, steady,
    Not as SLAVES, but as FREEMEN, our money we'll give

Our worthy *forefathers*, let's give 'em a cheer,
To *climates unknown* did courageously steer;
Thro' *oceans* to *desarts* for *freedom* they came,
And dying bequeath'd us their *freedom* and *fame.*

    Chorus.

Their generous bosoms all dangers despis'd,
So *highly*, so *wisely*, their *birthrights* they priz'd;
We'll keep what they gave,—we will piously keep,
Nor frustrate their toils on the land or the deep.

    Chorus.

The *tree* their own hands had to liberty rear'd,
They liv'd to behold growing strong and rever'd;
With transport they cried, " now our wishes we gain,
For our children shall gather the fruits of our pain."

    Chorus.

Swarms of *placemen** and *pensioners* soon will appear,
Like locusts deforming the charms of the year;
Suns vainly will rise, showers vainly descend,
If *we* are to *drudge* for what *others* shall *spend*.

Chorus.

Then join hand in hand, brave Americans all,
By *uniting* we stand, by *dividing* we fall,
In so righteous a cause let us hope to succeed.
For heaven approves of each generous deed.

Chorus.

All ages shall speak with *amaze* and *applause*,
Of the *courage* we'll shew *in support of our laws*
To *die* we can *bear*,—but to *serve* we *disdain*,
For *shame* is to *freemen* more dreadful than *pain*.

Chorus.

This bumper I crown for our *sovereign's* health,
And this for *Brit.·nnia's* glory and wealth;
That wealth and that glory immortal may be,
If *she* is but *just*, and if *we* are but *free*.

This song was published in the Boston Gazette. Mr. Dickinson sent an amended copy with the following letter.

" Dear Sir,

I inclosed to you the other day the copy of a song composed in great haste, I think it was rather too bold, I now send a corrected copy, which I like better. If you think the bagatelle worth publishing, I beg it may be this copy. If the first is published before this comes to hand, I shall be much obliged to you if you will be so good as to publish this with some little note, " that this is a true copy of the original."

In this copy I think it may be well enough to add between the fourth and fifth stanzas, these lines ;

---

* The ministry have already begun to give away in *pensions*, the *money* they lately took out of our pockets, *without our consent*.

How *sweet* are the labours that freemen endure,
That they shall enjoy all the profits secure.
No more such sweet labours *Americans* know,
If *Britons* shall reap what *Americans* sow.
In freedom we're born, &c.

I am, dear sir, with the utmost sincerity, your most affectionate and most humble servant,

JOHN DICKINSON.

Hon. JAMES OTIS.
Philadelphia, July 6th, 1768."

G. page 366.

Several articles relative to this affray were copied to form part of this appendix, but it is found necessary to omit them on account of their length. They may be found in the Boston Gazette and Boston Evening Post, at the period of the occurrence.

H. page 366.

VERDICT OF THE JURY.

James Otis, Esq. Plaintiff, vs. *John Robinson, Esq. Defendant.*
The Jury finds in this case that the defendant is guilty, and finds for the plaintiff two thousand pounds sterling damages and costs of suit.

Suffolk ss. &c. August Term, 1772.

Be it remembered, that this same term in a case here depending, wherein James Otis of said Boston, is appellant and original plaintiff, against John Robinson, late of said Boston, Esq. the said John Robinson, Esq. by James Boutineau, Esq. his father in law and attorney, comes into court, and on the behalf and in the name of said John Robinson, Esq. who is now in parts beyond sea, to wit, in the kingdom of Great Britain, being thereunto fully empowered as by his letters of attorney on file in the case may appear, freely confesses that in the assault committed by him, the said John Robinson, Esq. on him the said

James Otis, Esq. in presumptuously attempting to take him, the said James Otis, by the nose, was the first assault which occasioned and brought on all the consequent insults, wounds and other injuries, whereof the said James Otis in his declaration more particularly complains. He the said John Robinson, Esq. was greatly in fault, is very sorry for his conduct and behaviour that night towards the said James Otis, and asks the pardon of the said James Otis.

Signed, Ja. Boutineau, Attorney, and

James Robinson, Esq.

Done in court, and ordered that this paper be filed among the records of the court.

Sam. Winthrop, Clerk.

Whereupon the said James Otis, being personally present here in court, duly reflecting that he has ever been as ready to give, as to ask or demand gentlemanlike satisfaction for an insult, real or supposed, at the same time being fully conscious, and as he apprehends able abundantly to prove, that he then publicly offered that kind of satisfaction to the said John Robinson, Esq. previously to the said first assault, as on the part and in behalf of the said John Robinson, Esq. by his attorney James Boutineau, Esq. is above conferred. And the said James Otis, having always entertained a most consummate contempt of seeking a purse or pecuniary reparation for a personal insult, if any other more gentlemanlike could be obtained, by the consent of his parties, and that consistently with the laws of his country, accepts of the above submission here in court, in full for the assaults, insults, injuries, and damages above complained of in the declaration of the said James Otis and conferred as above. And upon the same submission so far as the said John Robinson, Esq. was concerned in the assaults, insults, and injuries above mentioned and confessed, as he thinks a gentleman and christian ought in such case, and on such submission, freely forgives the said John Robinson, Esq. and by these presents remiseth, releaseth, and acquitteth, and dischargeth him the said John Robinson, Esq. from all actions, suits and demands, by reason of, or occasioned by the premises, and also all right and cause of action in the declaration aforesaid.

Furthermore, the said James Otis, knowing full and right well that by the operation of the law hereupon, he releaseth and dischargeth the alleged and supposed confederates of the said John Robinson, from all demands supportable on the premises by our laws, but the said James Otis would by no means be understood to give up any other demands he may hereafter make by reason of the premises against alleged, or supposed confederates, [*should he ever meet with either of them in a state of nature, or without the reach of municipal laws,*] at the same time the said James Otis, of his own free will and meer motion, thinks fit to give it under his hand to remain on record in favour of the said John Robinson, Esq. as the said James Otis has often privately and publicly in the hearing of his friends and others, and even in the court of Common Pleas, *declared,* as he now does in this honourable court, that he looks on the said John Robinson, Esq. to be infinitely less to blame in this (for both parties in the suit) very unhappy affair, than those whom the said James Otis, were he inclined to give himself the trouble, thinks and is persuaded he could fully prove, artfully and most insidiously, as well as maliciously incited the said John Robinson, Esq. to so very unworthy an action.

Provided, the said John Robinson, Esq. by the said James Boutineau, Esq. his said attorney, pay the common costs of court, amounting to thirteen pounds, ten shillings and eight pence, with thirty pounds each, for the use of Samuel Fitch, John Adams, Esq. and Sampson Salter Blowers counsel, retained to the said James Otis in the case, and very diligently attending the business for three years, also the doctor's bills, amounting to seven pounds, twelve shillings. The sum of one pound eight shillings, for taking affadavits out of court, amounting in the whole to the sum of one hundred and twelve pounds, ten shillings and eight pence, lawful money, but not a farthing for the use of the said James Otis, he having (as before observed) a most thorough contempt for a pecuniary recompense when a better can be obtained.

JAMES OTIS.

N. B. The sum mentioned above, as agreed upon, viz. one hundred and twelve pounds, eleven shillings and eight pence was paid in court, and it is ordered by the court, that this paper be filed in the said case among the records of the Superior Court.

SAMUEL WINTHROP, *Clerk.*

The original release hastily drawn up by Mr. Otis himself in court, may be found in the files of the Supreme Judicial Court. The words in italics, between brackets, "should he ever meet with either of them in a state of nature, or without the reach of municipal laws," are perfectly legible, though he drew his pen through them, as the impropriety of such a reserve in a court of justice, no doubt occurred as soon as they were written.

I. page 451.

Though no human life was taken away during such a long term of agitation, suffering and revolution, yet there was another punishment that produced great notoriety, and a degree of dread that was rather increased by the mixture of horror and ridicule it occasioned. This was the strange punishment of *tarring and feathering,* by which invention, an English member of parliament, a few years since observed, that the Americans had destroyed Plato's definition of man; *animal bipes, implumis.* This outrage occurred but twice in Boston. The first time was in the case of Malcolm, a custom house officer, and it was universally believed that it would not then have happened, if it had not been for his brutality and cowardice, in drawing his cutlass and wounding a boy severely. The following account of this affair, is taken from the letters of Novanglus : "Malcolm was such an oddity as naturally to excite the curiosity and ridicule of the lowest class of people, wherever he went, and had been active in battle against *the regulators* in North Carolina, who were thought in Boston, to be an injured people. A few weeks before, he had made a seizure at Kennebec river, one hundred and fifty miles from Boston, and by some imprudence had excited the wrath of the people there in such a degree, that they tarred and feathered him over his clothes. He comes to Boston to complain. The news of it was spread in town

It was a critical time, when the passions of the people were warm. Malcolm attacked a lad in the street, and cut his head with a cutlass, in return for some words from the boy, which I suppose were irritating. The boy run bleeding through the streets to his relations, of whom he had many. As he passed the street, the people inquired into the cause of his wounds, and a sudden heat arose against Malcolm, which neither whigs nor tories, though both endeavoured it, could restrain, and produced the injuries of which he justly complained. But such a coincidence of circumstances might, at any time, and in any place, have produced such an effect; and therefore it is no evidence of the weakness of government. Why he petitioned the General Court, unless he was advised to it by the tories, to make a noise, I know not. That court had nothing to do with it. He might have brought the action against the trespassers, but never did. He chose to go to England and get two hundred pounds a year, which would make his tarring the luckiest incident of his life."

In the violent ferment that was created by the attempt to force the tea upon the country, threats that never would have been executed, were used to intimidate those, who, for the sake of a paltry gain, were willing to render useless all the sacrifices which had been made by the patriotism of the country. The following notice was sent from Portland, (then Falmouth) to the Boston Gazette. " Falmouth, Casco Bay, Feb. 10th, 1774. Many people being apprehensive that there will be a difficulty in preventing some individual persons from selling tea, even though this town should vote against it; we think proper to declare to you, that you need not doubt of your resolutions being carried into execution: for we whose names are hereunto subscribed, will engage that no person in this town, great or small, rich or poor, shall dare to counteract your designs.

THOMAS TARBUCKET,
PETER PITCH,
ABRAHAM WILDFOWL,
DAVID PLAISTER,
BENJAMIN BRUSH,
OLIVER SCARECROW,
HENRY HANDCART,

Committee for tarring and feathering.

It has been observed that only *two* instances of this irregularity ever happened in Boston. One by a mob, has been already described with its provocation. The other was by Colonel Nesbit, commanding one of the British regiments. The subject was a countryman, who was accused of attempting to purchase a soldier's musket; though the man declared that a regular plot had been laid to entrap him, and that he was innocent of any bad intention. However, this might be, the colonel seized him, gave him a mock trial, then tarred and feathered him, and carted him through the streets; he with a party of his men, all in uniform, and with drums and fifes, accompanying the procession in open day. The sudden violence of a mob was completely eclipsed by this deliberate, shameless outrage.

THE END.